Dying Right

Dying Right

THE DEATH WITH DIGNITY MOVEMENT

DANIEL HILLYARD AND JOHN DOMBRINK

ROUTLEDGE
New York and London

Published in 2001 by
Routledge
29 West 35th Street
New York, NY 10001

Published in Great Britain in 2001 by
Routledge
11 New Fetter Lane
London EC4P 4EE

Routledge is an imprint of the Taylor & Francis Group

Printed in the United States of America on acid-free paper
Design and typography: Jack Donner

Library of Congress Cataloging-in-Publication Data

Hillyard, Daniel, 1962–
Dying right: the death with dignity movement / Daniel Hillyard, John Dombrink.
p. cm.
Includes bibliographical references and index.
ISBN 0–415–92798–6—ISBN 0–415–92799–4 (pbk.)
1. Right to die—Law and legislation—United States. 2. Assisted suicide—Law and legislation—United States. 3. Euthanasia—Law and legislation—United States. I. Dombrink, John. II. Title.

KF3827.E87 H55 2001
344.73'04197—dc21

00–062814

To Harold, Doris, John, and Christine

—D. H.

For Maya, Paul, and Kara

—J. D.

Contents

Preface

Our analysis looks at how legal reformers have succeeded in raising the issue of the legalization of physician-assisted suicide and in passing the world's first law permitting the practice, advanced by public support for compassion and autonomy in an era of medicalized dying.

Dying Right examines how social reformers were successful in convincing a majority of voters in one American state (Oregon) to provide a safe harbor provision in the state's law prohibiting assisted suicide in cases of competent, terminally ill Oregon adults who repeatedly request physicians to prescribe a lethal dose of medication. This book describes the political conduciveness of the Oregon electorate to assisted suicide reform, the mobilization of proponent and opponent campaigns, the framing of issues within the opposing campaigns, and the planning and execution of strategies and counterstrategies. The roles of public opinion, organized medicine, organized religion, and key activists and their organizational bases are described in great detail. Our analysis of the motives, intentions, deliberations, and choices of organizational and citizen activists contributes to the sociolegal literature on the role of social agency in law, morality, and social change.

During the seven years of this study, it has been our good fortune to meet scholars from around the world with similar research interests. John Griffiths—a Dutch legal scholar whose book on euthanasia in the Netherlands is a sociolegal tour de force—once reminded us that regional controversies such as the one in Oregon are but local manifestations of a wider sea change taking place in the relationships between patients and physicians in industrialized countries around the world. To this end, this book depicts the nation's first state law to openly permit physician-assisted suicide, in the broader context of the social history of medical thinking and medical practice. We also connect the analysis to the rights consciousness of Americans that has been so prevalent since the 1950s and 1960s. Other areas of morality and criminal law formation—such as gambling, drugs, prostitution, homosexuality, and abortion—are explored for their relevance to social movements generally, and particularly to the death with dignity movement.

This book, therefore, is an important addition to a long history of sociolegal research on law, morality, and politics. It covers a ten-year period during which major legal and political events occurred throughout the United States and around the world. It is a thoroughly empirical case study based on data collected at the forefront and behind the scenes of the death with dignity movement.

Led by this resolutely empirical approach to studying the ebbs and flows of the criminal law in competition over relative moral standing, we describe the relation between the organized death with dignity movement, attitudes toward hastened death, and conflicts between divergent subcultures in American society. We show that while demands for hastened death cut across various social categories, legal activities concerning hastened death have been one way Americans have defined their own cultural commitments.

This thorough empirical case study, including in-person interviews at field sites, benefits from our exhaustive study of accounts of the topic in the media, professional journals, court documents, and legislative testimony. We also conducted seventy-one interviews with fifty-two key informants in Oregon; California; Washington; Washington, DC; and the Netherlands.

A primary source of data is the historical records stored at the home office of the campaign director for Washington's Initiative 119, consultant for California's Proposition 161, and consultant for Oregon's Measure 16 and anti-Measure 51 campaigns. The file boxes and crates of documents, videos, and audiocassettes are significant sources of the daily activities of the death with dignity movement from 1990 to 1997. From there and elsewhere, we had access to dozens of the paid television advertisements created for both the proponents' and the opponents' sides of the various campaigns.

We attended court hearings, listened to legislative hearings from Oregon on tape and on audio collections, and pored over the transcripts from hearings in the Oregon legislature and the United States Congress.

For the court cases, we collected and studied amicus briefs, preliminary claims and motions, original tapes and transcripts of oral arguments, and court opinions for all levels of the two assisted suicide test cases. Additionally, Dan Hillyard interviewed the Washington attorneys who argued against each other before the United States Supreme Court.

Finally, we collected, read, and archived a large number and variety of supplementary materials, published texts, and journal articles that address or report on the movement. Moreover, when we were not in the field, we maintained close contact with primary informants.

We think we have amassed a unique and rich perspective on the legal reform of assisted suicide. With access to the key players, we then combined an analysis of the existing record of memoranda, legislative hearings, and public statements—including the ads and arguments that formed the basis for the contestation of this issue. The book focuses on how the reformers framed what might be considered a radical notion in the context of already held beliefs about medicine and personal freedom.

Acknowledgments

During the course of the seven years that we have worked together on this project, we have benefited from the generosity and insights of many individuals.

Dr. Ralph Shambaugh, a Portland area physician, first opened the door for us to Dr. Peter Goodwin, who became the first person we interviewed in Oregon and was the perfect place to start.

Soon after meeting Dr. Goodwin, Dan Hillyard met John Duncan, then the executive director of the Oregon Death With Dignity Legal Defense and Education Center. As the institutional memory of the Oregon reformers, John has been most helpful in providing us access to the data his organization keeps on the movement. Fortunately for us, John's successor, Hannah Davidson, has been generous in offering us the same access, just as she was helpful in her earlier role as assistant director.

Another terrific source of data was Karen Cooper, who directed the Washington campaign and consulted on both ballot measures in Oregon. Karen gave us a few days of full access to the treasure trove of data she has archived, which we relied upon in Chapters 2, 3, and 4.

Dr. Katrina Hedberg, an epidemiologist at the Oregon Health Division, and Gary Schnabel at the Oregon Board of Pharmacy have also been very helpful. Katrina granted us multiple interviews and helped us understand the development of the Oregon Death With Dignity Act (ODDA) reporting procedures. Gary took the initiative to update us on significant events as they occurred.

Barbara Coombs Lee, director of the Compassion in Dying Federation, provided us with her firsthand insights on the clinical implementation of the ODDA. She also engaged us in lively discussions of the "safe harbor" concept and on the cultural and political distinctions between words like "suicide" and "hastened death."

We have been especially grateful for the political insights provided by Eli Stutsman, the general counsel and lead campaign strategist for the Oregon Death With Dignity Legal Defense and Education Center. Eli granted us several interviews and was most helpful in giving us an understanding of the finer points about the politics of law and social change as they applied to the two successful Oregon campaigns.

We are are also very grateful to those persons who sat for interviews on more than one occasion in Oregon, gave us great access to their files, or supplied key insights, including Scott Gallant, Mark Bonnano, Rep. Lane Shetterly, Ann Jackson, Dr. Bonnie Reagan, Daniel Field, Thomas Holt, Derek Humphry, Dr. Leigh Dolin, Kathleen Haley, Geoff Sugerman, and Sister Eileen Robleski. Mark Gibson shared with us important insights on the role of the governor in the implementation process. Kelly Hagan gave us substantive implementation issues to ponder. Senator Neil Bryant, David Fiskum, and Steve Telfer were instructive in providing us with roadmaps of how the key implementation bill of the 1999 Oregon legislature proceeded.

In Washington, medical ethicist Albert Jonsen gave a key early interview on the 1991 Washington initiative and his insights from a career in the emerging field of bioethics. We are also appreciative of the time and insight from Sister Sharon Park, John Lee, Peter McGough, and Morton Yanow.

From California, the insights of Robert Risley, Warren Bostick, and Hans Hemann were gratifying.

In Washington, DC, we benefited from the insights and files of John Budetti, Cynthia Haney, Lisa Geiger, Deborah Price, Susan Winchler, and especially John Giglio.

Interviews with Kathryn Tucker and William Williams, two lawyers who argued opposing sides before the U.S. Supreme Court, as well as before earlier courts, in the landmark Compassion in Dying test cases, gave us a nuanced insider's view of the constitutional issues involved in the assisted suicide court challenge.

A monthlong 1996 trip by John Dombrink to the Netherlands brought us firsthand accounts of the interplay of law and medical institutions in the evolving Dutch approach, and we are thankful to Professor John Griffiths, one of the authors of the commanding *Euthanasia and Law in the Netherlands* (1998), and Professor Maurice Punch for their advice and insight and to Corrine Bayley in the United States for her generous sharing of potential Dutch interview subjects. In the Netherlands, John Dombrink also benefited from the generosity and insights of Professor Paul van der Maas, whose empirical studies form the basis for much Dutch policy discussion; Dr. Rob Dillman of the Royal Dutch Medical Society (KNMG), who ably explained the KNMG's role and evolution; Professor Johann Legemaate, whose cogent analysis of Dutch euthanasia legal evolution informs Chapter 7; the centrally involved attorney Eugene Sutorius; and Heleen Dupuis, Kees Keeman, Karl Gunning, Cor Spreuuwenberg, Menno van Leeuwen, Maurice de Wachter, Egbert Schroten, Marius Aalders, Joseph Gevers, and Johanna Kits Nieuwekamp.

Across the world in the other direction, we have benefited from ideas shared with Australian law professor Roger Magnusson and his colleague Professor Harry Ballis, authors of the forthcoming *Angels of Death: Exploring the Euthanasia Underground.* From Canada, we are daily beneficiaries of the wide-ranging newsgroup that John Hofsess tirelessly operates for Last Rights.

At Irvine, we have learned from the advice of colleagues such as Dan Hillyard's doctoral dissertation committee members Kitty Calavita, Jim Meeker, and Valerie Jenness and from interested colleagues like Richard Perry, Dr. Ron Miller and Dr. Ronald Koons. In addition, Karen Bluestone, Laurel Alden, and Kelley Lunder of the School of Social Ecology's development office assisted us greatly. We are grateful to Jeffrey Ulmer for comments on an article published from this project. The scholarship of Jerry Skolnide, and his appreciation of the limits of the criminal sanction, influenced our framing of the issue.

Several UCI undergraduate and graduate students have contributed to our research project in various ways, digging out legal decisions and data, helping us sort our information, or even deriving their own honors theses from the topic. We thank Jojo Ma, Maichi Nguyen, Laura O'Toole, Patricia Torres, Richelle Swan, James Mowrey, Anne Sioson, Elsie Secoquian, Noemi Alvarado, and especially Thomas Haraikawa. Christopher Green added some important information from Washington, DC.

We are very grateful to Thomas Layton and the Wallace Alexander Gerbode Foundation for their support of research on the implementation of the Oregon Death With Dignity Act, which is reported here in Chapter 6. Finally, from the start at Routledge, we have appreciated the support and guidance of Ilene Kalish, and the production support of Nicole Ellis.

1

A Fate Worse than Death

CHALLENGING THE LEGAL TREATMENT OF DYING

> I have terminal cancer. To have a terminal disease drag on, to endure the pain is absolute hell. At the end, I want the choice to accept treatment, to refuse treatment, to die on my own terms in a dignified manner.
>
> —Pro-reform television advertisement from the 1991 Washington Initiative 119 campaign

INTRODUCTION: AMERICA'S FIRST LEGAL PHYSICIAN-ASSISTED SUICIDE, 1998

On March 27, 1998, an Oregon woman in her eighties who was near death from breast cancer legally ended her life with barbiturates supplied by a physician. Another fourteen persons would join her in utilizing the Oregon Death With Dignity Act (ODDA) in its first year of operation.

The Oregon woman was the first person to die under the provisions of the ODDA, a 1994 law passed by voter referendum. The ODDA provides a safe harbor from criminal and civil law for family members, counselors, and physicians who help competent adults with less than six months to live end their lives with prescription drugs. The law also protects patients from fraud and coercion. The ODDA is the world's first law of its kind.

The ODDA was drafted by attorneys in consultation with interested health care professionals and became effective on October 27, 1997, after three years of failed court challenges and an unsuccessful repeal effort. While these challenges were pending, the Oregon Health Division—the agency charged with overseeing and regulating ODDA practices—produced a list of requirements for physicians to follow in implementing the act (Oregon Health Division 1997:1). According to the Oregon Health Division, the attending physician has the following responsibilities (Oregon Health Division 1997:1):

1. to determine whether the patient has a terminal illness, is capable, and has made the request voluntarily;
2. to inform the patient of his/her diagnosis and prognosis, the risks and probable result of taking the prescribed medication, and the feasible alternatives including comfort care and pain control;
3. to refer the patient to a consulting physician for confirmation of the diagnosis and determination that the patient is capable and acting voluntarily;
4. to refer the patient for counseling if, in the opinion of either the attending physician or the consulting physician, the patient may be suffering from any mental disorder, including depression, causing impaired judgment;
5. to request that the patient notify next of kin (the patient does not have to comply); and
6. to offer the patient the opportunity to rescind the request at any time.

The division also produced detailed confidential report forms and a protocol for interviewing physicians who prescribe medicine under the provisions of the new law. These epidemiological data provided profiles of patients who received prescriptions, patients who actually used the prescriptions to end their lives, and the physicians involved and circumstances surrounding these events.

The fifteen reported deaths consummated eight years of tense political struggle over the expansion of patients' rights to control the time, place, and manner of death. The efforts included ballot measures in three states besides Oregon—Washington (1991), California (1992), and Michigan (1998)—and two cases decided by the United States Supreme Court—*Washington v. Glucksberg* (*Compassion IV* 1997) and *Vacco v. Quill* (*Quill III* 1997).

This book presents an analysis of how legal reformers succeeded in Oregon. Our analysis centers on how reformers framed what might be considered a radical notion—physician-assisted suicide—in the context of personal freedom. The long history of right-to-die reform enshrined the values of autonomy and choice in medical decision making, especially at the end of life. Around the country, public support for the following statement: "[A] person has the right to end his or her life if this person has an incurable disease" increased steadily from 38 percent to 61 percent between 1977 and 1996 (CNN/USA Today Gallup Poll 1996; Glick 1992). Popular beliefs about medicine and personal freedom, plus the maturing history of laws and clinical practices permitting control of the time, place, and manner of death, provided reformers with a proven political framework.

This book details the reformers' strategies. From the data that we have collected for more than seven years—at the front lines and from behind the scenes—we examine how the need for change was conceptualized, argued for, and communicated to a public that has been somewhat interested in but also quite wary of some of the implications of legalizing physician-assisted suicide.

As the Dutch legal scholar John Griffiths has stated, the events described in this book are indicative of a growing "sea change" worldwide in the relationships between patients, doctors, and the state. This book provides a thick description of modern death and the contested claims of rights related to dying in the modern era. In one sense, we chronicle the growing awareness of the shortcomings of medicalized dying and the concomitant perception that there exists a "right way"—meaning a desirable way—to die. In another sense, we detail the social processes by which personal desires about dying and death have been folded into the broader rights consciousness that exists in the United States—processes that have culminated in the so-called right to die.

The centerpiece of our analysis is the state of Oregon and its watershed passage of the ODDA in 1994. Oregon is the first place where death with dignity (physician-assisted suicide) was legalized.

The Netherlands has been the leading country in this approach toward the law and dying. The Dutch devised and overseen the evolution of a policy of nonprosecution of voluntary euthanasia within guidelines established by the legal system, the political parties, and the medical profession. However, the Dutch maintained their criminal statutes in this area (Griffiths et al. 1998; Legemaate 1995). Only in 2000 have the Dutch passed laws to fully legalize their twenty-five-year experience with euthanasia ("Dutch Take Step" 2000). Australia (Brough 1997), Colombia, and Switzerland (Associated Press 1999b) have instituted various decriminalization schemes, but Australia's was rescinded, Colombia's is not yet fully operational, and Switzerland's resembles the Dutch in a policy of nonprosecution. Thus Oregon is the first entity in the world to implement a regulatory regime for legalized physician-assisted suicide.

But Oregon does not stand alone in death with dignity reform efforts. Reformers in Washington and California attempted ballot initiatives several years before 1994 (and reformers in Michigan and Maine have failed since 1994). And while court challenges and a repeal effort blocked implementation of the ODDA, two court challenges moved through the federal courts and were finally decided by the U.S. Supreme Court. Each of these efforts—the three early proponent initiatives, the repeal initiative, and the federal court cases—is described in great detail in this book.

From a broader perspective, in this book we describe the dynamics of law and social change. Beginning with an empirical look at changes in the nature of dying, we explore the right-to-die movement in terms of changing relationships between doctors, patients, and the state. Autonomy and compassion are shown to be the two major themes that have been championed by reform proponents. On the other side of the debate, arguments that physician-assisted suicide is tantamount to killing patients, that legal change will result in the wrong persons using the law for the wrong reasons, and that the economically marginalized will be pressured to die against their will are closely considered. Other opposition arguments are also contemplated, including fears of a slippery slope to more active or involuntary forms of euthanasia and the potential for an erosion of trust and good care in the patient-physician relationship, as well as the ramifications of physician-assisted suicide on the reputation of the medical profession generally.

A final aspect of the book is discussion of the more nuanced ways in which the death with dignity movement is impacting law and society. Of primary interest is the growing recognition, at least among clinicians, that human intervention in the timing and manner of death is already as invasive as, and as risky, assisted suicide. Some people close to the debate argue that de jure decriminalization of assisted suicide is preferable to de facto decriminalization because only in the latter case are regulation and oversight truly possible. In this way, assisted suicide criminal law reform reflects the earlier debates over the proper use of the criminal law in the regulation of gambling, drugs, prostitution, and abortion.

Of related interest are the semantic arguments that in some measure have led to redefining suicide. Here our analysis draws several parallels with the abortion movement and with a variety of activities under the control of the criminal law—some of which have undergone significant change in recent decades. Besides the fact that abortion and physician-assisted suicide each deal with laws and policies that regulate death, they also have in common a divisive cultural struggle in which the changing conceptualization of a medical practice has accompanied a shift in public opinion and legal reform.

The last nuance that we explore is the rise of claims that death presents opportunities for life-enhancing experiences. Some suggestions include helping families and individuals to gain closure through death. Others include improving the care of the dying through clinical efforts such as better pain management. Better medical training has been targeted by some reformers, as has expanding hospice care. All of these suggestions are offered as ways of sidestepping the "need" to change the law to permit assisted suicide. In this way, the actors involved in the assisted suicide reform struggle share many features with other reformers in the broad area of law and social change.

Three functions are served by the various analytical perspectives taken in this book. In a limited sense, the book tells the stories of intense political struggles at the ballot box and in the courts. In a broader sense, we derive empirical explanations for why further death and dying reform is happening, why it is happening here in the United States, and why it is happening through direct legislation and litigation. Finally, *Dying Right* is a detailed account of how proposed changes in criminal law and medical practice are actually contested.

CHANGES IN THE NATURE OF DYING

> This isn't what Dad wanted—these machines. That's why he made a living will.
>
> —Pro-reform television advertisement
> from 1991 Washington Initiative 119 campaign

During the last fifty years, expectations about the role of medicine in society have stimulated widespread legal and normative change in America and other Western industrialized societies. Before the 1950s, the issue of killing patients was not of great concern because medical science was unable to appreciably extend the lives of terminal patients (Glick 1992). Common causes of death before the discovery of antibiotics included pneumonia, tuberculosis, and influenza. Those in a permanent unconscious state died quickly from additional illnesses and complications or because they were unable to eat or drink. Those with cancer and heart disease or victims of debilitating accidents frequently contracted pneumonia and died before their otherwise terminal condition took its toll.

During the 1950s, surgical techniques improved, and cancer patients, for example, could undergo surgery that might not cure but could postpone the ravages of illness. Developments during this period included intravenous feeding, new drugs to fight infection, and cardiopulmonary bypass machines and coronary angiography for open heart surgery and for studying coronary circulation (Jonsen 1990; Zussman 1992). In the 1960s, ventilators, cardiac resuscitation, kidney dialysis, organ transplants, artificial heart valves, and more antibiotics were added to the list of life-prolonging technologies (Porter 1998).

One repercussion of medical innovation has been a dramatic increase in the number of hospital admissions. Until mid-century, most people died at home without extraordinary medical equipment or treatment. Today, however, less than 20 percent of the population die outside hospitals or nursing homes (Foley 1996). As a result, more and more health care dollars have been spent on chronic care so that by the early 1980s some 30 to 35 percent of Medicare expenditures were devoted to the 5 percent of recipients who were in their last year of life.

As was the case with other technological advancements, medical innovation was often accepted on its face, saving legal, ethical, economic, and social considerations for later. At present, however, we know that one of the perceived detriments of the war on death and disease has been the prevalence of institutionalized dying (Foley 1996; Zussman 1992). Since many of these people do not want all the life-extending treatment they receive, it has been contended that to give them a greater choice, the right to say no would restore some of the dignity lost through the medicalization of life and death (Quill 1993; Shavelson 1995).

Table 1.1 illustrates where change in the locus of death falls in the epidemiology of the causes of death. As the table indicates, the age of pandemics receded as technological advancements transformed the immediate causes of death. But technological advancements, which had to be applied in institutional settings, ushered in a new age in the causes of death. In the new age, people died primarily from ailments such as heart disease and the advanced state of cancer, conditions that heretofore were rare, as people died well before reaching such chronic stages of illness.

The effects of these changes are presented in Table 1.2, which illustrates that institutionalized dying has led to greater physician control, a greater role for economic considerations, and greater patient ignorance about the law and ethics governing patient choice.

Prompted by these conditions of modern dying during the last quarter century, powerful social movements have emerged to create a new era of medical politics. At the center of the contemporary politics of medical practice have been intellectuals such as Ivan Illich, who maintained that "the medical establishment has become a major threat to health" (Illich 1976). Other movements include the patients' right movement (Macklin 1993); the right-to-die movement (Glick 1992); the women's movement (e.g., efforts such as the Boston Women's Health Book Collective's *Our Bodies, Our Selves* [1971] and the efforts it spawned); critics of for-profit, free-market, fee-for-service medicine; the independent living movement; and the emerging alternative medicine movement. Largely as a result of the public debate inspired by these movements, questions of individual and public harm, choice and consent, and constitutional rights have increasingly come to characterize the contemporary discourse on dying and all that surrounds it.

Table 1.1 Epidemiology of the Causes of Death

Dawn to 1850	Age of Pestilence and Famine
1850 to 1920	Age of Receding Pandemics
→	*Change in the Locus of Death*
1920 to 1960	Age of Degenerative Human-Made Diseases
Mid-1960s to Present	Age of Delayed Degenerative Diseases

(Foley 1996; Porter 1998)

Table 1.2 Change in the Locus of Death and Its Effects

1. During the period from 1920 to 1990, the development of advanced surgical techniques, antibiotics, intravenous fluids and drugs, respiratory support systems, and improved therapeutic and diagnostic techniques changed the locus of death from homes to institutions.
2. The institutionalization of death gave physicians even greater social control over the dying process.
3. Yet there is a strong consensus that physicians remain inadequately trained to care for the dying, and they are deterred economically from providing palliative care.
4. Moreover, patients typically do not understand their right to refuse treatment or to demand withdrawal of unwanted treatment, and advance care planning has barely been implemented.
5. Still, data from death certificates show that roughly 62 percent of the 2.3 million annual deaths occur in hospitals, 16 percent occur in nursing homes, and only 17 percent occur in homes.

(Foley 1996; Porter 1998)

These cultural changes exist in a dialectical relationship with clinical practices and their attendant discourse. As patients have demanded greater parity in the physician-patient relationship, including the right to die on their own terms, physicians have also struggled to preserve a level of nobility and autonomy based on expertise in the practice of medicine. The conflicts between patients, physicians, and medical ethics have often been resolved, at least temporarily, through changing discourse.

The term "mercy killing" is a simple example. Culturally, mercy killing is a beneficent act, as is denoted by the concept of the "coup de grace," or "blow of grace." But, mercifully or not, we do not go to a hospital to be killed. And killing is contrary to the cultural and professional role of physicians. The term "euthanasia" means simply "easy death." Yet it too is troublesome because of its connections to Nazi genocide. New terms such as "hastened death," "double-effect death," and "death with dignity" have been created by patients and clinicians to suit the needs and values of both and, most importantly, to legitimate prevailing practices.

The same processes have been essential to meet the challenges of technological advancements. The conflicts between patients, physicians, and medical ethics during the era of medicalized death have even led to having to create new clinical and legal criteria for establishing whether a person is living or dead. With the advent of cardiopulmonary resuscitation (CPR), defibrillators, and respirators, a determination of death based on heart and lungs became outdated. The brain became the organ wherein life or death could be established. But controversy arose between just what quantity of brain function, or more properly which parts of brain functioning, was required to establish valid clinical criteria.

A further element of establishing a criteria of death is the role of the state. One of the roles of physicians has been to prevent killing on behalf of the state. In the context of death and dying, the relationships between physicians and the state are fully evident in the fact that clinical criteria of death are statutory in every state. That is, the definition of death in a particular state is not merely a clinical matter—the definition of death is a legal definition.

A concept introduced by patients and taken up by ethicists is the notion of "quality of life." From a dying patient's perspective, quality of life is more important than the criteria of death, the role of physicians as healers, or the state's interest in preventing killing. A persistent vegetative state is not the same as being alive, even if a whole brain statute pretends otherwise. The relevance of this discussion to clinical practices and the social movements that have been and still are working to alter them is illustrated by the repeated shifts in the line between what actions are legal and not legal. The rationales for all of these distinctions reflect a balance between patients' senses about a right way to die, physicians' role as healers, and the state's interest in preventing killing.

The events described in this book may seem to portray the sea change in physician-patient relations as pressures that impinge upon clinical practices. But that is only half of the picture. The landmark court decision that gave Karen Quinlan's parents the right to disconnect her ventilator was borne out of their struggle against doctors operating under traditional medical ethics. The relevance of the dialectical relationship between clinical practices and reform efforts will become increasingly clear as we progress through this book. Underscoring all the regional contests detailed in this book, the central struggle in the right-to-die and death with dignity movements is how to define and safeguard the right of patients to orchestrate their own deaths according to their own morality and how to reconcile that with the healing role of physicians and the state's interest in preventing killing. This is the principal significance of the changes described in this section.

THE RIGHT-TO-DIE MOVEMENT ADVANCES

Historically speaking, the right-to-die movement resonates with other rights-oriented movements of the 1960s and the 1970s. The discursive themes proceeding from the "rights" movements of the 1960s and 1970s have formed the sociopolitical terrain that has inspired and fueled the contemporary death with dignity movement, while the conservative politics of the 1980s has presented obstacles for the movement. Ultimately, however, the death with dignity movement has succeeded in tapping into the discourse from each of these social movements and their attendant arenas of debate to frame its grievances, press its claims, and seek support for the movement.

In 1976, United States courts and legislatures began weighing the relative strengths of competing claims, as laws were created to address issues of treatment withdrawal, advance directives, surrogate decision makers, and the symbolism of artificial nutrition and hydration. Moreover, through judges and lawyers, states reinforced interests in preventing suicide, protecting the vulnerable, and promoting the health care professions. This bundle of interests was first presented to the U.S. Supreme Court in 1990.

For two reasons, the period from 1976 to 1990 is unique in the death with dignity movement. The first reason is that treatment withdrawal was legitimated during this period. The second is that the strategies and rhetoric of reformers stopped short of permitting assisted suicide and/or euthanasia. In many ways, the very opportunity for and processes of line-drawing set the stage for attempts to expand death with dignity beyond treatment withdrawal and into permitting assisted suicide and/or euthanasia.

The history of efforts to legalize euthanasia has occurred in three phases: the voluntary euthanasia movement, the right-to-die movement, and the death with dignity movement. Table 1.3 summarizes the major events in these movements' histories.

The voluntary euthanasia movement in the United States began during the first part of the twentieth century. It consisted primarily of scholarly, even esoteric, debate that had very little impact on public policy. There were several attempts before World War II to get laws passed in various state legislatures, but because of legislators' fear of political backlash, all failed, and euthanasia went virtually unnoticed on the professional, mass media, and public agendas (Garrett 1999; Hoefler 1994).

By 1976, however, when the New Jersey Supreme Court ordered Karen Quinlan's doctors to disconnect her ventilator, lawmakers, the media, and the public were engaged in a growing reinforcing cycle of concern and attention about changing definitions of euthanasia (Glick 1992).

The story of Karen Quinlan places these historical changes on another level: the ways in which medical technology affected the lives of ordinary people. Karen was a young woman who had lapsed into a permanent vegetative state. To keep Karen alive, doctors had implanted a feeding tube into her stomach and connected her to a ventilator. Her parents, having realized that the respirator could keep Karen clinically alive for another fifty or sixty

Table 1.3 Major Events in the American Movement to Legalize Euthanasia

1938

- The American Euthanasia Society is formed by elite academics in the behavioral, natural, and social sciences.
- They draw the line between voluntary and involuntary euthanasia.
- In New York, they write legislation but find no sponsor, yet commence the modern debate and politics.

1940s

- Nazi genocide stymies political efforts.

1950s and 1960s

- The goal to cure using high-tech medicine becomes the norm.
- Advances include antibiotics, CPR, respirators, and feeding tubes.
- A scholarly debate ensues about drawing the line between passive and active euthanasia.
- Societal reliance on hospital care for acutely and chronically ill and dying people becomes the norm.
- In a steadily significant number of situations, patients and their families experience high-tech medicine and the powerful role of physicians in terms of lost control, extended pain and suffering, loneliness and despair, false hope, and meaninglessness.
- In the political context of civil rights consciousness, right-to-die interest groups pique and win over media and public interest.

1970s and 1980s

- People in hospitals seek outside authority to control a family member's or sometimes their own waning life.
- In 1976 landmark case law (*In re Quinlan* 1976, in New Jersey) and legislation (a "living will" in California) are created.
- Elizabeth Bouvia's long legal battle in California foreshadows the issue of assisted suicide.
- Favorable court judgments and legislative enactments occur throughout the country.
- The limits of substituted judgment are tested in *Superintendent v. Saikewicz* (1977), *In re Storer* (1981), *In re Eichner* (1981), *In re Conroy* (1985), *Brophy v. New England Sinai Hospital* (1986), *In re Jobes* (1987), and *Cruzan v. Director* (1990).

1990–1993

- In 1990 Jack Kevorkian begins a well-publicized (e.g., appearing on *Donahue*) maverick effort to end medical suffering.
- The U.S. Supreme Court assumes (withhold ruling) that prior court decisions appear to protect a liberty interest in refusing unwanted medical treatment (*Cruzan v. Director* 1990).
- Ballot initiatives to legalize limited access to voluntary euthanasia ("physician aid in dying") are narrowly defeated in Washington (1991) and California (1992).
- Jack Kevorkian has publicized his part in at least fifteen suicides yet he evades prosecution.

Table 1.3 (Continued)

1994–1996

- In May 1994 Jack Kevorkian is acquitted in his first homicide trial.
- In May 1994 U.S. District Court Chief Judge Barbara Rothstein rules in favor of due process and equal protection challenges against Washington law banning assisted suicide.
- In November 1994 a ballot initiative to legalize limited access to physician-assisted suicide passes in Oregon.
- In December 1994 U.S. District Court Chief Judge Thomas Griesa rejects due process and equal protection challenges against New York law banning assisted suicide.
- In December 1994 U.S. District Court Judge Michael Hogan temporarily enjoins the Oregon law.
- In March 1995 in a 2–1 ruling a three-judge panel of the U.S. Court of Appeals for the Ninth Circuit reverses Judge Rothstein's ruling.
- In August 1995 Judge Hogan permanently enjoins Oregon's law.
- In March 1996 an eleven-judge panel of the U.S. Court of Appeals for the Ninth Circuit reinstates Judge Rothstein's ruling on due process grounds.
- In April 1996 a three-judge panel of the U.S. Court of Appeals for the Second Circuit reverses Judge Griesa's ruling on equal protection grounds.
- In May 1996 Jack Kevorkian is acquitted for a third time.
- In October 1996 the U.S. Supreme Court grants a hearing in both the Washington and the New York cases.

1997

- In January the Washington and New York cases are heard in the U.S. Supreme Court.
- In February a three-judge panel of the U.S. Court of Appeals for the Ninth Circuit holds that those challenging the Oregon law lack standing. Appeal is made to the U.S. Supreme Court.
- In April Jack Kevorkian burns a Michigan order to stop assisting suicides, calling the order "fascistic." Kevorkian has by now acknowledged participating in forty-five deaths, and bodies with notices to contact Kevorkian's attorney are continually found in Michigan hotel rooms.
- In April President Clinton signs the Assisted Suicide Funding Restriction Act of 1997, which prohibits the use of federal funds to cause a patient's death.
- In June the U.S. Supreme Court unanimously reverses both the Ninth and Second Appellate Court rulings.
- The day of the Supreme Court decisions, a body is found in a Michigan hotel room and Kevorkian's attorney publicly insinuates Kevorkian's involvement.
- In July the Florida Supreme Court follows the historical analysis of the U.S. Supreme Court and denies a right to physician-assisted suicide even under the privacy provision of the Florida Constitution.
- In October the U.S. Supreme Court refuses to hear the Oregon case.
- In October the injunction against the ODDA is lifted.
- In November the administrator of the Drug Enforcement Administration (DEA) determines that physician-assisted suicide with the use of federally controlled substances violates federal law.
- In November Oregon voters block repeal of the Oregon law by a 20 percent margin.
- The day after the election the state attorney general publicly announces that Oregon's law is in effect.

Table 1.3 (Continued)

1998

- In March the first death under the Oregon law is announced.
- In June U.S. Attorney General Janet Reno overrules the DEA administrator and rules that the federal Controlled Substances Act does not prevent Oregon physicians from prescribing medication in compliance with the ODDA.
- In June the Lethal Drug Abuse Prevention Act of 1998 is introduced by Senate Majority Whip Don Nickles and House Judiciary Chairman Henry Hyde. The act would outlaw federally controlled substances for use in assisted suicide.
- In August state authorities announce that eight people have died using the Oregon law.
- In October, the congressional session ends without the Lethal Drug Abuse Prevention Act of 1998 making it to the House or the Senate floor for a vote.
- In November CBS's *60 Minutes* airs a videotape shot by Jack Kevorkian showing himself injecting Thomas Youk. Kevorkian is charged with murder and delivering a controlled substance.
- In November an assisted-suicide reform measure fails in the Michigan ballot.

1999

- In February the Oregon Health Division reports that in its first full year of operation, twenty-three people requested prescriptions under the ODDA and fifteen used them.
- In March Jack Kevorkian is convicted of second-degree murder and delivering a controlled substance and begins serving a life sentence in prison.
- In June Hyde and Nickles introduce the Pain Relief Promotion Act of 1999, which sanctions the aggressive use of pain-control drugs even if death may result, and ensures a uniform application of the federal Controlled Substances Act notwithstanding state law.

2000

- The Pain Relief Promotion Act of 1999 continues to be considered in Congress.
- Oregon issues its second year report.
- An Oregon-like measure fails in Maine.
- The 106th Congress ends without the Pain Relief Promition Act making it to a floor vote in the Senate.

years, although in all probability she would never leave the vegetative state, requested that the ventilator be removed. They said they were not trying to kill their daughter, but if the ventilator were all that was keeping her alive, they could not permit or condone her continued existence in such a miserable, hopeless state. The hospital refused the request. If the Quinlans could obtain a court order absolving the hospital of wrongdoing, their directive could be granted. Without a court order, administrators were ready to maintain the current treatment.

The Quinlans filed suit, and the case wound its way up to the Supreme Court of New Jersey. There the court sided with the Quinlans, and ordered the removal of the ventilator (*In re Quinlan* 1976). The ruling was based on the right to privacy. Its impact on public policy was manyfold. According to philosopher Margaret Pabst Battin, it "brought home the possibility that situations like Karen's could happen to anyone" (Battin 1995:4). The Quinlan case became a focal point for agenda setting and innovation. It also became the starting point for the right-to-die movement.

The earliest calls for change had appeared in medical journals in the mid-sixties, when physicians began to question the desirability of prolonging lives with heroic medicine. Physicians began to distinguish between bringing about the death of patients actively—for instance, by injecting large doses of pain killers—or passively, by removing machines that maintain artificial breathing or blood flow (Griffiths et al. 1998; Jonsen 1990; Porter 1998; Sprung 1990). This distinction was quickly taken up by Catholic theologians. In fact, Catholic moral theologians had discussed euthanasia since the 1500s, probably because of the Church's long-standing work in the chaplaincy (Fletcher 1954; Vaux 1992). The Church has long distinguished between ordinary and extraordinary medical treatment, recognizing that some life-prolonging measures may place too great a burden on the individual; medical advances during the 1950s and 1960s made the distinction plainly salient (Wennberg 1989).

From 1950 to the early 1970s, the public agenda was concerned primarily with individual mercy killing cases as news events. In the early 1970s, reporting of other death-related issues began to converge: debates and resolutions on patients' rights, new definitions of death, polls of medical doctors, university and medical school seminars on death and dying, and cryonics. In 1974, NBC broadcast a television special on the ability of new medical technology to sustain life, mercy killing, and living wills. The news media sensationally reported stories about patients whose suffering was ended when, for example, a hospital orderly mercifully turned off life support machines. Some commentators accused the media of having practiced advocacy journalism. The result was an often sympathetic public response, which was itself an important agent of change.

Increases in the legal literature tended to follow increases in the medical, Catholic, and mass media literature, but not until the early 1970s—largely in reaction to public proposals for living wills. Legal literature tended to focus on traditional issues of legal analysis—liability, privacy, and the prospects for legislation. By the mid-seventies, legal literature focused on court cases and ways to improve legislation (Maguire 1984).

For some time the Catholic Church and even the American Medical Association (AMA) resisted legislative and judicial action because of fear that law inevitably would lead to government-sanctioned active euthanasia (Glick 1992). Nevertheless, public support for voluntary active euthanasia and the withholding and withdrawal of treatment grew steadily (Callahan 1993; Logue 1993). This growth stimulated further judicial and legislative recognition of a right to die. Hoping to limit expansive judicial policy, the Catholic Church reconsidered its opposition to some legislation, and issued guidelines of its own, and the AMA eventually endorsed passive euthanasia in most instances.

Although the right-to-die movement was increasingly visible by the early 1970s, the Karen Quinlan case made the death with dignity movement very prominent, and it has been a permanent agenda item since then. Other coverage that also kept the issue before the professional and mass publics included California's adoption of the first living will law in 1976, seven additional adoptions in 1977, and the *Superintendent v. Saikewicz* case (1977) in Massachusetts (in which it was ruled that state courts must retain authority in deciding to withdraw treatment in cases of incompetent patients). Following these events, at least several articles were published each year in medical, legal, and public medical literatures.

Table 1.4 lists the status of the right to die by 1990. From 1972 forward, the right to die had become a permanent item on the social agenda. As Garrett observes (Garrett 1999), several reformers took advantage of public support for the expansion of rights in this area to extend the fledgling right-to-die movement into an effort that would show greater success in the 1990s.

Table 1.4 The Right to Die Circa 1990

1. There are common law and constitutional bases for the right to refuse treatment.
2. The same bases apply to competent and incompetent patients.
3. Decisions for incompetent patients should apply, in descending order of preference, the subjective standard, the substituted judgment standard, and the best interests standard.
4. Advance directives may be used to ascertain an incompetent patient's preferences.
5. Food and water may be refused as any other form of medical treatment.
6. Active euthanasia and assisted suicide are morally and legally distinct from treatment refusal.

(Meisel 1992:315)

REFORM IN OREGON: PATIENTS, DOCTORS, AND THE STATE

> It felt as if my blood froze the first time a patient asked me to help them die. I realized that with all my technical knowledge about diagnosis and treating, I knew nothing about helping people die. And there was nowhere to turn—not to my colleagues, my association, the literature. There was literally no guidance anywhere.
>
> —Dr. Peter Goodwin, sponsor of the ODDA (Goodwin 1996)

This section chronicles the complex changes in social relationships and cultural values that inspired the death with dignity movement. Beginning with post–World War II changes in the nature of dying, the emergence of the death with dignity movement is explored in reference to claims about negative repercussions of the modern medicalization of life and death. How these processes were manifested in the cultural, political, and economic relationships between patients, doctors, and the state is a key consideration. The transformation of these relationships into claims for and against reforming assisted suicide law is developed.

An attorney behind the ODDA said he has never seen a law that intrudes into the patient-physician relationship as much as this law does (Stutsman 1996). This intrusion marks an amazing shift in power between doctors and patients during the last few decades. There are several reasons why this shift is taking place, including changes in the nature of dying, appeals to compassion and autonomy, the mobilization of support by key physicians and leaders, and the neutralization of some potential opposition.

Two sponsors of the ODDA were Barbara Coombs Lee and Dr. Peter Goodwin. Coombs Lee, a nurse, lawyer, and former legislative aide, and Dr. Goodwin, a practicioner of family medicine and professor of medicine, became involved in euthanasia reform because of their personal experiences in caring for dying patients. Each felt that many physicians have no penchant for, and some are even intransigent about, becoming intimate with their patients, especially with regard to helping them die. According to Dr. Goodwin, this is not the fault of physicians, for nothing in their training teaches them how to help a dying patient die:

> Traditionally, patients were generally given very high doses of morphine and left to die by the inch. The family was left waiting somewhere and in most cases not even informed that the patient was officially dying. Physicians were trained that it is harmful to give the family the bad news until it is over. These medical practices were deplorable. (Goodwin 1996)

Other data support Goodwin's claims about the negative repercussions of the modern medicalization of life and death. In 1961, the *Journal of the American Medical Association* (JAMA) published a study of physicians' practices in telling or not telling patients about a diagnosis of cancer. Results showed that 90 percent of the study's physicians reported a preference for not telling the patients of their diagnoses or prognoses (Oken 1961). In fact, patients were usually treated as children and were expected to submit in quiet deference. Patients who questioned paternalistic doctors were labeled as troublesome, and hospital staff often treated them accordingly.

Patients facing death were worse off. Physicians were not trained to treat patients and families facing death. Moreover, for both psychological and cultural reasons, they typically shunned the actual experience of death when it happened to their own patients. The inadequacies were personal and structural. Physicians labored under their own inadequacies whenever patients and families sought advice. And planning for death, and perhaps even hastening it, had no place in the discourse and practices of institutionalized end-of-life care.

But the very medicalization of life (and dying) that fostered social disparity between patients and doctors gave rise to new tensions and uncertainties in the patient-doctor relationship. As Roy Porter, the British social historian of medicine, observes:

> [N]ew tensions and uncertainties in the patient-doctor relationship are in many ways a response to the modern medicalization of life—the widening provision of medical explanations, opinions, services and intervention; the infiltration of medicine into many spheres of life, from normal pregnancy and childbirth to alcohol and drugs related behavior, in line with a philosophy that assumes the more medicine the better.... Today's complex and confused attitudes toward medicine are the cumulative responses to a century of the growth of the therapeutic state and the medicalized society. (Porter 1998:690–691)

On another level, the growth of the therapeutic state in a medicalized society has invited appeals to compassion and autonomy. There has been an emerging debate about the autonomy of the individual in the face of usually expensive medical options. Some analysts frame the issue in the context of power sharing and competition between physicians and patients. Patients' rights, which have expanded in many areas (Macklin 1993), and laws about informed consent characterize the rights consciousness that has grown around medical decision making as medical technology has expanded and forced many more people to make end-of-life decisions. And there has been a growing and changing consciousness regarding death itself among Americans.

The harmful burdens of heroic medicine became anecdotal inside and outside hospitals and nursing homes. People were angry with their own doctors and the medical profession for being so patronizing as to decide how they would live until death. Largely because of such tragedies, and reinforced by sympathetic media coverage, patients and their families began demanding more control over treatment decision making, especially at the threshold of death.

The attorney's remark about the intrusiveness of the ODDA signifies how much relationships between doctors and patients have changed and how radically the prospects for legal reform have shifted. The power shift that occurred as informed consent and similar ethical principles transformed physicians' practices left paternalism largely abandoned (Darval 1993; Jonsen 1993; Griffiths et al. 1998). For example, physicians have abandoned the assumption that patients do not really want to know what is wrong with them or that they cannot possibly understand.

According to the American Hospital Association, about 70 percent of deaths occur after discussion to forgo or withdraw treatment (Kolata 1997). In fact, norms have changed so dramatically that during the fifteen-year period between the seminal case of Karen Quinlan, and the time when reformers began using the ballot initiative to push for greater physician involvement in hastened death, it was estimated that each day in the United States, 6,000 deaths were "in some way planned or indirectly assisted" (Quill et al. 1992:1381). By that same time, all but six states allowed for some sort of living will and do-not-resuscitate provisions (Hoefler 1994). As mentioned earlier, national polls consistently have shown an increasing majority of public support for greater control over the situation of one's death.

As dying patients and their families have entered the professional aided-dying discourse, they have brought their own experiences and insights to bear on political analysis. They have sought to transform the cultural image of suicide as a violent, lonely, despairing act that leaves survivors confused and guilty for not having seen it coming, to a compassionate act of self-deliverance that honors choice and relieves suffering. According to these reformers, the fear of death in Western, Judeo-Christian culture, and the resulting laws for dealing with a person who no longer wishes to live, compound the disasters of heroic medicine. Viewed in this light, any facial ban against assisted suicide prevents dying people from deciding the circumstances of their own death, denigrates their moral judgment, and limits their freedom. Most importantly, choice in dying is more than an individual need, private crisis, or hospital staff problem—it is a collective issue because each of us will experience our own and probably a parent or other loved one's death some time or another.

Because it is a collective issue, choice in dying has shifted from the private sphere into the center of public debates (Battin 1995; Battin et al., 1998; Callahan 1987, 1990, 1992, 1993; Emanuel 1998; Englehardt 1989; Glick 1992; Jonsen 1990; Meisel 1992; Otlowksi 1997; Vaux 1992). For the past decade, legal scholars, medical professionals, public policy experts, ethicists, and ministers, as well as the general public, have grappled with the weighty and complicated issues of the ending of life in medical settings (Battin 1995; Dombrink and Hillyard 1998; Hoefler 1994; Quill 1996; Rothman 1991; Schneiderman and Jecker 1995). The proliferation of advance directives and living wills, following the 1990 United States Supreme Court decision in *Cruzan v. Director* (1990), has been one outcome of the rights consciousness of people considering end-of-life issues. But despite all the change, patients had still not been permitted to receive medical assistance with suicide until Oregon acted.

Ethicists such as Arthur Caplan have termed the legal referenda analyzed in this book as extremely important events in contemporary American medical ethics, calling Washington's 1991 assisted suicide initiative "the most important biomedical event in the United States" (Hoefler 1994:196). Caplan has even said that he sees the issue of euthanasia in the near future eclipsing that of abortion as a subject of moral and legal reform in the United States. Ethicist Peter Singer (1995:1) describes the euthanasia-related events in Britain, the Netherlands, and the United States as "surface tremors resulting from major shifts deep in the bedrock of western ethics. We are going through a period of transition in our attitude toward the sanctity of human life."

As Griffiths explains, physicians' practices are coming under greater legal control in all sorts of countries, and the legal position of patients is growing stronger. This general domestication of medicine is the major sea change that is taking place, and particular legal battles are but local manifestations (Griffiths et al. 1998). The impetus for medicine's domestication is the problem that brought bioethics into being, namely, who shall be saved when all cannot be saved? Moreover, several medical historians have explored the clinical and political aspects of this problem. Jonsen (1990) writes about the shift of moral probabilities from the absolute "Do everything possible for this patient" to the proportionate "Do everything reasonable for all patients." These questions suggest that changes in the doctor-patient relationship have been stirred by wider social movements to protect consumer and patient rights.

But patients, as sufferers and political actors, moved physicians to a more radical political position. Dying patients and their families insisted that the medical profession listen. Although there were few nasty debates or picket lines as with the abortion movement, much of the medical profession heard the general message as well as individual patients' demands. Communication and negotiation were taking place in public forums between institutions, organizations, and professional movements rather than in the seclusion of hospitals and courtrooms. What had been a private problem of death had become political, and what had been the subject of personal discussions became a fiery subject of public debate.

This context made it safer for key physicians and leaders to mobilize support for further legal reform. Polls of physicians, and the actions and statements of physicians' groups that have campaigned in favor of ballot measures and spoken in favor of federal claims, indicate that there are many physicians who treat dying patients who want to do more for them. But doctors like Timothy Quill in New York and Peter Goodwin in Oregon claimed they could not practice end-of-life medicine any better without professional and legal acquiescence in helping patients to exercise choice before death is imminent.

Some physicians said they were reluctant to help patients to die for fear of being drawn in—"It's difficult to act in the present legal climate." Some crossed the line. Operating in fear, they linked up with leaders in the legal profession, and this professional alliance advocated reform of assisted suicide law. For physicians who felt that the present legal climate put them at risk—professionally and legally—a decision by the people at large to change the law seemed both desirable and worth pursuing.

As patients demanded better end-of-life care, doctors who heard the calls for change lamented that their hands were tied by current law. Like physicians willing to challenge the abortion laws a generation before (Joffe 1995; Reagan 1997), some went public with the claim that legal change was needed, and soon public discourse included the subject of dying. Physicians who treated dying patients found themselves caught between several forces: progressive expectations of patients, laws prohibiting assisted suicide, and the professional bias against accepting death. As more physicians questioned current practices, public support for physician-assisted suicide expanded.

FRAMING ARGUMENTS FOR AND AGAINST REFORM

A major activity of the death with dignity movement has been to gain legitimacy for its claims by linking them with broadly accepted cultural values and beliefs. This linkage is a process known as "frame alignment" (Snow, Rochford, Worden, and Benford 1986). Snow et al. contend that the mobilization and activation of participants are contingent upon "the linkage of individual and [social movement organization] interpretive orientation, such that some set of individual interests, values, and beliefs and organization activities, goals and ideology are congruent and complementary" (Snow et al. 1986:464). To be successful, social movement organizations must mobilize potential adherents and constituents. To do this they identify events and conditions relevant to movement goals, interpret them in agreeable terms, and assign them favorable meanings. This is what is meant by framing. Frame alignment is successful when it succeeds in mobilizing potential adherents and constituents, garnering bystander support, and demobilizing antagonists (Snow et al. 1986).

Frame alignment processes differ between the constraints inherent in different reform strategies. As later chapters will show, proponents and opponents of reform resorted to different discourses and tactics depending on whether they were in court or running a ballot initiative campaign. However, despite these differences, social movements scholar Valerie Jenness makes it clear that "frame alignment processes nonetheless remain critical to the successful negotiation of the larger socio-political environment that crusaders of any type must participate in and ultimately be responsive to" (Jenness 1993:121).

Proponents of expanding the right to die continuously situated the death with dignity movement firmly within larger publicly legitimated issues and community values. As this book will demonstrate, the death with dignity movement has symbolically and literally linked the right to seek a physician's active, intentional assistance in causing death to principles and beliefs emanating from the right-to-die movement, the movement to decriminalize the harm caused by criminalization of activities that are happening anyway (e.g., drugs, abortion), and the larger efforts in this nation and others to bolster the position of patients against the harms of the medicalization of life. These issues and their attendant discourse constitute not only the political backdrop for the death with dignity movement but also a rhetorical and cultural resource for it.

As later chapters describe, the death with dignity movement has gained support from earlier legal changes based on compassion for suffering. As Schneiderman and Jecker have explained, "[M]edical treatment has come to be viewed by many as an unleashed menace rather than as a beneficent healing process" (Schneiderman and Jecker 1995:40). The perception that modern medicine does little to reduce suffering has been a major impetus for the right-to-die movement.

In 1958, Glanville Williams, a British scholar of jurisprudence, argued for legal reform of euthanasia laws as a way of preventing cruelty to patients and relatives: "Those who plead for the legalization of euthanasia think that it is cruel to allow a human being to linger for months in the last stage of aging, weakness and decay, and to refuse him his demand for merciful release" (Williams 1969:134). Williams's urgings seem to have anticipated the arguments by physicians like Timothy Quill and others who would lead American physicians in the movement for assisted suicide reform in the 1990s. Quill wrote: "A patient's request for assisted death often seemed simultaneously legitimate, heartbreaking, and terrifying to the caregivers. Watching patients beg for assistance that did not come seemed cruel, adding a final humiliation to a process that was already grueling and undermining" (Quill 1993:130–131).

Reformers argue that patients with terminal illnesses are primarily asking for refuge from suffering, which they characterize as unwanted, horrible, and essentially unproductive. This desire for compassion was articulated in campaign ads during all three state ballot initiative campaigns (Chapters 2–4) and in legal arguments presented in two federal court challenges (Chapter 5).

A second primary rhetorical and cultural resource that has been offered in support of reform is patient autonomy. Following the rulings of abortion cases from *Roe v. Wade* (1973) through *Planned Parenthood v. Casey* (1992) and contraception cases that preceded them, like *Griswold v. Connecticut* (1965), liberty and privacy concerns have dominated legal arguments. Many interest groups claim that *Planned Parenthood v. Casey* (1992) squarely affirmed the constitutional basis for liberty and privacy. A quote from *Casey* appeared in many amicus briefs when the issue of assisted suicide was taken up by the federal courts:

> It is settled now . . . , the Constitution places limits on a State's right to interfere with a person's most basic decisions about family and parenthood, . . . as well as bodily integrity. (Brief of Amici Curiae Legal Defense and Education Fund, Inc., et al., at 9, to the United States Court of Appeals for the Second Circuit 95–7028, citing *Casey* at 849 in support of reversing *Quill v. Vacco* 870 F. Supp. 78 [S.D.N.Y. 1994])

Judges also reasoned that principles of choice and autonomy provide a legal basis for reformers' claims. Federal Judge Barbara Rothstein rooted part of her 1994 District Court opinion in this manner:

> The liberty interest protected by the Fourteenth Amendment is the freedom to make choices according to one's individual conscience about those matters which are essential to personal autonomy and basic human dignity. There is no more profoundly personal decision, nor one which is closer to the heart of personal liberty, than the choice which a terminally ill person makes to end his or her suffering and hasten and inevitable death. (*Compassion I* 1994, at 16)

Rothstein's ruling was taken up by reformers: They used it as a powerful rhetorical source for framing briefs and oral arguments for the Supreme Court (Chapter 5).

Compassion and autonomy were the primary frames used by reform proponents. Compassion and autonomy evoke emotion, especially when linked to people's fears of a lingering death filled with pain and suffering. Emotional arguments made empirical frames seem less academic. The primary empirical claim asserted by reformers was that assisted suicide ought to be legalized because it happens already. That claim actually consisted of two arguments. One was that other medical practices at the end of life are essentially no different from assisted suicide. The other was that legalization would facilitate proper regulation of a now-secret practice.

Some of the argument for legalizing physician-assisted suicide has stemmed from the observation of Quill and others that with the practice of terminal sedation and the principle of double effect, de facto decriminalization already exists. Quill describes the basic premise of the ethical principle of double effect:

> In comfort care, unintended shortening of a patient's life can be accepted as a potential side effect of treatment, provided the primary purpose of the treatment is to relieve suffering. The underlying religious and ethical principle is called the "double effect," which absolves physicians from responsibility for indirectly contributing to the patient's death, provided they intended purely to alleviate the patient's symptoms. It places considerable weight on the physician's unambiguous intent to relieve suffering and not to intentionally shorten life. (Quill 1993:78)

Like prior reformers who successfully argued and mobilized for changes in abortion, gambling, or marijuana laws, the proponents of euthanasia legal reform have argued that the use of morphine at the end of life is a form of de facto decriminalization of assisted suicide. Under the "double-effect" theory, doctors are not considered to have acted unethically—nor are they subject to criminal prosecution—if they prescribe or administer potentially lethal levels of drugs with the intent to ease pain, not cause death. Activist physicians like Quill aim to bring secret practices into the open—employing a classic argument for the change of a de facto practice to a de jure legalized or decriminalized practice. In the words of a *New York Times* editorial, it is only a matter of sanctioning what already happens with "a wink and a nod" ("Assisted Suicide and the Law" 1997:A12). As we describe in Chapter 6, even Congress's Pain Relief Promotion Act of 1999, which undermines Oregon's assisted suicide law, sanctions the principle of double effect.

To date, the authority to define this distinction between killing and letting die has been kept within the boundaries of the medical profession. This is what sociologists of law mean when they refer to the "medicalized" approach, and the medicalized approach to laws regulating hastened death are very much a parallel to abortion law before *Roe v. Wade* (1973). For better or for worse, a medicalized approach to death and the law provides a powerful source for frame alignment efforts.

But the very same medical profession has enabled Dr. Quill and many other health care leaders to reject mainstream thinking. Here there is another parallel to abortion reform efforts:

> By the late 1960s, esteemed members of the [medical] profession no longer needed to attack abortion to prove their purity and could challenge laws promoted by their forebears without having their reputations questioned. The legalization of abortion gained great medical and popular support in these years. (Reagan 1997:234)

The right-to-die movement of the 1970s and 1980s brought the issue of hastened death onto public, professional, religious, and legal agendas. Physicians like Quill and Goodwin took calculated risks by framing their claims in generally held, historically meaningful values and beliefs.

As a final example of frame alignment processes, we consider the widely salient frame of economic discrimination. As will be discussed later, the typical economic argument against assisted suicide is that poor people will be enticed to choose death more systematically than people who can afford high-cost medical care. But a more novel argument advanced by legal philosopher Ronald Dworkin was presented in papers submitted to the Supreme Court (see Chapter 5). Dworkin contends that what we have currently is a two-tiered system that provides "a chosen death and an end of pain outside the law for those with connections and stony refusals for most other people" (Dworkin 1997:41). Dworkin's argument that laws that follow the medicalization of death favor "fortunate people who have established relationships with doctors willing to run the risks of helping them to die" can be seen both as a prediction of impetus for change and a resignation that the current system may prevail:

> The sense that many middle-class people have that if necessary their own doctor "will know what to do" helps to explain why the political pressure is not stronger for a fairer and more open system in which the law acknowledges for everyone what influential people now expect for themselves. (Dworkin 1997:41)

These debates are really debates about how to define what is happening already. But whether the principle of double effect as it is currently argued in legal, ethical, and clinical usage is biased or not, there actually is an empirical dimension to the claim that "it happens already." That dimension touts the benefits of regulation and oversight if all types of hastened death were decriminalized de jure. One of the principle assertions of this frame is that de jure decriminalization is the easiest road to reducing the harms that accompany criminalization of activities that occur irrespective of their legality. Powerful examples of this frame are laws regarding drug abuse and addiction and laws regulating abortion.

We want to illustrate this example of frame alignment with a rather low-key example that did, however, cultivate wide and serious scholarly interest. The Bay Area Network of Ethics Committees developed procedural guidelines for clinicians faced with a patient's request for a hastened death. Borrowing the concept of "harm reduction" from the field of addiction medicine and epidemiology, the network achieved a consensus:

> First, it is recognized that a potentially dangerous behavior is occurring and will likely continue regardless of legal and social prohibitions. Then interventions or other policies are offered that might lessen the negative consequences of the behavior without sanctioning the behavior itself. (Heilig et al. 1997:370)

As empirical examples of the harm reduction approach, Heilig et al. (1997) cited the use of methadone in the treatment of heroin addiction and needle exchange programs to quell the spread of HIV infection.

Opponents of death with dignity also must pursue frame alignment. They have linked assisted suicide with the potential for abuse, fear of a slippery slope, and a likelihood that alternatives to assisted suicide will be neglected. The history of euthanasia in the Netherlands is cited often.

The Achilles' heel of the death with dignity movement is the claim that the law would be used by the wrong people for the wrong reasons (Coombs Lee 1997). Some will resort to assisted suicide because they are depressed. Others will seek to avoid spending the family nest egg. That risk includes the possibility of coercion. Poor people with few options might be subtly forced into assisted suicide. Marginalized patients, such as the infirm elderly, the permanently disabled, and people with illnesses such as AIDS, might succumb to societal discrimination.

Opponents have aligned these potential abuses with people's memories of Nazi Germany. Even when proponents counterargue that modern proposals are grounded in compassion, not genocide, opponents turn to the history in the Netherlands—effectively arguing that any distinctions between compassionate euthanasia and genocidal euthanasia are more gray than black and white. Nat Hentoff, noted civil libertarian thinker and writer for the *Village Voice* and *Washington Post*, warns about "the small beginnings of death," observing that in every culture and time period, what began as help for a few people to achieve a good death in hard cases soon became a regular practice of controversial if not downright egregious hastening of death (Hentoff 1988).

In 1994 the New York State Task Force on Life and the Law, commissioned by New York Governor Mario Cuomo, issued a 217-page report—*When Death Is Sought: Assisted Suicide and Euthanasia in the Medical Context*—urging against legalizing assisted suicide and euthanasia. The Task Force warned that:

> The risk of harm is greatest for the many individuals in our society whose autonomy and well-being are already compromised by poverty, lack of access to good medical care, advanced age, or membership in a stigmatized social group. The risks of legalizing assisted suicide and euthanasia for these individuals, in a health care system and society that cannot effectively protect against the impact of inadequate resources and ingrained social disadvantages, would be extraordinary. (New York State Task Force on Life and the Law 1994:120)

The Task Force was careful to point out that:

> This risk does not reflect a judgment that physicians are more prejudiced or influenced by race and class that the rest of society—only that they are not exempt from . . . the prism of social inequality and prejudice that characterizes the delivery of services in all segments of society, including health care. (New York State Task Force on Life and the Law 1994:125)

A related set of opposition arguments and frame alignment processes is fear of a slippery slope. Here the fear is that laws that permit competent patients to voluntarily end their lives will eventually be expanded to incompetent patients who never asked for such "treatment." Distinguished law school professor Yale Kamisar asks:

> If personal autonomy and the termination of suffering are supposed to be the touchstones for physician-assisted suicide, why exclude those with nonterminal illnesses or disabilities who might have to endure greater pain and suffering for much longer periods of time than those who are expected to die in the next few weeks or months? (Kamisar 1996:88)

It is this opposition frame that most directly deflates proponents' framing efforts regarding compassion and autonomy. For if compassion and autonomy are the key reasons for permitting people to control the timing and manner of death, why should the law limit death with dignity to only a few?

University of Chicago Professor Leon Kass, M.D., urges that assisted suicide, once legalized, will not remain confined to those who freely and knowingly elect it:

> The enactment of a law legalizing mercy killing (or assisted suicide) on voluntary request will certainly be challenged in the courts under the equal protection clause of the Fourteenth Amendment. Why, it will be argued, should the comatose or the demented be denied the right to such a "dignified death" or such "treatment" just because they cannot claim it for themselves? (Kass 1991:473)

Kass points out that laws permitting competent patients to refuse treatment or to have treatment discontinued have been expanded to include nearly everyone, and he sees no reason why assisted suicide laws would not evolve (Kass would say "devolve") similarly: "With the aid of court-appointed proxy consenters, we will quickly erase the distinction between the right to choose one's own death and the right to request someone else's—as we have already done in the termination-of-treatment cases" (Kass 1991:473).

In *Cruzan v. Director* (1990), the Supreme Court tacitly approved the right of surrogate decision makers to act on behalf of permanently unconscious patients. The court cited a line of influential cases from California. That line of cases evolved into the concept that "by permitting the conservator to exercise vicariously a patient's right to choose, guided by his best interests, we do the only thing within our power to continue to respect him as an individual and to preserve his rights" (*Conservatorship of Drabick* 1988, at 855).

Drabick and *Cruzan*, therefore, provide widely accepted cultural values and beliefs that suggest there is a slippery slope. Opponents of death with dignity have aligned their arguments that physician-assisted suicide would not be limited to competent, terminal patients who make voluntary requests with known history.

Furthermore, again, the practices in the Netherlands have been used to frame opposition arguments about a slippery slope:

> During the past 2 decades, the Netherlands has moved from considering assisted suicide (preferred over euthanasia by the Dutch Voluntary Euthanasia Society) to giving legal sanction to both physician-assisted suicide and euthanasia for those who are chronically ill, from euthana-

> sia for physical illness to euthanasia for psychological distress, and from voluntary euthanasia to nonvoluntary and involuntary euthanasia. (Hendin et al. 1997:1720)

University physician Carlos F. Gomez, author of *Regulating Death: Euthanasia and the Case of the Netherlands*, states about the record of euthanasia in the Netherlands:

> What is becoming increasingly evident, as the bare outlines of their practice are fleshed out, is that the Dutch experience should serve as a cautionary tale, rather than a model program. What purportedly began as the ultimate exercise in patient autonomy has degenerated into the ultimate abuse in civil rights: innocent and unconsenting people are being killed, and the agents of their deaths are physicians, who are acting with the tacit consent of the courts. (Gomez 1992:6)

A final theme of frame alignment takes a middle-of-the-road approach. One medical ethicist who advocates this approach is Daniel Callahan, who sees a single moral obsession behind both medicine's attempts to overcome mortality and attempts to solve the problem of suffering by permitting euthanasia. Each seeks compulsively to solve the problem of human existence through control. But that control is illusory, says Callahan. Everyone dies, and we all live with mortality. Hence more effort ought to be made to enhance the likelihood of a good death (Callahan 1993).

Other analysts such as hospice advocate Ira Byock (Byock 1997; Wilkes 1997) and Elisabeth Kubler-Ross (Kubler-Ross 1969; 1978) add that dying presents an opportunity for family unification, fuller human realization, and other personal benefits. As de Hennezel explains: "[T]he last interval before death can also be the culmination of the shaping of a human being, even as it transforms everyone else involved. There is still time for many things to live themselves out, on a different plane, more interior and more subtle, the plane of human emotions" (de Hennezel 1997:xiv).

These arguments have come from many in the medical profession who hope to change the momentum of efforts to legalize physician-assisted suicide. They have attempted to blunt the arguments of death with dignity reformers by calling for better training in pain management and palliative care and better communication between physicians and patients and their families. Indeed, many practitioners, including the president of the AMA, have admitted that assisted suicide reform has been a wake-up call to the medical profession to do a better job.

Moreover, say proponents of the middle-of-the-road approach, legalizing physician-assisted suicide would actually hinder alternatives such as better pain care and hospice. Economic interests could lead health care providers to make suicide more available than long-term palliative care. There is some evidence that this has occurred in the Netherlands, where hospice has remained relatively rare.

These arguments are summed up well by a writer for *Christianity Today*, who said:

> Instead of seeking legal protection for euthanasia, we would do better as a society to develop our present resources. The hospice movement, for example, needs volunteers, money, and facilities to provide a less costly and more caring context for dying. And there is room for better use of our present knowledge in managing and eliminating pain. If we put our energies into these approaches, we may discover once again that we are all connected and that agony can have meaning. (Neff 1991)

In summary, these descriptions of frame alignment depict proponents and opponents actively debating the question of whether physician-assisted suicide should get legal protection. Proponents of legal reform have sought to capitalize mostly on previously proclaimed commitments to "freedom of choice" and the "right to self-determination." By contrast, opponents have persisted that assisted suicide would eventually worsen the problem of medicalized dying by reproducing societal discrimination. The formation of links such as these has facilitated frame alignment insofar as each side has invoked and employed select ideologies to justify its own position along preferred lines. Each side has attempted to keep the debate firmly situated in, and hopefully bound by, a set of values and discursive themes contained in the larger sociopolitical milieu.

CONCLUSION: CONTESTING THE LEGAL TREATMENT OF DYING

As this chapter has shown, during the last half of this century the war on death and disease gained momentum, and we entered the age of delayed degenerative diseases. Pain, suffering, and drug stupor became major side effects of medicalized death. Patients who valued quality of life more than just quantity of life began to demand the right to say no to modern medicine. Doctors who wanted to help lamented that their hands were tied by the law and professional ethics. A few doctors went public with the claim that legal change was needed, and soon the subject of better dying had a firm place in public, legal, and medical discourse and on reform agendas.

Treatment withholding and withdrawal became firmly entrenched in clinical practice. The principle of double effect has become more widely understood and accepted, and it is beginning to be sanctioned by legal authorities. But there are still those terminally ill people who do not want to be all doped up or who do not want to be in hospitals at all. They are making a claim that if the ends are the same—in this case death—why should the terminally ill not be permitted to request a lethal dose of medicine to hasten their deaths?

A great majority of people in the general public who think ahead to their own deaths agree that physician-assisted suicide ought to be available legally. That is why the early initiatives in Washington and California started off with strong voter support. Yet fears of abuse have never lost their importance. That is a primary reason why including injections in the early proposals led to their defeat. An injection requires direct aid in death; putting prescription medicine in one's own mouth and swallowing it puts the final act of inducing death in the hand of patients. The ODDA makes this distinction. As one of the reformers noted, "We knew we could not get social change if we tried a law which disregarded the people the law would govern" (Duncan 1996).

The chapters that follow examine the contestation of assisted suicide law in close focus. Chapter 2, "Death with Dignity: The Early States, 1991–1992," details the history of the first citizen initiative efforts—in Washington (1991) and California (1992)—to legalize "physician aid in dying," rhetoric which includes both assisted suicide and lethal injections. We discuss the individuals and organizations who formed the movement, political conduciveness, coalition building, campaign funding, campaign strategies and counter-strategies (including the use of opinion polls and focus groups), and media ads designed to sway voters. The chapter concludes with an analysis of why these initiatives failed.

Chapter 3, "Passage of the Oregon Death With Dignity Act," details and analyzes the passage of the world's first law legalizing physician-assisted suicide, a law passed by citizen initiative. The chapter is based on our interviews with principal proponents and opponents of the ODDA, comprehensive access to materials from the proponent campaign, and participant observation data from the campaign. Chapter 4, "A Movement to Repeal the Oregon Death With Dignity Act," focuses on the 1997 voter campaign to repeal the ODDA.

Chapter 5, "Compassion in Dying: The Assisted Suicide Test Cases" presents the history of two federal cases that were eventually ruled upon by the United States Supreme Court in 1997. The cases, *Vacco v. Quill* (1997) and *Washington v. Glucksberg* (1997), failed to get a *Roe v. Wade* (1973)-like ruling for the right to assisted suicide. The chapter describes the strategies as explained by the principal players in interviews and from their briefs, the supporting and opposition arguments written by the many amici organizations;

the rulings in the lower courts; and media, professional, and scholarly reactions to those rulings. Analysis of what the Supreme Court wrote and how it has been interpreted is also included.

Chapter 6, "Building the Safe Harbor: The Implementation of the ODDA," details the processes whereby health care associations and state agencies worked to fulfill the reporting and monitoring requirements in the ODDA. We also describe the efforts of many in the health care community to create guidelines for physicians who participate in the ODDA. Chapter 6 provides a complete picture of the negotiations that took place to achieve a consensus between many organizations to amend the ODDA and make it more workable in actual clinical practice.

Chapter 7, "Death with Dignity in Other States and Other Countries," provides a brief analysis of the failed 1998 Michigan and 2000 Maine initiatives, and an analysis of efforts in other states where various bills have been introduced but not passed. The chapter will also discuss the simultaneous emergence of anti–assisted suicide bills. In addition, we discuss the Dutch euthanasia experience in depth and provide information on legal efforts to reform the law related to end-of-life issues in many countries.

Finally, in Chapter 8, "The Good Death: Changing Moral Boundaries," we recapitulate the "natural history" of the death with dignity movement. That history includes efforts to overcome the cultural perception of those whose physical anguish supersedes their will to live as sick, inept, or despondent. It also includes efforts to remove the stigma from physicians who help patients expedite death, so that they would be viewed not as killers but as "midwives throughout the dying process," as one prominent physician activist has called himself.

2

Death with Dignity

THE EARLY STATES, 1991–1992

INTRODUCTION

When Dr. Jack Kevorkian assisted his first known suicide patient in June 1990, people all around the nation were expressing general support for the right to die. A poll conducted by the Times Mirror Center for the People and the Press indicated that eight in ten Americans believed that patients should be allowed to die in some circumstances, and half believed that incurably ill people should have a right to commit suicide (Associated Press 1990). The latter figure was up from 40 percent who expressed such a view in a 1975 Gallup poll. And that increase was even larger when respondents were asked what could be done with patients suffering great pain with no hope for improvement. In that instance, 55 percent said there is a moral right to commit suicide (Associated Press 1990). That number was up 9 percent from Gallup's 1975 survey.

Moreover, a May 1991 Roper Poll of 1500 people in California, Oregon, and Washington—commissioned by the Hemlock Society, a nationwide group that supports active voluntary euthanasia for the terminally ill—indicated that 60 percent of those polled thought the law should be changed to allow doctors to assist a suffering person in ending his or her life. Another 8 percent answered "don't know," leaving just 32 percent who believed the law should remain unchanged. Several other findings from that poll proved to be of significance in later movement efforts. For example, while on the one hand two-thirds of respondents approved of power of attorney statutes authorizing someone else to ask the doctor to administer drugs to end their lives if they are incompetent, fewer respondents would approve the giving of a lethal injection by physicians to end life (54 percent) than would favor the idea of a physician writing out a prescription for a lethal drug and the patient taking his or her own life (60 percent). These findings were unaffected by religious preference: physician "aid in dying" as a legal concept was favored by 67 percent of Protestants and 66 percent of Roman Catholics surveyed, as compared to 68 percent of the total public. Moreover, lesser educated and lower-income people were only slightly less likely to favor euthanasia.

The Hemlock Society, founded in California in 1980, had grown to be the most widely recognized organization fighting for the right to die. The organization had promoted many battles in courts and legislatures around the country and was greatly responsible for legal changes permitting the withholding and withdrawing of life-sustaining medical treatment and the use of living wills and durable powers of attorney for health care. Bolstered by this decade of success at legal reform, the Hemlock Society announced in July 1987 that it was ready to champion efforts to legalize more direct forms of euthanasia, including assisted suicide and mercy killing. Three states became the target for these efforts: California, Washington, and Oregon. Organization leaders predicted that getting a law passed in one state would lead to passage in a second state, and then a third, like a domino effect ("AAHS Moves Forward on Right-to-Die Legislation" 1987). The first effort was launched in California in 1988, but organizational disarray at the grassroots level ended in failure to gather enough signatures to qualify the proposed initiative for the ballot. Organizers then turned to the state of Washington.

CAMPAIGN BEGINNINGS IN WASHINGTON

Washington appeared to be a prime state for euthanasia reform. The state has a history of progressive public policy about death and dying (Jonsen 1991). The use of advance directives was authorized by statute as far back as 1979, at a time when only one other state (California) had a Natural Death Act statute. Later statutes authorized a list of surrogate decision makers to make medical decisions on behalf of both legally competent and incompetent patients.

Furthermore, Washington courts had been active. During the early 1980s, several Washington Supreme Court decisions endorsed the fundamental concepts that have become known as "the right to die," including total brain death as the clinical definition of death, the right of legally competent patients to forgo life support, and the right of surrogates to refuse life-sustaining care for patients in a permanent vegetative state. The only concept that had been rejected by Washington's Supreme Court was the withdrawal of nutrition and hydration from mentally incapacitated persons. In hospitals and ethics meetings all over the nation, this distinction between withdrawing medical treatment and withdrawing food and water was the focal point of debate about what was and was not included in the right to die. Hence, Washington's legal climate was at the cutting edge, a fact noted by Albert Jonsen, an eminent medical historian at the University of Washington (Jonsen 1991). That fact made proponents of euthanasia enthusiastic about Washington. A second factor they hoped would help their campaign was voter attitude.

In addition to the progressive legislation and judicial climate about death, Jonsen (1991) described Washington as having a high respect for autonomy and privacy. Moreover, he claimed, the state has a heritage of progressive, even radical, politics. This was just what euthanasia advocates were looking for. Perhaps most significantly, during the three years prior to the initiative campaign, state polls indicated that 61 percent of Washingtonians favored further euthanasia reform. In addition to these facts, the fact that about 14 percent of adults in Washington claimed no religious affiliation (only Oregon, at 17 percent, reported higher nonaffiliation; the national average was 8 percent) convinced social movement groups like the Hemlock Society that Washington would make an ideal bellwether state for the first major attempt in the nation to decriminalize mercy killing for certain terminal patients.

The initiative campaign began in the church basement of a Unitarian-Universalist community volunteer minister in Seattle, the Reverend Ralph Mero. Reverend Mero, who directed the pro-initiative campaign, was also the director of the Pacific Northwest Region of the Hemlock Society (Belkin 1993b, Biggar 1995). A flurry of national media coverage during the summer of 1991 renewed the prestige of the controversial topic and bolstered the campaign effort. The failure to indict Dr. Timothy Quill, who wrote an article in the *New England Journal of Medicine* detailing how he had prescribed a lethal dose of pain-killing medicine to help a terminally ill female leukemia patient commit suicide, was widely covered by the media. Spurred by this publicity, *Final Exit*, a book written by Derek Humphry, then leader of the Hemlock Society, and published by the Hemlock Society, became a national best seller (Belkin 1993b). The book received a good review in the *New York Times*. The *Wall Street Journal* ran a cover story on the book, including an interview with Humphry. Humphry also debated a representative of the American Medical Association on the *Today Show* (NBC-TV) (Cox 1993:32). The public intrigue surrounding the Nancy Cruzan story (the woman whose parents' request to remove her life support was the first to be decided by the United States Supreme Court) and the assisted suicides associated with Dr. Jack Kevorkian were also in the public eye at this time. In the wake of all this activity, the Washington chapter of the Hemlock Society threw its weight behind the Washington initiative.

Washington's initiative and referendum law allows an approved initiative to go before the state legislature for action. If the legislature fails to enact the initiative, it is to go on the ballot at the next general election. As expected, news of the initiative's certification was received coldly by Senate Republicans, who announced they would send the measure straight to the November statewide ballot. The legislature decided not to consider the initiative.

The campaign attracted a wide-ranging coalition of volunteers, including physicians, clergy, lawyers, citizens groups, and terminal patients (King 1991b). Among the many diverse civic organizations behind the campaign were: the Seattle-King County Bar Association, the Physicians for "Yes" on Initiative #119, the American Civil Liberties Union (ACLU) of Washington, the Northwest AIDS Foundation, the National Organization for Women of Washington State, the Puget Sound Council of Senior Citizens, the National Association of Social Workers, and the Washington State Democratic party. In addition, the following religious organizations lined up their followers in favor of the proposal: the Interfaith Clergy for "Yes" on Initiative #119, the Northwest Annual Conference of the United Methodist Church, the National Council of Jewish Women, and the Unitarian Universalist Association of the USA.

The group raised some $1.6 million, at the time one of the largest sums ever collected for an initiative campaign (King 1991b). A professional twelve-member phone bank dialed around the state seeking contributions. Other volunteers sent 125,000 pieces of mail around the nation. Each week, hundreds of checks arrived at the campaign headquarters in Lake Union (Simon 1991a). Most were for $25 or less (Public Disclosure Commission 1991). Many of the donations were accompanied with stories of pain and personal tragedy. One woman told the story of her husband's slow and painful death from prostate cancer. "I loved him so much, but not enough! Had it been me, instead of him, dying of cancer, he would have found a safe way to put me out of my misery," she wrote. The horror of his death is "what this insane world promotes by not allowing a civilized death as we do for animals," she continued. "We are long overdue for death with dignity." Another woman wrote about her sister, who died after a long battle with breast cancer. "Having seen what happened to Diane, I pray that Initiative 119 will pass. . . . I do not want to go through the pain and suffering that my little sister endured" (Ostrom 1991).

The campaign was part of the Hemlock Society's national agenda, and for the first time in an initiative effort nearly half of the money came from outside the state (Public Disclosure Commission 1991; Simon 1991a, c). Of the top forty-four contributions to the Washington Hemlock PAC, which ranged from $500 to $2000, only three were from local donors (Public Disclosure Commission 1991). Given the nationwide support, including donations from members and chapters of the Hemlock Society, the campaign chest for Initiative 119 swelled to a record level, making it the most successful fundraising effort supporting any state initiative since record-keeping began in 1975 (Ostrom 1991). Most significantly, the pro-campaign was raising double the amount raised by the opposition.

THE PROVISIONS OF INITIATIVE 119

As drafted, the Washington initiative (I-119) contained three provisions. The first defined "persistent vegetative state" and "irreversible coma" as conditions under which life support systems could be withdrawn if a patient requested withdrawal in a living will. The status quo provided for the withholding or withdrawal of treatment from patients with "terminal conditions" only. Since, from the medical perspective, irreversible coma and persistent vegetative state are not in themselves terminal conditions, the sponsors of I-119 sought, through this new language, to expand the conditions under which treatment could be legally withdrawn in Washington (McGough and Straley 1991).

The second provision listed artificial nutrition and hydration as life-sustaining procedures that could be refused or withdrawn. The 1979 Washington Natural Death Act refers only to "life-sustaining procedures" without naming specific types of life support machinery. While sponsors said this provision would merely "clear up confusion," in fact at that time forgoing food and water was one of the most controversial aspects of the right to die (Meisel 1992). Hence, any pronouncement of law could have been viewed as an effort to change the status quo.

The third and most controversial provision stated that physicians could provide assisted suicide and active euthanasia as medical services to competent, terminally ill adult patients who request them. Dubbed physician "aid in dying" by the initiative's sponsors, this last provision would make Washington state the only place in the world where the intentional killing of patients by physicians had been formally decriminalized.

The first two provisions were first proposed to the Washington legislature in 1988, three years before the initiative effort. The state's Natural Death Act had been criticized for its overly cautious definition of "terminal condition" and for its omission of explicit reference to nutrition and hydration as life-sustaining measures that may be forgone. The first two amendments sought to correct these deficiencies. This aspect of the initiative had generally been welcomed (Jonsen 1991:467). The changes had been supported by the Democratic-controlled House but had met resistance in past years among more conservative members of the Republican-controlled Senate, who managed to stall and kill the bill each time it appeared before the Health and Long-term Care Committee (Spencer 1991). The final provision, permitting aid in dying, was a radical departure from prevailing law and medical ethics. It was a political hot potato with damage potential as high as that associated with abortion reform measures. Hence, the idea of amending the extant Natural Death Act was politically astute. Associating the radical change with useful and broadly approved amendments made radical change seem less radical.

Additionally, the initiative included the following safeguards:

1. The aid-in-dying provisions of I-119 were totally voluntary for patients, physicians, and hospitals.
2. Only conscious, mentally competent, terminally ill patients with less than six months to live could voluntarily request aid in dying.
3. No one could request aid in dying for anyone else.
4. Two impartial people were required to witness the written request of the terminal patient for aid in dying. They could not be family members, heirs, or employees of the physician or health care facility.
5. A terminally ill patient could revoke his or her request at any time.
6. Two doctors had to indicate in writing that the terminally ill patient had less than six months to live. One of the physicians was to be the patient's primary doctor.
7. Physicians could require a psychological evaluation to ensure that the patient was mentally competent, not depressed, and that the request was voluntary.
8. Aid in dying could be requested at the time it was to be provided only, not in advance.
9. Terminally ill patients and their physicians could seek advice from any family members or clergy they chose (State of Washington Secretary of State 1991).

The pro-initiative campaign characterized these safeguards as "carefully written" and "strict."

FOCUS GROUPS

On March 14, 1991, two focus groups were held in Seattle to initiate voter opinion research on behalf of the proponents of Initiative 119 (Fairbank, Bregman, and Maullin 1991). Findings from that research were integral to the planning of the Washington campaign (Cooper 1998). Of most significance was the confusion about the phrase "aid in dying." The positive side of that confusion, claimed pollsters, was that voters were not necessarily associating the ballot title with hastening death, which was more controversial (Fairbanks et al. 1991). Conversely, confusion among voters could easily be exploited to spread misinformation about how aid in dying might be administered to play out negative scenarios. While participants generally supported the entire measure, they were clearly less comfortable and more anxious about the provisions allowing the hastening of death; the intensity of support seemed to waver when they were informed that the measure included that provision (Fairbanks et al.

1991). A related issue was the effect of the term "euthanasia." Proponents were urged to avoid the term at all times because of its negative connotations implying involuntary killing.

Another issue that troubled even strong supporters of euthanasia was the possibility that aid in dying may be used by the wrong people. The fear was that patients would opt for the procedure before all hope was truly exhausted. A related concern was that incompetent or malicious doctors might take advantage of patients, especially those with Alzheimer's disease. Nevertheless, much of the fear was assuaged when the focus group participants were told of the initiative's purported safeguards. But for those who opposed the initiative on religious grounds, nothing persuaded them to change their views. Religious opposition, declared voter researchers, appeared to be a nonnegotiable position. On the other side, the most powerful arguments voiced by supporters were freedom of choice, the desire to retain control of one's body, and the desire to end suffering.

THE PROPONENTS' CAMPAIGN STRATEGIES

Proponents began framing the campaign message with memoranda written by the campaign leadership. Reverend Ralph Mero and Reverend Marvin Evans suggested very similar approaches. Reverend Mero was sincere about the ability of voters to make the correct decision without proponents having to criticize the opposition. "We can occupy the moral high ground without involving ourselves in mud-slinging," wrote Mero (1991a). Instead, Mero suggested that the campaign should focus on the conditions of modern dying. Those conditions include expensive medical care; a big, impersonal health care industry; competing interests between doctors and hospitals in making money; and the decision-making power of doctors. Mero also stressed the favorability of families, not courts or the state, to make life-and-death decisions for patients. Given the entirety of these conditions, Mero sought to focus on the message that death is preferable to pain and suffering, irreversible coma, or a persistent vegetative state.

Reverend Marvin Evans suggested a similar framework for the campaign message. Reverend Evans wrote, "If we stick steadfastly to [the conditions of dying], we can sidestep our opponents' attempt to frame the debate their way by making inflammatory statements about the potential for abuse and our supposed lack of religious values" (Evans 1991). Similar to Mero, Evans remarked that physicians need to change the viewpoint that what they treat is disease, not patients. Evans described other conditions and facts about dying. The fact that many dying patients know they are dying should be owned up to, and when they have accepted the inevitable, their doctors should acquiesce and help them. Similarly, since the American Medical Association estimates that 70 percent of all deaths that occur in hospitals come after some decision to stop or forgo treatment, the law should permit as many reasonable options as possible. The campaign framework, Evans concluded, was that the guiding force should be patient choice, regardless of whether a patient chooses to have tubes left in to the bitter end or to have death hastened when death is imminent.

The two Reverends agreed to run a tame campaign, sticking to their own issues without maligning the opposition. However, their campaign director, Karen Cooper, suggested a far more aggressive approach. Cooper directly disagreed with Mero and charged that it was important to "identify the enemy" and assert that "we are the people, they are the bad guys" (Cooper 1991a). She also believed that Evans's approach was not proactive enough. Describing the status quo without revealing who the opposition is and pounding home what will happen if the opponent wins is not enough to win an election, she claimed (Cooper 1991b). Unlike Reverends Mero and Evans, Cooper had built a career around campaign directing and consulting.

Later in this chapter, the analysis of why the Washington and California initiatives were defeated will explore the claim that when voters are unsure, they vote "no." A pertinent quotation from a memorandum by Cooper sought to explain this point to Mero and Evans:

> We are the "yes" side of this ballot measure and therefore [we] are at a definite disadvantage. Because we are advocating a change from the status quo it is more time consuming and difficult to explain the reasons why we need a change. It is easy for the "no" side simply to seed confusion and doubt about the effects of any change. When voters are confused they vote no. They know what they have with the status quo. It may not be perfect, but it is known. For them to vote "yes" they must come to believe that the change is needed, that the intended change will be the result and that any unintended consequences will not be worse than the status quo. This is a lot for a voter to do. (Cooper 1991c)

The experience that Cooper brought to the campaign was further evident in her focus on voter perceptions. The modern conditions of dying are important, she agreed, but more important is what the typical voter *believes* the conditions to be. Thus,

> [a] well targeted campaign message must tap into what voters "perceive" about the issue with the one or two best arguments to keep the existing base of "yes" support intact (reinforcing what people already believe) and

> the one or two best arguments which move "undecided" or "no" voters to the "yes" column (tapping into doubts or uncertainties which undermine the "no" position). (Cooper 1991c)

Data that serve to create an accurate picture of the status quo are necessary yet insufficient if they fail to reveal voter perceptions, claimed Cooper. A campaign that does not maintain a correct view of voter perceptions simply cannot impact, let alone control, the changes in voter opinions that occur during a high-profile campaign: "To avoid or minimize [voter swings] (if we are ahead) or to cause movement to our side (if we are behind) we need to know how voters perceive the issues involved before the message delivery phase of the campaign begins" (Cooper 1991c).

On the basis of her expert knowledge, Cooper insisted that the proper way to frame the proponents' campaign would be to identify the campaign's enemies and attack them ruthlessly and, similarly, to create and maintain a wide gap between support for the proponents and enmity for their enemies (Cooper 1991d). But as politically astute as Cooper's views seemed, Mero responded with some insightful points of his own:

> We should be very careful about what we say about the opposition, especially the right to life movement and the Catholic Church. Describing Human Life of Washington as "right wing extremists" ignores the fact that they have not taken ultra-conservative positions on issues other than abortion, birth control, and death with dignity. The Roman Catholic Church is seen as "ultra-liberal" on many issues such as welfare, health care, education, non-reproductive women's issues, and child care. We must look soberly at what our Catholic opponents will argue, and develop counterarguments around our claim that an amorphous mechanized medical system that treats people like statistics and serves its own financial interests is the real opposition. (Mero 1991b)

Thus, even against his own campaign director, Mero championed the need to take the high road, warning that lambasting the opposition could result in an embarrassing situation in which proponents would have to backpedal. Mero insisted on a conservative framework within which the proponents would not appear to overstate their position with exaggerated claims about the opposition. The concluding section of this chapter explores how these different approaches played out, and how each may be useful in explaining the outcome of the initiative effort.

A second strategy by which the proponents sought to frame the debate was through a detailed media relations plan. Their primary goal was to reinforce what voters already believed. Those beliefs formed the basis of the memoranda by Reverends Mero and Evans quoted above. They include a conviction among many people that pain and suffering is often a fate worse than death and also the perception that modern medicine is impersonal largely because of technical training and economic competition between providers. They include a value system within which self-determination, choice, and autonomy are central to a sense of individual well-being. To reinforce these beliefs, the proponents set out "to control the media so that our story, not our opponents' story, is the one told all over the world" (Cooper 1991d).

A successful media plan required several important elements. At the local and state levels, the campaign planned to target the state's twenty-five daily newspapers, hundreds of weeklies, and dozens of special interest publications. This would be an arduous task, for it would not be enough to just blanket the press with generic letters and stories. Instead, the campaign would need to address the needs and interests of particular readers in specific political regions. Press coverage in these regions would have to be monitored carefully, so that questions and concerns could be addressed before the opposition had a chance to create or exploit misinformation. Also, local papers would pick up and report key messages and themes delivered by speakers from constituency groups such as doctors, clergy, nurses, lawyers, and social workers. In the same way, a successful national press strategy would be planned to "buy" millions of dollars of free advertising (Cooper 1991d).

Public speakers provided a third vital element of framing and reframing the campaign message. They would not only provide a rich source for local and national press coverage, as just described, but would also facilitate intimate meetings between interested voters and campaign representatives at the very local level. In fact, hundreds of engagements were scheduled from September through the first week of November. The formats included prepared talks, debates, and question-and-answer sessions. Primary groups recruited to speak included Physicians for "Yes" on Initiative 119, Interfaith Clergy for "Yes" on Iniative 119, the Hemlock Society, Unitarians for Death with Dignity, Nurses for Yes on 119, and Lawyers for Yes on 119. Forums targeted included county Republican and Democratic meetings, Republican legislative meetings, service clubs, state conventions and statewide organizations, chambers of commerce, Jaycees, League of Women Voters, labor union conventions, county labor council meetings, senior citizens clubs' and living groups, AARP, Catholics for Choice, and many others. From a strategic perspective, the campaign leadership impressed upon its speakers that everyone who speaks must deliver the same message. And for their part, leaders kept key opinion leaders around the state informed about the race. A small newsletter was planned to report the campaign highlights, a list of fundraisers, and good quotes from the media. Opinion leaders included the leadership of professional medical associations, of course, as well as the groups listed in Table 2.1.

Many of these groups provided endorsements for the proponents' campaign, and getting a distinguished list of endorsements formed a fourth factor in the campaign strategy. A general list of the groups sought included clergy and religious groups, elderly groups, AIDS support groups and gay and lesbian groups, health professionals and consumers, political and civic groups, business and service groups, women's/pro-choice groups, professional associations, labor groups, and minority groups. When the official campaign plan was published in May 1991, the groups that had endorsed the campaign included eight clergy and religious groups, five elderly groups, five AIDS support, gay, and lesbian groups, seven groups representing health professionals and consumers, ten political and civic groups, three women's and pro-choice groups, six professional associations, and a single labor group. Table 2.2 lists these groups by name, identifies groups that had declined support, and lists groups that the I-119 campaign was still targeting.

Table 2.1 Opinion Leaders Sought by I–119 Proponents

Anti-Defamation League staff	National Association for the Advancement of Colored People staff and board
Chambers of Commerce officers	Pastors of Black churches
City club officers, board, and members	Pastors of Protestant churches
City, state, and county boards and commissions	Pillipino youth activities officers
City, state, and county department heads and key staff	Political Action Committee directors and boards
Community council officers and members	Priests and Catholic laity
Democratic party chairs and officers	Rabbis and Jewish lay officials
Democratic PCs	Republican PCs
El Centro staff and board	Rotary Club officers
Elected officials and staff	School Parent Teacher Association officers
Environmental group officers	School principals and vice principals
Japanese American Citizens League staff and board	Senior center staff and officers
Jewish Federation staff and board	Senior citizen organizations
King County Bar staff officers and board	Small business owners
Kiwanis Club officers	Social service groups
Labor union officers and staff	Trial lawyers
League of Women Voters	Washington Education Association teacher representatives
Lions Club officers and staff	Washington Women United
Lobbyists	Women in Unity
	Women's Political Caucus

(Cooper 1991d)

Table 2.2 Endorsements Won, Lost, and Sought by the I-119 Campaign Six Months before the Vote

Endorsed	Declined
CLERGY AND RELIGIOUS	
Clergy for Yes on Initiative 119 Pacific Northwest District, Unitarian Universalist Association Unitarian Universalist Association—National Methodists of Washington State National Council of Jewish Women—Seattle National Council of Jewish Women—Washington State Temple De Hirsh Sinai—Social Action Committee Temple Tikvah Chadasha	None
Targets	
Anti-Defamation League Jewish Federation Young Jewish Leadership Organization	
ELDERLY	
Gray Panthers of Washington Gray Panthers of Kitsap County Older Women's League, Seattle-King County Older Women's League, Spokane Puget Sound Council of Senior Citizens	None
Targets	
AARP individual chapters Retired judges	
AIDS SUPPORT AND GAY AND LESBIAN GROUPS	
ACT-UP, Seattle AIDS Task Force, Plymouth Congregational Church Gay and Lesbian Democrats Northwest AIDS Foundation Olympia AIDS Task Force Seattle AIDS Support Group	Chicken Soup Brigade
Targets	
Greater Seattle Business Association SEAMEC [Seattle Metropolitan Elections Committee]	
HEALTH PROFESSIONALS AND CONSUMERS	
Group Health Cooperative of Puget Sound (HMO), Senior Caucus Nurses for "Yes" on Initiative 119 Health Information Network Physicians for Yes on Initiative 119 Washington State Nursing Home Residents Councils Patients for 119 Hospice Workers for 119	Alzheimer's Association of Puget Sound American Academy of Family Physicians American Cancer Society American Heart Association American Lung Association of Washington State American Medical Holistic Association Cancer Lifeline Muscular Dystrophy Association Nurses Local 1199 United Staff Nurses Union Washington State Psychological Association
Targets	
Washington Assembly for Citizens with Disabilities	

Table 2.2 *(continued)*

Endorsed	Declined
POLITICAL AND CIVIC	
American Civil Liberties Union of Washington Americans for Democratic Action—Washington Hemlock Society of Washington State Humanists of Washington Humanists of Portland—Vancouver metro area Libertarian party of Washington State Memorial Association of Spokane Metropolitan Democratic Club National Hemlock Society Washington State Democratic party	Daughters of the Pioneers Woodland Park Zoological Society
Targets	
Citizen Action WashPIRG [Public Interest Research Group]	
BUSINESS AND SERVICE	
None	None
Targets	
Chambers of Commerce Rotary Kiwanis Lions Jaycees Eagles Elks Veterans	
WOMEN'S GROUPS/PRO-CHOICE	
National Organization for Women—Washington State Women's Political Caucus, King County, Washington Evergreen Democratic Women's Club	Washington Women's Lawyers Northwest Women's Law Center Business and Professional Women
Targets	
Women's Political Caucus—Washington State and national Women's Business Network	
PROFESSIONAL ASSOCIATIONS	
National Association of Social Workers—Washington Subcommittee on Aging National Association of Social Workers—Washington State Lawyers for Yes on Initiative 119 Social Workers in Home Care Social Workers for Yes on Initiative 119 Washington State Society for Clinical Social Work	None
Targets	
Seattle-King County Bar Association American Association of University Women National Lawyers Guild Washington State Trial Lawyers	
LABOR	
Clallam County Retired Teachers	None

Table 2.2 *(continued)*

Endorsed	**Declined**
LABOR *(continued)*	
Targets	
Teamsters	
Seattle Education Association	
Sno-King Retired Teachers	
Washington State Labor Council	
Washington Education Association	
King County Labor Council	
Individual locals	
Communications Workers of America (CWA)	
Aero-mechanics	
Building Trades Council	
Carpenters	
Federal employees	
MINORITY ORGANIZATIONS	
None	Shanti
	Washington Association of Black Social Workers
Targets	
Women in Unity	
Black ministers and churches	
Asian groups	
Japanese American Citizens League	
El Centro de la Raza	
National Association for the Advancement of Colored People	
Urban League	
Chinese Tongs	
Vietnamese organizations	

(Cooper 1991d)

Some of the groups listed in Table 2.2 were selected for requests of their mail and phone lists. Contacting people from mail and phone lists was identified as another important strategy for reminding people to vote "yes." Moreover, contacts made from mail and phone lists provided an essential source of campaign donations. Appeals for money included a description of the initiative provisions, a declaration of the safeguards included in the initiative, and a statement of the expectation that Washington would serve as a model for other states. An example of an appeal for money is a letter sent to Hemlock Society supporters seeking start-up contributions to help with costs of printing petitions, mailing, and coordinating three hundred volunteers. The mailer sought contributions of $500, $250, or $100. Contributors were asked to make checks payable to the Washington State Hemlock Society. The letters were signed by Reverend Ralph Mero, President, Hemlock Society of Washington State.

These five strategies for framing the campaign message—framing the campaign message, managing a detailed media relations plan, managing public speakers, getting a distinguished list of endorsements, and maintaining mail and phone lists as sources of contributions and votes—formed the basis of the proponents' efforts to keep and win over new supporters and voters. Meanwhile, a similar campaign was being planned and waged by the campaign's opponents.

THE OPPOSITION

The first signs of opposition came from the Washington State Medical Association (WSMA), whose House of Delegates voted by an overwhelming majority at the annual meeting in 1990 to mount a vigorous campaign against the initiative. But by March 1991, an informal poll of 2000 members (50 percent responding) indicated that members were nearly evenly split over the issue: 49 percent favored WSMA support of Initiative 119, while 51 percent opposed it. In April, the WSMA board of trustees, without rescinding the earlier House of Delegates vote, decided officially not to recognize Washington Physicians Against 119, the private group formed to mount a campaign against passage of the initiative. The WSMA spokesperson stated that since the membership was divided, "there were other ways to oppose [the initiative] without getting directly involved" (Jonsen 1991:468).

Nevertheless, the WSMA did involve itself directly, pouring $40,000 into an anti-119 advertising campaign (Dority 1992; Public Disclosure Commission 1991; Robinson 1991). The association distributed a poster reading "Vote NO" and stressing the vagueness of the phrase "physician aid in dying," the inequities of choice inherent in the inequalities of socioeconomic status, the path to slippery slope arguments for further expansion of the law, and the social significance of the public trust that is secured by the core ethic of the physician's Hippocratic oath: not to kill one's patients, even when they plead for it (McGough and Straley 1991). An op-ed column in the *Seattle Times* written by a nationally syndicated columnist captured the sentiment of the association's opposition:

> There is good reason why the categorical Hippocratic taboo is so ancient, and so universal: A license to kill inevitably corrupts the doctor and endangers the patient. Euthanasia, once permitted, is not as easily contained as its promoters pretend. . . . The bright line must be drawn precisely between passive and active measures. Withdrawing treatment at a patient's request is one thing. No one is to endure the indignities of high tech medicine. But

> actively killing is quite another. It opens the gate to the most terrible abuses. First the terminally ill, then Down's syndrome children, then the Alzheimer's patients, and then anyone whose life we do not consider worth living. (Krauthammer 1991:A11)

The medical association pressured newspapers and TV stations across the state to oppose I-119 by pointing out the dangers of euthanasia. Both electronic and print reporters ran stories of how alarmed several hospitals and nursing homes had become over the prospects of the initiative's passage. The AMA Ethics and Judicial Council, at the national level, reaffirmed their continued opposition to doctor-assisted suicide and euthanasia by issuing statements in which Hippocrates—revered as the father of Western medicine and the author of the Hippocratic oath—was quoted (Cox 1993:162–163).

In conjunction with the opposition efforts of the WSMA, the group of doctors organized under the banner "Washington Physicians Against 119" issued a one-page flyer that listed ten reasons why their group opposed I-119 and implied that the voters should do likewise. The reasons were as follows:

1. "We want to care for our patients and not kill them . . . as doctors have been doing for 2,400 years."
2. "We want to offer terminal patients compassionate care and not death."
3. "Initiative 119 is not in the public's interest"—but rather offers the easy way out.
4. "It is intentionally vague because most people do not understand what 'aid in dying' and 'death with dignity' mean."
5. "Initiative 119 could easily destroy patient trust in doctors."
6. "119 would undermine the standard of care for everyone."
7. "The right to refuse to be kept alive by machines in Washington is already well established through the Natural Death Act of 1979."
8. "It establishes the fundamental right to die," but it would open the door to court challenges, allowing suicide on demand for everyone—even depressed teenagers.
9. "We don't want to be forced to participate in euthanasia."
10. "Doctors are human beings" and should not have the burden of killing other human beings.

The opposition's strategy was to turn the initiative on its head. The initiative's authors intended to write a law that maximized the values of autonomy and self-determination in health care decision making. To this end, they intentionally omitted any requirement that patients seek advice or instruction from counselors, doctors, or family members, since in many instances it is they who seek to change a patient's mind, often for self-interested reasons. Although the referendum was carefully crafted to avoid such conflicts, opponents cleverly recast it as "flawed" and "lacking in safeguards." They argued that even people who support the concept of physicians killing patients should vote against this proposal because it did not require patient counseling, a waiting period, consultation with a patient's long-term physician, a standard for determining a patient's mental or emotional competence, or family notification. Proponents could have focused on the absence of requirements as absolutely essential to the safeguarding of patient choice and accused the opponents of turning the intent of the proposed law against itself. Instead, the initiative's sponsors unintentionally legitimized their opponents' strategy by focusing their primary efforts on debating opposition claims.

To boost the opposition, an appeal was made to Catholic bishops and Catholic organizations around the country. The Catholic bishops of Washington and Oregon responded with a 5000-word joint pastoral letter expressing opposition to any effort to legalize euthanasia. The letter stated, "As a society we cannot and must not sanction the intentional killing of life" ("Northwest Bishops Denounces Euthanasia" 1991). Archbishop Thomas Murphy denounced the initiative during masses throughout the state, charging that the initiative "breaks the covenant of life which God has shared with us" and urging Roman Catholics to vote against the measure as a matter of "loyalty, stewardship, and simplicity" (Brown 1991).

Opposition mounted as the WSMA mailed posters and letters to 5000 physicians statewide requesting that they hang the posters and mail letters to patients urging them to vote against the referendum. Sample letters were drafted that said: "Death is an irreversible decision. Once effected, you cannot change your mind. Until a better solution is found, if there is ANY doubt in your mind on this important matter, you should vote against Initiative 119." One Washington resident, who received a variation of the letter from her doctor, said she had not had time to thoroughly study the issue, but generally agreed with her doctor's arguments: "Just reading [my doctor's] perspective on the issue was very helpful to me," said Amy Heinan. Two weeks later, 267 physicians had requested nearly 100,000 additional brochures (King 1991a).

In late September, the WSMA announced its reopposition to the referendum. The same day, in an apparently unprecedented action, the Catholic Church organized a major voter registration drive to swell the voting ranks before the general election. About one hundred volunteers from seventy parishes were recruited through notices placed in parish bulletins and through advertisements in the Catholic weekly newspaper *The Progress*. Although the Church's official position was that it was not pushing voter registration as a way to tell people how to vote, officials admitted that individual priests might link the two, given the Church's clear position on the initiative (Gilmore 1991). And in parishes across the state, inserts were stuffed into church bulletins, flyers were sent home with parochial school children, and clergy preached against the initiative. Their message stated:

> We are confronted here with a violation of the divine law, an offense against the dignity of the human person, a crime against life and an attack on humanity. Phrases such as "mercy killing," "rational suicide" and "aid-in-dying" or "death with dignity" should not be allowed to obscure the fact that euthanasia is killing an innocent human being. It is morally wrong. No civilized society should condone it. (Gilmore and Simon 1991)

Most significantly, by urging parishioners that it would take millions of dollars to educate the citizens of Washington, parish priests helped fund the opposition campaign by taking up special collections. The Washington State Catholic Conference's "No on 119" committee donated $334,000 ("Initiative Campaign Contributions" 1991; Public Disclosure Commission 1991). The Catholic conference and archdioceses nationwide contributed more than $150,000 (Public Disclosure Commission 1991; Simon 1991b). The Catholic Health Association donated another $50,000; the Sisters of Providence gave another $20,000 ("Initiative Campaign Contributions" 1991; Public Disclosure Commission 1991). The Archdiocese of Seattle and the National Conference of Catholic Bishops pledged $150,000 (Public Disclosure Commission 1991; Simon 1991c). Graham Johnson, executive director of the Public Disclosure Commission, said, "We cannot recall an organization of this kind taking such an active interest in this kind of campaign" (Simon 1991b).

AD WARS

Most of the money collected by the opponents was spent on hard-hitting television advertisements that invoked the fears of voters. The opponents' ads focused on three primary themes: (1) discrimination, (2) the fallibility of medical diagnoses, and (3) the lack of safeguards in the initiative. The ad about discrimination featured an older woman in a conservative orange dress. A hospice nurse, she claimed, "Those who can't afford healthcare and insurance could be pressured to have their lives ended." Moreover, "119 would be a bad law. It would prey on the fears of the aging and the underprivileged." The second theme, regarding the fallibility of medical diagnoses, showed an elderly man named Bill, who, like many senior citizens, believed I-119 would make bad law. He stated, "They diagnosed that I only had a couple weeks to live. It'll be four years ago this coming October. That's the problem with Initiative 119: they're giving some people too much authority to take someone else's life—it's more or less a right to kill."

The apparent goal of another ad was to question the proponents' claims about choice. "To have someone with a piece of paper and a pen saying what a good deal this is, you'd just slip right into it. And if somebody would have done that to me I would have gone 'okay take me,' and I would have been gone." Those statements were spoken by a woman playing with her teenage son. "I've had a lot of good times with my son," she stated. "I think he would have had a hard time forgiving me." A related claim was what opponents of I-119 called the lack of safeguards in the proposed law. "If you're depressed and ask to be put to death, no one has to give you a chance to change your mind," claimed a middle-aged woman in a conservative blue dress. Initiative proponents charged that what she said next stretched the truth about the initiative as far as possible. She stated, "And no special qualifications are needed; an eye doctor could put you to death." Finally, late in the campaign the opponents were joined by Dr. C. Everett Koop, former surgeon general of the United States. In his ad, Dr. Koop stated, "Death with dignity does not come by giving doctors the power to kill. For over 2000 years, doctors have been in the business of healing, not killing. Initiative 119 would end all that, because it would put inappropriate power in the hands of a few doctors willing to kill. The first victims would be the poor, the weak, the aging. Vote against medical homicide. Vote no on 119." Together, taken to their logical extreme, these hard-hitting television ads suggested that aid in dying could easily be abused by diabolical family members with the help of unscrupulous doctors.

In response, Kirk Robinson, president of the proponents' campaign organization, claimed, "Our opponents have launched an aggressive T.V. attack, distorting the facts about Initiative 119. These conservative religious groups are pouring in money from across the country. Thanks to your financial support, we can air ads which tell the truth about Initiative 119. We must protect the rights of individuals who are terminally ill to make their own medical decisions" (Robinson 1991).

Initiative 119 proponents sought to craft a television campaign that would engage, hold, and ultimately convince voters to vote yes on 119. But unlike many candidate and issue campaigns, voters' attitudes regarding the uncharted issue of physician aid in dying were not well defined. For this reason, the campaign hired a market research company—Greer, Margolis, Mitchell & Associates—to conduct focus group testing. Focus groups, although not a statistically valid representation of the voting population (because of the typically limited numbers of participants), are considered to provide insight into the preconceptions and thought patterns that voters exhibit as they consider an issue or candidate and choose a side. Issues that ask voters to examine their personal convictions on such a sensitive and emotional topic as physician aid in dying are particularly suited to focus group research.

The goal of the researchers was to explore several facets of voter attitudes. First was the initial impressions of the issues at stake if aid in dying became law. The researchers were notably interested in the concerns volunteered by focus group participants that had not yet been recognized by the campaigners. The concerns and hopes regarding all of the issues mentioned were a second point of interest. A third was how participants reacted to new information. Were first impressions solidified? Did participants change their minds? Did they become more confused and less unsure about their original opinions? What salience did various arguments have in solidifying or weakening the opinions of focus group participants? These questions were especially relevant to the third aspect of the focus group research—how participants responded on an emotional level. Television ads are short and transitory; therefore, they are most likely to capture voters' attention if they appeal to emotional convictions. For example, the focus group researchers tested whether the core message—that Initiative 119 protects patients' rights to make their own decisions about their own medical care—was too intense if portrayed in the first person (e.g., as if the camera were the patient taking in sights and sounds as a patient would), or whether the same images, captured reportorially, might be more tolerable to viewers. They also tested whether viewers responded better to patients in hospital beds or in their homes. Finally, they tested which message was resonating best with voters—the right to death with dignity, the right to end pain and suffering, or the right to choose when and how to die according to one's own beliefs.

Based on results from the focus group research, the campaign opponents chose to focus on three themes: (1) the inadequacy of current law, (2) rights consciousness and choice, and (3) voluntariness. In a video message to 119 supporters ("An Urgent Message from Initiative 119 Washington's Campaign for Death with Dignity"), Kirk Robinson, president of Washington Citizens for Death with Dignity, explained that the first ad aired by Initiative 119 was developed to explain the two parts of the measure ("adding artificial nutrition and hydration machines to the state's Natural Death Act, and permitting patients who have less than six months to live the right to choose to die on their own terms"). Two quotes summarize the theme of the first ad: "Most people don't know, but in Washington living wills are often ignored or overturned, and patients are kept alive by machines against their will" and "Initiative 119 will clarify the law."

The video portion of the ad depicted many machines, wires, lights, and tubes. A man lies unconscious, a ventilator forces air into his lungs, heaving his chest up each time it involuntarily sinks down. As this scene is viewed by the man's two daughters, one whispers, "This isn't what Dad wanted—these machines—that's why he made a living will." The ad concludes with a narrator admonishing voters to protect their rights by voting for Initiative 119.

The proponents' second and third television ads featured actual sufferers of terminal disease who wanted the choice to die according to their own wishes. In one ad titled "Pat Nugent," a somber, soft-spoken, middle-aged man stated, "I have terminal cancer. I don't know how much time I have left. I don't know if I'll be strong enough to ask for aid in dying or not. But, what I want is my own private choice to have control of what happens to me at the end of my life."

In the other ad, titled "Susan Baron," an articulate, mentally sharp, elderly woman lying in bed, stated, "I have terminal cancer. To have a terminal disease drag on, to endure the pain is absolute hell. At the end, I want the choice to accept treatment, to refuse treatment, to die on my own terms in a dignified manner." Each of these ads also stressed the voluntary nature of the proposed initiative. The ads claimed that the measure had strict safeguards designed to ensure that decisions were made by patients themselves. One example of the proposed safeguards was that under the law no one could request aid in dying for anyone else.

PROPONENTS AND OPPONENTS RESPOND TO ONE ANOTHER

As election day approached, pollsters in Washington estimated that 61 percent of the state's citizens favored Initiative 119. The estimation paralleled the results of a national opinion poll conducted by the *Boston Globe* and the Harvard School of Public Health in mid-October, which suggested that 64 percent of Americans favored physician-assisted suicide and active euthanasia for terminally ill patients who request it. Even 71 percent of American Catholics said they would support the Washington initiative if it appeared on the ballot in their state (Knox 1991).

To overcome the apparent 2–1 margin in favor of 119, the opposition bombarded voters with newspaper stories, campaign brochures, computer-generated mailings, and millions of dollars' worth of TV ads, most of which focused on the "no safeguards" debate. They stressed that the initiative did not require a waiting period or family consultations to make sure patients truly wanted to die. They claimed the poor would use aid in dying disproportionately so their families would not be burdened with large hospital or nursing home bills.

Both sides publicly accused the other of misleading voters. Opponents griped about the pro-initiative ad, which appealed to voters' emotions by depicting an elderly man hooked up to life support systems. Initiative backers pointed to misleading ads claiming that there were no safeguards in the measure. Supporters took their case to the attorney general and to court. Deputy attorney general Edward Mackie issued an opinion in which he agreed that the initiative spell out a variety of safeguards, although reasonable people could differ as to whether they were adequate. King County Superior Court Judge Carol Schapira agreed. "Someone else may say 'worthless safeguards,' and I won't quibble with them," she said, but no safeguards? "The initiative does contain safeguards" (Gilmore 1991b).

Initiative supporters focused on the people who might benefit. Their concern was for those who worry about how they would be perceived by friends and family in the event they become dependent on machines and caretakers for maintenance of routine bodily functions, for those who fear becoming a financial or emotional burden on others, and for those who fear being kept alive against their choice. "Principles of freedom," they said, "must include the right to choose a response to the unfortunate circumstances of disease or accident, including in some cases a self-determined death" (Canaday 1991). A group called Academics for Yes on Initiative 119 charged, "What opponents to 119 have lost sight of, in short, is real people with real problems. The woman wracked with bone cancer is not a theoretical construct—she is the victim of a painful, degenerative disease. So far as the disease is concerned, she has no rights."

To test the effectiveness of their ad campaign, I-119 proponents conducted tracking polls one week apart in mid-October. The polls results showed that during the week, more potential voters had seen both pro and con ads, and "don't knows" were drifting toward "yes." Survey questions designed to determine the reasons why potential voters would vote in favor indicated that voters indicating "yes" remained unchanged if their opinion rested on the conviction that the mentally competent should have the right to choose. However, voting yes on the basis of a belief in the right to die with dignity was down 9 percent. Nonetheless, voting yes on the basis of a conviction that dying people should have the right to end pain and suffering was up 6 percent.

On the other side of the debate, tracking poll questions designed to determine why voters were inclined to vote no indicated that some change was occurring. For example, the number of voters who agreed that people ought to die only when God wills their death was up 7 percent. Additionally, the number of voters reporting that the initiative language was vague was up 7 percent. But the number of voters reporting that aid in dying could or would be abused was down 6 percent. In general, more people believed that I–119 had strict safeguards to protect dying patients—up 6 percent; the percentage of people who believed that the law would be open to abuse was unchanged; and 11 percent more people felt that the law would protect against a lingering and painful death. Finally, the polls indicated that physicians, terminal patients, and nurses, respectively, were the most believable sources for information about the initiative, while the least believable sources of information were local newspapers and clergy.

On November 5, Washington voters defeated the initiative by a margin of 54 to 46 percent. Sixty percent of those eligible voted, a near record for an off-year general election in Washington. Given that October polls in the state showed 61 percent in favor of the initiative, the results befuddled many politicians and pundits. Whatever the reasons for the initiative's defeat, both sides claimed victory. Opponents claimed they had prevailed. Supporters claimed that such a showing during the first vote on euthanasia reform signaled an impetus for going beyond legalized removal of life support to some type of active killing. The faithful optimism of supporters resurfaced a year later in California (King 1991b).

THE CALIFORNIA INITIATIVE

In November 1992, a presidential election year, and less than a year after the defeat in Washington, euthanasia proponents offered a similar initiative for signatures for the ballot in California, a state with a tradition of common and protracted use of the initiative process (Magelby 1994). The players would be similar to the players in Washington, and the result would be the same.

The effort was started there by two Los Angeles attorneys, Michael White and Robert Risley (Parachini 1987). In 1984, Risley's wife, Darlena, was diagnosed as having ovarian cancer. She underwent two courses of chemotherapy, including one experimental treatment at University of California San Diego. She also underwent two operations in a year and a half, but her condition continued to decline steadily. After they got to a controversial clinic in the Bahamas, the couple reached what would become for Robert Risley a life-altering decision. Darlena asked Risley to help her take her life in the event she became totally incapacitated. Risley made up his mind to help her die, although it never came to that. After about two weeks of accelerating deterioration in the Bahamas apartment, Darlena Risley died.

After Darlena died, Risley became determined to change California law so someone in an analogous situation would not feel as legally powerless and at risk of prosecution as he had. He traveled to Sacramento and approached a series of legislators, including State Senator Barry Keene (D-San Rafael), a key backer of earlier successful efforts to pass legislation creating durable powers of attorney for health care. But Keene and other legislators agreed that Risley's proposal seemed too controversial and politically risky to stand any chance of getting through the legislature. It was at that point that Risley and

White decided to draft their proposed ballot initiative, formally called the "Humane and Dignified Death Act."

According to the act, a dying person would be able to make a written request to a physician to help him or her to die, that is, to seek assisted suicide or active euthanasia. The doctor would have to consult with at least one other doctor who would also have to agree that the suffering patient would probably die within six months or less. If both doctors agreed, then the primary physician would negotiate with the patient on how to die. A request to die would have to be in writing, unless the patient were comatose, and then the statute would have permitted a surrogate to act for the patient. Furthermore, the doctor could always back out if he or she desired. Hospitals were given the right to decline to permit euthanasia in their facilities, and forgeries of patients' signatures would be made a crime. Finally, doctors could not be sued, prosecuted, or lose their license to practice medicine for aiding a suicide or actively killing if they followed the law ("Supporters to Get Signatures" 1987:1).

Ironically, the referendum language on which the two lawyers finally settled would not have accommodated the situation Risley and his wife faced, since Darlena's condition was not incurable. Nor would it have applied to most comatose patients because they would not have signed a directive before the onset of their condition. Most Alzheimer's patients would not qualify, either, because they would not be competent to consent to their own deaths. The proposed change in the law would not, for that matter, have applied to Elizabeth Bouvia, the quadriplegic Riverside woman who fought to starve herself to death, since she would not die within six months (Parachini 1987).

With technical assistance from the Hemlock Society, Risley and White formed an organization called Americans Against Human Suffering (AAHS) (Parachini 1987). The Hemlock Society asked its California members to help collect the 450,000 signatures AAHS sought to get the initiative on the ballot. The huge task of getting 450,000 registered voters to sign the petition was divided between a direct mail campaign run by AAHS, which sought the previously uncommitted believer, and the door-to-door efforts of acknowledged grassroots supporters of active voluntary euthanasia ("Supporters to Get Signatures" 1987:1). Volunteers sealed envelopes, sorted mail, circulated petitions, and did whatever was necessary to see that the initiative succeeded. They mailed out 250,000 pieces of mail to people throughout the nation. Over 8 percent responded to the mailing and 40 percent of those included a contribution.

Risley began a nationwide campaign to achieve support for the initiative and a statewide signature-gathering campaign to qualify the initiative for the November 1988 election. He appeared on the CBS program *At Issue* and on

CNN's *Direct and Live*. He also addressed a bioethics committee of the Los Angeles County Bar Association ("AAHS Moves Forward" 1987:1,3). The Beverly Hills Bar Association endorsed the measure. However, the California Bar Association's advisory Conference of Delegates, which does not set association policy, defeated an endorsement in a close voice vote (Parachini 1987).

The proponents' television ads emphasized suffering, choice, and compassion. In an infomercial hosted by television actor Conrad Bain, proponents pleaded with hospital administrators and Cardinal Mahony to allow the terminally ill to decide for themselves. "Why should anyone else dictate how much suffering you should endure before you can end your life?" asked Bain. A short segment featured the story of Bob and Ginger Harper. Bob Harper was prosecuted in California for murdering his wife. "She couldn't take it anymore. She wanted to end it herself. But she wanted me there with her. I didn't want to lose her, I loved that woman." Harper was found not guilty, yet Bain protested that nobody should have to go through what he did. The banners at the end of the ad stated that Proposition 161 was for the terminally ill only and that terminal disease must be certified by two doctors. Moreover, only the patient could decide, the ad stated, and the law was written with strong safeguards.

The prospects of passing a euthanasia initiative in California appeared quite good. California is the first state that legislated the right to have life support withheld or withdrawn through the use of living wills. (Cal. Civ. Code §2500, Supp. 1990). Moreover, many opinions favoring passive euthanasia have been issued by the state courts (for example, *Bouvia v. Superior Court* (1986), in which a competent twenty-eight-year-old quadriplegic won the right to remove a nasogastric feeding tube inserted against her will; *Bartling v. Superior Court* (1984), in which a competent seventy-year-old seriously ill man won the right to remove a respirator; and *Barber v. Superior Court* (1983), in which the court decided that physicians could not be prosecuted for homicide because they removed a respirator and intravenous feeding tubes of a patient in a persistent vegetative state. Even California juries had taken a liberal stance toward issues in death and dying. For instance, in 1991 a jury acquitted a man who admitted he had pulled a plastic bag over his wife's face after she had taken an overdose of sleeping pills and fallen asleep. Derek Humphry, who testified in the California man's behalf and set up a defense fund that paid half of his attorneys' fees, said the verdict "sends a message to prosecutors that they're not going to get a conviction with this type of offense. The jury ignores the law and brings in a moral verdict" (Harrison 1991). Finally, from the mid-1980s, state polls suggested that nearly two-thirds of Californians believed doctors should have the right to give lethal medications to dying patients who request them ("Supporters to Get Signatures" 1987:1).

Two groups came out against the Humane and Dignified Death Act: the Roman Catholic Church and the California Medical Association (CMA). The CMA's House of Delegates voted unanimously to fight enactment of any law that would require a physician to provide medicines, techniques, or advice necessary for a physician to pursue a course of assisted suicide or that would require a physician who is unwilling to participate in assisted suicide to refer a patient to another physician who would ("CMA Resists Any Laws" 1987). A committee report listed the CMA's reasons for objection as being that it is the consensus of mental health professionals that suicide is almost always a psychologically abnormal event, carrying negative ramifications for family members and caregivers. The report also said that the ethical foundation of the medical profession would be seriously eroded if physicians became agents in the premature, unnatural termination of life. The doctors' leaders also claimed that the alternative of active voluntary euthanasia might undermine the hospice movement. At first the committee was divided equally, but a letter-writing campaign was started by opposing doctors throughout the state and, under this pressure, a sufficient number changed sides to approve opposition. The CMA also agreed to commit funds to opposing any such legislation (Humphry 1987:1).

The National Conference of Catholic Bishops designated October 4 as "Respect for Life Sunday." Congregations nationwide were given a leaflet that criticized the Hemlock Society, comparing its actions to the pro-abortion campaign of the 1960s. "Having won key court rulings authorizing withdrawal of food and water from disabled and seriously ill people, euthanasia proponents are demanding judicial recognition of a right to die by lethal injection," said the leaflet. Among other things, Catholics were urged to put anti-euthanasia flyers and posters in highly visible places in their communities (Humphry 1987:1).

The signature drive garnered only 130,000 of the 450,000 signatures sought. AAHS attributed the failure mainly to organizational problems and lack of money. AAHS announced that it would try again in two years and that it would try for similar initiatives simultaneously in Washington, Oregon, and possibly Florida. Robert Risley said that the initiative failed to qualify not through a lack of people willing to sign the petition but because there were not enough volunteers gathering signatures. "Within the next two years we are confident we can build our fund-raising base and volunteer organization so that there will be no problem getting sufficient signatures to qualify in 1990," Risley said ("Petition Failure Is Spur" 1988:1).

In October 1991, AAHS's state affiliate, Californians Against Human Suffering, succeeded in collecting more than the 385,000 valid signatures required (Capron and Michel 1992:16). The terms of the measure remained largely unchanged. A licensed physician would be able to help a terminally ill patient to die. The patient would have to be a mentally competent adult, and two physicians—one of whom would have to be the attending physician—would be required to certify that the patient suffered from an incurable or irreversible condition that would result in death within six months. The patient would have to have signed a directive requesting aid in dying that was witnessed by two people. If the patient were in a nursing home, one of the witnesses would be required to be a patient ombudsman. The request had to be communicated on more than one occasion. Aid in dying would be administered by the doctor or the appropriate means would be provided to the patient for self-administration. It would be up to the patient to determine the time, place, and manner of death. Aid in dying was defined as providing any medical procedure that would terminate the life of the qualified patient swiftly, painlessly, and humanely or providing the means to the patient for self-administration. The directive could be nullified orally or in writing by the patient. No health care professional or private hospital would be required to participate; their duty would be only to transfer the patient upon request. Physicians would be free from civil, criminal, and administrative responsibility. A request for aid in dying, or talk of one, could not be used by insurance companies to alter any insurance benefit. Aid in dying could not be deemed suicide, so insurance could not be withheld if a person died with assistance. A person could not be required or forbidden to sign a directive; no medical service could be conditioned on the presence or absence of a directive. Forging a directive would be prosecuted as homicide if death results (State of California Secretary of State 1992).

Responding to the successful lobbying campaign in Washington, which apparently convinced voters that there were no safeguards in the proposal, the California proponents put additional safeguards into their initiative. California required hospitals and other health care providers to report the number of euthanasia cases annually, including the ages and illnesses of those who died. The state also added a waiting period after a request for aid in dying was made, plus a mental competency check and family notification of the patient's intent. The California initiative also differed from its predecessor in Washington in that it contained special protection for persons in skilled nursing facilities, prohibitions against intimidation and tampering, provisions for psychological consultation, and limitation of fees (Cox 1993:173).

Nevertheless, as happened in Washington, more than one hundred powerful organizations united to fight the Risley-White initiative. The anti-161 side tried to portray the initiative as a flawed, even "kooky," measure masterminded by the leadership of a "ghoulish" Hemlock Society. Referring to the long and growing list of opponents to the measure, a No on 161 spokesperson said: "It's the civilized world versus the Hemlock Society." Meanwhile, the Yes on 161 campaign continued to point out that opponents received financial support from Roman Catholic sources, and accused the Catholic Church of trying to impose its view of euthanasia on others. "There would not be a campaign against 161 of any significance if the Catholic hierarchy were not leading the charge," said the campaign manager for Yes on Proposition 161. Lending credence to this argument was the sizable donations Catholic groups made to the measure's opponents. In addition, bishops called on parishioners throughout the state to contribute to the campaign to defeat the measure (Jacobs 1992c).

Curiously, although the national Hemlock Society's April 1987 newsletter described AAHS (Risley and White's first campaign committee) as Hemlock's "political wing" (Risley was president, Derek Humphry vice president), this time around Risley and White were careful to distance themselves from some views taken by Humphry, insisting that their new campaign committee, Californians Against Human Suffering, was independent of Hemlock and its chapters. Referring to Humphry's book, *Final Exit*, Risley stated: "His self-help book, we wish it wasn't there.... The legitimate problem with the book is that it can get into the hands of younger people, who are not terminal" (Risley 1994).

Just as the link with the Hemlock Society gave opponents a point of attack, so did the continuing activity of Dr. Jack Kevorkian. Because Kevorkian had long been licensed in California, the No on 161 committee charged that Kevorkian would be likely to "set up death clinics in California if Proposition 161 passes." The opposition campaign was led again by the state's medical association and was financed primarily by hundreds of thousands of dollars worth of small donations solicited by the Roman Catholic Church. The broad-based coalition included the National Right to Life Committee, the California Pro-Life Council, the California Association of Hospitals and Health Systems, the California State Hospital Association, the American Cancer Society, and the state Republican party (Jacobs 1992b).

Again, the political strategy was not to focus on the morality of euthanasia in general, but to hammer away at alleged flaws in the proposed law. There was, for instance, no "cooling off" period between the time the patient asked to be killed and the time the request was carried out. For that matter, they argued, although Proposition 161 talked of an enduring declaration, which implies a deliberative decision made over time, in fact it is possible, after a patient has made this declaration twice in a matter of hours, that doctor-assisted suicide could occur. In addition, there was no requirement for counseling about alternatives or for a psychiatric evaluation or other examination to rule out treatable depression as a cause of the request for mercy killing or assisted suicide. Nor was there any guarantee that others who know the patient well would be able to warn the physician, since the statute contained no requirement that family members be notified of a patient's request (Capron and Michel 1992:18).

Moreover, opponents argued, by borrowing the idea of an advance directive from existing law, the authors of Proposition 161 undermined voluntariness. That is because although a directive is supposed to be revocable, its very existence may make some patients feel obligated to follow through, they said. The existence of a directive may also alter the response of those who care for the declarant, by shifting the usual presumption that the declarant would want his or her life protected (Capron and Michel 1992:16–17).

Regarding the initiative's requirement that the directive must be witnessed by two people not linked financially with the patient and that, in particular, one of these two must be an ombudsman or patient advocate in the case of nursing home residents, opponents were concerned that this protection applied only to the directive (which could have been executed years before the active euthanasia), whereas no witnesses were mandated at the time of the actual request for euthanasia (Capron and Michel 1992:18). Moreover, although the statutory term "attending physician" may suggest a close, ongoing relationship, such connection and personal knowledge were not required by the statute and, indeed, are not characteristic for most people in a mobile society such as ours. Thus, "attending" connotes nothing more than the principal physician selected by, or assigned to, the patient (Capron and Michel 1992:19). Finally, there was nothing to take into account human error concerning the terminal diagnosis. Indeed, opponents argued, most physicians regard predictions of death more than a few days or weeks in the future as exercises in the grossest sort of guesswork.

In addition to these procedural objections, opponents also claimed that on the basis of previous court decisions, the proposal would almost certainly have been extended to incompetent patients as well. Advocates for such a change would certainly argue that it did not open the door to involuntary euthanasia but merely allowed patients who have lost the ability to express their wishes to obtain the "painless, humane, and dignified" death that they had already expressed a desire to have (Capron and Michel 1992:17). In addition, they argued that under California legal precedents, the California courts would have almost inevitably concluded that guardians of incompetent patients with terminal illnesses must be permitted to direct physicians to kill their wards. This example of nonvoluntary euthanasia would not be merely a likely abuse of the law, they claimed, but in fact would have been legalized by Proposition 161.

Finally, they argued that the provision's Declaration of Purpose, which stated that current state laws do not adequately protect the rights of terminally ill patients, falsely suggested that no legal mechanisms now exist for patients to avoid artificial prolongation of life. In other words, they said, by ignoring the state's Natural Death Act and Durable Power of Attorney for Health Care Act, as well as relevant case law, the Declaration of Purpose suggested that Proposition 161 was needed to fill a gap that did not exist.

Campaign spending reports indicated that the Catholic Archdiocese of Los Angeles spent $125,000 seeking to defeat Proposition 161. Other Catholic organizations and churches collectively gave several hundred thousand dollars more to defeat the initiative. Parish priests helped fund the opposition campaign by taking up special collections, imploring church members that the Church was "preparing them to make the kind of choice that will speak of compassion." By soliciting small contributions from its pool of millions of parishioners, the church offerings were not reported as "Catholic" money but were instead mixed in with other anonymous donations under $100. More than 80 percent of the funds that the anti-euthanasia campaign raised came from Catholic groups. And that was before the parish collections took place (Lostin 1992).

Other big donors against the initiative included the California State Council of the Knights of Columbus ($200,000) and Fieldstead and Co., controlled by Christian fundamentalist Howard Fieldstead Ahmanson Jr., which gave two donations of $50,000 (Jacobs 1992c). Altogether, opponents of the proposition collected almost $3 million.

The largest donor in support of the proposition was the Hemlock Society, which gave $15,000 in support of P-161. The contribution was insignificant. During the three months ending September 30, the initiative's opponents were able to raise $1.5 million—ten times the $146,000 raised by the pro-161 committee during the same period. The ability of the opposition to raise large sums of money quickly had the initiative's authors worried (Risley 1994). They were expecting a deluge of last-minute advertising, but they knew they would not have the money to respond. Initiative coauthor White said: "I feel like the guy standing on the beach waiting for that hurricane to hit Hawaii. . . . I can see it coming but there's not a damn thing I can do" (Jacobs 1992c:A3).

A 1991 poll conducted for the Hemlock Society by the Roper Organization found supporters of the concept outnumbered the opposition by more than 3 to 1. The ratio generally held up regardless of the age, religion, income, or education level of those responding. But by mid-October, the initiative's backers saw their support eroding. Although polls conducted a week before the election showed the initiative still leading by a narrow margin, support had decreased substantially over the course of just one month. A *San Francisco Chronicle* poll conducted in late September indicated that 70 percent of a random sample of six hundred Bay Area residents favored Proposition 161, and 22 percent opposed it (Olsyewski 1992a). Another September poll, by Mervin Field, found the physician-assisted death initiative had a 44 percent lead, with 68 percent in favor and 24 percent opposed. Within a month, that support had eroded. A Field poll in October indicated that support for the proposition had dropped to 55 percent, with 30 percent opposed. Two weeks later, a *Los Angeles Times* survey showed support among registered voters at 49 percent, compared to 45 percent opposed and 6 percent undecided.

A spokesperson for the No on 161 campaign claimed that the drop in the polls showed that once people looked at the initiative objectively, without the emotionalism connected with the issue, they were able to see it as not a good law (Kershner 1992). Lending credence to this argument was the additional finding of the early Field poll that indicated that only 32 percent of the people polled were familiar with the California initiative. In addition, opponents claimed, many voters mistakenly believed that Proposition 161 simply allowed doctors to disconnect terminally ill patients from life support systems (Kershner 1992).

As election day neared, opponents launched a huge advertising campaign based largely on scare tactics. The No on 161 organization spent $90,000 on an advertising campaign in the San Francisco area. The organization also announced that at least $30,000 would be spent on advertising in other parts of the state. By contrast, the supporters of Proposition 161 had already used up their entire advertising war chest on radio ads: $40,000 in the Los Angeles area and $15,000 in San Diego. Said the campaign coordinator for CAHS: "The ads could tip this whole thing toward the opposition at the end" (Olsyewski 1992a). The themes of the ads were much like the themes of the ads in Washington a year before. But this time around the ads were far more gruesome. The opponents had hired the advertising firm of Chuck Cavalier and Associates, a company known for the dramatic use of imagery and music.

Cavalier jumped at the opportunity to dramatize the proposition's provision that would have allowed doctors to give lethal injections. Syringes, poison, and executioners were the focus of two particularly gruesome ads. "You're about to see a secret suicide meeting, and unless you vote no on 161 it could happen to someone you know or love," said the narrator in one ad. Eerie music played in the background. Voices whispered indecipherably. An elderly woman sat alone in a small room with the blinds drawn. She appeared to be waiting sheepishly. A ghoulish-looking man in a black suit rapped on her front door. The man walked in and positioned himself behind the woman to prepare a syringe. He looked very sure of what he was doing, even sinister about it. Yet the woman appeared confused and unsure. The narrator continued, "161 allows physician-assisted suicide in secret, with no witnesses, no family notification, no psychological exam, and no medical specialists." The woman looked away and the image flashed between color and black and white, while the narrator implored voters to vote no on 161.

Other ads covered the charges that doctors make mistakes and that the proposition did not have adequate safeguards. They were less hard-hitting than the secret suicide and steel syringe ads, but still more base than the ads in Washington. In one ad, a banner claimed that Proposition 161 could have killed Jim Curly. An aging man stated, "I'm glad that thing wasn't around for me, 'cause when you get so depressed that I might have been stupid enough to say, 'all right, give me that needle,' and I wouldn't be here talking to you people today." Another ad featured a young pensive and distraught-looking woman who said, "Seven years ago I was told that I had a terminal illness and I would die. If Proposition 161 had been in the California law then, I would have asked the doctor to give me a lethal injection to kill myself. Obviously his diagnosis was wrong." Other ads featured banners such as, "Prop. 161 is badly written and has no real safeguards. Vote no on 161."

The opponents' ad attack was bolstered by strong media opposition. For example, an editorial in the *Orange County Register* recounted the flaws said to be in the proposed initiative and emphasized the prospect of poor or elderly patients being coerced to accept euthanasia as a way of relieving family financial pressures. It also argued that the drive to educate more doctors in advanced pain management would be set back if the counteroption of euthanasia were allowed. In an effort to secure the uncommitted voter concerned about taxes, the editorial pointed out that the measure would allow physicians in government hospitals to put people to death on the taxpayers' dime, adding that "given the wide range of beliefs among Americans about the morality of 'mercy killing,' it is hardly merciful to force taxpayers to finance the practice." Next to the editorial appeared a cartoon depicting a menacing pair of physicians looking like Dr. Frankenstein and his hunchbacked sidekick, Igor, with the caption: "We're from the government and we're here to help you" ("The Indignity of Prop. 161" 1992). Days earlier, another editorial declared that Dr. Jack Kevorkian would be able to start a cottage industry in California if Proposition 161 passed ("Kevorkian's Proposition" 1992). And just two days before the election a commentary compared the euthanasia reform movement to events in Germany leading to the Holocaust (Seiler 1992). Similar scare tactics were used on television. One ad depicted a monstrous-looking physician whose face moved closer and closer to the camera. Behind him was nothing but darkness. The connotation appeared to be that aid in dying would be practiced "in your face."

Moreover, in church services throughout the state, Catholic priests and fundamentalist ministers reminded churchgoers to vote down the initiative. Secular organizations hosted seminars and debates featuring some of the country's most prominent ethicists. Their arguments seemed to summarize the divergence of positions taken on the euthanasia issue. For instance, Margaret Pabst Battin, a University of Utah philosophy professor, described the choice to have one's life ended as "a new civil right," adding, "People ought to be architects of their own death" (Jacobs 1992d). University of Washington bioethicist Albert Jonsen argued, "If we abolish terminal misery from our experience, we will foolishly hide an essential measure of our humanity" (Jacobs 1992d). Dan Brock, director of the Center for Biomedical Ethics at Brown University, said: "While there are certainly differences between refusing life support and voluntary euthanasia, nevertheless the underlying values that provide the moral support for one also support the other" (Jacobs 1992d). Alexander Capron, codirector of the Pacific Center for Health Policy and Ethics at the University of Southern California, disagreed, claiming that while "withdrawal of treatment is a recognition of the limits to medicine, active euthanasia is a statement of medical power" (Jacobs 1992d). With the election just days away, Capron added that he worried that Californians would make their decisions without adequate reflection.

Poll results indicated waning support for the measure, which on election day was defeated 54 to 46 percent. White and Risley blamed the defeat on the inability of supporters to raise enough money for their own TV campaign (Olsyewski 1992b). Opponents, however, looked more to the substantive reasons for the measure's defeat than to the tactical. They claimed that it was not until the final days that people focused on the reality of Proposition 161. The television ads punctured the myths surrounding the proposal, they claimed.

Looking toward the future, proponents said they did not feel the need to add any more safeguards, adding that educating voters and calming fears—perhaps by small group discussions—might be more effective. Although disappointed, Derek Humphry viewed the fact that over five million people in the two Western states voted for reform as a strong indication that support groups needed to keep trying. Indeed, he reported, initiative plans were already underway in Oregon (Humphry 1992b).

ANALYSIS OF THE INITIATIVE DEFEATS

Political scientists have measured the ability of citizen initiatives to effect legal and social change (Bowler and Donovan 1998; Lowenstein 1982; Lupia 1992; Magleby 1984, 1994; Traynor and Glantz 1996). A general finding is that direct legislation is a valuable agenda-setting device (Magleby 1994). Many variables influence the success of initiative efforts. The political science literature analyzes the influence of money, election year and ballot length, credibility of the message and the people who communicate it, the malleability of voter intentions, and patterns of opinion change (Magleby 1992, 1994). This chapter and the next two chapters analyze the death with dignity campaigns in Washington, California, and Oregon in terms of some of these variables.

Many political pundits were surprised by the degree that voters' opinions changed during the early initiative efforts. (The next chapter shows how the same turnabout occurred in Oregon in 1994.) Even as national and state opinion polls indicated that a steady three-fourths of voters said they supported the notion of giving terminal patients the option of physician-assisted suicide, opposition campaigns in Washington and California encouraged about one in three supporters to change their minds when specific ballot proposals were considered. Scholars, campaigners, and pundits recognize that the most common pattern of opinion change is from "soft" early support for an initiative to a large majority in opposition to the measure on election day (Magleby 1994). That is why it is far more difficult to get a measure passed than it is to defeat it. Confusion, ambivalence, fear—these and similar emotions usually impel voters to avoid risk and support the status quo.

Knowing this, the proponent campaigns in Washington and California had to predict not only what factors could cause them to lose their soft supporters but also how to successfully counteract successful opposition tactics. If the opposition outspent proponents in the media, would voters come to believe that proponents could not collect enough money because their arguments were not as good? If the opposition came from physicians as strongly as is it was coming from clergy, would voters find opposing arguments more believable? How might other issues on the same ballot—such as abortion funding in Washington and congressional term limits in California—confuse or tire voters? How would news about the Supreme Court's decision in *Cruzan v. Director* (1990), the actions of Jack Kevorkian, and the revelation by Dr. Timothy Quill that he helped a patient die be spun into the death with dignity debate?

In Washington, a campaign insider said that the I-119 leadership never really appeared to expect to win. Perhaps that is why it appears that the campaign was overwhelmed by strategic considerations. Instead of developing and executing tactics to combat what everybody knew—that voters tend to change their minds about controversial initiatives—proponents thought they could use general voter sentiment to convince Washington voters to stay with them. The same strategy befell the proponents in California.

In Chapter 3, we will take a close look at how the nearly singular focus on public sentiment in the 1991 and 1992 campaigns contributed to their failures (by neglecting professionals who would eventually be asked to perform death with dignity). The remainder of this analysis of those early failures focuses on what analysts described as the reasons the early initiatives failed.

In Washington, the blitz of emotionally laden television ads and news coverage, combined with the all-out opposition from the WSMA and Catholic Church, was widely believed to have narrowed the margin between supporters and nonsupporters of I-119. Voter opinion can be affected by something as simple as ballot length. In Washington, for example, some analysts speculated that the presence of other complexly volatile issues on the same ballot—term limits, a tax rollback, and abortion—led voters to opt for the status quo. In addition to a presidential election, two Senatorial seats, and the usual Congressional and State legislative seats, the California ballot featured thirteen initiatives, including retirement and welfare reform, health care coverage, and state tax reform. Said Portland pollster Bob Moore, "People try to read the initiatives and to make judgments. They like this idea, but they don't like that one. But if you get too many measures on one ballot, a lot of people will end up voting against anything—unless it sounds like a tax cut."

Two other variables—these more difficult to predict during the early initiatives in Washington and California—were how voters would judge the credibility of either side's message and the person or persons who communicated them. Analysts of the loss in Washington conjectured that just weeks before the election, Dr. Jack Kevorkian's assistance in the suicides of two women in Michigan gave face to people's unspoken fears. Proponents claimed that the resulting front-page story helped undermine support for the initiative with frightening headlines about "Dr. Death's" latest escapade (King 1991b). In an article titled "Why Were They Beaten in Washington?" Derek Humphry downplayed Kevorkian's role, saying "Kevorkian . . . may have marginally affected the result, but not significantly" (Humphry 1992a).

Humphry went on to say that there were two chief reasons for the Washington defeat. The first reason was that the campaigners' avoidance of the words "suicide" and "euthanasia"—words used freely by the public and the media—sidestepped the crux of the debates. Karen Cooper, the I-119 campaign director, acceded that the campaign ads knowingly and willfully obscured the part of the initiative that included lethal injections. Cooper went on to state that this strategy ended up being a big mistake. The second reason for the I-119 defeat, charged Humphry, was that there really were too few safeguards. He was quoted as stating, "The Washington campaigners made the tactical mistake of painting their law with a broad brush, intending to sit down with the medical and legal professions after victory to hammer out the detailed guidelines under which euthanasia could be carried out. But the public did not want euthanasia laws on the books without built-in safeguards—a sign of the general distrust of the medical and legal professions" (Cox 1993:167–168).

In other interviews it was suggested that the proponents lost their liberal base of support in Seattle because they failed to effectively counter the opponents' primary point that the proposed law would be used by the wrong person for the wrong reasons. Opponents claimed the poor would use active euthanasia disproportionately so their families would not be burdened with large hospital or nursing home bills. An editorial declared that Kevorkian would be able to set up a cottage industry in California if an initiative passed there. In support of this charge, opponents declared that although the statutory term "attending physician" may suggest a close, ongoing relationship, such connection and personal knowledge were not required by the statute. Opponents were furthermore concerned that the proposed law contained no requirement for counseling about alternatives or for a psychiatric evaluation or other examination to rule out treatable depression as a cause of the request for assisted suicide or mercy killing. Together, these charges were intended to convince voters that even if they believe active euthanasia is desirable in some circumstances, decriminalization of the practice raises a specter of abuse that the measures before them failed to address adequately.

The proponents simply responded to the opponents' message too late, one insider said. Although they did conduct eight press conferences during the last week of the campaign, and polls showed support for the initiative started rising, the effort occurred too late. Observers also suggested that the proponents had not conducted enough opposition study. One observer also credited the opposition with creating ads that spoke to *pro* voters about pragmatic concerns, which polls showed affected pro voters more than issues of God, sanctity of life, and other moral issues. Each of these factors was offered as an alternative to the charge that poor spending patterns led to the initiative's defeat. But the organizer of two successful campaigns in Oregon—the only successful death with dignity campaigns—countered that spending patterns stand in the background of most other factors that contribute to an initiative campaign's success or failure. Effective organization was what this insider described to be a vital component of a successful initiative campaign.

Two variables, then—voter tendencies and responses to the messages and messengers—were further affected by campaign organization. In the wake of proponents' misfires during the early death with dignity campaigns, soft support grew softer, paving the way for the opponents' arguments that adequate alternatives to suicide and syringes already existed.

An editorial argued that if the option of active euthanasia were allowed, the drive to educate more doctors in advanced pain management would be set back. Others claimed the hospice movement would be similarly set back. Opponents argued that by ignoring natural death acts and durable powers of attorney for health care acts, the proponents' approach falsely suggested that no legal mechanisms exist for patients to avoid artificial prolongation of life.

In other words, passive euthanasia is a sufficient alternative to assisted suicide and mercy killing. This point was raised during the campaign in California by ethicist Arthur Caplan, who surmised that before the campaigns, many voters may have been ignorant of the distinction between passive and active euthanasia. The campaigns, therefore, gave voters their first chance to learn the difference, and when they discovered that the laws in Washington and California allow for passive euthanasia already, they dropped their support for the initiatives.

In conclusion, to determine if the time was right to sponsor state ballot initiatives, the proponents had to consider several questions. Would the legal and ethical consensus change merely because the public voted to change the laws? Is popular opinion alone enough to change the behavior of physicians, clergy, ethicists, and social movement groups? Can change be compelled by popular opinion? Perhaps early opinion polls in support of both state initiatives indicated that an equal cross section of the population believed there was a problem: that death can be preceded by undesirable suffering. On the other hand, perhaps the initiative defeats indicated that voters did not feel confident that the laws proposed would solve the problem, and perhaps might even exacerbate it. The latter became the so-called no safeguards (Washington) or too few safeguards (California) argument. "That strategy—support the goal but pick apart the proposal—usually works when voters view the ballot proposition as complex. When in doubt they vote no" (Skelton 1994). The proponents' near singular reliance on opinion polls has been called a poor strategy, since apparently opinion polls measured something other than what the campaign results indicated.

This analysis began with a statement of the general finding in the political science literature that direct legislation is a valuable agenda-setting device (Magleby 1994). Several variables have been described as possible reasons for the defeat of early death with dignity initiatives. Magleby's statement about the agenda-setting function of citizen initiatives suggests that defeat of an initiative may not be the same as failure of the public policy change being sought after. Chapter 3 develops the conjecture that the early initiatives in Washington and California did all they could reasonably be expected to do, which is develop grassroots pressure to sell the message that the status quo needed reexamination and change. It would be up to later campaigners to build a formidable coalition that could successfully use the ballot box to change law and public policy. That is just what happened in Oregon in 1994. The Oregon measure passed by a narrow margin and became the nation's (and the world's) first law to forthrightly permit physician-assisted suicide. Chapter 3 details the campaign strategies that led to the passage of the Oregon Death With Dignity Act.

3

Passage of the Oregon Death With Dignity Act

INTRODUCTION

Despite the losses in Washington and California, euthanasia reform advocates in Oregon sponsored an initiative for the November 1994 ballot. The Oregon initiative (Measure 16) restricted the role of a physician to providing a prescription for a drug such as Seconal to end one's life. In contrast to the proposed euthanasia initiatives in Washington and California, under Measure 16 the administration of lethalities would remain illegal.

Other distinctions between the Oregon initiative and its predecessors included the following. First, the attending physician would be required to inform the patient of the diagnosis, prognosis, and potential risks of the prescribed medication; the probable result of the prescribed medication; and the alternatives available, such as comfort care, hospice care, and pain control, as well as the right to rescind the request. The patient would also be required to make two oral requests fifteen days apart for life-ending medication, as well as one written request that would have to occur at least forty-eight hours prior to receipt of the medication. These stipulations were designed to ensure the authenticity and voluntariness of the patient's choice (Campbell 1994).

Second, physicians who participate in assisted suicide would have to be licensed to practice medicine in Oregon. This stipulation addressed the concern expressed during the first two campaigns that "even an ophthalmologist could put someone to death."

Third, the law would apply to Oregon residents only; hence state officials would not need to fear becoming "the suicide destination" of the United States. Having stipulated these and other safeguards, the proponents in Oregon sought to close the loopholes alleged during previous campaign efforts, allegations that effectively aroused doubt among the electorate and led to defeat.

Early indications from the Oregon campaign were that the narrowly written proposal and its attendant safeguards had captured public favor and neutralized potential opponents. Three months before the election, 63 percent of eight hundred registered voters surveyed supported the measure. The coalition opposing the measure included the Catholic archdiocese and Oregon Right to Life. Again the church was using the pulpit to campaign against the measure and to collect money to defeat it.

WHY OREGON? ELEMENTS OF STATE CONDUCIVENESS

Proponents of change could rest their hopes for success in Oregon. Given the sentiment of political independence held by many Oregonians and the state's progressive history of condoning various forms of death with dignity, the political climate in Oregon appeared more conducive than that in Washington and California to adopting an assisted suicide law. A national survey conducted by *Our Sunday Visitor* indicated that only 43 percent of registered voters supported Measure 16 nationally, but in Oregon the measure was supported by 60 percent early in the campaign (Bates and O'Keefe 1994). Additionally, Oregon is a unique state both in terms of the long history of citizens using the initiative power as a tool of legal and social change and in terms of citizens' defiance toward both organized religion and outside political pressure. Chet Orloff, the director of the Oregon Historical Society, claimed: "This measure is in keeping with Oregon. Throughout history Oregon seems to be out there ahead of other states in testing things" (Bates and O'Keefe 1994). John Pridonoff, executive director of Hemlock Society USA based in Eugene, said: "Oregonians tend to be more open-minded to a wide variety of opinions. That climate was very important" (Bates and O'Keefe 1994). Referring to the status of Oregon as a relatively secular place, historian E. Kimbark MacColl added, "Oregon has never been a strong church state" (Bates and O'Keefe 1994). Orloff supported this sentiment: "The fact that there has been no dominant religion has allowed a moral flexibility that a lot of states don't have" (Bates and O'Keefe 1994).

Furthermore, Magleby describes Oregon as an "initiative prone" state (Magleby 1994:232). Not only was Oregon the first state to adopt an initiative process, but citizen lawmaking has often been used in grand social movements. For example, Oregon is one of four states that adopted women's suffrage by initiative, Oregon was one of the early states to decriminalize marijuana possession and use (although it later recriminalized them), and Oregon has passed a number of municipal laws protecting gays and lesbians (and has defeated two anti-gay statewide measures).

As indicated by this representative history, many Oregon citizens view themselves as social progressives. Yet they do not feel that freedom is granted by government, and in fact many view centralized government as the bane of individual liberty. However, there is a solid sense of state sovereignty when Oregonians feel themselves pressured by "outside" political pressures. Whether or not Oregonians are in fact different, the fact that they believe they are different strongly impacts Oregon politics.

Oregonians also disdain religious pressure. Says Mary Jo Tully, a religious educator who serves as chancellor for the archdiocese of Portland in Oregon, "This diocese does not have the [human] resources of the larger and more Catholic archdioceses." In fact Catholics, although the largest religious group, are only about 12 percent of the population. Overall, Oregon is 62 percent "unchurched," making it more secular than most states. Hence Oregon is a unique state, both in terms of the long history of Oregon citizens' using the initiative power as a tool of legal and social change and in terms of Oregon citizens' defiance toward religious activism within the state and political pressure from outside the state. These factors make the state seem generally conducive to progressive political change from within. Moreover, its recent history with progressive changes in the rights of the dying and in the funding of health care made the state seem especially conducive to changing the laws governing hastening the deaths of terminally ill patients.

Starting with Oregon's early codification of living will legislation, Oregon law has increasingly reflected a right of consumers to give voice to their end-of-life values through effective legal planning. The state already had a detailed legal framework for using advance directives and for making decisions on behalf of incapable patients who lack advance directives. In addition, the issue of rationing the state's money for Medicare patients, which had raised ethical concerns of the same sort as are raised in the assisted suicide debate, had become a topic of public discussion in the late 1980s and early 1990s (Weiner 1992).

In Oregon, data were gathered from the general population to measure the relative importance of health outcomes. Individual values were assessed using a quality-of-well-being scale in a telephone survey of one thousand Oregon residents. Additionally, community values were solicited from 1048 citizens who participated in small group discussions at forty-seven community meetings held in all but two counties throughout the state. Participants were asked to prioritize nine categories of health services, to identify and discuss the values underlying their priorities, and to identify key shared values about health care. The assessment of community values on controversial health care issues was also a key factor in mobilizing public interest in the physician-assisted suicide debate in Oregon.

By 1994, thanks in part to the continued interest in Jack Kevorkian, people's understanding of the issues surrounding death and dying went beyond public knowledge during the earlier campaigns in Washington and California. Three things happened: (1) communities around the state were joined by satellite for a public debate on the merits of physician-assisted suicide; (2) a small group of prominent citizens (including the parents of Janet Adkins, who was the first known person to die with Jack Kevorkian's assistance) started an organization called Oregon Death With Dignity; and (3) a campaign to get the issue of physician-assisted suicide on the Oregon ballot was mobilized.

In 1994, there were slightly under 1.8 million voters in Oregon. Many of them had a strong record of going to the polls: the turnout for the previous statewide vote during a nonpresidential election year was 75 percent. The campaign would need to focus its efforts on the tricounty area of Multnomah, Clackamas, and Washington counties (with 753,288 registered voters), which includes Portland. This is the most important region of any statewide election (Cooper 1994), as it makes up approximately 42 percent of the overall voter turnout in Oregon. It was projected that securing 60 percent of the vote in that area would put the proponents in position to win the election (Cooper 1994). The proponents also sought to get campaign volunteers in this area. The tricounty area of Marion, Polk, and Yamhill counties (200,932 registered voters), which includes Salem—the state capital—was projected to be key in the campaign because of the strength of the pro-life movement there. Salem was also an important area because of the presence of the state's most political newspaper and the fact that much of the statewide media is generated out of the Capitol Press Bureau. According to campaign projections, winning in the low 50 percent of this region would be considered a victory for the proponents. Lane and Coos counties (218,362 registered voters), the second-largest population center in the state—which includes Eugene—was projected to be an important target because of the tendencies of voters there to vote for progressive issues. The area was targeted for signatures to qualify for the ballot, and proponents could hope to secure about 60 percent of the vote there. The population centers of Ashland and Medford, in Jackson and Josephine counties (131,906 registered voters), were projected to require a strong battle, but for different reasons. Voters in Ashland tended to vote progressively, but in Medford there were many conservative voters who reported regular church attendance. The overall area was becoming a retirement location for the state, putting voters there in the higher age brackets. The proponents had a difficult time assessing their chances of winning in that area. In smaller yet still key regions, including Benton, Deschutes, Umatilla, Klamath, and Linn counties (216,164 registered voters), local television stations and strong newspapers were expected to provide good resources for spreading the campaign message.

This county-by-county analysis, based primarily on media markets, appeared to make little difference according to the first opinion poll commissioned by the campaign proponents (discussed in detail later). Marion County indicated the least support, followed by the city of Bend, which had a low sample size. But Karen Cooper, the campaign consultant mentioned in Chapter 3 had a long career in campaigning for choice—primarily abortion. She pressed on with her opinion that knowing the media markets is an integral facet of winning a campaign.

CAMPAIGN PLANNING

The proponents had two ways to gauge the political environment. One was analyzing the wins and losses during the previous several elections. The other was assessing the other initiatives on the 1994 ballot.

In the 1992 Oregon election, only a term limits initiative passed. Among the initiatives that lost had been a proposal that would have narrowed the rights of gays and lesbians. To look back two years further, six of the eleven measures on the 1990 ballot failed, including a proposed law to ban abortion and another abortion initiative that would have required parental notification. In 1988, losing initiatives included a proposal to require the wearing of safety belts in automobiles and another that would have raised beer and wine taxes. Gauging from the outcomes of the past three election campaigns, therefore, the proponents speculated that choice would be a winning theme for Oregonians.

Looking next at the current 1994 election, which included eighteen ballot measures, a well-defined governor's race, and three hotly contested congressional races, the campaigners made the following assessments. First, in all three congressional races, democratic women candidates were running against male candidates from the radical right. Second, one of the measures, Measure 13, was a proposal to permit discrimination against gays and lesbians. They concluded that, on the one hand, these races were diverting some of the attention of the religious right away from the death with dignity campaign, yet on the other hand, these companion races and issues tended to pique overall voter interest in the 1994 ballot.

Five months before the election, Eli Stutsman, one of the directors of Oregon Right to Die, the political action committee that sponsored Oregon's Death With Dignity Act (ODDA), began soliciting campaign contributions to fund the signature-gathering phase of the campaign (Stutsman 1994a). Over eight hundred of Oregon Right to Die's most generous donors around the nation received letters from Stutsman. The letters contained a copy of the act, along with a summary of its provisions, related news stories, and literature for their review. They stressed that the campaign needed 66,771 valid signatures by July 8, 1994. They also identified the primary opposition to be the religious right. Nevertheless, Stutsman's letter declared, "We are currently better situated to win in November than any other citizen's group has been on this issue."

This claim was supported by a list of facts that the campaign had gathered. First, there was support from both Republicans and Democrats. Second, the campaign had already received endorsements from the Oregon American Civil Liberties Union (ACLU) and all of the West Coast right-to-die organizations and editorial support from some of Oregon's most conservative newspapers. Moreover, polls were indicating that 73 percent of Americans were claiming to support a measure such as the ODDA (Harris poll), and the Oregon Medical Association had refused to follow the American Medical Association's (AMA) stance in opposition to such issues. Additionally, the Oregon State Pharmacist's Association and the Ecumenical Ministries of Oregon had recently declined to come out against the measure.

The primary message of Stutsman's letter was to state that the Measure 16 campaign needed to receive $25,000 over the next five weeks. The letter assured potential contributors that the campaign had a strong and professional organization in place. Furthermore, it had received over 4500 financial contributions ranging from $5 to $5,000. This information was apparently chosen to assure contributors that their money would be well spent. Another letter, catering to a second set of contributors, distinguished the Oregon measure from the failed initiatives in Washington and California, calling the ODDA a "prescribing bill" only, meaning that it would allow a physician to prescribe medication to end the life of a dying patient under limited circumstances, but not to administer the life-ending medication; the letter further stated that physicians must also be qualified by specialty in the area of the dying patient's terminal disease (Stutsman 1994b).

Stutsman's letter campaign helped the proponents turn in 30 percent more signatures than required by law. After the signatures were gathered and the campaign was officially informed by the secretary of state that the ODDA would appear on the November ballot, Stutsman sent follow-up letters seeking further contributions to buy radio and television time. The letter stressed the importance of a media campaign to defend the proposed law against the expected well-funded tactics of the opposition. As with earlier letters seeking contributions to fund the gathering of signatures to qualify the measure for the 1994 ballot, Stutsman's next letter identified the Roman Catholic Church and its allied institutions as its opposition. It claimed to have learned much from the earlier efforts to pass death with dignity laws in Washington and California. It also reminded recipients that the opposition spent almost $2 million to defeat the Washington effort, and nearly $4 million in California. "Much of that money was used to purchase last minute television advertising to scare voters!," the letter stated. That strategy worked because in both cases supporters could not match opponents on the airwaves. Enclosed with the letter was a news story containing a quote from the church, which "vow[ed] an all-out fight to defeat" efforts to pass the ODDA.

Most importantly, Stutsman charged that the campaign for the ODDA was far better positioned to win than the earlier attempts were. One reason was that the campaign team knew the opposition and its strategy better than the teams in the prior states had, having learned from their experiences. A new tactic, Stutsman promised, was the use of lawyers to aggressively warn the opposition against making false publications about the ODDA, reminding readers that in Washington, the Public Disclosure Commission found that the anti-119 advertising contained serious misrepresentations. Stutsman charged that Oregon Right to Die would seek redress in the courts to keep false publications out of the Oregon campaign. Stutsman's efforts to stave off lies about the ODDA were a key to the campaign's success, said Karen Cooper, who had managed the Washington campaign and was later a codirector of the Oregon campaign.

Up to this point, the campaign had spent about $250,000 to get on the ballot. About another $500,000 would be needed for the radio and television advertising necessary to win the election. "The only hurdle left," declared the latest of Stutsman's campaign letters, "is to raise the money needed to purchase the radio and television advertising necessary to win passage of death-with-dignity legislation."

Another facet of the campaign plan was how to manage earned media. The media plan, which was prepared by Geoff Sugerman—the campaign's official communications and press director—was divided into two phases—defining the issue and actual persuasion efforts (Sugerman 1994). The first phase consisted of research and direct contact with the news media and editorial boards covering the issue. Special efforts were made to "work with" members of the Oregon press corps and the national media, including influencing the words they would use to cover the issue and the tack they would take in their stories and general education about the issue. The basis for these efforts would be poll and focus groups that would help the campaign form its message based upon what voters were thinking then and there.

The campaign decided to center earned media on personal stories of terminally ill people willing to come forward and speak on the issue. Those stories were told against the political claim that the Oregon initiative was the first to offer a limited form of death with dignity. Limitations included the omission of lethal injections from the law and the establishment of a process to ensure that the patient was capable and willing to end his or her life. Proponents would also attempt to play up the pride of Oregonians to be the first to find a better way to affect society's most complex problems (Sugerman 1994).

The plan for managing press and communications included daily, weekly, and monthly goals. The plan included contacting pollsters and media consultants for establishing national and local strategies—including sending out media packets and following up with phone calls or visits—keeping press logs, and establishing a policy for so-called yellow journalism. Timelines for each of these tasks were established early in the campaign.

The campaign plan also included an assessment of the strengths and weaknesses of both sides of the campaign debate, including appraisals of voter demographics and the political environment. Table 3.1 catalogues the propo-

Table 3.1 Proponents' Assessment of Their Own Strengths and Weaknesses

Our Strengths

- We have a good ballot title and even more important an excellent explanatory statement for the voter's pamphlet.
- We have supplemented the explanatory statement with five arguments in our favor.
- We have the experience of the Washington and California campaigns.
- We have excellent insight into the strategy of our opponents.
- Public sentiment is clearly on our side.
- Voters are very familiar with the concept and have had several years to form their opinions on the subject.
- We have a national fund raising list.
- Our telecontributing effort has been a remarkable success.
- We have designed a computer system that can track all of the data necessary for a professional modern campaign.
- Our press has been mostly favorable.
- We have employed one of the best public opinion research firms and one of the best media consulting firms in the nation.

Our Weaknesses

- We know that when the opponents claim that possibly the wrong person will die for the wrong reason, we lose our base of supporters. (This claim was restated several times during interviews with Karen Cooper three years after the campaign.)
- We are also vulnerable to the charge that our campaign is sponsored and supported by small fringe groups lead by people like Dr. Kevorkian and Derek Humphry.
- The *Oregonian*, the largest, most prestigious newspaper in Oregon, read by 70 percent of the voters, has so far written two negative editorials against us.
- Practically no one understands that this is a prescription bill only.
- The story of the lies and distortions of the Catholic Church has not caught the imagination of the press or they are uncomfortable reporting a negative story about the Catholic Church.
- Our biggest problem is money.

Table 3.2 Proponents' Assessment of Their Opponents' Strengths and Weaknesses

Our Opponents' Strengths

- A long history of political involvement
- A widespread, well-established organization
- A strong speaker's bureau
- A strong financial base
- Many Catholic medical professionals
- A clear and consistent emotional message

Our Opponents' Weaknesses

- Only half of self-identified Catholics support the Church's position
- Oregon has the lowest church attendance rate in the nation
- Vulnerability to accusations of lies and distortions in Washington and California
- Many voters view them as extreme
- Distracted by other issues (e.g., abortion, antigay)

nents' assessments of their own strengths and weaknesses. Table 3.2 lists their assessments of the strengths and weaknesses of the opponents.

OPINION RESEARCH AND MESSAGE DEVELOPMENT

The first opinion survey for Oregon Right to Die was conducted by Fairbank, Maslin, Maullin, & Associates between September 11 and 14, 1994. Overall, the results looked very good for the proponents. Supporters outnumbered nonsupporters nearly 2 to 1, and only 8 percent remained undecided.

Nevertheless, the opinion researchers also determined that these very positive results actually masked some important concerns. First was the fact that these results were nearly as good as the numbers in Washington and California, where earlier initiatives were defeated. The interpretation offered by the analysts was that polling by telephone most likely failed to capture the influence of the opposition's aggressive television ads, and it failed to validly gauge the decision-making process that occurs in the ballot box at the moment a voter decides to vote yes or no on a life-and-death issue (Fairbank, Maslin, Maullin, & Associates 1994). The industry cliché that people vote no when they are confused or feel ambivalent about a ballot measure apparently had a great effect on this issue. Analyzing the numbers, the solid base of support was only 30 percent. Nearly 10 percent who initially said they would vote in favor of the measure switched to no or undecided after hearing the opposition's arguments. Moreover, after hearing the opposition's arguments, those who were initially undecided split against the measure by a wide margin.

The previous experiences in Washington and California suggested that voters were vulnerable to opposition messages and unwilling to take a chance. In fact, 34 percent overall, including one in four of those who said they would definitely vote yes and nearly half of those who said they would probably vote yes, indicated that they did not want to take a chance on a law involving life and death. Hence this soft support for Measure 16 was a significant threat to the proponents' campaign.

Additionally, greater than two-thirds of the voters polled felt that existing laws governing the terminally ill were working well. The analysts reminded the campaign that awareness of a problem is highly correlated with support. Thus, the media plan would have to focus on getting out the message that there is a problem with the status quo and that that problem could affect everyone. Another problem for the campaign was the difference in support between voters who reported having voted on all ballot measures and those who said they had voted on only a select number of ballot measures. Those who said they always vote were far less supportive of Measure 16.

Messages used during the Washington and California campaigns were tested on the Oregon market, the goal being to pinpoint the messages that would keep swing voters from voting against the measure. Two themes predominated. The first was that the terminally ill could avoid a lingering, painful, and humiliating death. The second was that Measure 16 would prevent the imposition of religious views and would move control from the government to individuals. The message that Measure 16 provides safeguards against abuse carried some weight mainly among "soft supporters," half of whom said the assurance of safeguards would move them from the "probably yes" group to the "definitely yes" group. With regard to spokespersons whom voters trusted, nurses, doctors, and the terminally ill themselves were rated more highly than clergy, who thus far had carried the opposition's message. This finding was good news to proponents, who sought to maintain the perception that the sponsors of the measure were backing it because of personal experiences with terminal illness and the loss of loved ones. Messages that attacked the opponents had the least effect on those polled. Only a few at the margins were swayed by negative messages. Overall, one in ten no voters said they were more likely to support the measure after hearing about the opposition. Twenty-five percent of the undecided were similarly swayed. And among swing voters, especially those who said they may not believe the opposition yet did not want to take a chance on a life-and-death issue, nearly one-third were more likely to support the measure after hearing the negatives about the opposition (Fairbank, Maslin, Maullin, & Associates 1994).

Political affiliation, religious affiliation, age, and gender played other significant roles in voter attitudes toward the measure. Democrats and liberals generally favored Measure 16, while Republicans and conservatives generally opposed it. Voters who had identified with Ross Perot or independents in the 1992 presidential election were more likely to favor Measure 16 than to oppose it. Church attendance was highly correlated with voter opposition. Also, voter opposition was highest among Protestant fundamentalists, while support was highest among Jewish voters. Among Catholics, support and opposition were divided nearly evenly, until analysts took into account the factor of gender. Like men and women voters generally, Catholic women were far less supportive than Catholic men were. Combining these demographic variables, the core support consisted of Jewish, liberal, Democratic, highly educated men. The core opposition consisted of young Republican women, Catholic women, and lesser educated voters. Young women in general, especially Democratic women, independent voters, and those from the Eugene media market, were among the weakest supporters. Undecided voters tended to be younger women, older Republicans, Republican women, and independent voters.

From these data, the research team targeted two groups: older voters, especially Republican men fifty and older, and younger women. Each of these findings had to be tempered by the primary finding that apparently phone polls in Washington and California were poor measures come election day. Instead of framing the primary campaign themes around voter opinion polls, the proponents decided to pay close attention to internal issues of coalition and consensus building.

BUILDING A COALITION AND ACHIEVING CONSENSUS

The chief petitioners for Measure 16 were Barbara Coombs Lee, a nurse and attorney, and Dr. Peter Goodwin, a physician and university professor. Each had excellent community and professional standing with many years of experience and service in health care. Together they sought to build a coalition of people with professional and community integrity and reputations. Their goal was to secure voter confidence that the coalition truly aimed to achieve what is best for patients and physicians in terms of what could actually be accomplished by changing the law. As mentioned in Chapter 1, Coombs Lee and Goodwin became involved in euthanasia reform because of their personal experiences in caring for dying patients.

Dr. Goodwin's own life was profoundly affected the first time a patient asked him for assistance with dying. "It felt as if my blood froze," he said. "I realized that with all my technical knowledge about diagnosing and treating, I knew nothing about helping people die. And there was nowhere to turn—not to my colleagues, my association, the literature. There was literally no guidance anywhere" (Goodwin 1996). So Goodwin joined the Hemlock Society and served as a board director, just waiting for an opportunity like Measure 16 to come along.

When interest in a ballot initiative finally did come along in 1993, reformers started without a law in mind, believing instead that they should first learn what people actually wanted. To gain that knowledge, leaders of the newly formed organization Oregon Right to Die organized a forum for physicians, nurses, hospice workers, and pharmacists, as well as terminal patients and their families and people who had watched loved ones suffer protracted deaths or botched suicides. The goal was to get a bare-bones view of the problems surrounding the care of the dying and to develop possible options that could realistically work. The consensus was purportedly achieved without regard for the opposition. For example, Dr. Goodwin stressed that while omitting injections from the consensus and subsequent legislation had a very favorable political impact, that is not why they were omitted. "They were omitted because doctors overwhelmingly felt like they could not and would not provide them, and patients expressed very little interest in having them available" (Goodwin 1996).

CRAFTING A LAW AND FRAMING THE DEBATE

Coombs Lee and Goodwin teamed up with Eli Stutsman, a highly skilled attorney and campaign strategist, for help with crafting a law and running the campaign. The law would allow a patient with six months to live to ask a doctor to prescribe a lethal dose of drugs to end unbearable suffering. At least two doctors would first have to agree that the patient's condition was terminal. The patient would have to request the drugs at least three times, and the third request must be in writing. Most important, the law left it to the patient to take the final step and self-administer the drugs.

The Oregon ballot measure contained a strategic element that was aimed at correcting the concerns of opponents during the Washington and California initiatives. That strategy was to include numerous strict assurances of voluntariness. For example, in order to receive a prescription for medication to end his or her life, a patient must make two oral requests and one written request. At least fifteen days must pass between the oral requests, and at least forty-eight hours must pass between the written request and a writing of a prescription. Furthermore, no prescription could be issued until the patient was determined to be free of psychological or psychiatric disorder or depression causing impaired judgment. Additionally, only physicians who treat patients for terminal illnesses would be qualified to write prescriptions for life-ending medication. Moreover, all interactions between a physician and patient with regard to obtaining lethal drugs would be required to be documented in the patient's medical records, and there was a provision for random review of those records by the Oregon State Health Division. Most importantly, the law allowed physicians to prescribe life-ending medication only; in the end the medicine must be self-administered (i.e., lethal injections, mercy killing, and active euthanasia remain illegal).

Opponents set out to convince voters that ensuring voluntariness is not possible. They said that physicians are often accused of abandoning patients on the threshold of death because (1) they do not like to concede when death is imminent, and (2) they typically dodge communications with patients and loved ones concerning issues of death. Supporters counterclaimed, "The Oregon Death With Dignity Act is designed to foster communication between dying patients and their attending physician. The Act respects, and we believe will strengthen, the physician-patient relationship, by allowing unrestricted communication between the dying patient and his or her physician" (O'Keefe 1994f).

Coombs Lee framed the proponents' position: "You shouldn't have to suffer through a prolonged and agonizing death against your will. Measure 16 says decisions at the end of life are yours to make—free from unwanted unconstitutional government interference—with your family and physician at your side" (Coombs Lee 1996). Pat McCormick, spokesman for the Coalition for Compassionate Care, countered: "It's open to abuse because it fails to require mental health evaluations and family notification. It leaves those without access to good health care vulnerable to facing suicide as the least costly treatment option" ("State Demos Urge Party" 1994:9).

A spokesman for the Oregon Pharmacists Association explained the organization's opposition to Measure 16: "Pharmacists are educated in the healing arts to prolong life in the treatment and healing of illnesses and injuries. Our organization views Measure 16 as a direct contradiction to that" (O'Keefe 1994b:19). The Oregon Hospice Association opposed Measure 16, urging people to consider alternatives such as aggressive pain management and hospice care. Thomas Reardon, an Oregon physician and AMA board member, agreed, estimating that 90 percent of end-of-life pain could be treated (O'Keefe 1994b).

Stutsman, legal counsel for Oregon Right to Die, countered that the proposed law would merely "codify existing medical practice for the terminally ill." Dr. Goodwin concurred: "The physicians who are presently involved and have kept it secret, and who are in the closet, so to speak, will now be able to speak to their colleagues and say, 'I will do this in the future because I think it's appropriate care' " (Goodwin 1996).

As these statements illustrate, the debate presented numerous complex issues: compassion for suffering and the dying; fear that any exception to a total ban against assisted suicide would be abused; claims that the law is being skirted already, hence change would allow interprofessional and patient-physician candor; counterclaims that direct physician assistance in death would actually harm the image of the profession; claims that there would be even broader moral and social harms; and appeals to seek less controversial alternatives.

DISTANCING REFORMERS FROM THEIR RADICAL COLLEAGUES

Derek Humphry is widely acknowledged to be the initiator of the euthanasia reform movement in the United States. Humphry, himself an Oregon resident, is the primary founder of the Hemlock Society and author of the best-selling book *Final Exit*, a guide to self-help suicide. However, Measure 16 strategists saw him as a political liability, fearing his views might scare away voters worried that the measure was just the beginning of radical societal experiments to help people kill themselves (O'Keefe 1994c). Indeed, Humphry has advocated lawful assisted suicide not only in cases of terminal illness but also for sufferers of advanced rheumatoid arthritis and others who are "hopelessly ill." Moreover, he strongly argued that injections must be lawful because in some cases swallowing pills actually worsens a patient's condition. He characterized Measure 16 as but a step in the right direction and said it would be used as a lever to get lethal injections legalized (Humphry 1996).

Campaign strategists regarded Humphry's exclusion from the day-to-day politics as "necessary to get the Leigh Dolins of the world to the table" (Stutsman 1996). Dolin, incoming president of the Oregon Medical Association (OMA), was widely regarded as having been a key figure in the OMA's executive decision to take no official position on Measure 16. Professionally, Dolin was neither for nor against the measure; his view was that the issue of whether to legalize some cases of assisted suicide should be decided by Oregon voters (Dolin 1996). That deference to voters made Dolin's acquiescence in Measure 16 crucial, the proponents' campaign engineers believed. Hence they carefully maneuvered to alleviate his worries about being linked with Humphry.

The maneuvers to mobilize moderate state leaders like Dolin illustrate the role of social agency in legal change. Stutsman and Coombs Lee tensely balanced between extolling Humphry's enormous role in the assisted suicide reform movement and isolating their campaign from his "fringe" agenda. On the one hand, Stutsman and Coombs Lee met with Humphry to debate whether to include lethal injections in the measure. The meetings were long and laden with emotion (Humphry 1996; Stutsman 1996). Humphry lost the debates, he said, to the campaign strategists who think "this halfway measure will bring the medical professionals to their side" (O'Keefe 1994d). On the other hand, Coombs Lee publicly rebutted Humphry's suggestion that the proponents were playing to physicians. Nine days before the election, for example, Coombs Lee distanced the Oregon Right to Die campaign from Humphry, stating, "Measure 16 was designed to find the common ground with a moderate, rational and safe solution to a problem facing Oregonians. It was not designed to satisfy the fringe element on either side of this issue, not Derek Humphry and not the archbishop" (O'Keefe 1994d).

PHYSICIAN NEUTRALITY

Polls and surveys at regional and national levels have indicated that physicians are deeply split over the issue of active euthanasia (Cohen 1994). In survey results released in 1994, 46 percent of Oregon physicians said they might be willing to prescribe a lethal dose of medication if it were legal to do so, while 31 percent of the respondents would be unwilling to do so on moral grounds (Lee, Nelson, Tilden, Ganzini, Schmidt, and Tolle 1996). In another survey released along with the Oregon survey, 56 percent of Michigan physicians supported legalization of assisted suicide, and 37 percent preferred a ban.

When the campaign for Measure 16 commenced, Dr. Goodwin informally surveyed twenty Oregon family physicians. His longtime public interest in death with dignity, professional status as a teaching physician at Oregon Health Sciences University, and personal relationships with roughly six in ten family physicians in the state made him uniquely capable of accurately assessing the level of physician tolerance or support for various levels of physician-aided death (Goodwin 1996). Half of the respondents said they would be comfortable prescribing medication for a patient's use in suicide, but none wanted to give lethal injections. On the basis of this survey, Goodwin advised the medical association to neither support nor oppose Measure 16.

When the OMA House of Delegates convened to consider Measure 16, the common wisdom was that the delegates would vote to oppose the measure. But that sentiment changed during ninety minutes of intense, emotional debate. Dr. Goodwin reported his informal survey results suggesting an even split between physicians on the matter of prescribing lethalities. Other delegates spoke about their experiences with patients and with their own parents, siblings, and other relatives. An equal number of physicians shared personal experiences in which assisted suicide would have been a good option as would have been a poor option. Dr. Lee Dolin, then president-elect of the OMA, recalled the debate as the longest, most solemn that he could remember (Dolin

1996). When Dolin spoke, he reasoned that the wide differences of opinion among physician leaders suggested neither supporting nor opposing the measure. Instead, he advocated the position that patients and the general public should decide what they want from physicians. His sentiment might be accurately summarized as follows: If physicians cannot agree on what to do about the profoundly personal experience of dying, can we rightfully tell everyone else what they ought to do? Thus, the decision not to take an official position occurred probably not because physicians abdicated their moral judgment toward patients, as Campbell contends (Campbell 1994:147), but because the participants were evenly split over providing lethal prescriptions, just as were physicians in Dr. Goodwin's informal survey.

Physician neutrality accomplished a lot: It suggested to voters that at least half of physicians supported and would even implement physician-assisted suicide and it removed physicians from their previous opposition partnership with organized religion. Later it was considered by proponents and opponents alike as a key to Measure 16's passage.

DELIVERING THE MESSAGE

Voter opinion polls were used to develop the campaign messages and to determine how, when, and by whom they would be delivered. As described earlier, the "avoid pain and suffering" message used in Washington and California was one of the more effective messages with the base of support. Yet demographic variables including age, gender, and political attitudes appeared to play a large role in how voters accepted particular messages. For instance, the poll results indicated that men and women had different reasons for supporting the measure. On the one hand, men feared loss of control and humiliation. On the other hand, women feared that someone would take advantage of and hurt them. Both of these were highly emotional, very powerful messages capable of matching the emotion of the opposition, yet combining these themes in an effective way would require careful planning.

Careful planning would also be needed when attacking the opposition, especially Catholics. Poll results indicated that a frontal attack on Catholics would likely be unproductive. Even among supporters of Measure 16, the Catholic Church received a highly favorable name identification rating. Nevertheless, respondents said that ministers and pastors were significantly less trustworthy than doctors and the families of the terminally ill, and less still than nurses and the terminally ill themselves. These results indicated that while proponents needed to have their version become the framework for public discussion of Measure 16, that task could be quite difficult.

Defining the message was declared to be a threefold task (Cooper 1994). Foremost was to be the definition of the race in the minds of the media people assigned to cover the issue. That task involved defining the issues in terms favorable to the proponents and defining the opponents unfavorably. That meant convincing the press to use language chosen by the proponents and to ask questions that would put the opponents on the defensive. The second task was to utilize the free press to transmit doubts about the credibility of opponents to the voters. The third was to compel the opposition to spend as much of its resources as possible defending itself, as opposed to delivering messages that might hurt the proponents' campaign. To a degree, this approach may have strayed somewhat from the advice offered by the opinion research team—that is, focus on pain and suffering and individual choice and play down attacks against the opposition. Once again, however, it is important to note that Cooper, who offered the strategy, had years of professional experience, and even the pollsters conceded that their method of inquiry—telephone polls—may have been a poor indicator of voter attitudes. And to her credit, she advised the Washington campaign to take a more aggressive approach, although they lost. Moreover, the pollsters admitted that the more the issue of pain and suffering was presented to voters, the more uncomfortable they became with the stakes involved in taking a final position on this measure. Even though attacks against the opposition affected mostly marginal voters—those who indicated soft or no support for Measure 16—perhaps they were the voters who would be most likely to turn the vote in favor of the proponents. This conjecture is buttressed by the fact that the initiatives in Washington and California failed by a mere 4 percent.

Cooper's advice extended to keeping the active opinion leaders around the state informed about the race and its significance, and compiling a list of impressive endorsements. Opinion leaders were said to be two types of people. The first was a government official, staff person, or otherwise politically active person. The second was an opinion leader in his or her profession or community, although not necessarily a political person. These were the people who should receive regular mailings about recent campaign highlights, a calendar of fundraising events, good quotes from the press, and any other positive, upbeat information concerning the Oregon Right to Die campaign (Cooper 1994). Such mailings could be counted on to create an "echo chamber effect"; that is, political and community activists who tended to talk to, or even about, one another would communicate feelings of momentum and make sure that leaders were familiar with the campaign themes. The overall effect of opinion leaders sharing information would surpass the effect of individual opinion leaders.

Compiling a list of opinion leaders was the impetus for an effective endorsement program. Table 3.3 lists the opinion leaders/endorsements sought by the Measure 16 campaign proponents. The endorsement program was designed to give credibility to the issue and make yes a safe vote, especially in smaller towns.

Similar efforts included winning over free or "earned" press, meaning news stories and editorials—not paid advertisements. Articles and interviews would reach thousands of people, making it imperative that anyone who

Table 3.3 Opinion Leaders and Endorsers Sought by Measure 16

Medical/professional association leadership
Hospice staff
Anti-Defamation League staff
Chamber of commerce officers
City, state, and county board and commission members
Community council officers
Democratic and Republican party chairs and officers
Elected officials and staff
Environmental group officers
Jewish Federation staff and board
Labor union officers and staff
League of Women Voters
Lobbyists
Lions Club officers and board
National Association for the Advancement of Colored People (NAACP) staff and board
Civic group officers
Pastors of all Protestant churches (except Fundamentalists)
Parent Teacher Association (PTA) officers and other school district activists
Rabbis and Jewish lay officials
Rotary Club officers
School principals (especially high school principals in small towns)
Trial lawyers
Urban League staff and board
Oregon Education Association teacher representatives
Common Cause
National Abortion Rights Action League
Oregon Women's Political Caucus
Physicians for Social Responsibility (PSROR)
PeaceWorks
Thousand Friends of Oregon
United Seniors of Oregon
Association of Retired Citizens
American Association or Retired Persons

(Cooper, 1994)

spoke to the press stuck carefully to the messages chosen by the campaign leaders after expensive market research. Other activities of the leadership included statewide correspondence and meetings with newspaper, radio, and television reporters and editorial boards. They also conducted regular press conferences and press releases. Geoff Sugerman, the campaign's media director, kept regular records and offered periodic reports regarding these efforts. One of the more interesting findings was that the greatest concerns among media people were the potential for abuse of terminal patients and the lack of a requirement that patients requesting death with dignity would be required to undergo a mental health evaluation. In many cases, reporters and editors were swayed most by personal stories of people within their geographic area. As for paid advertisements—a medium through which proponents could exercise the greatest amount of control over the content of the messages—the campaign hired the firm of Zimmerman and Markham and authorized $300,000.

To test the impact of these activities, the Measure 16 campaign paid $13,000 to have Fairbank, Maslin, Maullin, & Associates conduct tracking polls during the last month of the campaign. As the name implies, tracking polls provide repeated assessments of voter opinions at short intervals. The results are compared to a baseline opinion poll so that analysts can detect sways in voter attitudes—hopefully detecting the immediate effects of proponent and opponent campaign efforts—and thus giving the campaign a chance to either accelerate its present efforts if the results are positive or change its course if the results are negative. These data are instrumental in detecting sudden changes in support, assessing the impact and effectiveness of pro and con media, and generating additional opportunities for soliciting financial support from committed donors (Fairbank, Maslin, Maullin, & Associates 1994b). A five-minute, four-hundred-sample track was conducted just days before the proponents began their television ad campaign, allowing the campaign to measure the damage of the yet unanswered attack lodged by the opponents and to establish a baseline for measuring the impact of positive messages that the campaign hoped would impact voter attitudes. This initial track was later followed by another five-minute poll of four hundred voters to measure the effectiveness of the proponents' ads, the aim being to determine whether the better strategy would be to respond to the opponents' ads nightly or to wait and run an onslaught of ads during the final week of the campaign.

At the time when the opinion researchers had suggested their $13,000 strategy for tracking voter attitudes, they had already identified the key targets of their analysis. The variables of most significance included sex, age, political affiliation, and place of residence. Women under age fifty (28 percent of the electorate) were targeted as the most likely to change their opinions after hearing the proponents' arguments for Measure 16. Democrats under age fifty (22 percent of the electorate) were predicted to be as easily swayable. Women voting in Portland were a more troublesome group (38 percent of the electorate), as they were most sensitive about the fear of taking a chance on a life-and-death issue. Nevertheless, 15 percent of them were estimated to be likely to switch to yes after hearing the proponents' arguments in favor of the measure. Older voters, those sixty-five and older (20 percent of the electorate), were assessed to be the most difficult to sway; in fact, 12 percent of them switched to no after hearing opposition arguments. Independent and nonaffiliated voters (about 14 percent of the electorate) were the most difficult group to assess.

At this point in the campaign, market analysts were still sure that the two most salient messages were pain and suffering and choice. Attacks against the Catholic Church, although effective in bringing more attention to the issue, continued to be an ineffective way of getting more people to vote yes. Arguments that the measure would legalize a practice that was occurring already, that is, that Measure 16 would actually prevent abuse, were suffering the same fate.

FUNDRAISING

The fundraising plan for Measure 16 included a wide array of strategies, smart planning, and skillful execution. Oregon campaign law allows donations from any source and in any amount as long as campaigners comply with reporting requirements. Already $300,000 had been raised to fund the gathering of signatures to qualify for the ballot. To get the campaign messages to voters, the campaign sought to raise between $500,000 and $700,000 using direct mail, telecontributing, house parties, individual solicitations, a major-donor fund-raising project, and solicitations from political action committees (PACs) and other supporting organizations. The direct mail plan included two phases: building a donor base and resoliciting past donors. An interesting quirk in the donor-building phase was that some of the mailings were actually anticipated to lose money after the costs of the mailings were accounted for. However, the professional experience of the campaign leaders and consultants had taught them that the people statistically most likely to respond to an appeal for money are not only those who contribute most frequently, but also those who have contributed most recently. Overall, therefore, going back to the donor base several times during the campaign was predicted to net $169,688 (Cooper 1994).

A phone room was set up to raise an estimated $9000 per week. House parties, in which a host agrees to pay the expenses for inviting guests who listen to speakers, watch campaign videos, and get asked to contribute to the campaign, were estimated to bring in a total of $39,000. Another $10,000 was solicited from PACs and big business, and the Hemlock Society USA was expected to use its donor lists to generate $150,000. Much of these funds were earmarked for a strong media advertisement campaign that would be carefully planned to spend money wisely right up to election day.

AD WARS

As was the case with the first two voter ballot initiatives in Washington and California, Oregon residents who proposed an expanded right to request and receive a physician's assistance in hastening imminent death identified compassion and choice as their most effective policy arguments. These themes were clearly present in their television ad campaign. One ad featured a former nurse who boldly claimed to be a criminal for obtaining the pills that her ailing daughter used to end her battle with bone cancer. "I'm a criminal. My twenty-five-year-old daughter Jody was in horrible pain dying of bone cancer. She wanted to end her life. I got her the pills. We both broke the law." "When did we give up our right to run our own life? Doesn't government have better things to do than to make criminals out of law-abiding citizens? Are we going to let one church make the rules for all of us?" she went on to ask. "And as she slipped peacefully away, I climbed into her bed and I took her into my arms for the first time in months," the woman said, suggesting that until this point her daughter's illness kept her from being touched by anyone—even her own mother. "I was a registered nurse, I know. Vote yes on 16."

The second ad theme, rights consciousness and choice, promised that Measure 16 would stop government interference in the lives of dying people and their families. This theme was poignantly depicted by an ad called "Faces," in which a series of fourteen faces of eight females and six males, mostly middle-aged professional people, faded in and out of the picture while they delivered the message:

> This is my body. I don't need you. I don't need government. I don't need any church playing politics with my choices, with my life. If I'm terminally ill, I'll decide how and when and in what way I will end my life. Measure 16 has all the safeguards you and I need. And it ends government and religious interference in a part of our lives that is strictly personal. Vote yes on Measure 16. Vote yes on Measure 16.

OPPOSITION STRATEGIES

Opponents of the proposed law included the Coalition for Compassionate Care, Oregon Right to Life, the Oregon Health Care Coalition, the Oregon State Council of Senior Citizens, and the Oregon Hospice Association. Religious organizations—particularly the Catholic Church—played prominent roles in defeating earlier aid-in-dying initiative campaigns in Washington and California, and they were the primary opponent in Oregon. The Church provided funds for the opponent campaign.

Pat McCormick, an opposition leader, said that more than 75 percent of the $1.5 million in contributions sent to his campaign to defeat Measure 16 came from Catholic sources, including $300,000 from donations in churches (O'Keefe 1994a:1). Parish priests, moreover, used their pulpits as a forum for sermons against the initiatives. An article in *The Oregonian* described one aspect of the effort: "Archbishop William J. Levada of the Diocese of Portland and Bishop Thomas J. Connolly of the Diocese of Baker have instructed their priests to preach against the measure on Sunday September 18, and to collect money a week later to defeat it" (O'Keefe 1994b). Priests were also encouraged to remind parishioners about the sanctity of life, especially in old age. Additionally, church membership rolls were used for distributing materials opposing the measures. For example, 200,000 copies of an eight-page voters' guide produced by the Oregon Family Council were distributed in 1600 churches (O'Keefe 1994b). Said Jeff Sugerman, executive director of Oregon Right to Die, "This politicking from the pulpit clearly shows our opponent's intention to promote Catholic religious doctrine by influencing Oregon voters" (O'Keefe 1994b).

Church leaders and other opponent organizations also executed a second, more secular, strategy. *The Oregonian* summarized the arguments: (1) doctors would become killers, contrary to their oath to the role of healer; (2) current methods for predicting the imminence of death are unreliable ("Misjudgment of a patient's condition could end life prematurely"); (3) family rights would be violated; (4) a slippery slope would be created, leading to court judgments allowing lethal injections when patients cannot swallow medication; (5) people may kill themselves to avoid financial costs ("The right to die may well become the duty to die"); and (6) depressed patients may be at most risk ("Depressed patients will likely go untreated"). Citing these problems, opponents claimed the proposed law lacked safeguards, a claim that became the key message of their ads and appeals.

The group Physicians and Nurses Against Measure 16, for example, placed a full-page advertisement in *The Oregonian* that read: "Need a second opinion?" The ad listed many names of those opposing Measure 16 and continued: "How about hundreds of them? Physicians and nurses from all parts of Oregon are speaking out in clear opposition to Ballot Measure 16. Former United States Surgeon General C. Everett Koop, M.D. says that 'Measure 16 is ripe for abuse.' The American Medical Association hopes 'the voters of Oregon will honor the healing role of physicians and vote against Ballot Measure 16.' Medical professionals are letting their voices be heard. On November 8, we need to hear yours."

In October 1994, the governing board of the AMA interceded in the debate with its announcement of opposition to Measure 16. Concurrent with this announcement, the AMA sent delegates to Oregon to join the opposition (O'Keefe 1994c). Thomas Reardon, a Portland physician and AMA national board member, explained the AMA's decision: "It's fundamentally inconsistent with the physician's professional role in taking care of patients. Our basic tenet is to do no harm.... There was a concern that this was a major issue not only for Oregon, but the country."

Leigh Dolin, then president-elect of the OMA, rebutted: "We'll see how Oregonians feel about outsiders trying to tell them how to vote" (O'Keefe 1994c). Dr. Goodwin characterized the AMA's action as "inappropriate and paternalistic" (O'Keefe 1994c). A spokesman for Oregon Right to Die agreed: "The fact is, this is just another out-of-state group coming in and saying this is wrong. What do Oregonians care what the AMA in Chicago says about this?" (O'Keefe 1994c).

The opponent group that entered the debate as the Coalition for Compassionate Care ostensibly attempted to broaden the conflict beyond the struggle between federal and local control. Rather than defining a nationwide professional organization such as the AMA as the local enemy, the Coalition for Compassionate Care pointed to the Hemlock Society and blamed its efforts to find at least one state that would legalize physician-assisted suicide for the current political approach (Coalition for Compassionate Care 1994). The question presented by the Coalition was whether physicians should be allowed to wield the kind of power that would be bestowed to them if Measure 16 passed. Attempting to disregard the political debate about whether physicians *should* be permitted to wield such power, the coalition claimed to focus on the fallibility of physicians' diagnoses and the depression experienced by patients told they are terminal. These two factors were said to support the greatest fears of those who remained wary of death with dignity—that Measure 16 did not require a mental health examination before lethal drugs were prescribed. This claim continued to worry undecided voters into the final weeks of the campaign.

FINAL WEEKS

In Washington and California, proponents misspent their funds during the crucial last ten days of the campaign—a time when TV, radio, and print messages and images are essential (Stutsman 1996). In those states, opponents blasted the media with frightening images and slogans, while the proponents had no money or failed to spend their remaining money to counterattack. Not so in Oregon, where Measure 16 strategists saved money to wage a strong media campaign during the final days before the vote.

They drove home two messages: Suffering people deserve better, and neither politics nor organized religion should dictate end-of-life choices. For example, a notable pro–Measure 16 radio commercial stated, "Who do you politicians and religious leaders think you are, trying to control my life?" It went on to emphasize the safeguards included in the measure. Proponents counterattacked with ads warning about the chances of misdiagnosis. They also rebutted what they called "the false assertion that only the Catholic Church opposed the initiative." But insiders complained that opponents remained too civil and failed to go for the political jugular vein, as they had in Washington and California. None of their ads had the impact of the award-winning ad in California, developed by the consultancy firm of Cavalier and Associates, which depicted a sinister-looking doctor entering an elderly woman's apartment and revealing a steely syringe that he used to euthanize her. Nevertheless, as in Washington and California, there was a narrowing of the initiative support as the weeks passed closer to the election, largely because of the opponents' claims that Measure 16 lacked adequate assurances of voluntariness (Park 1997). Yet opponents were never able to drive support for the measure below the 50 percent mark.

In early September, a viewer poll conducted by television station KPTY indicated that the measure was ahead 63 percent to 31 percent (Mapes 1994). Support was highest among young voters and lowest among older voters, and there was equally strong support among Democrats, Republicans, and independents. After the opponents' advertising blitz, however, a poll for *The Oregonian* and television station KATU showed the expected vote narrowing. The poll reported that the strongest opposition came from women, those over fifty-five, and those who considered themselves very religious.

Just days before the election, *The Oregonian*, the state's highest circulation daily newspaper, editorialized against the measure:

> Four realities are at the core of why the state should not become a co-conspirator in assisted suicide: (1) almost all pain experienced by the dying can be successfully managed; (2) virtually all clinical depression among

> the dying can be successfully treated; (3) such treatment is available to all Oregonians, rich and poor; and (4) when doctors control pain and relieve depression, suicide requests among the dying virtually vanish.

The editorial concluded, "Measure 16 places the most vulnerable at the greatest risk," and quoted from the New York State Task Force on Life and the Law Report: "No matter how well the guidelines are framed, this treatment would be delivered in the context of social inequality and bias that exists in society, including medical services. Those who are poor, elderly, lack access to good medical care or are members of minority groups will be at greatest risk" ("Offer Dignity without Death" 1994).

Nevertheless, a month before the election, polls continued to indicate that six out of ten registered voters supported the Oregon measure. Moreover, many of the Oregon counterparts of the political parties and medical associations that opposed the Washington and California initiatives either endorsed Measure 16 or adopted a position of "neutrality." For example, though the Washington State Medical Association and the California Medical Association opposed their respective initiatives as "fundamentally inconsistent" with the physician's role as healer, the OMA agreed to a motion "to neither oppose nor endorse physician-assisted suicide" (Campbell 1994; Dolin 1995, 1996; Goodwin 1996). On the other hand, the national board of the AMA announced that it strongly opposed the Oregon initiative and warned that if Oregon doctors participated in assisted suicide they would be performing an unethical act (O'Keefe 1994b).

On November 3, 1994, Measure 16 narrowly passed with only 51 percent of the vote. The voter turnout was 57 percent. A breakdown of the results by county showed that the vote was 55 percent for and 45 percent against in the population-rich Portland metro counties of Multnomah, Washington, and Clackamas. It passed in thirteen other counties throughout the state and lost in the most rural remaining twenty counties, which have smaller populations ("How Many Voted" 1994).

WHY THEY WON IN OREGON

In Chapter 2, our analyses of the initiative defeats in Washington and California restated Magleby's observation that citizen initiatives are a valuable agenda-setting device. Thus a defeat in one state may set a course for more successful action in another state. In fact, one insider from the Oregon campaign distinguished between first-stage and second-stage reform efforts. The first stage involves grassroots pressure to sell the message that the status quo needs reexamination and change. The second stage involves coalition building.

Perhaps the Washington and California reform groups were unable to achieve the second-stage politics of reform. That is not to say that there were not coalitions formed, especially in Washington. But second-stage coalition building in Oregon involved gathering a diverse group of many committed professionals to support the movement.

A related notion in the social movements literature is the distinction between adherent and constituent target groups (Snow, Rochford, Worden, and Benford 1986). Perhaps the early initiative efforts appealed largely to adherents—those who already fought for the death with dignity movement. Another concept from the same literature is the notion of frame alignment (Snow et al. 1986). The processes of targeting specific groups and of framing strategic arguments to win their support are useful concepts for analyzing the similarities and differences between earlier campaigns and the Oregon campaign and how these characteristics may help explain the different outcomes.

On the basis of these variables, our analysis in Chapter 2 suggested that campaign leaders in Washington and California failed to include constituent groups in their respective coalitions. If Oregon doctors are any indication, even physicians who expressed support for the concept of death with dignity were not prepared to inject patients with lethalities. Therefore, early campaigners either sought to use public opinion to force the hand of medical professionals or failed to genuinely consider the willingness of doctors to inject their dying patients (and the desire of patients to be injected) when they wrote their proposed laws. This is a bold conjecture derived from the Washington and California campaign data.

After the Washington defeat, Derek Humphry said that campaigners "made the tactical mistake of . . . intending to sit down with the legal and medical professions after victory to hammer out the detailed guidelines under which active euthanasia could be carried out." Humphry's remarks reveal the proponents' nearly singular focus on public opinion as a tool of social change. That strategy underestimated the roles of social movement, professional, and religious organizations who support the legal and moral consensus achieved during the last decade regarding the redefinition of killing in medical settings. The aim of the death with dignity proponents was to align the movement ideology, goals, and activities with voter interests, values, and beliefs. Instead, including injections in the proposed laws and calling them aid in dying gave salience to opposition arguments that proponents were attempting to put one over on the electorate. In the words of an insider in the death with dignity movement, first-stage reform efforts in Washington lacked an authentic connection with constituent groups, and thus failed at actual coalition building.

In California, the proponents' campaign was hobbled by perceptions that it was absolutist, especially on the issue of rights. Leaders were portrayed in newspaper articles as having personal incentives motivated by personal tragedy. They aligned their movement frame with the increasingly controversial Hemlock Society, which had added California to its movement agenda five years before the Proposition 161 campaign was waged ("Supporters Get Signatures" 1987). In their attempt to legislate all the concerns about legalizing euthanasia, the organization wrote a constitutional amendment from whole cloth that ended up being lengthy, tedious, and cumbersome—and therefore rich with challengeable provisions. The campaign rhetoric was regarded as packaged full of euphemisms, hiding undisclosed motives or principles, and treating voters paternalistically. Pitches to voters gave the impression that their role was to decide the battle of experts. But like the death with dignity movement's campaign in Washington, the California campaign created a false perception that the will of voters would control the practice of end-of-life care.

By contrast, the strategists in Oregon took negative voter perceptions at face value and set out to create contrary images about their campaign. From the organization's inception, multiple levels of support and a variety of constituencies were brought in. The leaders kept a professional profile, not disclosing personal stories but accompanying and advocating on behalf of others who did. They worked hard to portray their action frame as one developed from authentic assessments of the needs and desires of patients and health care professionals in their state. They wrote the law to be an extension of previous Oregon statutes defining and governing death with dignity in that state. They also allowed for a good deal of future clarification, the decision not to define the residency requirement being one example. Their campaign rhetoric portrayed them as empathic, rational people being demonized by church and state. Likewise, they talked in terms of inclusion, hoping that voters would feel they were deciding "our law."

The opponents also had to face the distinction between adherents and constituents. The primary bearers of opposition messages were Catholic organizations. On the one hand, the Church sought to educate believers about the immorality of taking human life in any instance, saying that life is sacred and humans are mere stewards of lives granted by God. That message appealed largely to religious believers. But Oregon is purported to be the most unchurched state in the nation. There was an anti-Catholic backlash. In fact, every issue on the ballot supported by Catholics went the other way. One was an antigay measure that aroused enough anger against the Catholic political machinery that some voters vowed to vote against the Church on every initiative regardless of its own merits.

But Catholics also ran a strong secular campaign geared toward educating voters about the potential dangers of doctors "killing" patients, especially when so many Americans cannot afford good health care. This argument—the wrong people may use the law for the wrong reason—was the death with dignity movement's Achilles' heel (Coombs Lee 1997). Only messages about choice and the adequacy of the measure's safeguards could be offered in opposition. However, the abuse argument also required voters to believe that physicians would become accomplices in illegal, unethical behavior. Two factors made that allegation dubious. First, patients tend to trust their own physician. Second, the political neutrality of the state medical association suggested that the physicians themselves did not believe such fears were credible.

The OMA decision to abstain from official debate had two immediate impacts on voter attitudes. Physician neutrality opened the way for the impression that Measure 16 may not have been as poorly written as its opponents claimed—at least in the official opinion of the physicians' organization. And it left the Church alone as the primary group against the proposed law (unlike in Washington and California, where the Church and physicians worked side by side). Given the antireligion sentiment of Oregonians, the appearance of religious groups standing alone helped the proponents' campaign. Ironically, perhaps, OMA neutrality also created another benefit for proponents because it led to intercession by the AMA, which played into Oregonians' opposition to "outside" pressure.

This analysis of strategic choices and their repercussions illustrates something more than just how voters' attitudes are affected by media messages and voters' feelings about those who communicate campaign messages. It also illustrates the significance of social agency in legal and moral change. For instance, the OMA's unexpected decision to remain neutral on Measure 16 changed the battlefield for both sides of the campaign. And it suggested that by omitting injections, the proponents had written a more sensible law—one that physicians could live with. In this campaign, therefore, the agenda-setting possibilities of lawmaking by initiative were partly influenced by campaign messages and communicators.

Another example was the struggle between campaign insiders to control which messages voters heard. Measure 16 leaders were terrified about the possibility of Humphry going public with his claim that, without the possibility of lethal injections, Measure 16 was seriously flawed. "If the true purpose of assisted suicide is to relieve suffering, patients and physicians will see for themselves that a law like Measure 16 that does not include injections is inadequate" (Humphry 1996). That message would almost certainly have killed the initiative. Aware of the leadership's fear, Humphry had to have a good reason for conceding to the narrower goals of the Measure 16 proponents. "In fact, Measure 16 will prove me right. So while at first I thought this [Measure 16] was the end of my book [*Final Exit*], in fact my book will be even more significant as people realize that obtaining drugs is not enough" (Humphry 1996). Humphry's comments indicate that he viewed his compromise with Measure 16 campaign strategists not as a concession, but as a maneuver toward vindicating his personal convictions about the need for lethal injections. This feeling of vindication was enough to keep Humphry from going public with his complaints about Measure 16, and again the contingent nature of social agency played a significant role in controlling voter attitudes and setting a public agenda.

On the other side of this insider controversy, Humphry's characterization of Measure 16 as a way to bootstrap social acceptance for active euthanasia was flatly contradicted by Stutsman, the central campaign strategist for the proponents of Measure 16. According to Stutsman and others, it was Humphry's persistence about injections that alienated people like Dr. Dolin, the incoming president of the OMA when the campaign for Measure 16 was launched. To secure nonresistance from moderate state leaders such as Dr. Dolin, Humphry was asked not to attend the deliberations between campaign strategists and wary community leaders. He was assured that the meeting participants knew his views already and was cautioned that his militancy might destroy the chance to cultivate key political support. The Measure 16 leadership was desperately trying to keep Humphry and his message out of the public eye.

Humphry reluctantly conceded that any level of lawful assisted suicide would be better than the status quo, so he agreed not to enter the meetings without invitation. He also made it clear in media interviews that he did not speak for the Measure 16 campaign. (By contrast, he was publicly perceived as a campaign spokesperson for Washington's Initiative 119 and California's Proposition 161.) Instead, he publicly proclaimed himself to be "more of the conscience of our movement." "I take a longer, historic view and a more honest view. But I'm not involved in day-to-day politics, so I can afford that" (O'Keefe 1994d). Humphry's concession allowed Measure 16 leaders to maintain their agenda and influence voter attitudes.

As this account illustrates, pro-campaign strategists had to achieve a fragile balance between satisfying Humphry's desire to be included in the overall assisted suicide movement and diplomatically distancing their campaign from his more aggressive agenda. Certainly, therefore, Humphry's exclusion from the coalition was much less a facade than a verifiable political strategy.

Then again, hardly anyone realized or paid attention to the fact that Humphry quietly helped raise about 20 percent of the $1 million dollars spent on the proponents' campaign. "It is a fact that I've written at least three fund-raising letters for them," Humphry said (O'Keefe 1994d). Although it was misleading to imply that the Hemlock Society funded the entire campaign—an insinuation that some opponents made in an apparent attempt to disparage the ODDA—"it is quite unlikely that the campaign could have succeeded without it" (Stutsman 1996).

In conclusion, only a carefully planned, tightly executed, and exhaustively guarded strategy enabled pro–Measure 16 tacticians to obtain everything they wanted: assent of moderate state leaders, Humphry's alliances with financial backers, and a majority of the votes. The lessons learned from earlier campaigns were successfully transformed into a significant instance of legal and social change. Oregon became the first place in the world to sanction some instances of physician-assisted suicide. Historically, Measure 16 reversed two thousand years of Western medical ethics and law. Academically, the passage of Measure 16 in the wake of the narrow failures of early efforts in Washington and California may be looked upon as some support for the general finding in the political science literature that legislation by initiative is a valuable agenda-setting device.

4

A Movement to Repeal the Oregon Death With Dignity Act

INTRODUCTION

Catholic organizations had repeatedly vowed to fight any and all efforts to implement assisted suicide (Park 1997). After the narrow success of Measure 16, Church affiliates joined with the National Right to Life Committee to begin planning how they could get Measure 16 back before the voters. First, they swayed the Oregon Medical Association to give up its position of neutrality on the issue of physician-assisted suicide. Next, they urged the Oregon legislature to send Measure 16 back for a second fight. Armed with an OMA resolution supporting the right of voters to consider repealing the law, the legislature put the exact measure back before the populace. Catholic organizations provided half of the more than $4 million spent to repeal Oregon's assisted suicide law. They invested in a political strategy that aimed to raise fear of so-called death with dignity. Television and radio ads, as well as illustrations in *The Oregonian*, sought to make suicide pills appear as frightening as a syringe. Measure 51 proponents sought to reproduce the erosion of support for assisted suicide that had occurred in Washington and California by convincing voters that even if they supported assisted suicide, the means that were legally justified by Measure 16 were inadequate to assure death with dignity.

"IMAGES THAT HURT US"

Barbara Coombs Lee spoke earnestly about three images that hurt the death with dignity movement. They are the needle, the bag, and the Netherlands. In 1994, the movement was hit by the very father of the right to die movement, Derek Humphry. Humphry penned a letter to the editor of the *New York Times* (Humphry et al. 1994). In the letter, he wrote about the needle, the plastic bag, and the studies coming out of the Netherlands. Humphry directly attacked the Oregon Death With Dignity Act (ODDA), charging that a law that forbids injections "could be disastrous." Humphry referred to a controlled study in the Netherlands, which, he claimed, left 25 percent of ninety patients who took pills lingering near death for as long as four hours. Fifteen of those patients required injections to end not just their own suffering, noted Humphry, but also the suffering of family members and physicians. In the Netherlands, Humphry explained, the law permits physicians to stand by ready to act with an injection if pills go wrong. But when pills do not work in America, physicians who fear leaving a needle mark must resort to putting a plastic bag over their patients' heads. Emphatically, Humphry concluded that he would prefer the injection over the bag (Humphry 1994).

Three years after Oregon voters approved the ODDA, State Senator Eileen Qutub, a Republican from Beaverton, helped lead the effort to send the law back to the voters, urging them to repeal it. Qutub and other senators claimed that there were issues that had become clear three years later that weren't clear before—life-and-death issues. During a speech on the Senate floor, mustering all the drama and flair that Derek Humphry had in his letter to the *Times*, Senator Qutub displayed a plastic bag, which she claimed would be necessary to make sure suicide by medication resulted in death (Rojas-Burke 1997). She successfully argued that rereferring Measure 16 to the voters would simply give them a chance to consider information about assisted suicide that had emerged since 1994.

Another appeal to voters was voiced by Nat Hentoff, a nationally renowned authority on the First Amendment and the Bill of Rights. Hentoff dramatically editorialized about the alleged incredibility of having to pull a plastic bag over one's head and bear death by suffocation.

> For $30, those planning suicide can buy a kit containing a clear, handmade, plastic Exit Bag—the size of a garbage bag—with a soft elastic neckband that has Velcro fasteners so it can easily be removed if the customer changes his or her mind.... For an extra $10, an illustrated brochure is available that tells the Exit Bag user how to get the best results. I'm surprised that the brochure isn't included in the basic package. (Hentoff 1988)

In Hentoff's concluding remarks, the Hemlock Society, Dr. Jack Kevorkian, and possibilities of a slippery slope were equated with Nazi Germany. This was more than hyperbolic editorializing. Studies from the Netherlands purporting a 25 percent failure rate became the repeal campaign's primary theme. The inference was that eventually death with dignity proponents would be pressed to seek to include injections in the law.

GETTING THE MEASURE BACK ON THE BALLOT

An article in *The Oregonian* by Mark O'Keefe just one month after the passage of Measure 16 sowed the seeds for the "Myth of the 25 Percent Failure Rate" (Smigelski 1997). O'Keefe's article stated that a seven-year Dutch study on the use of drugs to end the lives of terminally ill people showed that while 75 percent of patients die within three hours, the remainder can last two days or longer. That report simmered in the minds of policy makers during the next few years as conservatives successfully took over the leadership of the state medical association and the state legislature. The OMA's House of Delegates voted to support Measure 51, which would repeal Measure 16, in April 1997. The resolution before the 122 delegates stated, "Whereas proponents and opponents alike have determined physician-assisted suicide, as provided for in Measure 16, to be an uncertain procedure, which fails 25 percent of the time, often resulting in a prolonged death and increased suffering for patients, families and physicians ... be it resolved that the OMA will oppose legalization of physician-assisted suicide as provided for in Measure 16." During May and June, conservative legislators were said to have had the OMA resolution in hand when they successfully urged the Assembly and the Senate to refer the ODDA back to the voters for a second initiative contest.

Analysis of Measure 51 by *The Oregonian*'s Gail Kinsey Hill briefly described two reports that opponents cited to support their claim that pills do not always work. A 1994 report said that whereas 80 percent of those studied died within 5 hours of consuming lethal medication, the remaining 20 percent had not died within 5 hours, and they were injected with a muscle relaxant, which causes quick death. A 1971 report describes symptoms of barbiturate poisoning, but, Hill noted, it does not address doctor-assisted suicide (Hill 1997b). But other writers for *The Oregonian*, most notably Mark O'Keefe, said these reports showed that 25 percent of the suicides under Measure 16 would be botched. A writer for *Willamette Week* accused *The Oregonian* of "half-baked" reporting (Smigelski 1997). The same writer claimed that quoting proponents of Measure 51 for their claims that oral medication fails 25 percent of the time contributed to "a divisive campaign of deception that based on a misinterpreted Dutch study no one has bothered to read" (Smigelski 1997). Repeal opponents added that their own review of 24 terminally ill patients who died at home using prescription drugs contradicted the claims of Measure 51 proponents. Their study, conducted in 1996 by Compassion in Dying, reported that none of the patients took more than 10 hours to die, and on average, death occurred in three hours (Hill 1997b).

There was a lot of disagreement over the validity of O'Keefe's data. O'Keefe said his article was based on a phone interview with Dr. Pieter Admiraal.

Yet Admiraal's study showed that 96 percent of the eighty-seven people he studied died within five hours of taking life-ending medication. The other 4 percent died within two days. In response to O'Keefe's reporting, Admiraal made it widely clear that there are exceptionally few people who would live more than twenty-four hours after ingesting nine grams of barbiturates, which is three times the lethal dose, and most would die in less than half a day. Admiraal openly concluded that opponents of assisted suicide were badly misusing his research (Admiraal 1997). Moreover, Dr. Gerrit Kimsma, a Dutch researcher, addressed a letter to "the people of Oregon" in July 1997.

> To the people of Oregon: In the course of the on-going debate about assisted suicide in the United States, a particular claim has been made by the opposition . . . that in cases of physician-assisted suicide in the Netherlands the established failure rate is 25 percent. This is implied to mean that in 25 percent of the cases . . . through orally applied means, the effect would not be death. Instead, there would be widespread reawakening of suffering patients or some form of continued coma. This claim has no foundation whatsoever, is misleading and completely wrong. There are no scientific data nor hearsay to support it. (Kimsma 1997)

Additionally, Admiraal's letter stated, "The patient is in a deep coma without awareness and so without suffering." That, he wrote, is important for the family to realize. By and large, however, death with dignity proponents were unable to get this information out to voters without taking too much away from their limited manpower and money, which they were committing to push the claim that sending the ODDA back to the voters was wrong.

Oregon Right to Die hired GLS Research to measure the extent to which attitudes about Measure 16 had changed during the two years since the measure was passed and to assess reaction to the proposed repeal of the law by the Oregon state legislature. GLS conducted a telephone survey of six hundred randomly selected Oregon voters between February 20 and 23, 1997. The sample was drawn randomly from official state voter files. Voters strongly objected to legislative action that would send a repeal request to the ballot. Fully 80 percent of respondents strongly agreed that the legislature should never return any ballot measure approved by voters. Even among those who said they had voted no on Measure 16, 55 percent said the legislature should not overturn it. The results buttressed the confidence of Coombs Lee, a Measure 16 cosponsor as well as a campaign leader and spokesperson against Measure 51, that attacks on the legislature would prove effective (Coombs Lee 1997). Coombs Lee was also delighted to hear that voter approval of the ODDA had grown from 52 percent when the vote passed in 1994 to 61 percent in 1997.

Voter sentiments supporting Measure 16 and opposing a second vote were manifested in editorials from media around the state. From February to May, twenty-two newspapers printed forty-three editorials against referral of Measure 16 back to the voters, while only two (*The Oregonian* and the *Catholic Sentinel*) wrote six in favor. Examples of editorial titles from the opponents of repeal included "Hands Off Suicide Issue," "Let's Not Vote Again on Assisted Suicide" (Albany *Democratic-Herald*); "Give Right to Die Law a Chance, First," "Voters Are Ahead of OMA on Suicide" (Ashland *Daily Tidings*); "No Confidence: Legislators Confuse Religion with Matter of Free Will" (Astoria *Daily Astorian*); "Lawmakers Should Uphold Voters' Policy" (Corvallis *Gazette Times*); "Listen to the Voters" (Gold Beach *Curry County Reporter*); "Dear Legislature: Leave Our Voter Initiative Alone" (Grants Pass *Daily Courier*); "Don't Put Assisted Suicide Measure on Ballot Again" (Klamath Falls *Herald and News*); "Bogus Attack: Measure 16 Foe's Tactic Misleads" (Madras *Pioneer*); "Daffy Docs: The OMA Just Doesn't Get It" (Medford *Mail Tribune*); "Blocking Assisted Suicide Violates the Will of the Voters" (Salem *Statesman-Journal*); "Suicide Law Affirms Basic Freedom" (Sandy *Post*). On the other side, editorial titles in support of repeal included "Death without Dignity: Legislature Should Give Voters a Chance to Repeal an Assisted-Suicide Measure That's Too Flawed to Fix" (Portland *Oregonian*); and "Measure 16: Repeal Is Overdue," "Assisted Suicide's Perils Roll On" (Portland *Catholic Sentinel*).

Politically, the widespread feeling against referral was largely ignored by Oregon politicians who wanted to block implementation of Measure 16. Moreover, this block of state leaders estimated that they could safely ignore media opinion. But they also knew they could not ignore Governor Kitzhaber's word that he would veto a legislative move to block the will of voters who voted for Measure 16. The decision to refer Measure 16 became a matter of politics: The only way to avoid the governor's veto was to send Measure 16 back to the voters for a second campaign and vote.

Despite the widespread media sentiment against referral, in May (House) and June (Senate) the Oregon legislature passed the referral measure. Never before had a ballot measure been sent back to voters in its exact form. Commenting on this first-time event for the legislature, Bill Lunch—respected both as a political science professor at Oregon State University and as a political analyst for Oregon Public Broadcasting—said:

> One of the reasons this came back to the ballot was that the legislative leadership did not like the law. They wanted to just repeal it straight away in the 1997 legislative session rather than fix it. There was a bill to clean up the glitches and so forth, and deal with the implementation problems, that went through committee but which never emerged on the floor because

> the leadership just wanted to kill the assisted suicide law altogether. They didn't have the votes for that when the governor told them that he would veto a bill to repeal it altogether so they bypassed the governor and took it to the ballot for a referral as a second alternative, one that they didn't prefer. (Lunch 1997)

Many people quietly protested that legislators—a few who are strong right-to-life supporters—were openly deceptive in their scheme to either repeal Measure 16 themselves or get it back before the voters for another multimillion-dollar attack against it. But it worked, and the alleged 25 percent failure rate became the theme of the Yes on 51 Committee.

EDUCATING VOTERS

Repeal proponents contended that the issues surrounding assisted suicide are so delicate and profound that voters should be given another chance to vote given this new information about a 25 percent failure rate. On that basis, their role in the repeal campaign would be to educate voters about the studies from the Netherlands. That turned out to mean raising doubts about whether barbiturates work, whether people will choke on their own vomit, whether they will linger for more than five hours, and whether some may need a lethal injection. Colin Fogarty, radio reporter for Oregon Public Broadcasting, commenting on this focus on clinical issues, noted with interest how much the repeal debate differed from the 1994 debate about patient autonomy, the right to die, the health care system, and whether assisted suicide should be available to patients (Fogarty 1997a). Diane Dietz, reporter for the *Eugene Register Guard*, concurred, saying "And completely missing from the debate this time are the thoughtful, moral arguments that we heard in 1994." She also noticed that repeal proponents had put religion aside to focus on the clinical aspects (Dietz 1997).

Indeed, Catholic leaders lowered their public profiles and played down the moral arguments that dominated their 1994 effort. "We have stayed in the background," said Auxiliary Bishop Kenneth Steiner of the archdiocese of Portland. "We didn't want this to backfire on us as it did in 1994, when they said this is the Catholic Church, or the religious right or religious extremists, or conservatives" (Religion News Service 1997). In August, the Catholic Health Association's (CHA) Board of Trustees donated $180,000 in response to a solicitation from the U.S. Catholic Conference, Oregon Catholic Conference, and Oregon members of CHA to the "Yes on 51 Committee," which spearheaded the Oregon repeal effort. "CHA opposes assisted suicide wherever people are trying to legalize it," said CHA's general counsel Peter Leibold

(Religion News Service 1997). The three Catholic sponsors agreed to ensure that CHA's contribution would be used in a communications campaign that would be faithful to Catholic values, said CHA president/CEO Jack Curney (Religion News Service 1997). CHA executive vice president Bill Cox described opinion polls still showing support for Oregon's assisted suicide law as disappointing "because the educational efforts to show its dangers have been going on for some time" (Religion News Service 1997).

Thus, the education campaign included playing down religious affiliation and moral arguments, as well as sticking to clinical issues like failure rates and increased suffering. Death with dignity activists countered by reminding voters who was driving the opposition effort and by declaring that organized religious principles should not usurp individual moral choices. They focused most, however, on the popular belief that government should not be involved in end-of-life decisions, aiming to align their campaign with the popular view that Oregon legislators had no business sending back a law legitimately passed by a majority of voters for a second vote.

THE MEDIA CAMPAIGN

The proponents of repeal hired Chuck Cavalier to run their ad campaign. Cavalier had helped defeat the 1992 California campaign by producing spooky television images of doctors and needles. This time around, Cavalier would have to do without images of needles, but that did not stop him from creating surrealistic commercials aimed at scaring voters. For example, in one ad backed by scary music with deep bass chords and screechy keyboards, a pill bottle sat alone on a glass shelf in a medicine cabinet. The writing on the label was obscured. The label itself obscured the contents. The obscurity and lighting made the bottle of pills appear ominous, and the overall picture suggested doubt, deceit, and confusion. As the camera panned closer to the bottle, an announcer said in monotone: "According to Measure 16, if terminal patients swallow these capsules, they'll die. But what 16 doesn't say is that the pills don't work nearly 25 percent of the time." At that point, the word "poison," then a skull and cross bones, then the face of an agonizing middle-age woman flashed on the bottle. A quote attributed to Derek Humphry, cofounder of the Hemlock Society, faded into the picture: "Evidence . . . shows that about 25 percent of assisted suicides fail." Various pictures were flashed onto the bottle: a distraught older woman, a sad mother and son, a depressed middle-age woman, and, finally, the face of a despondent young man. Simultaneously, the announcer claimed: "The patient may be left in painful convulsions, lingering for days at a time. There's no family notification required, no mandatory psychiatric exam—even your diagnosis doesn't have to be right. Because Measure 16 isn't about dying, it's about killing. And only you can stop it." The ad concluded with a claim that Measure 16 is fundamentally and fatally flawed.

In an ad called "Billy" which drew the most ire from death with dignity proponents, a disheveled old woman and a very young man in a surrealistically lit room with tables and magazines—apparently a doctor's waiting room—sat waiting to receive medicine prescribed under Measure 16. The man/boy is not hospitalized and doesn't appear sick. He could be an AIDS patient, but he looks mostly like a teenager making a tragic choice. The announcer stated: "Billy won't die right away. He'll choke on his own vomit, in painful convulsions, and linger for days."

ABC affiliates in Eugene, Medford, Klamath Falls, and Portland, as well as Portland's two other big network stations, refused to run the "Billy" ad, citing issues of credibility. "When they hired Chuck Cavalier, we expected it," said Coombs Lee. "His method is to find something scary and buy a lot of TV time."

At the same time that the repeal proponents began running their aggressive ad campaign, they also offered soundbites for television and print news stories accusing the death with dignity camp of being anti-Catholic. "It's popular to bash Catholics," said Auxiliary Bishop Kenneth Steiner, of the archdiocese of Portland. "If they did it to any other minority, they wouldn't get away with it." Trish Conrad, the campaign manager for the Measure 51 campaign, said, "To single out the Catholic Church from the hundreds of endorsements we've received is blatant bigotry." Coombs Lee, spokesperson for the anti-51 campaign, explained that she only criticized the Church's political machinery, not its spiritual views. "This has nothing to do with bigotry," she said. "This is not about the people of the Catholic faith. This is about a very powerful and wealthy political machine." Coombs Lee added that she was offended by being called a bigot.

But neither Coombs Lee nor the rest of the anti-51 campaign got sidetracked by the accusations of Catholic-bashing. Instead, they remained focused on the messages that opinion polls had repeatedly shown were most likely to keep voters on their side. Most Oregon voters were indignant over the legislature's action of sending a measure back to voters for a second vote. Numerous polls even indicated that voters' anger over rereferral went beyond the particular issue of death with dignity. The percentage of voters polled who said they would not reelect a legislator who required a second vote ranged from 40 percent to 66 percent. And when asked what they believed to be the primary reasons for the legislators' actions, voters said politics and pressure from the Church and right-wing ideologues influenced legislators more than concern about dying patients.

Strong opposition to repeal crossed all religious, political, and demographic boundaries. In fact, pollsters concluded that there was an actual consensus on this issue. The anti-51 campaign's main goal, therefore, was to assess their best media strategy for maintaining their lead. They started by testing three ads. One featured a physician, Dr. Glen Gordon, identified as a past president of the Oregon Medical Association, sitting at his desk making sober declarations about the usefulness of assisted suicide.

> Sometimes my patients and their families have to make very difficult choices about life and death. When we passed Measure 16, we guaranteed that all patients would have a choice. But now some politicians in Salem are making us vote on this all over again. Measure 16 has every safeguard patients and doctors could want. Now all we need is protection: from the politicians.

Another ad featured a widow arguing for why assisted suicide would have made her husband's death better.

> My husband Emerson had terminal cancer. But politicians took away any chance he had to use Measure 16. He died a horrible death. Now the Catholic Church is spending a fortune to repeal Measure 16. They want to impose their views on the rest of us. The choice about using Measure 16 was taken away from Emerson. Don't let them take that choice away from you.

The final ad tested featured a widower identified as a chief petitioner of Measure 16 making an emotional demand that his wife should have had the right to assisted suicide.

> I led the campaign for Measure 16 and when it passed I said, "Now, people will have a choice." I never thought the legislature would do the bidding of the Catholic Church and the OCA. I never dreamed they'd make us vote on this all over again. I'm 80 years old and I intend to live a long time. But how I die is up to me, not some crackpot politicians in Salem.

Twenty-nine participants at a market research facility were asked to view the ads and answer questions about them. Results showed that antipolitician and choice messages received a much higher response than the anti-Catholic message. On the basis of those criteria, respondents rated the physician ad better than the widow ad, and both of those much better than the widower ad. From these data, death with dignity proponents decided that the

Dr. Gordon ad was best because it almost certainly would cross over into swing and pro-51 voters. But they also decided that the widow ad would be good to run because it was clearly the most emotional, believable, and memorable of the ads, and people, especially women, seemed to relate to the widow. On the basis of tests of these two ads, repeal opponents projected that nearly three-fourths of the people who viewed the ads would respond positively to one or more of the opponents' messages.

Another strategy was to attack the claim that studies cited by the state legislature indicated that 25 percent of all assisted suicides would fail. The anti-51 campaign created an ad showing different physicians asking the pro-51 campaign to "show me the study."

> The politicians and the Catholic Church claim there's a new study that shows Measure 16 is fatally flawed. So Oregon doctors are saying, "Show me the study." The truth is, you could look forever and you won't find that study—because it doesn't exist. It's simply not true. And any campaign not based on the truth is fundamentally and fatally flawed.

A greater impact of that ad was that it became widely reported that the anti-51 campaign had managed to steal the Measure 51 campaign's slogan, "It's fatally flawed." Tim Hibbits, the most often quoted pollster during the campaign, called the tactic of stealing the opponent's slogan "one of the cleverest moves in politics in a long time" (Hill 1997c:A14). *The Oregonian* reported the goal of the tactic as twofold: One was to portray the legislature and the Catholic Church as political powerhouses willing to bend the truth, while the other was to create confusion by co-opting the Measure 51 campaign's slogan. Anti-51 forces countered that the goal was not to create confusion, but to spotlight the proponents' reckless interpretation of studies that they viewed to be unrelated to the debate. "Whether it will change votes or not, I don't know," Hibbits said, "but as a campaign tactic, it's very clever" (Hill 1997c:A15).

OMA AND MEDIA PRESSURES

One of the factors that had been claimed to tilt Measure 16 in favor of the proponents back in 1994 was the position of neutrality taken by the state medical association. For one thing, unlike what happened in Washington and California, medical association neutrality left Catholic organizations alone in fighting the measure. Additionally, although there were physicians' groups who campaigned hard against Measure 16, there was not the general specter of physicians being opposed to performing a service that they would be charged with providing. But when the OMA's leadership changed, so did the association's official position on assisted suicide. In early 1997, the OMA's House of Delegates voted to support referral of Measure 16. In fact, the OMA's proposal was part of the package presented by legislators who convinced their colleagues to send the ODDA back to voters in 1997.

To test the effect of the OMA's change of position, the anti-51 campaign asked GLS Research to conduct a telephone survey measuring voter reaction to the OMA's decision to oppose Measure 16. Five hundred voters were randomly polled on May 4 and 5, 1997. The results were compared to results of a poll of six hundred random voters conducted in April, before the OMA decision was made public. Only 7 percent of voters said that knowing the OMA's position would affect their votes. The rest said the OMA announcement would have no effect on their vote. Moreover, voters were cynical about the validity of and the reasons for the official change. Thirty-six percent of the respondents believed that the OMA reversal was the result of an organized effort by a small number of doctors who were religiously opposed to Measure 16. Only 31 percent said that the decision fairly represented the views of most doctors in the association. Regarding the motives for the reversal, 48 percent identified malpractice suits as a major factor in the OMA decision. Thirty-nine percent said that politics played a major factor. Thirty-six percent said that money and profits were a factor. But just 35 percent said that concern about the welfare of dying patients was a major factor. Based on these results, the researchers concluded that fierce opposition to legislators sending the measure back to the voters was not dampened by the OMA's announcement; in fact, voters were cynical about it.

Given these results, what worried the anti-51 campaign more was the apparent bias of some of the state's leading print media. While pro-51 campaigners were busy circulating the message that studies from the Netherlands showed that a pill-only law such as Measure 16 would lead to botched suicides in 25 percent of the cases, anti-51 campaigners circulated an article written by David Smigelski for *Willamette Week* called "To Die For" (Smigelski 1997). We talked at length about Smigelski's charges with the director of the Oregon Death with Dignity Legal Defense and Education Center (Duncan 1997b). Smigelski accused *The Oregonian*'s Mark O'Keefe with "sloppy reporting" about the studies from the Netherlands. He further accused David Reinhard, an associate editor of *The Oregonian*, of slanting the facts even further. In a June 8 column, Smigelski reported, Reinhard said: "We now know that Measure 16's drugs-only regime fails up to 25 percent of the time. The pills don't always kill, leaving patients to wallow in vomit and experience convulsions, brain damage, persistent coma or vegetative states and lingering death" (Smigelski 1997:32). In our interview, Duncan stated that Reinhard was going beyond the data from euthanasia studies and was including in his claim data from a 1971 report on the effects of barbiturate poisoning. The 1971 report was from emergency room data regarding people who overdosed on barbiturates either because they accidentally took too much prescription medication or because they were drug abusers. This is the same report cited by Gail Kinsey Hill, who accurately stated that the 1971 report did not address doctor-assisted suicide (Hill 1997b).

When Smigelski interviewed Reinhard two days before publishing "To Lie For," Reinhard claimed "It would be stupid to suggest these people don't die. Of course they die" (Smigelski 1997:32). Yet Smigelski found a May 8 editorial in which Reinhard said, "Should Oregon doctors be allowed to give terminally ill patients drugs that will end their lives in only three cases out of four?" (Smigelski 1997:32). Measure 51 opponents charged that Reinhard's bias and willingness to distort the facts was a tactic shared by news and editorial writers for *The Oregonian.* Duncan, the director of the Oregon Death with Dignity Legal Defense and Education Center, verified several facts about key personnel from *The Oregonian.* One was the fact that Mark O'Keefe, who first generated the claim of a 25 percent failure rate, attended Pat Robertson's Regent University and was a religion reporter assigned to cover Measure 16 on his very first day at *The Oregonian.* Another was that Fred Stickel, a Catholic and longtime publisher of *The Oregonian,* had strongly opposed Measure 16 since its beginning. These facts were stated by Smigelski and corroborated by Duncan, both of whom suggested that Stickel was using his paper to push his crusade against assisted suicide. Barbara Coombs Lee, a chief petitioner of Measure 16, told Smigelski that *The Oregonian* "has given the entire issue [of the failure rate] the credibility it has" (Smigelski 1997:31). Other evidence of the paper's bias included 13 anti-suicide commentaries in 1997, as well as the fact that besides the *Catholic Sentinel,* only *The Oregonian* supported the legislature's decision to send the Death With Dignity Act back to voters (twenty-two newspapers were opposed).

By October, Reinhard had carefully changed his rhetotic. On October 17, Reinhard appeared on the television program "Seven Days" to discuss the repeal effort (Reinhard 1997a). On October 19, he wrote a column for *The Oregonian* titled "Liar, Liar" (Reinhard 1997b). In both forums, Reinhard's evaluation of the data from the Netherlands was far more tempered. He no longer claimed that a pills-only regime would cause patients to wallow in vomit and experience convulsions, brain damage, persistent coma, or vegetative states and lingering death. In lieu of that claim, he said that studies from the Netherlands indicated that up to a quarter of patients who take oral medication to end life could fall asleep before finishing the drugs, and that 10 to 20 percent would be unable to swallow oral medications. Overlooking the fact that patients who couldn't swallow oral medications wouldn't qualify to use the law, now Reinhard used data from the Netherlands to claim that Measure 16's ban against injections would prevent many patients from experiencing the "sweet death that Sixteen's defenders pledge" (Reinhard 1997a, 1997b).

Although Reinhard had backed away from his earlier claims about reports from the Netherlands, his political attack was now more virulent. He accused the anti–Measure 51 campaign of outright bigotry and fraud. He began his column titled "Liar, Liar" with these words: "Measure 16 author Barbara Coombs Lee denies she's a religious bigot or Catholic basher. The heart wants to believe her—no one wants to think someone so savvy would traffic in such raw intolerance—but the mind has doubts" (Reinhard 1997b). The column went on to attack several of the anti-51 campaign ads. Reinhard took ODDA backers to task for linking Measure 51 to Lon Mabon and the Oregon Citizens Alliance—an ultra-conservative group that has been widely castigated in Oregon. Anti-51 leaders conceded to us that their campaign had overreached with this rhetoric.

Reinhard also criticized an anti-51 television ad challenging pro-51 claims about studies from the Netherlands. The ad featured three physicians asking indignantly, "Show me the study." "It's showtime!," Reinhard exulted (Reinhard 1997b). That, and his accusations of bigotry, became Reinhard's new hook for presenting more tempered claims about euthanasia in the Netherlands.

Reinhard's appearance on "Seven Days" and his October 19 column coincided with a four-day series of editorials in *The Oregonian* urging voters to approve Measure 51. The editorials claimed that the best evidence suggested that drugs used under the law fail about a quarter of the time. Death with dignity under Oregon's Measure 16, they said, may be anything but dignified. They questioned whether terminal patients who suffer from depression can make good death with dignity decisions. They hailed hospice care for becoming widely available and asked, "Is suicide really the only answer?" Finally, they argued that Oregon's "sham safeguards" won't protect the terminally ill, but they will protect health care providers who engage in assisted suicide.

Media bias added to voter cynicism. Even *The Oregonian* published letters to the editor from readers who reacted with anger and disbelief. "You did a tremendous disservice to Oregon with the shrill illogic of your editorial series demonizing Measure 16 and those who supported it for humanitarian reasons," said Jerry Shurman, a reader from southeast Portland. "Usually, when *The Oregonian* endorses a position, it does so with some semblance of calm and cogency," he said. "If you want to support Measure 51, you should do so reasonably" (Shurman 1997). Another reader said, "The drawing of a doctor wearing a hangman's noose is particularly repugnant. In a newpaper of *The*

Oregonian's stature, an occasional statement of reasoned opposition or support should be enough" (Benson 1997). Another reader summed up the response: "One word—biased—describes your editorials on Measure 51. In addition, you omitted the main issue of this measure—it is the individual's choice" (McAtee 1997).

THE DEATH WITH DIGNITY MOVEMENT WINS BIG

Proponents of the ODDA gathered in an elegant hotel and anxiously awaited the news of the first ballot returns. There were television screens, one on each wall, and in the middle of the room, television, radio, and newspaper reporters stood ready to record the action. The early ballot count was so lopsided that television stations called the defeat of Measure 51 just minutes after the polls closed. The room erupted in raucous cheer. Clicks and lights from more than a dozen cameras did not just record this moment in history; they helped create it. Coombs Lee took the podium to announce the defeat. "Oregon voters didn't just say 'No.' They said '*Hell No*'!" The mood turned jubilant. Among those gathered around Coombs Lee were two women with terminal disease, a man whose personal experience of the death of his wife prompted him to initiate Measure 16, a woman whose husband had fought for Measure 16 yet suffered and died just months after it was enjoined, a physician who treats dying patients, and staff people from local movement organizations. The group was assembled to illustrate that it was ordinary people who fought for this law. Coombs Lee praised their courage and the courage of Oregon voters. And she spoke of the need for all sides to work together on improving care for the dying.

ANALYSIS

The last two chapters analyzed the ways in which campaign messages and voter perceptions of the communicators of those messages affected voter opinion. In each campaign, initiative sponsors had the burden of persuading voters that there was a problem with the status quo and that their measure was a desirable remedy. Forced to address concerns that their initiative contained too few safeguards, each proponent began on the defensive. They also sought, at least in California, to distance themselves from the Hemlock Society and from Dr. Kevorkian. In Washington, they also argued against the tactics of opponents before the state attorney general and the courts. And the Oregon proponents struggled to walk a fine line between courting and distancing themselves from Derek Humphry. These efforts drew energy from the proponents' efforts to "stay on message" (Cooper 1997). They also gave opponents several opportunities to use media time to take shots at the death with dignity people.

For death with dignity proponents, much of the problem of staying on message and controlling the messengers was missing from the repeal campaign. A large majority of voters believed that issues like Jack Kevorkian were irrelevant in 1997 because they had already been considered by voters in 1994. The Hemlock Society did not arouse the same suspicion as it had a few years earlier. And although Derek Humphry was cited by the repeal campaign for his congressional testimony regarding the 25 percent failure rate, Humphry himself did not back the repeal measure. For the first time, therefore, the death with dignity movement was not having to operate from a defensive position. In fact, given voter resentment about the legislature's decision to command a revote, the movement saw early on that it could quickly take the offensive.

Campaign messages, and deciding who would communicate them, mattered most during the late stages of the campaign—when soft supporters began moving toward undecided. The fact that this was a mail-in election had a significant impact at this point in the campaign battle. The significance to the campaigners was that they had adequate time to conduct exit polls of voters who voted early and, more importantly, to assess the attitudes of unsettled voters. As has been stated in previous chapters, on average, about 70 percent of voters change their opinions on ballot measures, compared with 26 percent who shift in candidate elections (Magelby 1994). Voters on ballot initiatives are more susceptible to short-term forces, are more likely to decide later in the campaign, and rely heavily on political advertising to make up their minds.

As the Measure 51 campaign came to a close, the anti-51 camp watched its lead in the polls erode fairly rapidly among all demographic categories, especially women. With less than two weeks remaining, the percentage of voters polled who said they would definitely vote to reject Measure 51 had dropped an average of 21 percent (34 percent among women ages eighteen to thirty-nine, and 28 percent among women sixty-five and older). Additionally, many voters remained confused about what a yes or no vote would mean. Five percent of the electorate planned to vote yes on Measure 51 yet thought they were approving Measure 16. Only one percent of the electorate planned to vote no on Measure 51 yet thought they were repealing the law. This gave the proponents of Measure 51 a 4 percent lead going into the election. Furthermore, anti-51 support was dropping rapidly among voters who reported having seen a yes on 51 ad but not a no on 51 ad, which in one large media market was five times as many voters who had seen a no ad only. These numbers began to alarm death with dignity supporters.

Polls of early voters revealed that 28 percent had voted yes, 49 percent no, and 20 percent said they were undecided (the researchers conjectured that many of those who said they voted "undecided" were apprehensive about revealing how they voted to the pollsters). Of greater importance (because of the unreliability of the "undecided" response of early voters) was the split between voters who said they had not yet voted. Thirty-five percent said they would vote yes, thirty-eight percent said they would vote no, and twenty-eight reported that they had not decided.

These results were especially significant to the anti-51 campaign. What they indicated was that as the campaign—and especially the ad wars—wore on, erosion of support for the anti-51 campaign did not inure to the benefit of the pro-51 campaign. In fact, the percentage of voters in the yes campaign remained stable. Instead, voters were sliding from the no category to the undecided category. Surprisingly, the category of undecided voters had climbed 13 percent since baseline measures were taken. Yet in an odd way, this was good news to the death with dignity camp. To repeat a theme from previous chapters, undecided voters usually vote no. If that general tendency held in this election, the poll results in the waning weeks of the election may not have been as troubling as they seemed. The anti-51 proponents would not have to move undecided voters into the yes column; they simply had to keep them undecided. The distribution of undecideds was even across the demographic spectrum, giving the anti-51 campaign a chance to target any number of demographic groups. The campaign had reserved plenty of money to keep their ad campaign running until the last minute, and with a wide range of ads and plenty of tracking poll data to determine which ads worked best with different voter groups, they had a strong chance of winning.

For reasons that were probably more sentimental than tactical, the anti-51 campaign had run the ad depicting an angry widower blaming the Catholic Church, the Oregon Citizens Alliance, and "crackpot" politicians for putting the law back before the electorate, even though opinion polls indicated a general distaste for attacking the Church and rated this ad well below two others. After all, Al Sinnard, the man featured in the ad, was not just a chief petitioner for Measure 16; he had also initiated the Oregon death with dignity movement in the basement of his home. In the last weeks of the campaign, older women were especially put off by the message against Catholics. Negative reactions to anti-Catholic sentiment among women sixty-five and older had gone up 21 percent. Moreover, this was the largest demographic group to have moved from the no to the yes side, or to undecided. Thus, more television was devoted to the calmer, more emotional ad featuring an older widow. The ad featuring an older male physician remained a staple of the ad wars, since voters had repeatedly responded well to the calm, professional demeanor of the doctor.

Surprisingly, the anti-51 campaign found itself on shaky ground regarding the message that Measure 51 was not based on the truth. Early in the campaign, political strategists had hailed the campaign for stealing the opponents' message. But within a period of just one week at the campaign's end, this message had lost ten points—the greatest decline of all the anti-51 messages. The most competent strategy, therefore, was to keep reminding voters of how they got to the point of having to make this decision in the first place: because the state legislature had second-guessed them. Not only did that basic message continue to receive high support in voter polls during the final weeks (60 percent agreed, a slip of only two points from baseline), but it avoided negative messages against Catholics, the opposition, and politicians. (Regarding the latter, the percentage of people who believed that politicians should have no hand in life-and-death decisions had decreased 7 percent.) Apparently these strategies worked, and the rule of thumb that undecided voters vote no followed the tendency. Oregon voters, who enjoy their political independence, upheld Oregon's tradition of social innovation.

Our analysis of the death with dignity movement's successful use of opinion polls to fight off strong opponents involves the significance of campaign organization, including spending patterns. Proponents of death with dignity have consistently complained about the disparity between the proponents' rather small coalition of volunteers and the opponents' large organizational base. Whether the opponents were the state medical association, the Catholic Church, or the state's largest newspaper, opponents have enjoyed widespread voter recognition and prestige.

The Oregonian used its news stories and editorials to campaign hard against Measure 16. Catholic churches distributed brochures and delivered sermons in thousands of parishes throughout the three states, and collected hundreds of thousands of dollars in individual donations. Physicians' groups were similarly well organized. Form letters and posters made their way from the state medical associations through physicians and their staffs to patients. The success of these efforts was indicated by the comments of one Washington resident who decided to vote no: "Just reading (my doctor's) perspective on the issue was very helpful to me."

On the other hand, during the early campaigns the proponents' accessibility to committed voters and campaign contributions was largely limited to the four thousand mostly elderly members of the Hemlock Society. Proponents had only a relatively small group of capable yet loose-knit volunteers. Moreover, their campaign efforts started off so splintered (Washington) or became so splintered (California) that an effective campaign strategy was never executed. By 1994, the Compassion in Dying organization and all its expansion efforts had become very well organized, yet its leaders still portrayed themselves as David and the opponents as Goliath (Coombs Lee 1994, 1997b; Duncan 1994). Yet the opponents' ready access to captive audiences was eventually overcome by the tightly organized group in Oregon. Key organizational efforts included achieving a consensus, which included the views and attitudes of the various professionals that would be directly affected by changing the law (the omission of injections was a key difference from the early death with dignity campaigns), and forming and executing campaign messages and strategies from rigorous, longitudinal assessments of voter attitudes using repeated focus group sessions and opinion polls. The effects of these efforts are difficult to quantify. But Oregon proponents like to point to their success in overcoming a 5–1 spending ratio during the Measure 51 effort to repeal the ODDA.

The issue of uneven spending was noted in Chapter 2. The opposition in California outspent the initiative backers by a margin of 10–1. "We just didn't have enough money to refute their allegations of too few safeguards," said Robert Risley, founder of the California campaign. "Their last minute ad campaign finally wiped us out: we just couldn't respond" (Risley 1994). Risley's comments found support in the lay perception that unequal spending can result in too much political influence by affluent contributors and can weaken electoral competition. This belief translated into charges such as Risley's that Proposition 161's opponents, especially the Catholic Church, spent far too much to permit a fair campaign. (But in Washington, campaign contributions to both sides were nearly even, with proponents spending slightly more.)

A pivotal political strategist who organized the successful 1994 Oregon campaign proclaimed that more important than unequal spending is spending patterns. He second-guessed the Washington campaign's failure to plan and execute a stronger media battle in the final days of the campaign. Responding to that charge, another campaign insider doubted whether Reverend Ralph Mero and the Hemlock leadership ever really expected to win, given that this was the first initiative effort. If it is true that the initiative's leadership missed crucial opportunities because they underestimated the movement's chances of success, perhaps the expert from Oregon correctly conjectured that it was not so much unequal spending as the campaign's poor spending patterns that contributed to the loss in Washington.

But variables such as unequal spending and the delivery and defense of a campaign message appear to have been subsumed by a broader set of cultural variables—namely, the effects of legal change on the broad range of people who would be directly affected. In the everyday world of end-of-life care, affected interests include health care practitioners, patients, professional standards and ethics, payment providers, patient advocates, and political action committees, including religious and right-to-life influences and right-to-die advocates. Arenas of debate have been established by each of these interests. Thus, for consensus to be achieved, many variable interests must be accounted for: patients and families; health care administrators, physicians, and other health care professionals; and the clergy and lawyers who counsel them. Moreover, law and morality are influenced by policy statements promulgated by medical associations and academic and governmental reports, as well as by many other groups and individuals. It has been said, in short, that clinical practice exists in an iterative relationship with the law, and vice versa (Meisel 1992).

Given the iterative relationship between law and social practice, the efforts of proponents in Washington and California may have failed in part because they focused almost exclusively on opinion polls as indicators of public opinion. Initiative supporters in both states focused on the few people who might benefit from active euthanasia. Their concern was for those who worry about how they would be perceived by friends and family in the event they become dependent on machines and caretakers for maintenance of routine bodily functions. That concern extended to those who fear becoming a financial or emotional burden on others and those who fear being kept alive against their choice. "Principles of freedom," they said, "must include the right to choose a response to the unfortunate circumstances of disease or accident, including in some cases a self-determined death" (Canaday 1991). These are legitimate concerns with which the public could certainly identify.

Nevertheless, this singular focus on public sentiment side-stepped equally significant interests of the physicians, clergy, ethicists, judges, legislators, and administrators who would be affected by changes in the law. The opponents of the aid-in-dying initiatives objected on several grounds. Physicians, clergy, and ethicists urged voters to compare the probable consequences of decriminalizing active euthanasia in terms of value preferences: "We want to care for our patients and not kill them ... as doctors have been doing for 2,400 years"; "We don't want to be forced to participate in euthanasia"; "Doctors are human beings and should not have the burden of killing other human beings"; "As a society we cannot and must not sanction the intentional killing of life." Ethicist Alexander Capron claimed that while "withdrawal of treatment is a recognition of the limits to medicine, active euthanasia is a statement of medical power" (Jacobs 1992c:A28).

Underscoring these sentiments of physicians, clergy, and ethicists was the fear of the slippery slope phenomenon. Opponents in California argued that under legal precedents in that state, the courts there would almost inevitably conclude that guardians of incompetent patients with terminal illnesses would have to be permitted to direct physicians to kill their wards (Parachini 1987).

Variables measured by political scientists have helped us analyze the wins and losses in each of the West Coast states. The broader implications of each campaign have been addressed in terms of how direct legislation has fared as an agenda-setting device in the death with dignity movement. The book now turns to a different forum where debate has occurred—the courts. State courts and legislators have resisted being saddled with the burden of deciding the sticky issues of assisted suicide. But that did not stop Compassion in Dying from going to federal court with constitutional claims. The next chapter describes and analyzes the two cases that were eventually decided by the U.S. Supreme Court.

5

Compassion in Dying

THE ASSISTED SUICIDE TEST CASES

> The right of a competent, terminally ill person to avoid excruciating pain and embrace a timely and dignified death bears the sanction of history and is implicit in the concept of ordered liberty. The exercise of this right is as central to personal autonomy and bodily integrity as the exercise of rights safeguarded by this Court's decisions relating to marriage, family relationships, procreation, contraception, child rearing and the refusal or termination of life-saving medical treatment.
>
> —Legal Brief of the American Civil Liberties Union

> Excluding people from the protection of the homicide laws based on the condition of their health is a particularly serious departure from the principle of equal justice for all. Indeed, withholding such protections is an injustice of unspeakable magnitude, for it leads to the literal destruction of the very lives that government is charged with protecting.
>
> —Court Brief of Catholic Conferences and other religious organizations

1997: NO *ROE V. WADE*

On June 26, 1997, the U.S. Supreme Court determined that there would be no *Roe v. Wade* (1973)–like protection for assisted suicide in the near future. In a 9–0 decision in *Washington v. Glucksberg* (*Compassion IV 1997*), the justices held that the respondents' asserted "right" to assistance in committing suicide is not a fundamental liberty interest protected by the due process clause. In a second decision (*Vacco v. Quill* [*Quill III*] 1997), again 9–0, the court held that a state's policy distinguishing between letting a patient die and making a patient die is rational and therefore a state ban against assisted suicide does not violate the equal protection clause. In so deciding, the justices closed the door opened by the 1994 ruling in the Western District of Washington in *Compassion in Dying v. Washington* (*Compassion I* 1994), but they noted that the debate would go on and encouraged the states to be the laboratories for change.

GENESIS OF THE COURT CASE

While campaign strategists were busy trying to get Measure 16 passed in Oregon, some of them began a separate legal reform effort in the federal courts. Their effort was led by the organization Compassion in Dying, which was one of the driving forces behind Measure 16, and their goal was to establish that the "right to die" and therefore physician-assisted suicide are protected under the United States Constitution. Using *Roe v. Wade* (1973) as a stepping stone, they fashioned their legal claims around the issues of individual freedom and liberty and drew parallels from legal principles about abortion and the right to make highly personal decisions regarding reproductive choice. They challenged two state laws banning assisted suicide, one in Washington and the other in New York.

Each challenge was ultimately rejected unanimously by the United States Supreme Court. Nevertheless, the challengers had won in a Washington trial court and in appellate courts in federal appellate circuits covering both Washington State and New York. During the three years from 1994 to 1997, while the two cases moved through the federal courts, implementation of the ODDA had been enjoined by a federal judge in Oregon. That injunction was lifted just days before the ballot measure to repeal the Oregon Death With Dignity Act (ODDA) was defeated.

Although the Supreme Court rejected Compassion in Dying's claims against assisted suicide bans in Washington and New York, the court battles were an important effort at lawmaking to assisted suicide advocates because they further raised public consciousness about choice and end-of-life care and because the Supreme Court's rulings on privacy and liberty have been central to the expansion of individual rights in the United States. Moreover, the decisions in the two cases may yet prove to be victories of sorts for death with dignity advocates, as Chief Justice William Rehnquist, who wrote the court's leading opinion in each case, explicitly encouraged the states to be the laboratories for change on this hotly contested national issue. This chapter details the strategies of activists and interest groups involved in the two court cases and the role of organizations in shaping the arguments before each court. We also analyze the court opinions at each level of adjudication, and we end the chapter with a discussion of constitutional adjudication as a tactic for contesting assisted suicide laws.

TRIAL AND APPELLATE COURTS

We want to begin with a brief history of the court decisions at the trial and appellate levels and put them in the historical context of simultaneous court decisions enjoining the ODDA in Oregon. This description is admittedly cumbersome because it depicts five hearings—three in the west and two in the east—that overlapped. This overlapping description, however, truly depicts the multiple directions that the death with dignity movement took during this three-year period. A few of our primary informants played key roles in all of the events taking place during this period: the injunction against the ODDA in Oregon, the federal court challenges against two state laws banning assisted suicide, and the ballot initiative seeking to repeal the ODDA. Our research became similarly multifaceted.

We should also mention that Jack Kevorkian was in the news quite a bit during this period, as he was acquitted in three trials before Michigan juries. The juries' history-making shows of compassion were a good gauge of public sentiment on the increasingly popular issue of physician-assisted suicide. Kevorkian's acquittals increased the confidence of death with dignity proponents involved with Compassion in Dying although that organization and its affiliates have steadfastly distanced themselves from Kevorkian and his extralegal strategies for changing clinical practices on physician-assisted suicide.

In May 1994, just six months before Oregon voters passed the ODDA, Jack Kevorkian was acquitted in his first homicide trial. That same month, Compassion in Dying won a judgment from U.S. District Court Chief Judge Barbara Rothstein, finding Washington's assisted suicide law unconstitutional on due process and equal protection grounds. We will refer to this decision as *Compassion I* (1994). But in December 1994, a month after the ODDA was passed, Compassion in Dying and its affiliates began suffering a series of big blows. In New York, U.S. District Court Chief Judge Thomas Griesa rejected the very same claims that Judge Rothstein had accepted in Washington. We will call this decision *Quill I* (1994). The same month, U.S. District Court Judge Michael Hogan granted a temporary injunction against the ODDA (*Lee v. State of Oregon* 1994). This effort was led by the National Right to Life Committee, which presented a formidable foe for Compassion in Dying's legal affiliates.

Then in March 1995, Judge Rothstein's ruling was reversed in a 2–1 ruling by the U.S. Court of Appeals for the Ninth Circuit. This decision we call *Compassion II* (1995). Compassion in Dying's situation worsened in August 1995, when Judge Hogan permanently enjoined the ODDA (*Lee v. State of Oregon* 1995). Proponents dug in their heals, however, and six months later, in March 1996, they won a reinstatement of part of Judge Rothstein's ruling. This decision we call *Compassion III* (1996). In *Compassion III*, an eleven-judge panel of the U.S. Court of Appeals for the Ninth Circuit supported Judge Rothstein's ruling on the due process challenge. Judge Stephen Reinhardt, writing for an eight-member majority, wrote:

> Like the decision of whether or not to have an abortion, the decision how and when to die is one of the most intimate and personal choices a person may make in a lifetime, a choice central to persona dignity and autonomy. A competent, terminally ill adult, having lived nearly the full measure of his life, has a strong liberty interest in choosing a dignified and humane death rather than being reduced at the end of his existence to a childlike state of helplessness—diapered, sedated, and incompetent. (*Compassion III* 1996, at 3161–3162)

Following the lead of the district court judge in *Compassion I* (1994), Judge Reinhardt's opinion found the U.S. Supreme Court's ruling in *Planned Parenthood v. Casey* (1992) authoritative. That and other reproductive freedom rulings provided the basis for the Ninth Circuit's finding that liberty includes the right of competent individuals to ask for and receive a physician's assistance in dying. But, having found sufficient reason in that analysis to declare the Washington law unconstitutional, the Ninth Circuit declined to consider the equal protection claim.

The following month, however, in April 1996, a three-judge panel of the U.S. Court of Appeals for the Second Circuit reversed the earlier decision by Judge Griesa in New York, which we designated *Quill II* (1996). That court based its reversal on the equal protection claim only, saying that permitting physicians to assist those on life support but not those who are similarly ill yet not on life support is tantamount to discrimination. Speaking for the court, Judge Roger Miner wrote:

> [I]t seems clear that New York does not treat similarly circumstanced persons alike: those in the final stages of terminal illness who are on life-support systems are allowed to hasten their deaths by directing the removal of such systems; but those who are similarly situated, except for the attachment of life-sustaining equipment, are not allowed to hasten death by self-administering prescribed drugs.... It simply cannot be said that those mentally competent, terminally-ill persons who seek to hasten death but whose treatment does not include life support are treated equally. (*Quill II* 1996, at 22–23)

In rejecting the state of New York's claims for the overarching interest of the state in preserving life, Judge Miner added:

> At oral argument and in its brief, the state's contention has been that its principal interest is in preserving the life of all its citizens at all times and under all conditions. But what interest can the state possibly have in requiring the prolongation of a life that is all but ended? . . . And what business is it of the state to require the continuation of agony when the result is imminent and inevitable? (*Quill II* 1996, at 22–23)

Nevertheless, the same opinion forcefully rejected the due process claim, which seemed to put some doubt on the vitality of the opposite decision on due process grounds rendered in the Ninth Circuit. Two other significant events occurred in 1996. In May Jack Kevorkian was acquitted in his third trial. Five months later in October 1996, the U.S. Supreme Court granted a hearing in both the Washington and New York cases, which took place on January 7, 1997.

All of the federal court actions came to a close in 1997, which was a busy year for death with dignity advocates. Back in Oregon, in February 1997, in a rehearing of Judge Hogan's injunction against the ODDA, a three-judge panel of the U.S. Court of Appeals for the Ninth Circuit held that the plaintiffs who had sought the injunction lacked standing to have their claims heard in federal court. Appeal was made to the U.S. Supreme Court, which in October 1997 refused to reconsider the case. Four months earlier, in June 1997, the Supreme Court had unanimously overruled both the Ninth and Second Appellate Court rulings in landmark decisions (*Washington v. Glucksberg* [*Compassion IV*] 1997 and *Vacco v. Quill* [*Quill III*] 1997). In the first 9–0 decision, the justices held that the respondents' asserted "right" to assistance in committing suicide is not a fundamental liberty interest protected by the due process clause. In the second decision, also 9–0, the court held that a state's policy distinguishing between letting a patient die and making a patient die is rational and therefore a state ban against assisted suicide does not violate the equal protection clause. In so deciding, the justices closed the door opened by the 1994 ruling in the Western District of Washington in *Compassion I* (1994). But they noted that the debate will go on and even encouraged the states to be the laboratories for change.

Finally, in November 1997 Oregon voters blocked the Measure 51 repeal campaign, and the next day the state attorney general publicly announced that Oregon's landmark law had taken effect. The first death under the Oregon law was announced just four months later, in March 1998.

CAUSE LAWYERING: KATHRYN TUCKER AND THE COMPASSION IN DYING ORGANIZATION

In this section, we detail the strategies of activists and interest groups involved in the two court cases and the role of organizations in shaping the arguments before each court. We begin with a profile of the leading attorney and how she became involved with Compassion in Dying. We focus on the development of the legal arguments proffered by Tucker and Compassion. We also profile the plaintiffs in the cases. This discussion leads to our description of the first disposition by Judge Barbara Rothstein in Washington. That disposition closely paralleled the court briefs and oral arguments offered by Tucker, especially with regard to its extension of the liberty interest protecting abortion and reproductive rights, to the issue of physician-assisted suicide.

In a 1997 interview, Seattle attorney Kathryn Tucker, who argued the reformers' case to the Supreme Court in 1997, explained how she got involved in the death with dignity movement (Tucker 1997). As a law student at Georgetown University Law Center, Tucker was active in environmental protection litigation. Her first job out of law school was with a powerful law firm in the east. So widespread was the firm's clientele that whomever Tucker brought in as a potential new client, her proposals were rejected on the grounds of potential conflict of interest between Tucker's representation and previous representation by the firm. Tucker grew tired of the inertia of that job, so she looked west.

Tucker had heard about the 1991 assisted suicide initiative effort in Washington. She made some calls and offered to volunteer her legal services. In fact, she was an active advisor during the ballot initiative campaign for Initiative 119 in Washington in 1991, which we examined in Chapter 2. This was not really Tucker's issue, however, so when the campaign was over she went on to work for other clients. Yet Reverend Ralph Mero—the Unitarian minister who formed the Compassion in Dying organization and commenced Initiative 119—periodically sent Tucker information about Compassion's hands-on assistance with dying. Realizing that members were in real danger of being prosecuted for assisted suicide, Tucker suggested a judicial preemptive strike. She sought to secure a federal court ruling declaring that antiquated assisted suicide laws cannot govern end-of-life care in the context of modern medicine, and the terminally ill have no less a right to control the time, place, and manner of death than a woman has a right to control her reproduction. Mero approved Tucker's proposal, and with Compassion's support, the lawsuits were started.

Tucker's legal strategy was straight from the pages of *Planned Parenthood v. Casey* (1992). In *Casey*, the Supreme Court's benchmark decision regarding abortion rights, the prevailing justices backed away from the privacy rationale of *Roe v. Wade* (1973) and decided instead that the right to obtain an abortion is a fundamental liberty, which generations of women have relied upon the judiciary to protect. A quote from *Casey*, written by Justice Kennedy, appeared to squarely support Tucker's approach:

> These matters, involving the most intimate and personal choices a person may make in a lifetime, choices central to personal dignity and autonomy, are central to the liberty protected by the Fourteenth Amendment. At the heart of liberty is the right to define one's own concept of existence, of meaning, of the universe, and of the mystery of human life. Beliefs about these matters could not define the attributes of personhood were they formed under compulsion of the State. (*Planned Parenthood v. Casey* 1992, at 2791)

Tucker reasoned that if one's own view of the mystery of human life permits inducing the abortion of a live fetus, it surely must permit assisting someone to voluntarily end his or her own life before the final, most painful stages of his or her imminent death. Abortion involves the life or death of potential others; suicide doesn't. Therefore, if choices central to personal dignity and autonomy include abortion, they also include physician-assisted death.

As for the Compassion in Dying organization, the declarants in the Washington and New York lawsuits indicated various reasons why they have sought to change the law. The framing of the personal autonomy issue within the lineage of privacy rights from *Griswold v. Connecticut* (1965) to *Roe v. Wade* (1973) to *Casey* (1992) is paramount to the arguments of the pro-euthanasia legal forces. As the appellees stated in their brief in *Compassion I* (at 11–12):

> Appellants and amici assert that reproductive rights jurisprudence has no application to this case.
>
> ... To the contrary, these cases explore the protection afforded by the United States Constitution to decisions that are motivated by intensely personal concerns, that deal with the individual's own body, and that will determine the course of the individual's life. That is exactly the kind of decision at issue in this case. *Roe* and, most recently, *Casey* recognize that the Constitution's guarantee of liberty protects such decisions from unjustified state interference. The guarantee of liberty recognized in these cases has equal application to the decision at issue in this case. The abortion cases are not just about abortion, but about the very basis of what it means to be a free person in a free society.

This novel legal reasoning was presented to the court by three patient plaintiffs, the Compassion organization, and several physician plaintiffs. The patient plaintiffs made two claims: first, that they had a right to seek a physician's assistance with suicide without undue government interference, and second, that Washington's ban against assisted suicide unconstitutionally discriminated between assisted suicide and withholding or terminating lifesaving medical treatment. Plaintiffs from the Compassion organization claimed that the law put their staff members in jeopardy of criminal prosecution for assisting dying persons as they exercise their constitutional rights of choice in the face of imminent death. The physician plaintiffs alleged claims on behalf of their own patients, as well as on behalf of their own right to practice medicine according to their own consciences and professional judgments.

Harold Glucksberg was a Seattle oncologist who was also a clinical professor at the University of Washington. He had written in his declaration for the first Compassion case in the District Court:

> I occasionally encounter patients dying of cancer who have no chance of recovery, whom I know to be mentally competent and able to understand their condition, diagnosis, and prognosis who desire to hasten their deaths and avoid prolonged suffering. These patients cannot hasten their death without assistance or could do so but only at the risk of increased pain and anguish to themselves and their families.
>
> It is my professional judgment that the decision of such a patient to shorten the period of suffering before death can be rational and on occasion my professional obligation to relieve suffering would dictate that I assist such a patient in hastening his or her death.
>
> Under the statute prohibiting assisting suicide, fulfillment of this professional responsibility might expose me to criminal prosecution. The statute deters me from treating these patients as I believe I should. (Glucksberg 1994:5)

Eventually, the plaintiffs Jane Roe, John Doe, and James Poe would die, and Glucksberg would be the lead respondent at the Supreme Court level.

Another plaintiff, Thomas Preston, M.D., would author a *New York Times* op-ed article on the "morphine drip" and the assisted suicide that exists under normal practice of medicine in the United States. In it, Preston asserted that the two practices differ only in time and stated intent.

Preston critiqued the New York Task Force on Life and the Law, a group that eschewed the need for legal reform including assisted suicide, when he wrote: "[T]he panel didn't acknowledge that the physicians routinely end patients' lives with morphine drips. The necessary regulation will be possible only if we admit that euthanasia is widespread now" (Preston 1994:A15). The plaintiffs were joined by a long list of organizations and individuals who filed friend-of-the-court briefs with the court.

On behalf of Compassion in Dying were groups interested in civil liberties and personal autonomy, like the American Civil Liberties Union (ACLU), and those connected to potentially affected groups, including the Gray Panthers, the Older Women's League, the Northwest AIDS Foundation, and the Seattle AIDS Support Group. In addition, they were joined by the Hemlock Society; the National Organization for Women, Seattle Chapter; the Humanists of Washington; the National Lawyers Guild; Local 6 of Service Employees International Union; and Temple de Hirsch Sinai. In the brief, the amici concentrated on the argument that the Washington statute unduly burdened the right of persons to commit "rational suicide" (American Civil Liberties Union of Washington et al. 1994:10). They acknowledged that the state had an interest in preventing suicides by those who had mental illness and could therefore not make a rational decision to end their lives, but argued that

> at the other end of the spectrum, where a person's quality of life is significantly impaired by a medical condition that is extremely unlikely to improve, and that person, after careful consideration and without undue influence, has made the decision that suicide is a more appropriate and dignified alternative than continuing to live without an acceptable level of quality of life, such a decision cannot be considered irrational. (American Civil Liberties Union of Washington et al. 1994:5)

On behalf of the state of Washington were amicus briefs from the National Right to Life Committee and the United States Catholic Conference.

JUDGE BARBARA ROTHSTEIN'S RULING (*COMPASSION I*)

In an opinion issued May 3, 1994, in the United States District Court for the Western District of Washington, Chief Judge Barbara Rothstein found for the reformers. Rothstein found the reasoning in *Casey* (1992) "highly instructive and almost prescriptive" on the due process issue (*Compassion I* 1994, at 1459). She quoted from *Casey* (1992), "The underlying constitutional issue is whether the State can resolve these philosophic questions in such a definitive way that a woman lacks all choice in the matter" (*Planned Parenthood v. Casey* 1992). Judge Rothstein reasoned that "profound spiritual and moral questions surrounding the end-of-life" cannot be resolved so definitively that the State may absolutely prohibit a terminally ill, mentally competent person from committing suicide under the guidance of a physician. She concluded that choices about abortion and imminent death are equally as intimate and personal, and so is the potential for suffering without protection from unwarranted governmental interference. Both a woman's right to abort an unwanted fetus and a terminally ill person's right to orchestrate the time, place, and manner of death fall "within the realm of the liberties constitutionally protected under the Fourteenth Amendment" (*Compassion I* 1994, at 1460).

Judge Rothstein read the State of Washington's argument to be that removal of life support leads to a "natural" death, while physician-assisted suicide leads to an "artificial" death. Judge Rothstein did not accept that argument. Instead, she concluded that the fundamental rights of terminal patients not on life support are burdened, while the rights of patients whose death can be hastened by removal of life support are not so burdened. Having ruled that these two groups are similarly situated, Judge Rothstein concluded that Washington's absolute ban against assisted suicide (RCW 9A.36.060) violates the equal protection guarantee of the Fourteenth Amendment (*Compassion I* 1994, at 1467).

Judge Rothstein also found *Cruzan v. Director* (1990) instructive. In *Cruzan* a majority of justices held that for purposes of deciding the issue before the court—whether Missouri could require clear and convincing evidence of an incompetent patient's prior wishes concerning removal of life support—they assumed that a competent person does have a constitutionally protected right to refuse lifesaving treatment, even artificial nutrition and hydration. Judge Rothstein said she was confident that faced squarely with the issue, the Supreme Court would reaffirm the court's tentative conclusion in the *Cruzan* case. "The question then becomes whether a constitutional distinction can be drawn between refusal or withdrawal of medical treatment which results in death, and the situation in this case involving competent, terminally ill individuals who wish to hasten death by self-administering drugs prescribed by a physician" (*Compassion I* 1994, at 1467).

Judge Rothstein concluded that no constitutional distinction could be drawn between treatment refusal and physician-assisted suicide by an uncoerced, mentally competent, terminally ill adult. Her rationale was that in both situations the decision whether to hasten death is profoundly personal—the kind of decision that is essential to personal autonomy and basic human dignity. And decisions essential to autonomy and dignity are within the liberty interest protected by the Fourteenth Amendment (*Compassion I* 1994, at 1467).

Having recognized physician-assisted suicide to be a constitutional right, Judge Rothstein looked to review the Washington law against the undue burden standard. In this case, that standard of judicial review, which was set forth in *Casey*, calls for the court to first examine the alleged state interests in maintaining a total prohibition on all assisted suicides, and then to determine whether the challenged statute places a substantial obstacle in the path of individuals seeking to exercise a constitutionally protected right (*Compassion I* 1994, at 1464). Judge Rothstein concluded that the Washington law places an undue burden on the exercise of a protected liberty interest in voluntarily committing physician-assisted suicide, and ruled that the law is unconstitutional.

REACTION AND AN APPEAL

The state of Washington appealed to the Ninth Circuit, and briefs were filed in 1994. In its opening brief, the state of Washington challenged the basis upon which Judge Rothstein made her decision. In her opinion, Rothstein stated:

> The liberty interest protected by the Fourteenth Amendment is the freedom to make choices according to one's individual conscience about those matters which are essential to personal autonomy and basic human dignity. There is no more profoundly personal decision, nor one which is closer to the heart of personal liberty, than the choice which a terminally ill person makes to end his or her suffering and hasten an inevitable death. (United States District Court Order at 16)

The state's brief argued that Judge Rothstein's decision ignored "the state's legitimate interests in preventing suicide and in protecting vulnerable individuals from abuse or undue influence" (at 16). Moreover, the brief said, Judge Rothstein's decision was "contrary to the holding of virtually every court that has dealt with end-of-life issues" (at 16). As for Rothstein's holding regarding the degree of the individual's interest at stake, the state argued that Rothstein "improperly analyzed assisted suicide under the principles of reproductive rights" (at 19).

This was also a central argument submitted by the National Right to Life Committee in a friend-of-the-court brief. The National Right to Life Committee filed an amicus brief which argued that Judge Rothstein had misapplied the law when she read *Cruzan* and *Casey* to favor the reformers.

Several other organizations supported the state of Washington as friends of the court with amici curiae briefs. The American Medical Association (AMA) presented several arguments about how a change in the law would adversely affect the medical profession. The association's key argument was that "physician-assisted suicide, properly defined, has long been recognized, and continues to be recognized, as unethical and contrary to the responsibilities of physicians to their patients" (American Medical Association 1994:2–3).

The traditional role of physician as healer is enshrined in the code of the medical profession and has long been argued to be central to the integrity of the physician-patient relationship. *Cruzan*, the AMA's brief stipulated, did in fact accord constitutional status to the right of individuals to make private medical decisions. But the right of patients to make their own medical decisions has long been recognized in the United States, and it is firmly grounded in the ethics of the medical profession, which makes patient autonomy a key principle of the physician-patient relationship. "That right, however, has limits" (American Medical Association 1994:2). Citing language from various codes that govern physicians' practices in the United States, the AMA's brief focused on how Judge Rothstein's ruling, if upheld, would change their code and the role and prerogatives of physicians, and thereby affect the nature of the doctor-patient relationship negatively.

To the AMA, "the option to assist a patient's suicide will likely cause some physicians to divert their attention from what should be their primary and most critical mission—to provide care and comfort to their patients, including adequate relief from pain" (American Medical Association 1994:9).

Further, the brief argued that "the term physician-assisted suicide must be carefully defined to avoid criminalizing a wide array of medical practices that are ethically proper and indeed constitutionally protected" (American Medical Association 1994:3). They noted that the AMA's Code of Medical Ethics states: "[The] principle of patient autonomy requires that physicians respect the decision to forego life-sustaining treatment of a patient who possesses decision-making capacity. Life-sustaining treatment is any treatment that serves to prolong life without reversing the underlying medical condition" (American Medical Association 1994:3). Thus, the thrust of the AMA's brief was that "the views of the medical profession on physician-assisted suicide should be considered in any analysis of whether individuals have a constitutional right to this practice" (American Medical Association 1994:3). In the opinion of the AMA, Judge Rothstein's ruling, which was based on jurisprudential principles regarding choice and on an extension of the Supreme Court's rulings on abortion, gave too little weight to how physicians' practices, which are steeped in ethical traditions, could be adversely affected. While opposing the legalization of physician-assisted suicide, the AMA has been consistent in its briefs and lobbying efforts to protect the efforts of physicians currently assisting end-of-life decisions under the "double-effect" doctrine. In Chapter 6, we will explore how they eventually placed this language explicitly and squarely in the second version of federal legislation meant to block the ODDA.

In addition to the issues of the misreading of *Casey* and *Cruzan*, the International Anti-Euthanasia Task Force hammered at the idea that there was no legal or cultural tradition in the United States supporting suicide as a basis for legalizing physician-assisted suicide. They also challenged the ruling in Judge

Rothstein's opinion that voluntariness characterized the choosing of assisted suicide. Citing studies showing that a large percentage of those committing suicide to have had a major psychiatric illness at the time of death, they argued that "it is impossible in practice to assure that a suicide is wholly 'free' or 'voluntary'" (International Anti-Euthanasia Task Force 1994:31).

The Washington State Hospital Association argued that the reform would impair important functions of hospitals, increase the risk of malpractice litigation, and expose both hospitals participating in physician-assisted suicide and those choosing otherwise to an "increased threat of litigation" (Washington State Hospital Association 1994:11).

The United States Catholic Conference, in a brief joined by their Washington, Oregon, and California counterparts, argued that Judge Rothstein's likening of assisted suicide to "personal decisions relating to marriage, procreation, contraception, family relationships, child rearing and education" was misguided; that suicide is not constitutionally protected because it is a choice central to personal dignity and autonomy" and that the voluntariness of suicide is overstated (United States Catholic Conference 1994:7,18,28).

On behalf of the reformers, a group of amici filed a brief in support. Joining the American Civil Liberties Union (ACLU) were the Northwest AIDS Foundation; the Seattle AIDS Support Group; the Northwest Women's Law Center; the Older Women's League; the Gray Panthers Project Fund; the Hemlock Society of Washington State; the National Organization for Women, Seattle Chapter; the American Humanist Association; the National Lawyers Guild; Local 6 of the Service Employees International Union; the Temple de Hirsch Sinai; the AIDS Action Council; the Lambda Legal Defense and Education Fund, Inc.; the Unitarian Universalist Association; and the Seattle Chapter and the Pacific Northwest District Council of the Japanese American Citizens League. The amici argued that the Fourteenth Amendment "protects the personal choice of a mentally competent, terminally ill person to commit suicide" (American Civil Liberties Union et al. 1994:11). Further, they argued that Washington's "blanket prohibition" of assisted suicide "unduly burdens" the rights of terminally ill persons to make "rational end-of-life decisions," an argument that roots the reformers' pleas in the established jurisprudence from the reproductive rights cases (American Civil Liberties Union et al. 1994:21).

THE FIRST APPELLATE DECISION (*COMPASSION II*)

On March 9, 1995, a three-judge panel of the Ninth Circuit Court of Appeals voted 2–1 to reverse Judge Rothstein's ruling (we call this first Ninth Circuit ruling *Compassion II* 1995). Judge John Noonan, writing for the majority, found the language of *Casey* inappropriate in the situation of assisted suicide:

> To take three sentences out of an opinion over thirty pages in length dealing with the highly charged subject of abortion and to find these sentences "almost prescriptive" in ruling on statutes proscribing the promotion of suicide is to make an enormous leap, to do violence to the context, and to ignore the differences between the regulation of reproduction and the prevention of the promotion of killing a patient at his or her request. (*Compassion II* 1995, at 590)

Noonan also rejected Rothstein's reading of the *Cruzan* decision:

> The district court found itself unable to distinguish between a patient refusing life support and a patient seeking medical help to bring about death and therefore interpreted *Cruzan*'s limited acknowledgment of a right to refuse treatment as tantamount to an acceptance of a terminally ill patient's right to aid in self-killing. The district court ignored the far more relevant part of the opinion in *Cruzan* that "there can be no gainsaying" a state's interest "in the protection and preservation of human life" and, as evidence of that legitimate concern, the fact that "the majority of States in this country have laws imposing criminal penalties on one who assists another to commit suicide." *Cruzan*, 497 U.S. at 280. Whatever difficulty the district court experienced in distinguishing one situation from the other, it was not experienced by the majority in *Cruzan*. (*Compassion II* 1995, at 591)

THE SECOND APPELLATE DECISION OF THE NINTH CIRCUIT (*COMPASSION III*)

The Noonan panel's decision was appealed by the *Compassion* plaintiffs. They argued that the three-judge panel overlooked or misapprehended points of law or fact, by misreading *Casey* and *Cruzan*, and their applicability to the reformers' claims. The Ninth Circuit agreed to conduct an en banc hearing, which took place on October 26, 1995.

On March 6, 1996, the eleven-judge en banc panel voted 8–3 to affirm Judge Rothstein's ruling *(Compassion III* 1996). Regarding the liberty interest under *Casey* the panel said: "The district court found [three sentences in *Casey*] 'highly instructive' and 'almost prescriptive' for determining 'what liberty interest may inhere in a terminally ill person's choice to commit suicide. (*Compassion In Dying*, 850 F. Supp. At 1459). We agree" (*Compassion III* 1996, at 813). Moreover, the panel found Judge Rothstein's reading of *Cruzan* compelling:

> [W]e conclude that *Cruzan*, by recognizing a liberty interest that includes the refusal of artificial provision of life-sustaining food and water, necessarily recognizes a liberty interest in hastening one's own death. [Footnote 70]: Prior to the court's decision in *Cruzan*, more than 15 states specifically prohibited implementing an advance directive that would have led to the termination of artificial nutrition and hydration. Alan Meisel, The Right to Die 369 & n.63 (1989). A few years after *Cruzan*, however, only a few states still prohibited the termination of nutrition and hydration as part of a living will, a prohibition that is probably unconstitutional under *Cruzan*. Alan Meisel, The Right to Die; 1994 Cumulative Supplement No. 2 395–99 (1994). (*Compassion III* 1996, at 816)

QUILL V. VACCO

Meanwhile, across the country in New York, a similar challenge was taking place. The state of New York, with its large medical and legal communities, had engaged in an extensive consideration of the utility of current assisted suicide prohibitions and the possible options for reform. The broad-based New York State Task Force on Life and the Law had weighed in against assisted suicide, arguing instead that greater attention be paid to patient complaints of pain and the training of medical personnel in palliative care.

For this lawsuit, three terminally ill patients who wished to have the assistance of physicians in committing suicide, and three physicians who claimed it would be consistent with the standards of their practices to prescribe life-ending medication, filed a complaint against the attorney general of the state of New York, G. Oliver Koppell.

The Quill plaintiffs were Timothy E. Quill, M.D.; Samuel C. Klagsbrun, M.D.; Howard A. Grossman, M.D.; Jane Doe, a seventy-six-year-old cancer patient; George A. Kinglsey, a forty-nine-year-old publishing executive with AIDS; and William A. Barth, a twenty-eight-year-old fashion editor with AIDS.

In 1991 the lead plaintiff, Dr. Timothy E. Quill, wrote an account of his role in a patient's hastened death by barbiturate poisoning, and it was published in the *New England Journal of Medicine*, sparking widespread debate in medical circles.

He wrote at that time: "I wrote the prescription with an uneasy feeling about the boundaries I was exploring—spiritual, legal, professional and personal. Yet I also felt strongly that I was setting her free to get the most out of the time she had left, and to maintain dignity and control on her own terms until her death" (Quill 1991:691).

An internal medicine specialist at the University of Rochester in New York, Quill has since then written other books and articles and is presented as a more reasonable physician-spokesperson for the death with dignity movement than Jack Kevorkian. The other physician plaintiffs, Samuel C. Klagsbrun and Howard A. Grossman, claimed they were desisting from prescribing lethalities for fear of prosecution. During the course of the litigation the three patients died, leaving only the physician plaintiffs. Also, Attorney General Koppell was succeeded by Dennis C. Vacco, and thereafter the case was known as *Quill v. Vacco.*

Joining Quill and all as amici curiae were the Lambda Legal Defense and Education Fund, Inc.; the National Association of People with AIDS; the Unitarian Universalist Association; the Americans for Death With Dignity; the Death With Dignity Education Center; the Gray Panthers Project Fund; the Hemlock Society; Minna Barrett; and the Euthanasia Research and Guidance Organization (ERGO).

Joining the state as amici curiae were: the United States Catholic Conference; the New York State Catholic Conference; The National Right to Life Committee, Inc.; the New York State Right to Life Committee; and some members of the New York state legislature.

The challenged statutes were §125.15(3) and §120.30 of the New York Penal Law. The first section provides in relevant part that "a person is guilty of manslaughter in the second degree when [h]e intentionally . . . aids another person to commit suicide." Section 120.30 provides that "a person is guilty of promoting a suicide attempt when he intentionally . . . aids another person to attempt suicide." Violation of either statute is a felony. The plaintiffs challenged these statutes only insofar as they apply to situations when a physician aids the commission of suicide by a mentally competent, terminally ill adult wishing to avoid continued severe suffering by prescribing a death-producing drug that the patient takes. The constitutional right the plaintiffs claimed would apply to both patients and physicians under these circumstances.

THE DISTRICT COURT RULING (*QUILL I*)

On December 15, 1994, Chief Judge Thomas Griesa dismissed the action. Griesa's rationale illustrated what Ronald Dworkin characterizes as the party of history (Dworkin 1996). In seeking to determine the contours of personal liberty and the bounds between individual and collective interests, Griesa analyzed physician-assisted suicide independently from the cases about abortion, procreation, and child rearing, and his rationale centered on the cultural and legal history of suicide and assisted suicide in the United States, a major argument of the legal opponents of assisted suicide reform in the courts.

First, Griesa narrowly read the holding in *Cruzan*. He recognized that the Supreme Court had not stated a single convenient statement of the issue before the court. So Griesa described the issues broadly: whether Nancy Cruzan had a federal constitutional right to withdraw life-sustaining medical treatment, whether her right could be exercised by her parents, and whether her parents' offer of proof regarding Nancy's intent was being unconstitutionally hampered by Missouri's requirement that her parents present clear and convincing evidence of Nancy's wishes. Chief Judge Griesa read the court's rationale to be that in order to get to the analysis of the constitutionality of Missouri's requirement of a higher standard of proof than is required in most civil cases, the court merely *assumed* a constitutional right of a competent terminally ill patient to withdraw treatment that leads to death. "With regard to *Cruzan*, . . . the Court did not actually make the holding upon which plaintiffs seek to rely" (*Quill I* 1994, at 83).

Second, Griesa declared, "[T]he trouble is that plaintiffs make no attempt to argue that physician-assisted suicide, even in the case of terminally ill patients, has any historic recognition as a legal right" (*Quill I* 1994, at 83). Recent studies, including the one undertaken by the New York State Task Force on Life and the Law (1994), have reexamined the issue and reaffirmed the historic ban against assisted suicide. That ban has existed since English common law, and was reestablished in the American colonies. Changes in the law regarding suicide merely abandoned the practice of punishing the family of the suicide; however, assisting suicide has remained illegal in a majority of state laws and under the Model Penal Code, the comments to which state:

> The fact that penal sanctions will prove ineffective to deter the suicide itself does not mean that the criminal law is equally powerless to influence the behavior of those who would aid or induce another to take his own life. Moreover, in principle it would seem that the interests in the sanctity of life that are represented by the criminal homicide laws are threatened by one who expresses a willingness to participate in taking the life of another, even though the act may be accomplished with the consent, or at the request of the suicide victim. (Model Penal Code § 210.5(2) and comment, at 100; see American Law Institute 1980)

Upon these bases, Chief Judge Griesa held that there is neither a constitutional right of physicians to prescribe lethalities to terminally ill patients nor a right of terminally ill patients to receive them (*Quill I* 1994, at 84): "In any event, it would appear clear that suicide has a sufficiently different legal significance from requesting withdrawal of treatment so that a fundamental right of suicide cannot be implied from *Cruzan*" (*Quill I* 1994, at 84).

EQUAL PROTECTION ANALYSIS

New York law distinguishes between a patient who can hasten death by requesting withdrawal of life-sustaining medical treatment and a patient who is not on life support and therefore must seek a lethal prescription to hasten death. The issue is whether this distinction has a reasonable and rational basis (citing *Dandridge v. Williams* 1969).

Reasonable minds differ about whether ingesting a lethality is distinct from refusing treatment. Hence it is rational for the state to distinguish between "intentionally using an artificial death-producing device" and "allowing nature to take its course" (*Quill I* 1994, at 84). Finally, under the Constitution and the federal system it establishes, the resolution of the present sincere and conscientious public debate about physician-assisted suicide is properly left to the democratic process within the states (*Quill I* 1994, at 85). On the basis of this analysis, the court dismissed the plaintiffs' challenge.

Griesa's decision was appealed to the Second Circuit, where arguments were taking place on a parallel course to those in the *Compassion* cases.

QUILL IN APPELLATE COURT (*QUILL II*)

In an amicus brief, several members of the New York state legislature (in a brief prepared by Americans United for Life) took issue with several of the challenges by the reformers, concluding, "There is no medical reason to legalize assisted suicide. Nor is there any legal basis for recognizing a right to suicide under the Constitution" (Members of the New York State Legislature 1995:12). They argued that the right to assisted suicide was not a fundamental right, that assisted suicide cannot be equated with the refusal of medical treatment, and that therefore the New York state policy to allow withholding or withdrawal of treatment was not an equal protection violation (Members of the New York State Legislature 1995:30).

The legislators started their brief with a quote from the New York State Task Force on Life and the Law, which had concluded: "The risks of legalizing assisted suicide and euthanasia for these individuals, in a health care system and society that cannot effectively protect against the impact of inadequate resources and ingrained social disadvantage, are likely to be extraordinary" (Members of the New York State Legislature 1995:1).

The Catholic Church, as mentioned in Chapters 2, 3, and 4, had been very involved in opposing assisted suicide legal reform. In this case, the United States Catholic Conference warned of the "dark import" of the reformers' claim (United States Catholic Conference 1995:3).

On behalf of the reformers, a group of amici joined in a brief—Lambda Legal Defense and Education Fund, the Death With Dignity Education Center, the Unitarian Universalist Association, the Gray Panthers, and the Hemlock Society. The amici challenged the state's asserted interest in preserving life as justifying a ban on assisted suicide. In opposition, they argued that New York's "blanket prohibition against aid to suicide unduly burdens the right of the terminally ill to make rational end-of-life decisions" (Lambda Legal Defense and Education Fund et al. 1995:22). In conformity with the reformers' briefs, the amici group argued that the Fourteenth Amendment protects "the personal choice of a mentally competent, terminally ill individual to terminate unendurable suffering and hasten inevitable death" (Lambda Legal Defense and Education Fund et al. 1995:11).

On April 2, 1996, a three-judge panel of the Second Circuit Appellate Court overturned Griesa's decision (*Quill II*). Judge Roger Miner, writing for the two-judge majority, embraced the equal protection argument.

REACTIONS TO THE NINTH CIRCUIT AND SECOND CIRCUIT RULINGS

Reactions to the two appellate rulings was substantial from many quarters, with some ethicists and legal scholars commenting on the surprising rapidity of the emerging legal reform.

Seattle Unitarian Minister Ralph Mero of Seattle's Compassion in Dying, the plaintiff in the original lawsuit, stated that the ruling put "profoundly personal end-of-life decisions in the hands of dying patients and their doctors, rather than in the hands of the state" (Weinstein and Stammer 1996:A19).

The public policy director of a Seattle AIDS organization exulted, saying: "Hallelujah. I'm not sure if this will lead to more physician-assisted suicides by those with AIDS. But for those who are facing death with AIDS, or even having to think about it, court recognition of their private right to die with dignity will give them a lot of peace" (Weinstein and Stammer 1996:A16).

Derek Humphry, the head of ERGO the Oregon-based Euthanasia Research and Guidance Organization and the former head of the Hemlock Society and author of the best-selling "how-to-commit-suicide" book *Final Exit*, discussed the implications of the Ninth Circuit's ruling in the context of the right-to-die movement:

> The assisted suicide movement never has sought approval of accelerated death for the mentally or physically handicapped, the depressed or for the poor or elderly.... What we are now close to getting in America is choice

> in dying for those unfortunate few—perhaps 5 percent of all who die—whose suffering and/or indignities the medical profession is unable to alleviate. Legalizing assisted dying will remove it from the present secret crime of the bedroom and enable doctors to stop acting covertly. (Humphry 1996:B11)

Burke Balch, director of National Right to Life Committee's Department of Medical Ethics, represented the view of one of the amicus parties opposing liberalization:

> No one should think that this ruling can be applied only to those who "voluntarily" say they seek death. Court decisions in virtually every state have established that when a competent person is given a "right," an incompetent person must have the same "right," which may be chosen for him/her by a guardian or other third party. Thus, this decision threatens people—like those with Alzheimer's disease and other conditions that fog their mental abilities—with death, even though they never asked for it and may not wish it. (Weinstein and Stammer 1996:A16)

Elsewhere, Balch warned: "The so-called right to die will quickly become the duty to die" (Lewin 1996:A8).

Mark Chopko, general counsel of the U.S. Catholic Conference, labeled the ruling "a novel and dangerous expansion of the law.... The decision has pushed the law into obliterating a distinction that has long been recognized—not just in the law but in medicine—between withdrawing medical assistance and taking active steps to hasten death" (Weinstein and Stammer 1996:A16). Notre Dame law professor Douglas Kmiec questioned the Ninth Circuit ruling: "Reinhardt's newly minted suicide has no support in the two centuries of our constitutional existence ... [B]eyond its distortion of the Constitution and disregard of the 'self-evident' truths in our declaration of national purpose, the invested suicide right is a serious affront to the democratic process" (Kmiec 1996:B11). Kmiec was ominous about the implications of the rulings:

> Tragically, the existence of the putative suicide right puts enormous psychological pressure on the elderly and the disabled. We do what the doctor orders, and as a New York commission found, "Once the physician suggests suicide or euthanasia, some patients will feel that they have few, if any alternatives, but to accept the recommendation." This is especially true of the poor.... Pain can be a strong encouragement for suicide, and the poor have far less means of alleviating severe pain. In these days of reduced

> public expenditure, there is but a short distance between the false proclamation of a personal suicide right and the generalized calculation that this might well reduce the overall cost of public assistance. (Kmiec 1996:B11)

Dr. Jack Lewin, chief executive of the California Medical Association, stated, "Doctors are not in the business of speeding people on their way out of their lives. . . . This act has a tremendous potential for abuse. In today's for-profit health-care world, one could imagine in the future a corporation wanting to save money on hospital beds by hastening a patient's death" (Monmaney 1996:A1). David O'Steen, speaking for the National Right to Life Committee, said the ruling meant that euthanasia wouldn't be voluntary, which "threatens every grandmother, grandfather and medically dependent or disabled person" (Casteneda 1996:1A). Dr. Nancy Dickey, AMA president, responded: "Stepping over that line [to assist a suicide] is not in the best interest of patients or society" (Savage and Weinstein 1996:A19).

Placing the two decisions together, plaintiff attorney Kathryn Tucker found significance in the fact that: "It's the population of about half the country between these two decisions." She added: "Looking forward to possible Supreme Court review, I would say that the 2nd Circuit has done us a favor by applying the alternative constitutional ground [equal protection] that wasn't reached by the 9th Circuit" (Savage and Weinstein 1996:A19).

University of Southern California law professor Erwin Chemerinsky made note of the differing constitutional bases for the two rulings, noting, "The fact that the 2d Circuit ruled on equal protection might be important at the Supreme Court, at least in terms of Judge Ginsburg's vote. Ginsburg has been very hostile to protecting unenumerated substantive rights under the due process clause. I think she is much more likely to find a right to physician-assisted suicide under equal protection than under due process" (Savage and Weinstein 1996:A19).

NOVEMBER 1996: AMICUS BRIEFS TO THE SUPREME COURT

The Legal Center for Defense of Life and the Pro-Life Legal Defense Fund argued that, in accepting the reformers' framing of their case in the 1992 *Casey* decision, the court had missed another connection—the failed *Bowers v. Hardwick* (1986) case, in which the Supreme Court failed to find fundamental constitutional protection for homosexual sodomy. *Bowers*, not *Casey*, was what pertained here, they charged (Legal Center 1996). The same group also charged that the Ninth Circuit had distorted the historical record to justify the creation of a new fundamental constitutional right.

The National Right to Life Committee a very active group in opposition to the reformers at earlier stages, also hammered away at the Ninth Circuit's use of *Casey* as being inapplicable to the assisted suicide case. They argued that while *Casey* dealt with "potential life," the assisted suicide case dealt with "born persons," and cases in which the state's interest to protect life were indeed compelling (National Right to Life Committee 1996:17).

The National Right to Life Committee also criticized the Ninth Circuit for giving too much weight to the reformers' interpretations of the Supreme Court ruling in the withdrawal of life support case of *Cruzan* in 1990, a point that would resonate in the justices' own rejection of the reformers' interpretation of the previous Supreme Court decision. They argued that the Supreme Court drew a bright line between the "right to die"—which it "did not even speak of" (National Right to Life Committee 1996:19)—but had couched its analysis solely on the issue of a "right to refuse treatment."

The National Right to Life Committee concluded that compelling state interests in four areas "overrule any asserted interest in assisted suicide" (National Right to Life Committee 1996:iii):

1. An interest in preserving life outweighs any interest in assisted suicide.
2. An interest in protecting third parties outweighs any interest in assisted suicide.
3. An interest in preserving and maintaining the ethical integrity of the medical profession outweighs any interest in assisted suicide.
4. An interest in preventing suicide outweighs any interest in assisted suicide.

The New York–based group Choice in Dying came from a different perspective. While the right-to-life groups had not been involved in end-of-life care, Choice in Dying had been so involved. It was described in its amicus brief as "the oldest and only national organization devoted solely to a broad range of end-of-life issues . . . [with a mission] to secure the rights of patients to make decisions about end-of-life medical care and to promote quality care of dying patients" (Choice in Dying 1996:1). Based on its stature, Choice in Dying took on a separate set of issues: that pain was not adequately managed at end of life that there was public and professional confusion surrounding end-of-life care.

For one thing, Choice in Dying argued that the Ninth Circuit had mistakenly considered "double-effect" deaths and physician-assisted suicide to be equivalent, which it did not. They even raised the idea that there was a lack of professional consensus about the definitions of terminal illness, a theme hit home by the ads in Oregon's Measure 51. On palliative care, Choice in Dying argued that technology is available to manage the pain associated with terminal illness. Not to be accused of simply supporting the status quo or of suggesting the viability of a "third way" of pain relief, Choice in Dying also criticized the medical profession for currently overusing approaches and treatment that led to too much "potentially painful life-sustaining treatment in dying patients" (Choice in Dying 1996:15).

The American Suicide Foundation added in a brief with its expertise. It focused on the issues of misdiagnoses of depression and mental illness. It sought to detach the notion of the terminally ill seeking suicide as a special deserving case, in which depression would not be an important factor. On the contrary, it argued, problems from physical illness play a part in 25 percent of all suicides and rise with age (American Suicide Foundation 1996:5) It singled out depression as the primary cause for suicide and argued that offering physician-assisted suicide to the terminally ill may mask the symptoms of treatable depression.

The American Suicide Foundation attacked the Dutch experience in the rest of its brief, charging that physicians would not be able to distinguish those who would have the rights to assisted suicide from those who would not. It also raised an issue touched upon by others, that the Dutch experience indicates the likelihood of a slippery slope, with "the virtual impossibility of regulating physician-assisted suicide or limiting it to competent, terminally ill individuals" (American Suicide Foundation 1996:iii). It argued that "virtually every guideline established by the Dutch to regulate euthanasia is routinely violated in practice" (American Suicide Foundation 1996:21).

The anti-euthanasia organization the International Anti-Euthanasia Task Force, headed by Wesley Smith, author of *Forced Exit* (1997), put forward a set of arguments that complemented its fellow amici by concentrating on the economics surrounding coerced physician-assisted suicide. In addition to focusing on the economic pressures that would "force individuals to accept assisted suicide" (3), the organization criticized the Second Circuit for underestimating this problem and presuming that proper state regulation would protect against it.

A second line of argument proposed by the International Anti-Euthanasia Task Force was that the advent of managed care would be the worst situation into which to initiate physician-assisted suicide, since cost containment issues would lead to coerced deaths. Reading like a manifesto from single-payer system health care reformers, its argument chided managed care programs for ignoring patients rights and operating "in a manner that indicates a quest for only short term effectiveness and maximum cost containment" (International Anti-Euthanasia Task Force 1996:17). Moreover, the group charged that the chronically ill, particularly those are elderly or poor, are the hardest hit by cost containment.

The National Hospice Organization (NHO), founded in 1978, is the national organization representing 2200 hospice programs and forty-seven state hospice organizations (National Hospice Organization 1996:7). NHO's history was interlinked with that of Catholic health providers. With physician-assisted suicide seen as a surrender to death when it sees the opportunity for growth and closure through the dying process, NHO argued that "hospice care provides a proven, effective alternative to assisted suicide that is ideally suited to ameliorate the factors underlying the desire for suicide among the terminally ill" (National Hospice Organization 1996:5). The NHO elsewhere stated an organizational position against assisted suicide. Not surprisingly, the brief of the NHO argued that the Ninth Circuit and Second Circuit failed to consider the "opportunities to find value during the last stage of life" (National Hospice Organization 1996:6). The NHO argued that allowing physicians to end life would "irrevocably change the way care is perceived and undermine hospice care as a more appropriate option for care of the terminally ill" (National Hospice Organization 1996:17)

Disability rights groups, like Not Dead Yet, have been prominent opponents of assisted suicide legal reform in the states where reform has been considered. Some groups added briefs against the reformers. In its brief, the National Center for the Medically Dependent & Disabled, Inc. argued centrally that "recognition of a due process liberty or equal protection right to assisted suicide would result in nonvoluntary killing of persons deemed to have a diminished quality of life" (National Center for the Medically Dependent & Disabled, Inc. 1996:16). James Bopp and Thomas Marzen, authors of the brief, had gained attention with their editing of the journal *Issues in Law and Medicine* and other writing on this and aligned topics. They were also the lawyers who convinced Judge Hogan to enjoin the ODDA from 1994 to 1997, as we describe in the next chapter.

The American Hospital Association, in its brief (American Hospital Association 1996), reiterated the arguments of the main briefs and other amici, that there is a rational basis for distinguishing assisted suicide from withdrawal of treatment and that the Ninth Circuit misread *Casey* and *Cruzan.*

Several members of the New York and Washington state legislatures argued for continuing the bright line distinction between states' decriminalization of suicide or attempted suicide and that of assisted suicide. They offered a similar argument in supporting the continued distinction between the refusal of treatment and the choice of assisted suicide (Members of the New York and Washington State Legislatures 1996:15,23). Representatives of nineteen states, including New York and Washington, argued in a brief authored by the California attorney general's office that the Ninth Circuit was wrong in finding a liberty interest for assisted suicide and had improperly underweighed the relevant state interests present in prohibiting assisted suicide (States of California et al. 1996).

The chairs of the U.S. Senate and House Committees on the Judiciary, Senator Orrin Hatch and Representative Henry Hyde, argued in their brief that the judiciary—unlike legislative bodies—was ill-suited to carve out the needed compromises in such a heated area (Hatch 1996:13). These arguments were also addressed in briefs by the Legal Center for Defense of Life, the National Spinal Cord Injury Association, the American Geriatrics Society, and the Project on Death in America.

The Project on Death in America (PDIA) was not an unexpected opponent of the reformers, but it did have an unusual pedigree. The director of the PDIA, Dr. Kathleen Foley, had a firm reputation in the world of palliative care medicine and has been an articulate and well-published commentator on end-of-life issues. However, PDIA was a project of the Open Society Institute, part of the policy network developed by financier George Soros, one of the world's most influential investors. By comparison to its related organization the Lindesmith Center, which argues strenuously and articulately for reassessment of the American system of drug control, the PDIA did not challenge the status quo on end-of-life care in a similar direction. While one could argue that PDIA was innovative in its support of palliative care programs throughout the country, Foley, individually and with critics like Herbert Hendin, spoke out in Congress (Foley 1996) and elsewhere and wrote essays and articles often about the dangers of legalizing assisted suicide. Meanwhile, Soros ended up donating funds to the assisted suicide reformers in Oregon for their successful 1997 effort to stave off repeal.

PDIA's amicus brief, penned by Yale scholar Robert Burt, argued that the Supreme Court should not "pre-empt public debate and legislative action by premature constitutional resolution of issues with such complex dimensions as physician-assisted suicide" (Project on Death in America 1996:4). It also argued that constitutional resolution was premature because adequate safeguards had not been developed for physician-assisted suicide (Project on Death in America 1996:12).

Seventeen briefs by amici curiae in support of the reformers were filed by leaders in the fields of medicine, law, bioethics, religion, and others. Among the participants were the Center for Reproductive Law and Policy, the American Medical Student Association, a Coalition of State Legislators, the Washington Psychological Association, a Coalition of Mental Health Professionals, Prominent Americans with Disabilities, a Coalition of Hospice Professionals, The National Women's Health Network, the Northwest Women's Law Center, 36 Religious Organizations, Leaders and Scholars, The Episcopal Diocese of Newark, the Gay Men's Health Crisis, the American Counseling

Association, Americans for Death With Dignity, and Family Members in Support of Physician Assisted Dying.

With the *Compassion* rulings so rooted in the jurisprudence of *Roe* and *Casey*, it was expected that a group like the Center for Reproductive Law and Policy would file an amicus brief for the reformers. The center, whose attorneys had been counsel or amicus for every reproductive rights case for twenty years, argued in an interesting manner that abortion rights review standards were indeed as high as *Casey* established, but that it was not clear that assisted suicide rights were equal. Instead, they argued that *Cruzan*, more than *Casey*, provided the important grounding for the reformers.

The unique aspect of the surviving family members rested in the declarations provided by surviving family members, who spoke of their family members' choices of self-deliverance, of the last painful days of AIDS, and of desperate suicides by shotgun of terminal patients who couldn't find a way within the medical and legal system to arrange more appropriate methods of dying (Surviving Family Members 1996).

The support of AIDS activists and AIDS service organizations had been prominent in the reformers' challenges from the first level of *Compassion* onward. There had been support for assisted suicide reform among AIDS activists, and Magnusson and Ballis, among others, have described the active underground euthanasia network operating in certain American cities (Magnusson and Ballis 2000). The Lambda Legal Defense and Education Fund, which had been an amicus in the Second Circuit *Quill* appeal, joined at the Supreme Court level with the Gay Men's Health Crisis and several individuals with disabilities to challenge the impression that all disability groups were lined up against the reformers. To them, the proposed reform would have drawn a bright line between those with terminal illness and those with other disabilities, thus challenging the notion of the slippery slope that Not Dead Yet and other groups had made (Gay Men's Health Crisis et al. 1996:16). Indeed, Hugh Gregory Gallagher, one of the individual amici, was a polio quadriplegic and historian who had written a book, *By Trust Betrayed: Patients, Physicians and the License to Kill in the Third Reich* (Gallagher 1990), which examined the horrors of the Nazi euthanasia regime. Gallagher distinguished the current reforms efforts as a clear difference: "The case of assisted suicide is quite different: the patient with a terminal illness retains complete choice over whether to live or to die. Neither the state nor the physician may decide, based on their conceptions of the individual's quality of life; the individual must assess his or her own quality of life. This is true whether or not the individual has a disability" (Gay Men's Health Crisis et al. 1996: appendix).

In addition, amicus briefs were submitted by groups of experts—legislators, bioethicists, hospice professionals—who disagreed with opponent briefs by their counterparts or, in the case of hospice, with their national organization.

The hospice professionals challenged the arguments of the opponents by claiming that the availability of physician-assisted suicide would support the integrity of the medical profession, would protect the interests of family members and loved ones, and would promote the states' interest in promoting life. They took on the safeguards issue by declaring that physician-assisted suicide occurred in secret at that time, suggesting that "appropriate procedural safeguards to protect terminally-ill patients from coercion and untoward influence can be established" (Coalition of Hospice Professionals 1996:15).

A group of state legislators—including some who had introduced reform legislation—challenged the position of the New York and Washington legislatures, and the several state attorneys general, in a brief that asserted that the state's interest in preserving and protecting life, preventing suicide or coercion, or protecting the handicapped or maintaining the ethical integrity of the medical profession did not justify a ban on "physicians rendering assistance to a mentally competent, terminally ill patient" to end his or her life (State Legislators 1996).

Where the opponents had powerful institutional religious organizations, such as the United States Catholic Conference, the reformers claimed the support of several mainstream Protestant ministers and dioceses. The amici argued that there was a diversity of religious opinion in the United States on the topic of assisted suicide, and that "A terminally ill person's decision to hasten death is the sort of personal, intimate, often spiritual decision" that the Fourteenth Amendment supported (36 Religious Organizations 1996:10).

The American Civil Liberties Union (ACLU) and other amici who had offered briefs in *Compassion* and *Quill* at the lower levels added a brief arguing against a "blanket prohibition" on physician-assisted suicide and for the key equal protection and liberty claims of the reformers. For example, they argued: "The right of a mentally competent, terminally ill person to choose an end to suffering by hastening an inevitable death is implicit in the concept of ordered liberty" (American Civil Liberties Union 1996:9).

A group of psychologists and counselors, with individual and institutional contributions, argued against the brief of the American Suicide Foundation and the opponents, claiming instead that a terminally ill person can indeed make a competent decision to choose assisted suicide, without the overriding issue of depression clouding his or her judgment (Washington State Psychological Association, et al. 1996).

A group of law professors, including those like Charles Baron, Norman Cantor, and Alan Meisel, who had written extensively on end-of-life issues (Baron et al. 1996; Cantor 1993; Meisel 1989), centered their brief on the issue of de facto legalization that existed, taking on the "double effect" as an unregulated regime open to abuse. To them, "The state regimes of regulation . . . are unconstitutional because they have become irrational means for advancing the state interests that are alleged to justify them" (Law Professors 1996:4).

A group of prominent bioethicists, many of whom had written important works on the topic, argued that the law indeed needed to be updated to address the concerns of the reformers and that competent terminal patients should be able to exercise the right to assisted suicide. They rooted their arguments in "four basic principles of biomedical ethics: autonomy, nonmaleficence, beneficence, and justice" (Bioethicists 1996:2).

Finally, jurisprudential scholar Ronald Dworkin, one of the world's most respected legal scholars, joined with a group of other similarly respected legal philosophers in arguing for the correct reading by the Ninth Circuit of *Casey* and *Cruzan*. Dworkin, who had offered his own analysis of the meaning of the appellate courts' opinions, in the same way as he had charted numerous abortion decisions (Dworkin 1996), joined with the others in arguing: "If . . . this Court reverses the decisions below, its decision could only be justified by the momentous proposition—a proposition flatly in conflict with the spirit and letter of the court's past decisions—that an American citizen does not, after all, have the right, even in principle, to live and die in the light of his own religious and ethical beliefs, his own convictions about why his life is valuable and where its value lies" (Dworkin et al. 1996:21).

JANUARY 1997: ORAL ARGUMENTS TO THE SUPREME COURT

On January 8, 1997, the historic oral arguments in the two cases took place before lawyers and historians inside, while outside, disability rights groups protested and prayed (Blumenfeld 1997). The opening argument for the state was presented by William C. "Willie" Williams, a senior assistant attorney general of the state of Washington. In the context of end-of-life care, he argued, there is a clear line between permitting patients to demand nontreatment when nontreatment will result in death, on the one hand, and the provision or administration of lethalities by physicians, on the other. He argued that such a line was consistent with the clear line that is necessary to distinguish between conduct that is permissible because it is consistent with the concept of ordered liberty, and conduct that is not. To the state of Washington, the "new line" that the challengers asked the court to draw was unstable, for they suggested that the right to refuse treatment that was assumed in the *Cruzan* case provided a seamless web of constitutional rights flowing from that decision. In Williams's words, that challenge faltered for two reasons.

First, in the state of Washington's view, the challengers sought to supplant the social policy developed by Washington voters. The Washington statute prohibiting assisted suicide was forged at common law, had been upheld by centuries of legal traditions, and was recently ratified by a direct vote of the people of Washington (referring to the defeat of Initiative 119 in 1991). The same prohibition had been legislated in virtually every state and is strongly supported by the organizations of health care professionals who care for the sick and dying every day.

Second, the state of Washington argued that the liberty the challengers proclaimed is itself inconsistent with the concept of liberty. It is limited to very few people. Those very few must justify their exercise of the so-called constitutional right. And the so-called right must be closely regulated. In sum, it is incongruous that a so-called liberty should be applied so narrowly and be so difficult to exercise. In an interview with Mr. Williams, he stressed this point (Williams 1997). He also stressed that he was executing the will of the electorate. He made it clear that when and if a majority votes in favor of assisted death, he could surely stand before a court and make the opposing arguments.

The *Washington Post* would report the next day that the justices were skeptical of the assisted suicide reformers' legal claims (Biskupic 1997). It would not be an easy day for Kathryn Tucker.

Justice Sandra Day O'Connor asked Mr. Williams to explain why the state's interests suggest that the court should uphold Washington's total ban against assisted suicide even if the court declared there is a liberty interest in attaining and providing physician-assisted suicide in the case of the competent terminally ill. Williams named three interests: first, preserving life, which Williams suggested could be the basis for people organizing into communities; second, preventing abuse and undue influence, which Williams urged is more of a risk with assisted suicide than with treatment withdrawal; and third, regulating the medical profession, which he said is necessary particularly because physicians have the power to kill. Justice Souter asked Williams to focus on the second state interest, preventing abuse, and asked whether there is any empirical way to calculate the probability of such a risk. Williams could offer none, citing the fact that the practice has never been legal in the United States. There was some discussion between Williams and a few justices about the Dutch experience and also changes in law in the Northern Territory of Australia. None of this satisfactorily addressed Justice Souter's concerns, however, so Justice Stevens changed the subject.

What Justice Stevens, and the justices who asked follow-up questions, wanted to know was whether Williams believed that state legislatures have the power under the Constitution to make laws permitting physician-assisted suicide. Williams answered yes, under the states' police power to define the laws of homicide. This branch of questioning seemed to be of particular interest to Justices Stevens and Kennedy and to Chief Justice Rehnquist. Next Williams fielded a series of questions from Chief Justice Rehnquist and Justices Kennedy and Scalia about the propriety of assuming a liberty interest yet upholding a total ban. Mr. Williams's responses seemed rather ineffective judging from the justices reactions in addressing this "conundrum," as the Chief Justice called it.

Although Solicitor General Walter Dellinger agreed that the court should uphold the Washington ban against assisted suicide, he offered an argument that the court should nonetheless declare a liberty interest in being free from state interference in alleviating severe pain and suffering. Chief Justice Rehnquist pointed out that such an interest was not the basis of the Ninth Circuit Court's opinion. Dellinger conceded that, and was quick and careful to add that the parties before the Supreme Court were not claiming a general liberty interest in controlling the time, place, and manner of death. Chief Justice Rehnquist wanted to know how the liberty Dellinger was suggesting differs from the liberty assumed by the plurality in *Cruzan*. Dellinger responded that it is less than the interest assumed in *Cruzan* and, therefore, just as in *Cruzan* the court could assume a liberty yet uphold the law based on a finding that the state's interests outweigh liberty interests.

Justice Ruth Bader Ginsburg introduced the next line of questioning, one that turned out to be a central point in the court's refusal to declare the Washington law unconstitutional. Justice Ginsburg wanted to know Dellinger's opinion about whether the issue of a liberty to control one's death should ever be a judicial decision rather than legislative. Dellinger answered that it would be a grave mistake for the court to impose on all fifty states a transformation that has not even been experienced in one state. Yet Dellinger stopped short of stating that the issues should be limited to legislative action, given it was his brief and only his brief that urged the court to reject the legal challenge yet declare a narrow liberty when the state imposes a rule that prevents someone from the only means of relieving severe pain and suffering.

In Dellinger's closing statements, he referred the court to two sentences from the New York State Task Force on Life and the Law Report:

> [In ideal cases] [p]atients would be screened for depression and offered treatment, effective pain medication would be available, and all patients would have a supportive, committed family and doctor. Yet the reality of existing medical practice in doctors' offices and hospitals cannot generally meet these expectations, however any guidelines or safeguards might be framed. (*Quill III* and *Compassion IV* Transcripts 1997a:10; quoting The New York State Task Force on Life and the Law 1994:120)

Dellinger offered these remarks from the Task Force Report to help Justice Souter with his yet unanswered questions about the reality of the risk of abuse and undue influence.

At the completion of the states opening argument, Kathryn Tucker rose and began her argument by defining the scope of the liberty she was arguing for. The liberty to choose a humane and dignified death, she claimed, belongs to people at the threshold of death from terminal illness who are in full possession of their mental faculties. Justice Scalia wanted to know why the liberty is limited to those on the threshold of death. He posited that the distress of a person enduring severe pain for ten years is more compelling than a person who will soon die. Why should not the person in chronic pain have a right to suicide? Scalia asked. Tucker tried to distinguish between chronic pain and imminent death, but Justice Scalia teased her by interjecting that the dying process has begun for everyone. Tucker persisted that imminence is the key factor in defining the liberty to choose how and when to die.

But, Tucker was next asked, what about the person who is either too sick or just too scared to administer the lethality, is not that person in a more sympathetic situation? Such a person may draw more sympathy, Tucker agreed, but requiring a patient to self-administer a lethality provides that extra assurance that death is truly voluntary. Again, Tucker was asked, under a grand due process clause, why should not a competent person who is not terminally ill and who has no pain have the same right to choose when and how to die as a person who is very close to dying? Again Tucker tried to distinguish between a person with a long life expectancy and a person with no choice about whether to live or die in the near future. What seemed to be bothering the court was that a liberty based on autonomy, which is an inherently expansive concept, could be so narrowly drawn. The claim seemed incongruous.

Throughout this line of questioning, Tucker worked hard to inform the court that the liberty asserted by the challengers comprises really three interests: avoiding unwanted pain and suffering, decisional autonomy, and bodily integrity. As she did so, the questioning turned to the problem of the proverbial rush to the courthouse doors that would surely result if the court upheld the challengers' claim—the abortion controversy being the best example. Tucker could not convince Chief Justice Rehnquist and Justices O'Connor and Ginsburg that regulation would be ironed out in the legislatures. Chief Justice Rehnquist reminded Tucker that as long as there are people who strongly support and people who strongly oppose physician-assisted suicide, and those factions are constantly fighting it out in every legislative session, ultimately more issues than not will be claimed to be of constitutional magnitude and therefore be left to the courts to decide. Said Justice O'Connor, "I think there is no doubt there would be a flow of cases through the court system for Heaven knows how long" (*Quill III* and *Compassion IV* Transcripts 1997a:14).

Next came a critical series of questions asking why all of these issues should not be resolved by legislatures. Justice O'Connor raised the important point that traditional equal protection analysis is based on the premise that the group suffering discrimination is politically powerless and therefore cannot seek relief in the democratic process, which is what prompts the judiciary to step in. The justices seemed especially deferential to the fact that, unlike gender or skin color, everyone dies. Tucker responded that the cultural denial of death was oppressive enough to suggest that political processes do not work as usual regarding issues of death and dying. But the justices challenged her further, noting that her own brief and supporting amicus briefs indicated that opinion polls show consistent public support for physician-assisted suicide, as well as solid political support. The best response that Tucker mustered was that de facto physician-assisted suicide is available primarily to the educated and the affluent who can access a physician willing to help with an illegal act. But the court was not buying it. And apparently Tucker saw that, for she changed the subject to what she saw as the court's duty not to leave the protection of vital liberties to the legislative process.

That transition touched off the most volatile dialogue between Tucker and the court. Justice Kennedy began:

> [This] matter of defining [a] liberty ... is a question of ethics and of morals and of allocation of resources and of our commitment to treat the elderly and infirm. And surely legislators have much more flexibility and a much greater capacity to absorb those kinds of arguments and make those decisions than we do. You're asking us in effect to declare unconstitutional the law of fifty states. (*Quill III* and *Compassion IV* Transcripts 1997a:15)

Tucker tried to answer, but she was interrupted by Justice Souter's exhortation that the claimed constitutional issues surrounding the rights of the dying are so modernistic that they may be impossible for courts to assess without more real-world experience from which to weigh the competing interests. Tucker confidently disagreed with Justice Souter, and for that she cited the court's analysis in *Cruzan.* But what she said—that the court found the withdrawal of a feeding tube to be a significant liberty interest—upset Justice Kennedy. As Tucker apologized again and again, Justice Kennedy drilled her with the notion that all the court had done in deciding *Cruzan* was *assume* a liberty interest *for the purpose of deciding the broader issue* of whether the state's interests in preserving life could substantiate a heightened evidentiary standard.

"That's a rather critical point, is it not?" asked Justice Kennedy. Tucker backpedaled and agreed. "And," continued Justice Kennedy, "that makes this case worlds apart from *Cruzan*: in *Cruzan* we explained why what the legislature had done was reasonable; by contrast, you are asking us to overturn the laws of all the states but one" (referring to the passage of Measure 16 in Oregon) (*Quill III* and *Compassion IV* Transcripts 1997a:16).

Tucker attempted to substantiate her posture by saying that *Cruzan* essentially safeguarded the individual's right to make life-and-death decisions, free not only from interference by the collective but also from interference by those close to the individual. For a person interested in public policy, that is a fair reading of *Cruzan*, but Justice Kennedy was dissatisfied with that reading from a legalistic viewpoint: There is no language from *Cruzan* that could *explicitly* support Tucker's point.

Finally, Justice Scalia set the tone for Tucker's final argument:

> Declining medical treatment is something quite different from suicide. In saying you have a right not to have your body invaded, if you choose not to receive it, you're following a common law tradition that goes all the way back. You're opposing a common law tradition when you say there is a right to kill yourself. Why can't a society simply determine as a matter of public morality that it is simply wrong to kill yourself just as it is wrong to kill someone else? What in the constitution prevents that moral judgment from being made in this society's laws? (*Quill III* and *Compassion IV* Transcripts 1997a:17)

Tucker answered "This [decision] has to do with one's own body, one's own medical care, and suffering in the face of death. And that brings it within—if any decision falls within the private realm of decision-making, which this Court has indicated the government may not enter, it would be this decision" (*Quill III* and *Compassion IV* Transcripts 1997a:17).

Finally, once again Tucker was asked to define the liberty interest at stake. Tucker succinctly reiterated that she propounded a liberty that involves bodily integrity, decisional autonomy, and the right to be free of unwanted pain and suffering, and that that liberty is at least as vital as the liberty assumed under *Cruzan*. But once again, Tucker was contradicted, this time on the basis that the liberty she proclaimed is questionably limited to a narrow class: the competent terminally ill. Tucker attempted to explain that the limitation is because the liberty does not ripen until one is certifiably terminal. Why? the justices wanted to know. Again, explained Tucker, unlike people who are about to die, people who are not medically terminal may go on to lead a fulfilling life and contribute to society. At that stage of life the state's interest is greater. But once a person is expected to die, especially if such expectation is despite modern medical interventions, the interests shift such that individual liberty is paramount. Conversely, a patient who has a temporary condition that can be resolved through a short period of life-sustaining treatment and then go on to a healthy life is not eligible for withdrawal of life-sustaining treatment in Washington. The justices wanted to know how the element of autonomy in decision making could differ between the terminally and not terminally ill. Once again, Tucker stressed that the important distinction is between *how* to die versus *whether* to die, with only the former demanding constitutional protection. Tucker's response, as meritorious as it sounds, seemed to be lost in the sounds of laughter that followed the court's final ribbing comments.

Presenting a legally rigorous argument, Dennis C. Vacco, the attorney general of the state of New York, stuck to basic constitutional principles. Vacco's thesis was that persons who wish to procure lethalities from physicians are not similarly situated with people who wish to withdraw treatment: There is no equal protection issue because *neither* person has a right to procure a lethality from physicians. He explained that the right to refuse treatment springs from common law doctrines such as the right to be free from unwanted bodily interference, the right to be free from battery, and the right to be left alone. By contrast, he explained, the right of patients to have a third party, in this instance physicians, help them kill themselves has never been tolerated, medically or legally; hence these two acts are clearly distinguishable.

Justice Ginsburg interjected that it would be nice if the issues could be tucked so neatly into just two distinct categories. But as many of the briefs described, there is this sizable gray area in which patients are taken off artificial food and water and drugs are used to sedate them and perhaps render them unconscious while they wither away and die, not within hours, but over the course of days and days. Unlike Tucker, Vacco was permitted to offer long answers. He began by explaining that the challengers had wrongly described the practice of sedation in their briefs. The correct medical phrase, he insisted, is sedation in the imminently dying, not terminal sedation. That's because patients are not sedated so as to induce death, as the challengers would contend. The standard practice is to use sedatives during the last hours of death for treating nausea, shortness of breath, delirium, and excruciating pain.

Then with Justice Breyer's coaching, Vacco described the standard practice he was referring to. Under the law and according to patients' rights in hospitals, patients are permitted to stop eating and drinking. But they are not abandoned for making that choice, he said. Instead, they are aggressively treated for pain and suffering. Then only during the last hours are drugs that may render them comatose or even hasten death used to treat the final ravages.

Most importantly, the drugs are used not to induce death but to aggressively treat the final symptoms of dying. All this is necessary given that patients have a right to stop eating.

This standard medical practice is far different from purposely prescribing a type and amount of drugs designed specifically and solely for patients to kill themselves, Vacco continued. That has never been embraced by the medical profession, nor by the courts or legislature of the state of New York, nor by the New York State Task Force on Life and the Law, which studied these issues for nine years. And for the record, he asserted, the challengers' claim that death is brought upon by virtue of a coma coupled with the termination of food and water is simply wrong. Most medical professionals will agree that long before death comes from starvation it will come from suppressed respiration, which is treated with other drugs, or from the underlying illness.

Next came a series of inquiries about just where the line has been drawn. Vacco provided answers. Can a state totally forbid withdrawal of treatment just as it totally forbids assisted suicide? No, not constitutionally. Can a state force-feed a person who goes on a hunger strike to protest something? Yes, the state's interest in preserving human life is highest when a healthy person would go on living but for his or her suicidal conduct. Indeed, most states, Vacco explained, have deemed it appropriate for the state to intervene in such circumstances. The court itself said that is proper in *Cruzan*.

What about a person who learns she has a kidney disease yet refuses to undergo dialysis and but for that refusal she would live—can the state treat her forcefully? No, not constitutionally, because terminality does not matter in the context of refusing to accept treatment for an illness, as distinct from refusing to eat as a form of protest.

During his final minute, Vacco reemphasized that the risk of abuse is of primary concern to the state. He also acknowledged the risk that physicians take when operating in the gray area of aggressive drug treatment leading to sedation, coma, and eventually death. But that is not criminal conduct in New York if the physician intends only to treat pain—pursuant to the principle of double effect.

Next, on behalf of the challengers, Professor Laurence Tribe began with an analysis of the tedious differences between individual patients and between patients and nonpatients. One might have even thought they heard Tribe say that once a feeding tube is implanted in a nonterminal patient, that patient cannot ask to have the tube removed if her intent is to die. In an interview with Tucker, and after reading her legal briefs, it is not clear that she agrees. After nearly ten minutes of this, Tribe was chided: If the court were to go into this sort of intricate analysis it wouldn't decide any other case than New York's, and then the court would have to make the same analysis for forty-nine other states. Speaking as if the court were suggesting the contrary extreme, Tribe ended that line of argument by stating that the issues are too complex for a simple solution applicable nationwide.

Justice Breyer prodded Tribe toward more routine constitutional issues by asking him why the court should snatch this debate from the legislative process and what liberty interest is at stake. Tribe's answer was nonresponsive. He said the states are operating with the lights out. He described current medical practice as being Kafkaesque: The principles of double effect and treatment withdrawal logically collapse into the practice of slow euthanasia—unregulated and without witnesses as to the patient's wishes. Again Tribe was asked whether his arguments were better left to the legislature. Again he was nonresponsive, going back to Justice Ginsburg's concern about the risks to physicians operating in fear of criminal prosecution. Justice Kennedy prodded Tribe to consider the issue of autonomy, particularly the Task Force Report's suggestion that physician-assisted suicide would result in *less* autonomy as a result of poor patients being offered assisted suicide in lieu of costly treatment. He did not answer the question, but instead merely restated his yet to be constitutionally substantiated claim that the line between treatment withdrawal and physician-assisted suicide is a dubious one. "Dubious?" Tribe was asked rhetorically. "Are you not impressed with the study that shows that in Holland, where they have the line you want us to draw, there were but three centers for treating pain, yet in England where they have the New York rule, there were 185 pain centers?" asked the justices. "Yes, but. . . ." Professor Tribe seemed unwilling to concede any legal point contrary to his normative argument that New York law is just not fair.

Tribe drew some ire when he suggested that the court could rule for the challengers primarily because the New York legislature has not visited the issue of assisted suicide under the current regime of end-of-life care. A voice from the bench shouted, "Well, why on Earth would [the analysis] be any different unless you buy Judge Calabrese's idea?" Hasn't the court specifically disclaimed the notion of legislative due process? Tribe argued with the Chief Justice, but to no avail.

As Tribe's time was running out, he was asked again to define the liberty interest. Finally, he did. What he said is that when death is imminent a person has the liberty to be free of state laws that would result in his or her having to choose only between excruciating pain and suffering or a drug induced coma. "Why only when death is imminent?" Scalia demanded once again. This is when Tribe turned to the words used by his co-counsel, Tucker, whose opening sentence talked about the "threshold" of death. The court's jurisprudence, claimed Tribe, reveals that life has certain critical thresholds: marriage, birth, childrearing, for example—that get special deference under due process and equal protection analyses. "All of this is in the Constitution?" Scalia asked acerbically. "You see," Scalia continued, "this is lovely philosophy." "But you want us to frame a Constitutional rule on the basis of that—Life has various stages: birth, death . . . ?" Tribe backpedaled to *Casey*, and Justice Breyer called him on it, charging that Tribe's position is an amalgam of several precedents. "One part of your claim is freedom from pain and suffering; where is that in the law?" Justice Breyer asked (*Quill III* and *Compassion IV* Transcripts 1997b:18). For his final statement, Tribe admitted that, alone, the interest in avoiding pain and suffering is too nebulous. But you add to it the interests in shaping one's life and avoiding state control, then you have a special liberty.

REACTION

Those in attendance at the oral arguments did not miss the points of the justices' skepticism. Only the most stalwart optimists came away with the hopes that there were five votes for upholding either the Ninth Circuit or Second Circuit opinion. The *Los Angeles Times* reported that the justices left little doubt they would reject the notion. Its reporter, David Savage, described every justice as expressing wariness of creating "a new, untested, and practically unlimited right to assisted suicide" (Savage 1997:A1). Another legal analyst thought:

> [Y]ou could certainly sense from the questioning that the Justices in the middle who the plaintiffs really need to get the votes of in order to establish a right to physician-assisted suicide, Justice O'Connor, Souter, Ginsburg, and Kennedy, for example, all had very great concerns about opening Pandora's box, about creating a new constitutional right. . . . This isn't something that just affects some discrete minority like a racial minority somewhere that might not be fairly represented in the democratic process. Why can't we leave it to legislatures to work this out? They know more about it than we do. They are more flexible than we are. (Taylor 1997:3)

The *New York Times* characterized the justices' consideration as "an unusually personal session," and its correspondent, Linda Greenhouse, described the justices as "fascinated by the issue and deeply engaged by the arguments—but at the same time eager to keep the Court out of yet another momentous question of life and death" (Greenhouse 1997:A1).

THE SUPREME COURT'S JUDGMENT AND OPINIONS

It was therefore not a surprise when the opinions in *Vacco v. Quill* (*Quill III* 1997) and *Washington v. Glucksberg* (*Compassion IV* 1997) were handed down on June 29, 1997. While the 9–0 votes in the two cases could not have been more lopsided, the complexity of issues addressed by the justices, and some ambivalence on the part of some of them, made the opinions more extended than the votes might indicate.

Washington v. Glucksberg (*Compassion IV*)

The court's majority opinion, written by Chief Justice Rehnquist and joined by Justices Scalia, Thomas, Kennedy, and O'Connor, refused to strike down the laws of almost every state, laws that reflect centuries of legal doctrine and practice. The court found it prescriptive that assisted suicide has been rejected consistently, continually, and almost universally throughout this nation's history. There has never been an exception even for terminally ill, mentally competent adults. The court's decision in *Cruzan*, wrote Rehnquist, does not suggest otherwise. That ruling was not based on some abstract principle of autonomy, but on the nation's long-standing recognition that an unwanted touching, including forced medication, is a battery. Rehnquist rejected the Ninth Circuit's reading of *Casey* as well. *Casey* does not suggest that any and all important, intimate, and personal decisions are protected by the due process clause, wrote Rehnquist.

Moreover, said the chief justice, the legitimate government interests that are clearly rationally related to Washington's total ban against assisted suicide are many. They include prohibiting intentional killing and preserving human life; preventing the serious public health problem of suicide, especially among the young, the elderly, and those suffering from untreated pain or from depression or other mental disorders; protecting the medical profession's integrity and ethics and maintaining physicians' role as their patients' healers; protecting the poor, the elderly, disabled persons, the terminally ill, and persons in other vulnerable groups from indifference, prejudice, and psychological and financial pressure to end their lives; and avoiding a possible slide toward voluntary and perhaps even involuntary euthanasia.

Vacco v. Quill (*Quill III*)

The court's majority opinion, written again by Chief Justice Rehnquist, found no basis in the claim that New York's law discriminates against those not on life support. *Every* competent person can refuse treatment withdrawal; *no one* is permitted to assist a suicide or receive assistance in committing suicide. The court, moreover, disagreed with the Second Circuit Court of Appeals that ending or refusing life-sustaining treatment is the same as assisted suicide. The distinction comports with fundamental legal principles of causation and intent, and it was recognized, at least implicitly, in *Cruzan*. Moreover, the distinction has been, and is, widely recognized and endorsed by the medical profession, the state courts, and the overwhelming majority of state legislatures.

As for whether New York law bears a rational relation to some legitimate end, the court found the following to be valid and important public interests that easily satisfy constitutional scrutiny: prohibiting intentional killing and preserving life; preventing suicide; maintaining the physician's role as healer; protecting vulnerable people from indifference, prejudice, and psychological and financial pressure to end their lives; and avoiding a possible slide toward euthanasia.

O'Connor's Concurrence

First, Justice O'Connor agreed with the chief justice's opinion on the basis that there is no general right to suicide. That was on the basis of framing the issue as a "right to commit suicide which itself includes a right to assistance in doing so." But she further noted that the challengers asked the court to consider the narrower issue of whether the state could stand in the way of someone controlling the circumstances of their imminent death in the face of great suffering. And although Justice O'Connor said there was no reason for the court to consider that question, given that the laws in Washington and New York did not forbid sedation of the terminally ill—even to the point of hastening death—she appeared to be suggesting that given a different law and a different issue, the position of Solicitor General Dellinger, that there is a cognizable liberty interest in controlling the time, place, and manner of death, would sway her. In the meantime, she decided, the difficulty with establishing both terminality and assurances of voluntariness justifies each total ban against assisted suicide that the court upholds.

Perhaps Justice O'Connor's most poignant point was that the ubiquity of death assures that the democratic process will draw a proper balance between individual autonomy and the state's interest in assuring voluntariness. She wrote: "There is no reason to think the democratic process will not strike that balance" (*Quill III* and *Compassion IV*, at 2303). Finally, it has been widely stated that a related statement by Justice O'Connor may have been intended to urge people to use state legislative processes to strike the proper balance: "[T]he ... challenging task of crafting appropriate procedures for safeguarding ... liberty interests is entrusted to the 'laboratory' of the States ... in the first instance" (*Quill III* and *Compassion IV* 117 S.Ct. at 2303).

Stevens's Concurrence

Justice Stevens's concurrence seemed far more nuanced than the court's opinion. Stevens agreed with the court that the distinction between withdrawing treatment, thereby permitting death to ensue from an underlying natural disease, and causing death to occur, by providing or administering lethalities, is a constitutionally sufficient basis for the state's classification. Nevertheless, debate is still open regarding the limits of state power to intervene in end-of-life choices. That debate is not foreclosed by the decisions in these cases, said Stevens, since the challengers mounted a facial challenge of the state laws. The court's holdings, he continued, apply to all or most cases in which the state bans against assisted suicide might be applied. But that does not foreclose a different decision regarding particular terminally ill patients and their doctors.

Justice Stevens wanted to make clear his views regarding the limits that the Constitution places on the power of the states to punish physician-assisted suicide. Individual autonomy regarding the decision to end one's life is tempered by the value that a person's life has to others. For that reason, Justice Stevens sided with the court's judgment that the liberty protected by the Constitution does not include a categorical "right to commit suicide which itself includes a right to assistance in doing so" (quoting the court's rendition of the question presented) (*Quill III* and *Compassion IV* 117 S.Ct. at 2305). However, there are situations in which hastening death is constitutionally protected.

Stevens read the court's precedent in *Cruzan* quite broadly, much like Tucker had. The trial court, argued Stevens, in essence authorized affirmative conduct that would hasten Nancy Cruzan's death. The source of that decision, insisted Justice Stevens, was not just a common law rule allowing refusal of medical treatment. The source of that decision included a person's interest in dignity and in determining the character of the memories that will survive long after one's death. Thus, at least implicitly, the rationale in *Cruzan* was a fundamental right to make deeply personal decisions regarding not whether to die, but how. Moreover, avoiding intolerable pain and the indignity of living one's final days incapacitated and in agony is certainly "[a]t the heart of [the] liberty . . . to define one's own concept of existence, of meaning, of the universe, and of the mystery of human life," citing the exact language that Tucker relied on from *Casey* (*Quill III* and *Compassion IV* 117 S.Ct. at 2307).

As for the state interests, Justice Stevens analyzed four: the contributions that each person makes to society; preventing suicides that occur because of depression or coercion, encouraging better efforts at pain management and palliative care, and safeguarding the healing role of physicians. The interest in the contributions that an individual makes to society has less force when a terminally ill patient is faced with the decision of how to die, not whether to die. This does not mean that such persons have less value, Stevens argued; rather, it gives proper recognition to the individual's interest in choosing a final chapter that accords with her life story, instead of one that demeans her values and poisons memories of her. Moreover, the state's legitimate interest in preventing abuse does not apply to an individual who is not victimized by abuse, who is not suffering from depression, and who makes a rational and voluntary decision to seek assistance in dying. Additionally, palliative care does not relieve all pain and suffering. Thus, an individual adequately informed of all of the care alternatives might rationally choose assisted suicide, and the state's interest in preventing abuse is but minimally implicated for such an individual. Finally, contrary to the defendants' position that physician assistance in suicide is always contrary to the physician's healing role, Stevens cited the fact that accepted practice includes treatment withdrawal, withholding lifesaving procedures, and sedating the terminally ill, all of which point to the fact that physicians are already involved in hastening death. Thus, Justice Stevens supported the argument that in some cases a physician's refusal to dispense lethalities that would ease suffering and make an otherwise painful death more tolerable and dignified would be inconsistent with the physician's healing role.

To look at his concurring opinion overall, Justice Stevens appears to be advocating a sort of sliding scale for balancing individual versus state interests regarding the circumstances of one's death. He wrote, "The state interests supporting a general rule banning the practice of physician assisted suicide do not have the same force in all cases." That is because, properly viewed, the sanctity of life is not a collective interest, but rather an aspect of individual freedom, said Justice Stevens (*Quill III* and *Compassion IV* 117 S.Ct. at 2307).

Souter's Concurrences

Justice Souter offered the most expansive view of what Dworkin refers to as the party of principle. He said that the nation's history and traditions include not just the specific rights that have been recognized in the past but the "basic values" that are revealed when we interpret those rights to see which more general principles of political morality they represent. If we apply reasoned judgment to the assisted suicide issue, Souter argued, we can identify arguments of what he called "increasing forcefulness for recognizing some right to a doctor's help in suicide." There can be no stronger claim to a physician's assistance than at the time when death is imminent, a moral judgment implied by the state's own recognition of the legitimacy of medical procedures necessarily hastening the moment of impending death, for example, terminating life support and allowing pain relief that advances death. But Souter was not prepared to recognize a constitutional right "at this time"

(*Quill III* and *Compassion IV* 117 S.Ct. at 2293). He agreed with assisted suicide opponents that it could be impossible to regulate against abuse, citing studies from the Netherlands. Souter acknowledged the dispute over those studies, but said that legislatures are better positioned to take testimony and make factual findings regarding them.

Breyer's Concurrence

Justice Breyer disagreed with Justice O'Connor's concession to frame the issue before the court as to whether there is a right to commit suicide with another's assistance, yet he joined the remainder of her opinion. He would view the contested liberty interest as one involving personal control over the manner of death, professional medical assistance, and the avoidance of unnecessary and severe physical suffering—combined. He referred to the court's prior decisions, especially Justice Harlan's dissenting opinion in *Poe v. Ullman* (1961), which said that "certain interests" require particularly careful scrutiny of the state needs asserted to justify their abridgment. One such special interest may, said Justice Breyer, be a "right to die with dignity." But, he said, he would conclude that an element of any such right would be the interest in being free from state inflicted pain and suffering, and since the Washington and New York statutes do not impose such hardship, in the final analysis of these cases he agreed with the court's judgments.

To summarize, Rehnquist wrote the majority opinion in which Scalia, Thomas, Kennedy, and O'Connor joined. That opinion was grounded in a historical analysis that inquires whether the particular right in question has been historically recognized. This view of due process analysis is grounded in the judicial philosophy that inconsistency in judicial sanctions for seemingly similar liberty interests is preferable to judicial expansionism. Dworkin notes that probably only Scalia and Thomas subscribe to Rehnquist's historicist analysis (Dworkin 1997). That is suggested by their joint opinion with Souter in the 1992 *Casey* abortion decision endorsing the interpretive view of due process. Kennedy and O'Connor, Dworkin surmises, probably joined Rehnquist out of institutional courtesy, avoiding the inelegant result of a unanimous decision with no majority opinion.

O'Connor's concurring opinion said that changed circumstances might cause her to reconsider. And Ginsburg, who joined O'Connor's opinion rather than the court's, agreed. Breyer also left room for reconsideration. So did Souter. And Stevens would have found for assisted suicide proponents now, had the issue been properly raised to the court, he said. Thus five justices appear ready to recognize at least a constitutional limitation on the right os states to prohibit assisted suicide in every case. However, O'Connor, Ginsburg, and Breyer suggested they would limit such a judgment to relief from pain.

CONCLUSION

The *Los Angeles Times*, which like the *New York Times* had supported the reformers' court challenges, acknowledged in an editorial in the aftermath of the 9–0 decisions in *Quill* and *Glucksberg* that assisted suicide "is not a subject for clean constitutional resolution," but saw hope for its continued discussion and evolution in the fifty states. ("Justices' Ruling Won't End" 1997:B8)

Dr. Jack Kevorkian's lawyer indicated that the ruling wouldn't make any difference to Kevorkian (Hughes 1997). The International Anti-Euthanasia Task Force, while applauding the ruling, warned, "In declaring that assisted suicide is a matter for states to decide, the U.S. Supreme Court today rang the opening bell in the next battle over assisted suicide" (International Anti-Euthanasia Task Force 1997:1).

In Oregon, reformers like Barbara Coombs Lee predicted that voters would still support the ODDA, as they indeed would in a few months by the large 60 percent to 40 percent margin (Price and Mauro 1997:4A).

Clearly, the work of the reformers would be much different today had *Quill* and *Glucksberg* been decided in their favor. In the same way that *Roe v. Wade* (1973) made unnecessary the continued liberalization reforms in state after state that had characterized the immediate pre-*Roe* period, a pro-reformer opinion by the Rehnquist court would have changed the landscape of end-of-life care dramatically. Instead, even as the United States Congress has attempted to effectively block Oregon and other states from indeed being "laboratories" for the type of studied reform that Rehnquist refers to in the majority opinion, other states like Michigan and Maine have arisen to vote on Oregon-type reform, however unsuccessfully.

As it was, the Oregon reform remained untouched by the *Quill* and *Glucksberg* opinions. The major Supreme Court action for Oregon would come later in 1997, when the Supreme Court denied certiorari to the *Lee v. Oregon* (1997) case, which had blocked implementation of the ODDA. Thus, while 1997 began with oral arguments in the United States Supreme Court that indicated to all observing that the justices were not inclined to follow the path of the Ninth and Second Circuits, 1997 ended with the way clear for Oregon to begin use of the ODDA. The following chapter takes up that issue.

6

Building the Safe Harbor

THE IMPLEMENTATION OF THE ODDA

> The real story is that many of the stakeholders who got interested during the campaign have taken ownership of the issue according to their own organizational interests.
>
> —Oregon Death With Dignity Defense and Education Center General Counsel Eli Stutsman (Stutsman 2000)

> I feel it's our responsibility as a legislature to properly implement an initiative even though we don't agree with it.... It's an emotional issue. But when people realize you're not talking about a referral or a repeal, hopefully that will take the emotion out of it.
>
> —Oregon State Senate Judiciary Chair Neil Bryant (Hoover and Lednicer 1999)

INTRODUCTION

Between the time Measure 16 was passed in November 1994 and the time the first Oregon Death With Dignity Act (ODDA) death was reported in March 1998, the status of the Oregon assisted suicide reform remained in some doubt, as assisted suicide opponents made several maneuvers to invalidate the law. In Chapter 4, we chronicled the unsuccessful efforts in 1997 by anti-reform forces to repeal the ODDA by the same initiative process that was used to pass it. This and other legal maneuvers to thwart implementation of the ODDA began in earnest soon after the law's passage in 1994, and not until 1997 were the anti-reform forces finally defeated, paving the way for the first ODDA death. This chapter details the various stages in the efforts to block implementation. This description includes many overlapping events that occurred in multiple legal arenas. It also examines how the ODDA proponents were successful in keeping their revolutionary reform afloat in the face of multiple legal contests in multiple arenas of challenge over the course of these forty months. Table 6.1 provides a timeline for these years.

Table 6.1 Implementation Timeline

1994	Measure 16 passes (November) Litigation to block ODDA begins (November)
1995	Task Force to Improve the Care of Terminally Ill Oregonians begins (January)
1997	Oregon legislative session Litigation to block ODDA fails (October) Measure 51 (Repeal) Fails (November) Drug Enforcement Administration intervenes (November) Governor's Task Force begins
1998	Interim Oregon legislative session First ODDA Death (March) Congress: Hyde/Nickles I
1999	First-year Oregon Health Division report (February) Oregon legislative session (SB 491) Hyde/Nickles II begins
2000	Second-year Oregon Health Division report (February) Hyde/Nickles II continues

LITIGATION AGAINST THE ODDA

Fifteen days after the November election in 1994, several plaintiffs filed an action seeking a judicial declaration that the ODDA violates the United States Constitution, and a court order blocking state officials from recognizing or acting under the law (*Lee v. Harderoad*, later changed to *Lee v. Oregon* 1994).

The plaintiffs were represented by the lead counsel for the National Right to Life Committee, Inc. The plaintiffs claimed that an assisted suicide regime for the terminally ill would create a class of people who are not protected from the traditional criminal barrier against assisted suicide. NRL lawyers claimed that the ODDA violated the equal protection and due process rights of terminally ill people who might feel coerced to use the law. They further argued that the ODDA violated statutory and First Amendment rights of individuals and organizations who would not wish to participate in the law. They also claimed the law violated the Americans with Disabilities Act.

In the United States District Court for the District of Oregon, Chief Judge Michael Hogan ruled in favor of the claimants. "The problem," Chief Judge Hogan reasoned, "is that the procedures designed to differentiate between the competent and incompetent are not sufficient," which undermines the basic premise underlying the state's argument that the ODDA is constitutional: that only competent persons can consent to the drug overdose *(Lee v. State of Oregon* 1994, at 10) Moreover, the judge added:

> Measure 16 withholds from terminally ill citizens the same protections from suicide the majority enjoys. In the process, it has lowered standards and reduced protections to a degree that there is little assurance that only competent terminally ill persons will voluntarily die. The majority has not accepted this situation for themselves, and there is no rational basis for imposing it on the terminally ill. (*Lee v. State of Oregon* 1994, at 21)

First by restraining order, then by preliminary injunction, and finally, on August 3, 1995, by permanent injunction, Judge Hogan blocked the Oregon District Attorney and the State Board of Medical Examiners from recognizing any exceptions from law or regulation created by the ODDA (*Lee v. State of Oregon* 1995).

ODDA supporters quickly appealed their case to the Court of Appeals for the Ninth Circuit. On July 9, 1996, a three-judge panel of appeals court judges heard arguments regarding the permanent injunction.

Seven months later, on February 3, 1997, the judges ruled 3–0 that no plaintiff had successfully alleged a "particularized concrete and imminent injury in fact" to challenge the constitutionality of the ODDA *(Lee v. State of Oregon* 1997). The judges added a long list of other constitutional requirements regarding the jurisdiction of the courts (e.g., "premature adjudication," "entanglement in abstract disagreements," "standing," "ripeness," "sufficient injury or endangerment," and "case or controversy"). The unanimous court characterized the plaintiffs' alleged injuries as based upon a "chain of speculative contingencies" *(Lee v. State of Oregon* 1997, at 1388). In the absence of the threshold requirement of plaintiffs' standing, the District Court could not proceed to exercise its powers. Accordingly, Chief Judge Hogan's judgment enjoining the implementation of the ODDA was vacated, although stays were granted pending further review (*Lee v. State of Oregon* 1997, at 1392).

The National Right to Life Committee plaintiffs appealed to the United States Supreme Court, which, on October 14, 1997, denied further reconsideration of the case. The Supreme Court (No. 96-1824) remanded the case to the Court of Appeals for the official order to lift the injunction and dismiss the case. The Court of Appeals vacated District Court Judge Hogan's injunction and ordered Hogan to dismiss the case on October 27, 1999, and on that date, the ODDA went into effect.

REFORMERS' APPROACH: KEEPING THE FIRES GOING

During this time, the implementation of the ODDA was moving forward on different fronts, however haltingly. The ODDA reformers, in order to see their ideas through to full implementation, maintained their involvement through all stages of the process. These stages included tracking the work of creating guidelines and rules for implementing the ODDA; tracking the activities of, and lobbying, lawmakers in Washington, DC; commenting on OHD reports on the ODDA; and participating in the legislative process of clarifying the ODDA. The details of these stages in implementation are reported in later chapters. The main point of this chapter is to establish the implementation strategy of reformers as but one step in a broad reform plan they mapped out back in 1993.

On the surface, it may appear that the central figures behind passage of Measure 16 were closed out once implementation efforts commenced. For example, no one from the Measure 16 campaign was invited to join the Task Force to Improve the Care of Terminally-Ill Oregonians. Yet this turn of events was in fact anticipated by Measure 16 organizers. In an interview, Eli Stutsman stated that many terms in the ODDA had purposely been left vague (Stutsman 1996). He explained that part of the strategy for using law to generate social change includes permitting room for people to clarify the language of the law to fit the needs of those who will implement and use it. In other words, not only were Measure 16 strategists aware that many reform efforts fail because a small group tries to exert too much control at the expense of including the actual people whose varying interests are affected by proposals for change, they actually built this contingency into their reform framework.

Stutsman had faulted reformers in other states for trying to include every contingency in the law they wrote. The wholly legalistic approach to writing California's Proposition 161, for example, backfired, in Stutsman's opinion, by opening the door for the opposition to lead the proponents into defending the specifics of the law during the time when they should have been championing the reasons for the law. In Stutsman's view, most of the people who were likely to vote actually supported the California proposition, but the proponents were unable to remain on-message while they defended against the opponents' attacks. Late in the campaign, the opponents' most general argument—that even those who support the concept of physician-assisted suicide should reject the California proposal—gained in salience and helped narrow the margin of support. And because reform leaders in California had written their law as a constitutional amendment (which could be amended only by another constitutional amendment) there seemed to be little chance of salvaging it.

By contrast, while some commentators faulted the Oregon law for seeming vague, its authors and primary backers, having learned from the California defeat, decided that fighting for a simple, understated statute would push the movement beyond its efforts to get a law on the books, and into the actual medical practice of providing prescriptions for the purpose of ending life to qualified patients with terminal disease. Once the law went into effect, reformers maintained pressure for its full enactment, yet remained somewhat detached from efforts of stakeholders to hash out the details of implementation. Rather than try to control these efforts, the reformers stood by and let others deal with areas of the law that they perceived to be too ambiguous. The reformers moved in only when it seemed that access to the law might be constrained. Eschewing the drive to win every battle, they picked their battles carefully, and kept their eyes on their long-range goal of assuring patient access.

This strategy was effective because it allowed ideological conflicts to be expressed in and become part of the law. The negotiations surrounding SB 491 are the best example. The right to opt out of the ODDA now includes the power to sanction employees and agents who violate policies prohibiting involvement in the ODDA, yet those same powers are carefully circumscribed so as to ensure that all patients and health care professionals are free to use the law outside the context of their relationships with conscientious objectors. The point to be taken from this discussion is that the strategy of maintaining pressure for change, while leaving room for others to hash out the details, differentiates the Oregon reformers from others before them, and this strategy appears to account for the changes we see in Oregon.

TASK FORCE FORMATION

Soon after Oregon voters passed the ODDA in November 1994, the Oregon Health Division formed a work group to craft emergency administrative rules. The "Death with Dignity Task Force" included administrators from the Oregon Health Division (OHD) and the Medical Examiner's office, and representatives from the Oregon Hospice Association, the Oregon Nurses Association, the Oregon Association of Hospitals, the Oregon Health Care Association, the Oregon Board of Pharmacy, and the Oregon Senior and Disabled Services Division, as well as chief petitioners of Measure 16.

There was a sense of urgency because the ODDA mandates OHD involvement. The mandate is to "make rules to facilitate the collection of information regarding compliance with this Act" and to "annually review a sample of records maintained pursuant to the Act" (Oregon Revised Statutes 127.865). Adoption of emergency rules commenced with incorporation of definitions from Measure 16, documentation requirements, data collection forms, and assurances of confidentiality and shielding from liability. But the proposed rules were held in abeyance when Chief Judge Michael Hogan enjoined the ODDA in late December 1994. Instead of disbanding the work group, however, most members agreed to continue meeting under the auspices of the Center for Ethics in Health Care at Oregon Health Sciences University.

THE TASK FORCE TO IMPROVE THE CARE OF TERMINALLY-ILL OREGONIANS

In January 1995, the Center for Ethics in Health Care at Oregon Health Sciences University convened the Task Force to Improve the Care of Terminally-Ill Oregonians. Besides its overall goal to promote excellent care of the dying, the Task Force took on the duty of formulating professional standards and regulations for the eventual use of the ODDA.

The Task Force included physicians, representatives of hospitals and other health institutions, representatives of the Oregon Bar, the Oregon Board of Medical Examiners, the Oregon Board of Pharmacy, the Oregon Health Division (OHD), the Oregon Hospice Association (OHA), the Oregon Medical Association (OMA), the Oregon Nurses Association, the Oregon Psychiatric and Psychological Associations, and the Oregon State Pharmacists Association. Our interviews with seven members of the Task Force have aided in illuminating the Task Force's approach.

The Task Force identified its overall goal as "to thoughtfully consider how to improve end-of-life care in Oregon." The Task Force stated four goals as constituting its mission: to "share information, experience and understanding of available resources for the care of terminally ill Oregonians"; to "facilitate the development of professional standards relating to the Death With Dignity Act"; to "develop and coordinate educational resources on all aspects of the competent and compassionate care of terminally-ill patients"; and to "foster relationships and networking on issues related to compassionate care of the terminally-ill' (The Task Force to Improve the Care of Terminally-Ill Oregonians [hereinafter The Task Force to Improve] 1998:3). The Task Force and its subcommittees and working groups began meeting in 1995.

The Task Force's work was published as a guidebook, *The Oregon Death With Dignity Act: A Guidebook for Health Care Providers*, in March 1998. The guidebook "tries to tease through some of the very challenging issues and explain the tensions that exist for a provider trying to work through these issues with patients and families," said Dr. Patrick Dunn, chairman of the panel that produced the guide (Associated Press 1998a). The report represented months of consensus building and careful analysis of implementation issues by the group of physicians, other health providers, ethicists, and attorneys.

The guidebook suggests how to respond when a patient asks about physician-assisted suicide. Citing AMA ethical guidelines, the Task Force asserts that physicians have the obligation to openly discuss the patient's concerns, feelings, and desires about the dying process regardless of the physician's moral views on physician-assisted suicide. To help the patient make rational choices about dying, physicians should discuss the range of available options for end-of-life care, including advance directives, do-not-resuscitate orders, and hospice or palliative care (The Task Force to Improve 1998:5). The guidebook describes the range of actions a physician may take when asked about physician-assisted suicide.

After exploring the issues and alternatives, physicians may decide to honor a request for lethal medication, they may decide that participating in such deaths violates their personal values and/or professional ethics, or they may decide that there are reasons to reject a particular patient's request. What is important here is that the Task Force guides physicians to consider their own moral and ethical principles as fully as they consider the patient's. This is known under the guidelines as "conscientious practice." The guidebook devotes a full chapter to the subject of conscientious practice.

The Task Force grounds its discussion of conscientious practice in language from the ODDA: "No health care provider shall be under any duty, whether by contract, by statute or by any other legal requirement to participate in the provision to a qualified patient of medication to end his/her life in a humane and dignified manner" (ORS 127.885 §4.01[4]).

In order to effectuate this provision, the Task Force declared that "All health care providers have a right to know whether their care of patients involves actions that would be morally objectionable for them" (Task Force to Improve 1998:8), including the right to know whether they would be participating in physician-assisted suicide. The right to know extends to institutions and health care systems, as well as to hospital staff and pharmacists.

The right to know raises several potential conflicts. The Task Force addressed the patient's right to know what options are legally available, the patient's right to privacy, the institution's or system's right to prohibit its agents and employees from participating in the practice, and the patient's right to continuity of care in the event a transfer is needed from a provider unwilling to participate in physician-assisted suicide to another one who is. As stated above, all providers have a right not to be unknowing participants. Nevertheless, the guidelines state, "attending physicians must respect the confidentiality of the patient's request unless otherwise waived" (The Task Force to Improve 1998:38). Moreover, systems that choose not to participate should notify patients and providers, including prospective employees, in advance. The Task Force also suggests that non-participating health systems may need to develop policies regarding transfers. Related suggestions are the development of multidisciplinary forums for staff discussions about controversial procedures and practices, and processes for resolving conflicts.

A reading of the Task Force guidebook suggests that the toughest conflict to resolve is between a provider's desire not to discuss the ODDA with an inquiring patient, and the obligation to openly explore the patient's concerns, feelings, and desires about dying. Again the Task Force cites the AMA's 1992 report, "Decisions Near the End of Life," which urges physicians to examine "the needs behind the demand" for an active end to life (The Task Force to Improve 1998:7). The guidebook stops short of stating that providers must have this discussion, but it does state that providers "must" transfer care, for "to do otherwise would be abandonment" (The Task Force to Improve 1998:7). To meet this burden the provider may decline to find a physician who will fulfill the patient's request, but he or she "must not hinder the transfer" (The Task Force to Improve 1998:7).

Thus far we have reported on the Task Force guidelines regarding a physician's obligation to communicate, from the standpoint of the patient's right to be informed of the options legally available, and the physician's duty to discuss the underlying concerns of patients who inquire about the ODDA. Another reason the guidelines call for open communication is to assess the degree to which psychological or existential distress may be affecting the patient's decision making.

The ODDA mandates a mental health evaluation if the attending or consulting physician believes that the patient may suffer from a psychiatric or psychological disorder, or depression causing impaired judgment. The Task Force guidebook includes a chapter on mental health consultation and referral. The chapter states: "The mental health consultation as outlined by the Act is a form of competency evaluation, specifically focused on capacity to make the decision to hasten death by self-administering a lethal medication" (Task Force to Improve 1998:30).

The guidebook warns about the difficulty of assessing impaired judgment in terminally ill patients. Sadness, hopelessness, and difficulty experiencing pleasure are mild psychological symptoms that can be expected when patients are given a terminal prognosis. These are also characteristic symptoms of patients coping with the physical limitations that accompany illness. Other symptoms may be feelings of isolation, guilt, low self-worth, anger, and the sense of being a burden on others (The Task Force to Improve 1998:31). The role for psychiatrists and psychologists is to determine whether any of these symptoms may limit the patient's competency.

"Mental disorders, knowledge deficits, and coercion" are factors that limit competency (The Task Force to Improve 1998:30). To determine whether any of these factors exist, the guidebook encourages physicians to review the patient's medical records, to discuss the patient's medical history with the attending physician, and to assess the patient through personal interviews. Understanding the patient's overall situation should be the goal of the mental health professional. This includes the factors underlying the patient's request for medication to end his or her life. According to the guidebook, these factors may include "the patient's access to or attitudes about medical care, communication with the attending physician, his or her quality of life, belief system, life history, financial and family issues" (The Task Force to Improve 1998:30).

According to the guidebook, one of the functions of the mental health professional can be to counter negative thinking and reframe alternatives for the patient. Patients who are attempting to cope with loss of control may have a distorted sense of their options. Other factors that may affect a patient's ability to think flexibly include prior experiences with death, personality factors, and attitudes of family members. Regarding the latter, the mental health evaluation should include interviews with caregivers and family members (with the patient's consent) (The Task Force to Improve 1998:30).

The guidebook devotes a chapter to the issues of family needs and concerns (Chapter 6). This was a point of debate during the Measure 16 campaign. Some opponents faulted the ODDA for failing to include a requirement that family members be notified of a patient's request for medicine to end life. The proponents of the ODDA rejected such a requirement for the reason that in some cases it could inhibit patients from using the law. To this end, the ODDA only requires physicians to encourage patients to notify family, but the patient can decline to do so. Other references to family in the ODDA include a provision that a family member can be one of the two witnesses to the patient's written request, and a provision granting family members the same legal immunity from prosecution as health professionals have under the act for being present when the patient ingests medicine to end life.

The Task Force defines the term "family" to include all of a terminally ill individual's most intimate relationships, including spouses, common law partners, unrelated living companions, close friends, children, and family of origin (The Task Force to Improve 1998:17). The Task Force acknowledges the centrality of patient self-determination in the decision to end life with the help of a physician, yet it states further:

> The Act reads as if the doctor-patient relationship exists in isolation. In fact, patients exist in a social network, and that network provides a foundation that empowers the patient to exercise autonomy. Family members can provide dialogue, feedback, and knowledge of [a] patient's values and priorities when a patient is considering an important decision. Physician-assisted suicide impacts the patient's intimate friends and family, whether they know about it in advance or not. (The Task Force to Improve 1998:17)

According to the guidebook, family notification may lead to reassurance that a patient is not an emotional or a financial burden to family members.

Notification may also prevent complicating the grieving process. It may also prevent family members from unwittingly becoming involved in the suicide if they discover the patient before death has occurred. Most important, family notification may enhance the process of gaining closure if conflicts can be resolved, final conversations can occur, and services for honoring the deceased can be arranged (The Task Force to Improve 1998:17).

Physicians are urged to encourage engaging a person's closest social network early in the dialogue. For those patients who do want family involvement, the guidebook encourages discussion of whether family should be present when the prescription is ingested. If family members will be present, the guidebook calls upon the attending physician to explain the potential complications and what to do and not do if they occur. The guidebook also encourages a plan for notifying the physician, who can notify the funeral home that the death was expected and that he or she will sign the death certificate, so that investigation by the medical examiner will be avoided (The Task Force to Improve 1998:18).

The Task Force's caution to avoid an investigation by the medical examiner is grounded in the attending physician's obligation to document ODDA deaths and report them to the Oregon Health Division (OHD), and the obligation of all health professionals who hold state licenses to report incompetence or unprofessional conduct (The Task Force to Improve 1998:43;40). The ODDA requires the OHD to make rules to facilitate the collection of information regarding compliance with the ODDA and to annually review a sample of records maintained pursuant to the act.

The OHD has taken three steps to meet these requirements. First, it has written administrative rules regarding reporting requirements. Second, the OHD has created several standard reporting forms. Third, the Health Division has designed a questionnaire for all prescribing physicians to be conducted in person or by telephone after the death certificate is received. The guidebook notes that while the physician questionnaire is not specified in the ODDA, "the Health Division has the authority to conduct special morbidity and mortality studies under which such a survey would be conducted" (The Task Force to Improve 1998:44).

Finally, the guidebook declares that "The Act does not assign enforcement authority to the Division and is silent on what the Division should do when non-compliance is encountered" (The Task Force to Improve 1998:44). Under the guidelines, individuals who violate the Act will be reported to the appropriate licensing board. A separate chapter is devoted to professional non-compliance (Chapter 12). That chapter states that "The Board of Medical Examiners does not consider good faith compliance with the Act [to constitute] unprofessional conduct" (The Task Force to Improve 1998:40). However, the obligation to report non-compliance is established by prior law and extant ethical guidelines (The Task Force to Improve 1998:40).

We have described a weighty effort to consider issues central to the implementation of the ODDA. The Task Force to Improve the Care of Terminally-Ill Oregonians created a useful guidebook for health care providers whose practice may be affected by the decision of Oregon voters to permit a patient to request, and a physician to deliver, a lethal dose of medication which both physician and patient know is intended to hasten impending death. Central to these guidelines are issues of patient self-determination, conscientious practice, assurances of voluntariness, reporting requirements, and remedies for non-compliance. We have detailed nearly all the chapters in the guidebook. Other chapters present elaborations upon the primary issues we've detailed. These issues include access to comfort care, hospice, and palliative care (Chapter 4); the roles and responsibilities of the attending physician and consulting physician (Chapter 7); pharmacy information (Chapter 10) and emergency department and emergency medical services (Chapter 11); and issues of civil liability and negligence (Chapter 15).

Overall, the Task Force sought to represent a wide range of experience, perspectives, responsibilities, and opinions regarding end-of-life care. It noted in its final report: "Without endorsing or opposing the principles embodied in the Death With Dignity Act, the Task Force has developed this guidebook as a collective response to its enactment" (The Task Force to Improve 1998:3).

Although the guidelines were generally acclaimed by assisted suicide supporters, some opponents of the ODDA denounced their very existence. For example, Dr. Greg Hamilton, a Portland psychiatrist and head of Physicians for Compassionate Care, which opposes the ODDA, said that in his mind guidelines for an immoral practice are not helpful. "I suppose in the death camps in various military movements there have been rules and guidelines about how to carry out the procedures at death camps, but that doesn't make it right," said Hamilton (National Public Radio 1998a).

The reformers, on the other hand, praised its progress, and its marshaling of people with disparate interests and viewpoints into a collaborative and pragmatic enterprise. Hannah Davidson, who was director of medical and education programs for the Oregon Death With Dignity Legal Defense and Education Center, said, "They've done a really professional job of creating a document that will generate the kind of data that everyone has been asking for, but at the same time protect the patient's confidentiality." Similar sentiments were expressed by an *Oregonian* reporter who observed that passage of the ODDA both forced wider thought about the reality that some patients would rather end their lives than endure the dying process, and brought together a task force whose members were unlikely to collaborate otherwise (Hoover 1998).

Finally, the leader of the Task Force, Dr. Susan Tolle, director of the Center for Ethics in Health Care at Oregon Sciences University, which convened the Task Force, praised the work:

> By convening 25 health care organizations—including competing health systems with different views on assisted suicide—to grapple with end-of-life care, the task force did more than produce the country's first practical guidebook on the practice: It uncovered gaps in end-of-life care where more change is needed. And it galvanized some organizations on the task force to better care for the dying. (Hoover 1998)

RULE PROMULGATION

The day after 60 percent of Oregon voters affirmed the Oregon Death With Dignity Act in November 1997, the OHD returned to the project it had begun three years earlier to write rules fulfilling its mandate under the ODDA. But by contrast to the situation in 1994, when no one really knew how implementing the ODDA should proceed, in 1997 there were key people in the health care community who were fulfilling numerous roles in institutionalizing the voter initiative. People charged with promulgating state rules were also members of the Task Force to Improve the Care of Terminally-Ill Oregonians. They had worked closely with other professionals whose practices are directly affected by the ODDA. With production of a guidebook for health care providers well under way, promulgating rules for assuring compliance with the terms of the act could proceed with greater assurances that they would be followed.

To begin with, many of the definitions contained in the ODDA were incorporated into the OHD rules. But two changes were made, the most significant of which was the definition of who may use the act. Under the ODDA definition of who may initiate a written request for medication, there is a requirement that the person must be "capable." However, in the language of the ODDA "capable" is defined in terms of who is "not incapable." A patient is defined as "incapable" if he or she "lacks the ability to make and communicate health care decisions to health care providers" (ORS 127.800 §1.01[6]). The OHD was dissatisfied with this approach to the determination of capability, and instead chose to determine who may use the act in terms of who is "capable," not who is "incapable." Under the OHD rules,

> "Capable" means that in the opinion of a court or in the opinion of the patient's attending physician or consulting physician, psychiatrist or psychologist, a patient has the ability to make and communicate health care decisions to health care providers, including communication through persons familiar with the patient's manner of communicating if those persons are available. (OAR 333–009–0000 [4])

The second change involved the definition of "counseling." Under the terms of the ODDA, counseling means "a consultation" (ORS 127.800 §1.01[6]). The OHD was dissatisfied that a single consultation could render a patient eligible to use the Act, so it adopted slightly different language which says that counseling means "one or more consultations as necessary" (OAR 333–009–0000 [6]).

Public hearings on the administrative rules proposed by OHD were held on March 20, 1998. In attendance were representatives who appeared on behalf of the chief petitioners of the ODDA, the Oregon Medical Association, the Oregon Catholic Conference, and the opposition group Physicians for Compassionate Care. Each of these groups provided oral or written comment on the proposed regulations.

In general, the hearing raised easy issues regarding clarification of the administrative rules. The OMA representatives wanted assurance that providing access to patient records was just a secondary, not a required, method of providing the OHD with the information it needs to monitor ODDA deaths. The OHD rules require access to patient records only in the event that an attending physician who writes a prescription for medication to end life elects not to fully and accurately complete, date, and sign a report form developed by the OHD (OAR 333–009–0010). Representatives from the Oregon Catholic Conference recommended minor additions to the demographic data collected on the reporting forms. But they also added that their comments "should not be construed as support for the adoption of rules to implement Measure 16" (Oregon Health Division 1998:4). They objected to the process of adopting administrative rules implementing the reporting requirements under Measure 16, because, they testified, "the rules institutionalize and attempt to 'professionalize' the act of physician-assisted suicide" (Oregon Health Division 1998:3–4). The objections were entered into the record, but the rule-making process was completed.

To summarize the rules, a physician who writes a prescription pursuant to the ODDA must submit several items to the OHD. The first is a copy of the patient's written request for medication to end life. The second is a signed and dated report, entitled "Request for Medication to End Life, Attending

Physician's Report and Medical Records Documentation," which is either completed in full or indicates that the required information can be retrieved from the patient's medical records. The third is a signed and dated copy of the consulting physician's report. The fourth is a signed and dated copy of the counseling referral report, if the patient is referred to counseling. In addition, physicians may be asked to complete a confidential form which solicits information concerning the circumstances of the patient's death. Physicians who receive the form are required to complete and return it (OAR 333–009–0010[1]). Next, any health care provider who dispenses medication pursuant to the ODDA must submit to the OHD a copy of the dispensing record, which must include the patient's name; the prescribing physician's name and phone number; the dispensing health provider's name, address, and phone number; the name and quantity of the medication dispensed; and the date it was dispensed (OAR 333–009–0010[2]).

Along the way, other rules had to be hashed out for including pharmacists in the opt-out provisions of the ODDA. The Oregon State Pharmacist's Association, concerned with the ability of individual pharmacists and pharmaceutical organizations to avoid participating in the act, wanted prescriptions for life-ending medication to state their purpose on the label. The OMA objected to the pharmacists' proposal on grounds it could jeopardize patient privacy and interfere with patient-physician confidentiality. The medical association filed suit, but the governor's office stepped in and convinced the two sides to compromise.

The result of these efforts is that patients have only two ways of receiving medication to end life. The first is to receive medication directly from the prescribing physician. This method of dispensation is likely to be rare because, according to the Oregon Board of Medical Examiners, only about 100 of the 11,000 physicians in Oregon are licensed to dispense prescription medicine. The more common way to receive medicine to end life is to have the prescribing physician communicate the request to a dispensing health care provider. The main point is to prevent a situation in which a patient presents a prescription directly to a pharmacist. The rationale is that pharmacists who do not want to be involved in physician-assisted suicide should never be confronted with having to refuse a patient on the spot. This issue was also taken up by the Task Force to Improve the Care of Terminally-Ill Oregonians, which stated in its guidebook:

> When an attending physician writes a prescription for medication pursuant to the Act, personal communication with a pharmacist in order to determine his/her willingness to dispense it will help insure confidentiality and avoid presentation of the prescription to a pharmacist unwilling

> or unable to participate. We strongly encourage this advance communication to work out any necessary details, to allow the attending physician and pharmacist to concur regarding any questions about drug, dose or route of administration, and to discuss important patient medication counseling issues. (The Task Force to Improve 1998:33)

As we alluded to above, Governor John Kitzhaber played another key role in the rule-formation process. Kitzhaber convened a work group of officials from agencies who would be involved in implementing the ODDA. The governor's task force included many people from the same organizations and state agencies that developed the guidebook by the Task Force to Improve the Care of Terminally-Ill Oregonians. The governor's group met in January and February of 1998, and the guidebook was released in March 1998.

From the beginning, the group members agreed that they would not use the forum to rehash the arguments debated during the campaign. Nor would they reduce the scope of the ODDA, as twice passed by voters. In an interview, an aide to the governor reported that everyone was briefed that as members of the governor's task force, they were there to execute the voters' will and make it work. "Everyone stayed in bounds after that was established" (Gibson 1998). Kitzhaber's goal was to generate debate on how to make the law work. His sense was that the focus of the group's work was less about assisting suicide than about carrying out the will of Oregon voters.

Kitzhaber's public stature and medical credibility impacted the implementation process significantly. He is a former emergency room doctor and is highly respected by the medical profession. He is also highly respected by the electorate. Kitzhaber could talk the talk with physicians on the task force he convened, and when he reminded the task force members that as leader of the executive branch his job was to execute the will of voters, they honored that and worked with him (Gibson 1998).

Kitzhaber had in fact voted against Measure 16, and during the 1994 campaign he had openly opposed the measure. But in a 1997 interview with Gail Kinsey Hill of *The Oregonian,* Kitzhaber revealed that it was not the concept of assisted suicide that he opposed, it was the potential implementation issues and the tactics of both sides in the campaign (Hill 1997a). Revealing for the first time that he personally sympathizes with the concept, he said he thought the ad campaigns in 1994 were atrocious and failed to get to the fundamental issues (Hill 1997a). Yet once voters passed the law, Kitzhaber wanted to "come to terms with those implementation questions" (Hill 1997a:A20). He criticized the Oregon legislature for referring the law back to voters instead of working to improve it. "There are some huge ethical and medical and legal questions about this, and they're not going to go away," Kitzhaber said. "They're with us as long as people continue to live longer, as we continue to make advances in medical science" (Hill 1997a:A20).

This being the governor's sentiment, he made it clear that he would not allow state officials to dilute the law as twice passed by voters. The governor's task force completed its work in February 1997, and in March the OHD conducted public hearings on its administrative rules and adopted them. The Task Force to Improve the Care of Terminally-Ill Oregonians published its guidebook in March, and on March 27, the first death under the ODDA was reported. Governor Kitzhaber also put lawmakers on notice that their attempts to dilute the law would be vetoed. This was the state of affairs when Senator Bryant formed a work group to clarify implementation issues in the law in 1999. The threat of a governor's veto was an important chit for reformers, for while they were willing to negotiate, they could rest assured that access to the law could not be thwarted.

THE DEA INTERVENES

Once Judge Hogan's injunction was overturned on October 27, 1997, and Measure 51 was soundly defeated about a week later, anti-suicide forces turned to the United States Drug Enforcement Administration (DEA). They received a favorable ruling by the administrator of the DEA, Thomas A. Constantine, who agreed with the sentiment of many members of Congress that administering a drug to deliberately cause someone to die is not a "legitimate medical purpose" within the meaning of the Controlled Substances Act. Barbiturates—the physician-assisted suicide movement's drugs of choice—are regulated under the Controlled Substances Act.

Constantine's letter stated that the DEA

> has conducted a thorough review of prior administrative cases in which physicians have dispensed controlled substances for other than a "legitimate medical purpose." Based on that review, we are persuaded that delivering, dispensing or prescribing a controlled substance with the intent of assisting a suicide would not be under any current definition a "legitimate medical purpose." As a result, the activities that you described in your letter to us would be, in our opinion, a violation of the [Controlled Substances Act]. (Constantine 1997:2)

A few months later, however, Attorney General Janet Reno exercised her oversight of the DEA and issued a conflicting opinion. Reno ruled that the Controlled Substances Act is enforceable against the use of controlled substances for assisted suicide only to the extent that states have not authorized assisted suicide:

> The State of Oregon has reached the considered judgment that physician-assisted suicide should be authorized under narrow conditions and in compliance with certain detailed procedures. Under these circumstances, we have concluded that the [Controlled Substances Act] does not authorize DEA to prosecute, or to revoke the DEA registration of, a physician who has assisted in a suicide in compliance with Oregon law. (Sutin 1998)

Justice Department Official Joseph Onek explained:

> We found that in looking at the statute [that it was] unlikely that Congress would have intended that this difficult moral, social, and medical issue would be resolved by the DEA. . . . We are concerned that this legislation will embroil the DEA in decisions about the use of pain medication for terminally ill patients which it is poorly equipped to make. (National Public Radio 1998b)

CONGRESSIONAL LEGISLATION TO BLOCK THE ODDA: HYDE/NICKLES I

On the very day in 1998 that Reno sent her letter, House Judiciary Chairman Henry Hyde (R-Illinois) introduced the Lethal Drug Abuse Prevention Act of 1998 (H.R. 4006). Hyde is widely renowned as a longtime pro-life supporter and author of the Hyde Amendment, which cut off federal Medicaid funds for abortions; he would later be prominent for his role in leading the impeachment effort against President Clinton in 1998 and 1999.

At the same time, the United States Senate considered S.B. 2151, introduced by Senator Don Nickles (R-Oklahoma). Hearings were held on that bill on July 3. In a 1998 interview, Nickles staff aide Debbie Price explained that Nickles had a record on legislation circumscribing assisted suicide. That record includes the bill that prohibits using federal monies to fund assisted suicide. Thus, sponsorship of the 1998 bill was "a natural extension of his previous work."

The Pain Relief Promotion Act was intended to conflict with the one-of-a-kind Oregon law that permits federally controlled substances to be used in physician-assisted suicide. The Pain Relief Act would have punished physicians who prescribe federally regulated drugs with intent to cause a patient's death. To prevent a chilling effect on end-of-life care, the Pain Relief Promotion Act would also have legalized aggressive pain management, specifically, the clinical administration of large quantities of drugs that control pain but pose a risk of death. The prevailing clinical and legal bias is that death is a bad outcome. Therefore, intending to cause death is criminal.

The Hyde/Nickles bills were not the first time that Congress had acted on the issue of assisted suicide since the Measure 16 vote. In 1997, Congress had almost unanimously approved the Assisted Suicide Funding Restriction Act (42 U.S.C. §14401 et seq.) stipulating that federal funds, health facilities, and health programs are not to be used for assisted suicide or euthanasia. Signing this bill into law, President Clinton said it "will allow the Federal Government to speak with a clear voice in opposing these practices"; he warned that "to endorse assisted suicide would set us on a disturbing and perhaps dangerous path" (Doerflinger 1999).

Hearings were held on July 14, 1998, at which time a variety of witnesses testified. In opening the hearings on July 14, 1998, Hyde stated:

> I introduced H.R. 4006, the Lethal Drug Abuse Prevention Act of 1998 ... to clarify that intentionally dispensing or distributing a controlled substance with the purpose of causing the suicide or euthanasia of any individual is not a legitimate medical purpose and will subject an applicant or registrant to revocation or suspension of their DEA registration to provide and dispense controlled substances.
>
> I was concerned that doctors not be hindered in their palliative care of patients, because provisions in this bill may present a situation where pain alleviation that results in death is confused with actions that are taken to assist in a patient's suicide. (Hyde 1998)

American Medical Association (AMA) President Thomas Reardon brought the considerable influence of the AMA against the bill:

> The AMA is sympathetic to the concerns that have motivated the introduction of this measure. We agree with the sponsors that physician-assisted suicide is ethically incompatible with the physician's role as healer. Yet the AMA, after considerable internal consideration, has decided that we must oppose the bill before the Subcommittee today. That decision is based on a disagreement over means, rather than ends.
>
> We understand that the sponsors are attempting to assure that no controlled substances are available to persons seeking suicide. In fact, however, we fear the "real world" consequences of the bill would be to discourage the kind of appropriate aggressive palliative care that can dissuade patients in pain from seeking just such an early death. Recent promising

> advancements in the care of people at the end of life could be set back dramatically, to the detriment of patient care. In addition, the AMA believes that expanding the DEA's authority in this matter would be an unacceptable federal intrusion over matters of state law regarding the practice of medicine. (Reardon 1998)

Herbert Hendin testified in favor of the bill. Hendin, a psychiatrist who believes that reformers underestimated greatly the prevalence of treatable depression among those requesting suicide, was the medical director of the American Society for the Prevention of Suicide and a critic of Dutch euthanasia practices, as we will discuss more deeply in Chapter 7. He stated:

> Surprisingly, and contrary to the expectations of its proponents, sanction for assisted suicide and euthanasia increases the power and control of doctors, not patients. This happens because the doctor can suggest assisted suicide or euthanasia, which has a powerful impact on patients' decisions, can ignore patient ambivalence, not present suitable alternatives, and even end the lives of patients who have not requested it. (Hendin 1998)

Hendin also took a swipe at the AMA, which was not supporting the legislation.

> Sanction of assisted suicide is therefore bad for patients, bad for medicine, and bad for society. The American Medical Association recognized this in the strong amicus curiae brief opposing assisted suicide it submitted to the U.S. Supreme Court. Yet it is difficult for the AMA to be of help to us with the legislation you are considering. Some of the AMA leadership are uncomfortable at supporting government restriction of doctors' privileges to prescribe controlled substances even in response to a practice that the AMA condemns. This seems to be a case where public interest must prevail over the understandable but nevertheless parochial interests of some in the profession to be free of outside regulation. (Hendin 1998)

Also speaking against the bill was the American Pharmaceutical Association, which feared the vulnerability of pharmacists to DEA investigation and prosecution because of the wide net the bill employed. A past president of the organization stated:

> I understand that HR 4006, the Lethal Drug Abuse Prevention Act of 1998, was developed to eliminate health care professional involvement in suicide. The impact of this law, however, will not be in the realm of assisted

> suicide or the voluntary termination of life by terminally ill patients. The impact, rather, will be felt by every pharmacist, every physician, every health care provider and the patients they serve. Each one of us will feel the impact of these regulations—and see the physical and emotional impact of the further degradation of our already abysmal management of chronic pain. (Knowlton 1998)

Governor John Kitzhaber of Oregon testified at the hearing, warning that the bill would displace the role of Oregon—and other states—as the appropriate bodies to determine what is standard medical practice:

> Whether intended or not, H.R. 4006, through its amendment of the Controlled Substances Act, "displaces the states as the primary regulators of the medical profession" and supersedes "a state's determination [of] what constitutes legitimate medical practice." Furthermore, H.R. 4006 achieves its policy objective—of prohibiting states, through their constitutional processes, from permitting physician assisted suicide—by indirection. It does not say to the American people, "Suicide at the end of life, assisted or otherwise, is not legally condoned in this country!" Rather, H.R. 4006 establishes a less-than-benign process of intimidation, threat or significant professional risk to practicing physicians attempting to alleviate the pain and suffering of terminally-ill patients. (Kitzhaber 1998)

FORMATION OF THE NATIONAL PAIN CARE COALITION

Even with the AMA in opposition, one key to the eventual failures of the Hyde/Nickles bills was the work of a coalition of health organization calling themselves the Pain Care Coalition. At the time, one key player, John Budetti, was the legislative director for a Washington, DC, law firm whose clients included the American Academy of Pain Management, the American Association of Head Ache, and the American Pain Society. While attending the second mark-up of Hyde/Nickles, he found unexpectedly that representatives of many other concerned organizations were in attendance. Spontaneously and informally, these concerned parties began sharing their concerns with each other, and soon there was talk of forming a coalition with John Giglio of the National Hospice Organization as the de facto leader. The result of these events was the formation of the National Pain Care Coalition. The coalition began a series of lobbying efforts, including letter-writing.

The American Pharmaceutical Association (APA) is a good example of why a particular organization joined the coalition. Organized pharmacists are neither for nor against assisted suicide, but they were opposed to an expanded police role of the DEA. One of the empirical reasons for remaining neutral on assisted suicide is the Oregon experience. In Oregon, very exclusive networks of physicians and pharmacists have emerged to service those very few patients who desire to make use of the ODDA. Most importantly, it is so easy to opt out of participation in the ODDA that there is no concerted impetus for pharmacists' associations to take an advocacy position. The APA had no immediate plans to expend many resources on the issue of assisted suicide. Yet when Hyde/Nickles came along, the time, money, and energy expended on the issue exploded (Geiger 1998).

The coalition determined that the primary problem with Hyde/Nickles was the determination of a physician's intent. The primary mission of the DEA under the Federal Controlled Substances Act has been to control the diversion and abuse of controlled substances. DEA investigations of such incidents occur after the alleged illegal act. By contrast, and to the consternation of the coalition, Hyde/Nickles I would have permitted DEA investigations *before* any action occurred. Thus, whether a physician intended to cause death (illegal) or relieve pain and suffering (legal) would be the focus of federal inquiry. In August 1998, while Hyde/Nickles I was being debated, 959,798 physicians were federally registered and hence subject to the Federal Controlled Substances Act.

For some groups, one of the driving forces for membership in the coalition was opposition to any expansion of the Federal Controlled Substances Act. More specifically, some groups claimed that Hyde/Nickles went beyond the immediate issue of assisted suicide, in that, if anything, legal change would narrow federal power in the context of patient choice.

Coalition leaders asked physicians, lawyers, hospice directors, nurses, and insurance providers to review Hyde/Nickles. They communicated through conference calls and e-mail. One by one the organizations determined that Hyde/Nickles would not do what it proposed to do.

At first, coalition players sought advice from medical groups: How could Hyde/Nickles be amended to make it work? The response was that better management was needed. Yet there was not enough time to recast Hyde/Nickles in that way, so it was decided that the bill was irreparable and that advocating for an amendment was the wrong approach.

Worried that the effect of Hyde/Nickles I would be too broad and would undercut current efforts at palliative care, the National Hospice Organization led a number of health care organizations in opposition to the bill.

NHO president John Giglio testified:

> And we're here not to discuss physician-assisted suicide or to debate physician-assisted suicide. What we're here today to talk about are the

> unintended consequences of this legislation. That if it goes forward, it's going to have serious negative impacts on patients who suffer pain in America and the doctors and nurses and hospice administrators and others who care for those patients. (Giglio 1998a)

He added:

> [W]hen groups like ours looked at the unintended consequences of this legislation, we fear that there'll be a significant chilling effect on the practice of aggressive pain management in the United States.
>
> As a result, more patients will suffer pain, more patients won't get the types of strong pain medications that they need, and this legislation will have the perverse effect of increasing the demand for physician-assisted suicide, because more patients are going to be in pain if this bill gets passed. (Giglio 1998a)

The NHO had argued in its brief opposing assisted suicide reform in *Vacco v. Quill* in the Supreme Court, as we saw in Chapter 5, that "the acceptance of assisted suicide as a way to deal with terminal illness would undercut further efforts to increase the public's awareness of hospice as a life-affirming option" (National Hospice Organization 1996).

In the end, the work of the Pain Care Coalition and the opposition of the AMA combined to thwart the passage of Hyde/Nickles I. Having passed the House Judiciary Committee and the Senate Judiciary Committee, it stalled before votes on both house floors and died with the end of the Congress in 1998. Plans were made to revise it for subsequent introduction, as we will see later in this chapter.

1998 OREGON INTERIM LEGISLATURE

The Oregon legislature convenes every other year, during odd-numbered years. However, the judiciary committee and some others remain convened during interim sessions. Senate Bill 19 came out of a 1998 interim committee charged with fine-tuning the ODDA. Representative Lane Shetterly (R-Dallas), chairman of the committee, said Providence Health System and the OMA met with him and former Senator Ken Baker (R-Clackamas) to discuss whether a doctor could be sanctioned for participating in an assisted suicide at hospitals that forbid it, such as Providence Health Systems, the state's Catholic hospital network (Barnett and Lednicer 1999).

During the 1997 legislative session, there had been a majority report and minority report. The majority report became Measure 51—the voter referral.

There was also a minority report that would have implemented Measure 16. Bryant introduced the minority report at the beginning of the 1999 legislative session (Bryant 1999).

Meanwhile, in March 1998, the first ODDA death took place.

OREGON HEALTH DIVISION'S FIRST-YEAR REPORT ON THE ODDA (1999)

The ODDA requires the OHD to perform routine surveillance and evaluation of physicians' practices under the law (ORS 127.865 [2]). This has been a sensitive endeavor requiring deep probing into the private relationship between patients and physicians while fiercely protecting their privacy. Surveillance depends entirely on voluntary reporting by physicians; thus any slip causing physicians to mistrust the OHD could have thwarted the surveillance effort and functionally prevented successful implementation of the law.

On February 17, 1999, the OHD released its first report on ODDA practices. (No prescriptions were filled during the two-and-a-half months after the law became effective in October 1997, so the division decided to issue its first report on all ODDA prescriptions filled during 1998.) Before describing how the information was collected, we present a brief summary of the findings:

- The concern that a large number of people would use the law appears to be unfounded.
- The concern that patients would suffer lingering, painful death appears to be unfounded.
- The concern that vulnerable populations would become victims of the law appears to be unfounded.
- The concern that patients would choose death to spare their families financial hardship appears to be unfounded.
- ODDA patients were more concerned than non-ODDA patients with personal autonomy and control.
- ODDA patients were more likely than non-ODDA patients to be single.

Details regarding these findings and the study limitations are included after we complete our description of the data collection process.

The first level of data measured compliance with the act. OHD administrators reviewed the twenty-three attending physician compliance forms. These forms, or the relevant portions of a patient's medical record submitted in lieu of them, must include patient and physician information, the action taken to comply with the law regarding both the oral and the single written request, the consulting physician's name and a copy of his or her report, the results of the mental health evaluation (if necessary), and the medication prescribed and accompanying information provided to the patient (ORS 127.800–ORS 127.897). All physician reports were in full compliance with the law. To determine the number of ODDA deaths in 1998, the OHD, through its routine review of death certificates, matched death certificate data with the completed compliance forms.

During this inaugural year, the division decided to expand its data by interviewing attending physicians about the conditions under which, and the reasons why, patients decided to use the ODDA. They also asked about the specific effects of the prescribed medication, such as how quickly the medication acted and whether there were any unexpected or adverse effects. Other information they sought included the patients' insurance status, end-of-life concerns, end-of-life care, and functional status at the time of death.

To determine whether the deaths of ODDA patients were significantly different from all other deaths, the division compared ODDA data with two control groups. The first control group included people who died from similar underlying illnesses (e.g., lung cancer, ovarian cancer, congestive heart failure). The second included people who were matched for major demographic variables (e.g., age, underlying illness, date of death). Additionally, characteristics of the fourteen physicians who participated in the fifteen deaths were matched with a control group of physicians who treated non-ODDA patients who died during the period.

The concern that a large number of people would use the law appeared to be unfounded. Twenty-three people requested ODDA prescriptions. Fifteen died after taking the medications. Of the eight remaining, six died of their illness, and two were still alive at the end of 1998. To determine what proportion of those who died in Oregon used the ODDA, the division established the denominator from 1996 data—the last year for which death certificates are complete. The number of Oregonians who died in 1996 was 28,900. Using these numbers, ODDA deaths accounted for only 5 out of every 10,000 annual deaths in Oregon.

The concern that ODDA patients would suffer a lingering death was the basis for the very expensive, and very contentious, repeal effort. But during the first year, the average time to unconsciousness was five minutes (range three to twenty minutes), and the average time to death was twenty-six minutes (range five minutes to eleven and one-half hours). The division interpreted these data to say that at best, those thinking about using the ODDA should realize that the time to death is unpredictable. ODDA proponents add that these results, although preliminary, lay to rest the exaggerated claims that were the basis of the death with dignity opponents' $5-million repeal campaign, as we saw in Chapter 4.

ODDA patients were not disproportionately poor, less educated, uninsured, or lacking access to hospice care, as proponents vigorously claimed during the Measure 16 campaign in 1994, as we explained in Chapter 3. ODDA patients were similar to others with regard to sex, race, urban or rural residence, level of education, health insurance coverage, and hospice enrollment. Eight were male; all were Caucasian; eight were from the tri-county Portland area; twelve had at least a high school diploma, and four were college educated; fourteen had private or public insurance; and ten had hospice care. The median age of ODDA patients was sixty-nine years; the mean age of other non-ODDA patients was seventy-four years. Thirteen of the fifteen were suffering from terminal cancer—about 87 percent; the rate of cancer deaths among non-ODDA patients was 23.5 percent. A similar important finding is that ODDA patients were four times less likely than non-ODDA patients to be disabled (21 percent to 84 percent). Contrary to opposition claims, disability was not a reason for choosing an ODDA death.

Next, although concerns about the financial impact of treating terminal illness did not appear to be a critical factor in seeking assisted suicide, more ODDA patients than non-ODDA patients were concerned with personal autonomy and control. The only significant difference between the fourteen ODDA attending physicians and the forty physicians who provided end-of-life care for the forty-three control patients was the attitude toward writing an ODDA prescription. Fully two-thirds (twenty-nine out of forty-three) of the physicians who treated control patients would have refused to write a prescription for lethal medication had the patient requested it (Chin et al. 1999a). The data about autonomy and control may be affected by two factors: (1) Perhaps physicians who will write a lethal prescription are more likely to initiate and/or respond to inquiries regarding the importance of autonomy and control to the patient and (2) perhaps physicians who will not write a lethal prescription are less likely to remember and/or report the importance of autonomy and control to the patient.

Before moving on to a consideration of how the limitations of the study design may affect these findings, a consideration of marital status at the time of death—the only significant demographic factor that distinguished ODDA patients from others—is in order. Significantly, only two of the ODDA patients were married at the time of death. Five of the others were widowed, four were divorced, and four were never married. The rate of being widowed was the same as in the total population of those who died in 1996—the last year for which death certificate data are finished. But ODDA patients were almost twice as likely to be divorced (27 percent to 16 percent), and they were just more than

25 percent more likely to have never be married (27 percent to 5 percent). Overall, almost four times as many ODDA patients were less likely to be married at the time of death (13 percent to 47 percent). This population is less likely to be married overall, and widowhood is the usual reason why.

The validity of these five general findings may be affected by the small number of assisted suicide cases; the use of physician interviews to report on patients' thoughts, feelings, and actions; and the inability of the study design to account for no reporting. Taking these issues one at a time, the significance of marital status is unclear at this time.

Some high-profile opponents of physician-assisted suicide argue that the finding regarding marital status is an important factor in the ongoing debate about public policy. On the other hand, ODDA proponents claim that maybe it is to be expected that marital status is relevant to concern with personal autonomy and control; this situation is satisfactory given (1) only 5 in 10,000 people who died in one year used the law and (2) the fifteen people who used the law were the types of dying individuals for whom the Oregon law had been championed.

The second concern about the validity of these first-year findings is the method of determining the conditions under which, and the reasons why, fifteen people chose to use the ODDA—physician interviews. The data gathered from physicians are subject to quite a number of challenges, none of which is yet testable given the totally voluntary nature of ODDA reporting requirements. It is far too early in the implementation phase of the ODDA to take a heavy-handed approach toward ensuring full compliance with the law. This forced state regulators to take a standoffish approach—one in which the only message was: We want to do our job the best we can and to get full cooperation; we'll protect the identity of ODDA patients and physicians tooth and nail. Although this attitude is probably significantly related to why the OHD received full cooperation from the fourteen ODDA attending physicians—both in terms of completing and submitting forms and answering interview questions—there is still no way to determine whether or how much these data may have been affected by the contingencies of memory, ethics, and/or emotion.

Finally, the study design is admittedly totally nonresponsive to the issue of nonreporting. Without a tip from a third party, the OHD has no way of discovering instances in which a physician provides someone with a lethal prescription in total secrecy. In reporting how this issue has played out in the political activities of assisted suicide opponents, state regulators have suggested during interviews that even if there have been (or there will continue to be) a few cases of lawbreaking, no one suggests that lawbreaking occurs any more (or less) often than before the ODDA was passed and its implementation commenced. Also, since this change in the law makes it easier to assist a patient's death without the threat of civil or criminal penalties, it may be that physicians are less likely to break the law because, if they follow this law, they are provided a safe harbor from the general proscription against and punishments for assisted suicide.

REACTIONS TO THE REPORT

Negative reaction to the first-year report included the issue of noncompliance. For example, an op-ed article in the *Detroit News* stated: "The report gives us nothing approaching a full picture of the extent to which physicians (and others) both have and have not complied with the law" (Spindelman 1999).

The author of the article, Marc Spindelman, was teaching a seminar on assisted suicide as a visiting instructor of law at the University of Michigan Law School in Ann Arbor. He went on to say: "To their credit, the authors of the report explain that because of the obligation to report any noncompliance with the law to the Oregon Board of Medical Examiners for further investigation[,] we cannot detect or collect data on issues of noncompliance with any accuracy" (Spindelman 1999).

Other negative reactions included an editorial in AMA's *American Medical News* and a similar commentary in the *Wall Street Journal*. The *American Medical News* editorial stated: "Assuming Oregon's experience is truly meaningful—the caveat being that the numbers are small—then it signals we are moving another step closer to that slippery slope ("Assisted Suicide Lesson" 1999). The editorial was especially concerned with the fact that only one ODDA patient reported having intractable pain and that ODDA patients were more likely to be concerned about loss of autonomy and loss of bodily functions.

> Fears over loss of autonomy or of bodily function are dramatically different than intractable pain. They represent perception, fear, anticipation, abstraction. The more such standards are accepted, the deeper the slide into the utterly false notion that physician assistance is, in the Hemlock Society's words, "part of the continuum of care." ("Assisted Suicide Lesson" 1999)

A similar view was expressed by Wesley J. Smith, a lawyer for the International Anti-Euthanasia Task Force: "Yet pain wasn't a factor in a single one of the Oregon suicides. Thus, rather than being a limited procedure performed out of extreme medical urgency, legalization in Oregon has actually widened the category of conditions for which physician-hastened death is seen as legitimate" (Smith 1999).

Smith is the author of *Forced Exit: The Slippery Slope from Assisted Suicide to Legalized Murder* (Smith 1997), in which he passionately warns that allowing legalizing assisted suicide for any group, no matter how small, will create a caste of disposable people. He raised that issue again in response to the OHD first-year report: "Disability-rights advocates point out that allowing assisted suicide based upon fear of needing help going to the toilet, bathing and performing other daily life activities will involve far more disabled and elderly people than terminally ill ones" (Smith 1999).

As Smith read the first-year report, the United States is headed down the same slippery slope as the Netherlands, where Dutch policy on euthanasia is "beyond effective control," according to a study published in the *Journal of Medical Ethics* in early 1999 (Smith 1999). "Rather than alleviating concerns," Smith charged, "the study reveals that assisted suicide is bad medicine and even worse public policy" (Smith 1999).

Other commentators were more moderate. One letter to the editor of the *New England Journal of Medicine* focused on the secondhand accounts from physicians instead of patients or their families (Fins and Bancroft 1999). Another focused on the report that patients who chose physician-assisted suicide were more likely to have been divorced or never married, opining that this was "perhaps a predictable response for persons who lack emotional attachments to and a comfortable dependency on caring others" (Edwards and Connor 1999).

These reactions prompted a reply from the authors of the first-year report. They told about carefully considering how much additional intrusion into the lives of patients and their families was acceptable during an emotional and important decision-making time.

> [W]e were especially concerned about the consequences of an inadvertent breach of confidentiality that might result from a more invasive approach, one that involved interviews with other health care providers or family members. We believed that our decision—to conduct additional in-depth interviews with the physicians who wrote prescriptions for lethal medications—best balanced the need for immediate information and evaluation with the need to respect the privacy and confidentiality of those involved. . . . Any perceived lapses in this commitment, especially in the current atmosphere of intense public scrutiny, would render our reporting system ineffective. (Chin et al. 1999b)

On the finding regarding marital status, they simply stated that the data on marital status "should be viewed as speculative" (Chin et al. 1999b).

Other commentary focused on the patients who want a law like the ODDA (Boehm 1999). There will "continue to be people for whom the loss of independence is, truly, a fate worse than death." Still others claimed that the unwillingness of many doctors to prescribe deadly drugs is creating a roadblock. As we reported earlier, the OHD's sampling of physicians revealed that 67 percent of doctors who treat terminally ill patients said they would refuse to participate in suicide. Similarly, an Associated Press article pointed out that "six of the 15 terminally ill people who used the law to end their lives last year were turned down by at least one doctor" (Cain 1999). Further research is warranted for a possible connection between these findings and other findings regarding the importance of autonomy and control.

"The small numbers should be reassuring to the critics," according to Peter Rasmussen, a Salem oncologist who had helped two patients with assisted suicide and said that he had discussed the issue with perhaps a hundred others. "A year of relative inactivity with very few patients, without scandal, has made everybody rest easier, myself included" (Vitez 1999).

"It's not the harbinger of destruction that people thought it was going to be, but it's still bad social policy," said the Reverend John F. Tuohey, a Catholic priest who oversees health care ethics at Providence Health System, the state's Catholic hospital network. "We'd rather people didn't choose it, but it challenges us to provide better care so they won't choose it. . . . It's being implemented thoughtfully and carefully" (Vitez 1999).

An early opponent, Ann Jackson, the head of the OHA said that the ODDA is "working well": "[T]he law is giving Oregonians one more option at the end of life. It's just one of many choices. We have seen how hard it is for most people to [request] the drugs" (Vitez 1999).

An editorial in the *Times Union* (Albany, NY) stated:

> So much, for now anyway, for all the "slippery slope" predictions and fears about such a practice. There's no evidence of botched suicides or a widespread rush among the sick or suffering to move to Oregon for the right to be put to death. Nor is there any sign of Dr. Kevorkian–like abuses of someone's will to end a life of incurable agony. ("Mercy in Oregon" 1999)

A *New York Times* editorial made a similar endorsement of the first-year report:

> The Roman Catholic Archbishop in Portland has denounced their deaths as cause for "sadness and shame." Moral conscience is always grounds for disagreement. But Oregon seems to have shown, on this most personal

> and final of issues, that it is possible to make law and bureaucratic rules that allow people to take responsibility for themselves, without the state, or anyone else, abusing them. That is cause for relief. (Assisted Suicide, in Practice, 1999)

A United Press International writer interviewed selected prominent scholars of the right-to-die and death with dignity movements. Dr. Timothy Quill, professor of medicine and psychiatry at the University of Rochester School of Medicine and Dentistry in New York, said the Oregon findings are what he expected. "The data are reassuring. Nothing in the data says the process is out of control or people are being coerced. It shows physician-assisted suicide is being used as a last resort in the context of good end-of-life care" (United Press International 1999:2). James Hoefler, chairman of the political science department at Dickinson College in Carlisle, Pennsylvania, and author of the book *Deathright: Culture, Medicine, Politics and the Right to Die* (Hoefler 1994), stated: "People were predicting Oregon would become the "fly and die" state. But that isn't going to happen. A relatively small number of people took the prescriptions. They were concerned about quality of life and they cut across all demographics" (United Press International 1999). Both Quill and Hoefler said they didn't expect the one-year report to cause other states to rush to adopt similar physician-assisted suicide laws. Said Hoefler, "There isn't enough data or enough patients for other states to adopt this. And it's not the answer to death in America" (United Press International 1999:3). Hoefler also made comments like those in *The Oregonian*: "Doctors and care givers are seeing the Oregon initiative in assisting suicide as a sort of indictment against their ability to treat people at the end of life. There are alternatives to improve the quality of life" (United Press International 1999).

Since the report was issued, there has been concern about the validity of data based on memory. For example, when physicians are asked why patients chose death with dignity, they may remember more about autonomy and dignity than about the patients' complaints about pain. Hence, the data that suggest patients used the law for reasons other than pain may be biased to an unknown degree. It hasn't been decided how this problem will be dealt with as the Oregon Health Division continues to profile patients and doctors who use the ODDA.

Confidentiality between patients, their families, and their physicians remains paramount. Some people have questioned whether epidemiologists should be the ones collecting the data that many interested people and organizations would like to analyze. But since that's what the law calls for, says Hedberg, they'll keep doing it.

The issue of underreporting doesn't seem to have much weight. And it's still Hedberg's belief that there is very little incentive to do what is allowed under the ODDA without heeding the reporting requirements. Breaking the law by nonreporting or underreporting makes little sense. For instance, a family member who disagrees with the patient's choice could report the doctor who broke the law. Meanwhile, the incidence of hoarding pills for suicide is as unknown today as it was before the ODDA. In fact, said Headberg, what the fifteen people who committed suicide under the ODDA in 1998 represent in terms of overall suicide among the terminally ill remains as unknown as ever.

OREGON HOSPICE ASSOCIATION JOINS IN SUPPORT

With many ODDA clients having been in hospice programs, one of the interesting developments in Oregon has been the integration of hospice and the ODDA. While we noted earlier that the NHO had argued against physician-assisted suicide, including to the Supreme Court, the OHA has taken a different tack (Jackson 2000). While hospice organizations generally have seen the promise of assisted suicide reform as undercutting the support for hospice programs, the OHA has begun to work with the Oregon ODDA reformers, moving forward from its 1994 opposition to Measure 16.

In 1994, the OHA began neutral on Measure 16, wanting more information, wanting robust debate, and not wanting to be used by either side; the OHA came out opposed late in the campaign (Jackson 2000). OHA Director Ann Jackson became very involved in the Task Force to Improve the Care of Terminally-Ill Oregonians, Oregon Health Decisions, and public presentations. She came around to accepting physician-assisted suicide to honor patients' choice, yet still believes most patients' concerns can be handled by hospice and that physician-assisted suicide should remain a final resort.

CLARIFYING THE ODDA IN THE 1999 OREGON LEGISLATURE—SENATE BILL 491

Senate Bill 491, a group of amendments to help clarify some of the provisions of the 1994 referendum, was the key implementation legislation of the Oregon legislature. Among other provisions, S.B. 491 cleared up issues over residency requirements, mandated against suicide in public places, and required pharmacists to report ODDA prescriptions to the OHD, establishing a second check against abuse. The Oregon Catholic Conference tried to bar all talk about assisted suicide anywhere on its hospital grounds. What resulted was a fragile political compromise based on the shared conviction that the law must be kept from failing. Even consensus group members who were morally opposed to assisted suicide and/or the ODDA favored the clarity provided by S.B. 491 over the status quo. Over a two-year span, the Oregon state legislature had gone from being the locus of anti–assisted suicide politics to an effective mechanism for shoring up ambiguities in the law.

Senate Bill 491 was introduced in January 1999 by a Republican senator from Bend, Neil Bryant, the chair of the Oregon Senate Judiciary Committee. In an interview (Bryant 1999), Bryant described S.B. 491 as the product of a collaborative effort involving the Providence Health System, the OMA, the Oregon Health Care Association, the Oregon Health Division, the Oregon Pharmacists Association, Oregon Right to Die, and the Oregon Senate Judiciary Committee, which he chaired. The purpose of S.B. 491, said Bryant, was to clarify certain areas in the law and to improve its implementation.

The bill contained ten sections. The primary issues included physician responsibilities (Section 3), residency requirements (Section 8), and the right to opt out of the law (Section 10). Other issues included the tightening of a few definitions used in the ODDA, qualification for use of the ODDA (it cannot be based solely on age or disability) (Section 2), state claims in case of use of the ODDA in public, notification of next of kin (the physician must recommend this), and reporting requirements (a copy of the record that a physician is required to create and keep upon dispensing medication pursuant to the ODDA must be filed with the OHD) (Section 9).

The collaborative effort that Bryant directed and carefully guarded is reflected in the breadth of the issues addressed in S.B. 491. Bryant told how he brought a diversity of players to the table and started off by soliciting each one's wish list (Bryant 1999). That produced a collective list of nine requests. Bryant proposed four items himself: tightening the definition of residency, discouraging use of the ODDA alone, prohibiting use of the ODDA in public places, and defining who may use the law in terms of who is "capable" in lieu of who is "not incapable," plus adding new language saying "no one shall qualify for the law solely because of age or disability" (Bryant 1999). Three other items that made it into Bryant's bill were proposed by pharmacists, doctors, and Oregon Right to Die. The two others were clearly unacceptable to Bryant and others at the table. One item by the Catholic Church would have effectively abrogated the ODDA (Bryant 1999).

The work group for S.B. 491 included representatives of Providence Health System (Alitha Leon Jenkins), the OMA (Scott Gallant and Mark Bonnano), Oregon Health Care Association (Gwen Dayton), OHD, Oregon Pharmacy Association, Oregon Right to Die (Steve Telfer), and the Senate Judiciary Committee.

Bryant handled the recalcitrance of Catholic organizations swiftly. Single-handedly, he excluded the lobbyist from the Oregon Catholic Conference from the collaborative effort. The lobbyist's views were well known, and Bryant expected him to remain strident and unyielding. Predicting that the Catholic Conference would hinder efforts to build consensus, by Bryant's own admission he virtually dictated that the lobbyist not be permitted to attend the group's meetings. This parallel between Bryant's handling of Catholic opposition and the exclusion of Derek Humphry from the meetings of movement activists who wrote the ODDA is worth noting.

Oregon Right to Life (ORL) is another group whose involvement in S.B. 491 was of import. The apprehensiveness of ORL members to legitimize the ODDA by participating in procedures to amend it rendered Bryant's decision to exclude ORL from the work group as a decision with very little political consequence for Bryant. Yet during S.B. 491's homestretch through the Senate, ORL (through Gail Atterbury) was admitted to the consensus group in exchange for the consensus group's acquiescence in an amendment requiring pharmacists to report ODDA prescriptions to the OHD. Along with the physician reporting requirements, the additional requirement that pharmacists report incidents of use of the ODDA established a second check against abuse of the law, and it was this addition to the regulatory scheme that was widely reported to have legitimated ORL's eventual move to join the consensus (Bryant 1999).

S.B. 491 would have passed easily without ORL's endorsement. But that does not dampen its significance to our study of Stutsman's strategy of leaving the language of the law vague enough so that those who did implement and use it could overcome different cultural meanings of killing, such as physician-assisted suicide and death with dignity, and fit the law to their concrete practical needs.

THE CONSCIENCE CLAUSE PROVISIONS

The proposed amendment with language that reflected the most complex collaboration clarified the scope of health care provider organizations to punish health care provider practitioners who provide ODDA services. A delicate balance was achieved between real people who champion very different cultural meanings of ODDA practice. A powerful religious minority still views any form of physician-assisted suicide, whether or not it is performed legally and in a dignified manner, as a form of direct killing. Proponents of legalizing such an option are currently willing to concede narrow qualifications in exchange for a safe harbor from police, prosecutors, and administrative officials. Inside the safe harbor, qualified patients and dutiful physicians can make and perform competent arrangements for physician assistance in death, without the prospect of prosecutions and/or civil actions arising under assisted suicide and homicide laws. The consensus group that developed S.B. 491 worked hard to build the safe harbor approved by Oregon voters.

It will help to begin with a look at the fragile compromise produced by the consensus group:

1. The right of health care providers to exercise their consciences and opt out of ODDA practice includes the right to impose sanctions against leasees, employees, and independent contractors who violate valid agreements not to practice death with dignity.
2. On the other hand, the scope of such agreements, from which the right to impose sanctions arises, is limited by principles of agency. A principal cannot sanction a physician who is off the principal's property and acts outside the scope and course of their employment arrangement or independent contract.
3. Most importantly, these rules embrace the right of qualified patients to negotiate their own agency relationships with physicians acting outside the scope and course of other property, employment, and contract relationships. This agreement could not have been reached without serious splintering between key Catholic organizations.

DELEGATING STATUTORY CONSTRUCTION

Bryant's response to a question we posed about who were the consensus drivers revolved around the role of lawyers for the various organizations in the work group. The task of closing the deal between the parties became tedious once lawyers began hashing out the desired language. That effort reached a point when changing a mere word here or there threatened the consensus, which could have killed the bill—either by a governor's veto or even a decision by Bryant to withdraw it. So once bargains were reached and language was hammered out, there was understanding between Bryant and House representatives that nothing would be changed. Representative Shetterly (Shetterly 1999) acknowledged that the bill was hard fought and well thought out during the Senate proceedings and that it contained very careful language; therefore, the only way to make it work was to maintain the bill as passed by the Senate, and that is what he successfully worked to do.

The fact that more doctrinal Catholic organizations were excluded from the work group permitted the group to cultivate nondoctrinal and politically volatile policies driven by clinical realities. In hindsight, the Catholic Conference may have underestimated the chances of S.B. 491's success. The work group that met once or twice a month during the summer of 1998 had as a central concern to clear up an ambiguity in the ODDA arising from the following: On the one hand, ORS 127.885 says that no health provider shall be under any duty, whether by contract, by statute, or by any other legal requirement, to participate in the provision to a qualified patient of medication to end his or her life in a humane and dignified manner. To some observers, the original ODDA was not well crafted, which is often thought to be true of initiative laws because they lack the rigorous process of rewriting that occurs for legislative proposals as various concerned parties weigh in with prepared and oral testimony while the proposal moves through several committees.

Providence Health System was concerned about an ambiguity between two provisions in the section of the law granting immunities. At the same time that no health care provider shall be under any duty to participate in the ODDA (ORS 127.855[4]), no professional organization or association or health care provider may subject a person to penalty for refusing to participate in the ODDA (ORS 127.855[2]). In the words of prepared testimony by Alitha Leon Jenkins:

> By definition, a "health care provider" is either an individual practitioner or a "health care facility" [ORS 127.800(5)(6)]. The ambiguity in the existing law arises in the [penalty] provision, which could be interpreted to mean that a facility cannot enforce its contracts or discipline a practitioner for participating in assisted suicide procedures, even if the participation is on the facility's premises or within the scope of an employment or independent contractor relationship between the facility and the individual practitioner. (Jenkins 1999)

According to interviews, five strategies were used to address this problem.

1. Some members of the group identified who they thought could be the strongest opponent—they identified the OMA because of its political influence and clout. Identifying who was in the best position to kill a proposed bill and winning that association's support was the key action during the presession.
2. Two prominent leading legislators—Shetterly and Bryant—were approached, and Providence unequivocally disavowed any motive to overturn the law or otherwise block implementation. Its aim was to clarify the law. While this was an absolutely untenable position for the Catholic Conference to take, with its role as advocate, the tenuous position of the hospitals and health systems as implementation proceeded urged pragmatism and certainly not detachment.

3. The reform proponents were implored to play a positive role in consensus formation. This would require them to give some ground on the issue of permitting a facility to sanction a provider who breaches a contract that bars participation in assisted suicide, or who violates facility regulations that bar assurances that patient access to the law, as it was passed and affirmed by voters, would not be diluted.
4. Language was hammered out between Providence, the OMA, and the right-to-die group, with the governor's office kept informed of these efforts by the various parties.
5. At the point at which the proposed bill was ready for introduction in the legislature, Providence again disavowed any effort to overturn or block the law.
6. The bill was ushered through the legislative process through contacting a range of legislators and working to mollify critics (Bryant 1999; Fiskum 2000).

Early on in the negotiations, Providence had compromised with the OMA and agreed to permit referrals by keeping them out of the definition of "participation" in the ODDA. Much later, during the tenth and eleventh hour negotiations, the Catholic Conference and the archbishop wanted Providence to change their position, providing an ethical analysis based on the Catholic principal of "agentry," whereby one is said to constructively participate in an unethical act merely by referring one to someone who will perform it. In meetings at the capitol, which included the working group, the leading legislators did not embrace that position and the OMA wouldn't support the change. Moreover, the reformers "had the governor's veto in their pocket." Operating from a politically pragmatic position, which couldn't fully embrace the Church's ethical concerns, Providence focused on the clinical responsibilities to patients and acquiesced in keeping the amendments on the subjects of ownership, employment, and contracts (Fiskum 2000).

Here, literally every word mattered. Bryant supplied the key phrase "course and scope of employment/independent contract." Moreover, referral is to made to "a physician," not to a physician who will be known to help. This is a vital distinction—one that suitably honors Catholic concerns with "agentry." The language also does not apply to insurers—again, the bill focused on ownership, employment, and contracts.

> Ethicists, lawyers, and of physicians agreed to it. Allied groups such as OAHHS [Oregon Association of Hospitals and Health Systems] played a good role. Most of all, it bridges gaps, it reflects good faith and good will, and it makes winners instead of losers. On the other hand, the same sec-

> tion of law says that no professional organization or association, or health care provider, may subject a person to censure, discipline, suspension, loss of license, loss of privileges, loss of membership or other penalty for participating or refusing to participate in good faith compliance with ORS 127–800 to 127.897. (Jenkins 1999)

Faced with this ambiguity, Providence worked to clarify the law in a way that would allow its health system to live out Catholic values within it facilities and within its employment and contractual relationships (Fiskum 2000).

PROTECTING LIFE AND SAFEGUARDING PATIENT AND PHYSICIAN AUTONOMY

S.B. 491 had several key provisions, many of which went through several revisions, and most of which were the subject of intense discussion.

Section 1

This section deals with definitions used in the act. Subsection (3) defines "Capable" and replaces "Incapable." It defines in positive terminology a patient's ability to make and communicate health care decisions to health care providers. In Subsection (5), the definition of "counseling" has been modified to change "consultation" to "one or more consultations as necessary" for the purposes of determining that the patient is capable. Subsection (6) has been modified by adding "or dispense medication" to clarify pharmacists' inclusion as health care providers.

Section 2

Subsection (2) amends ORS 127.805 to clarify that qualification for use of the act cannot be based solely on age or disability. Qualifications must be based on terminal illness diagnosed by two independent physicians, residency, demonstration of capability as an adult to perform informed decision making, and the ability to carry out all other provisions of the act.

Section 3

This section addresses physician responsibilities. The intent of these amendments is to strike a balance between burdening the attending physician with unenforceable responsibilities and protecting the patient by providing appropriate information through counseling. Specifically, Subsection (1)(b) requires that the attending physician request that the patient demonstrate Oregon residency based on *indicia*. Subsection (1)(g) directs the attending physician to counsel the patient about the importance of having another person present when the patient takes the medication to end his or her life and to not do so in a public place. This counseling provision will become an item on the check list the State of Oregon Health Division has prepared for use by physicians. Subsection (1)(1) codifies the existing rule adopted by the Board of Medical Examiners to ensure appropriate confidentiality between physician and pharmacist in the delivery of prescriptions for the purposes of the act. Subsection (2) is added at the request of the state health officer. It permits the attending physician to sign the patient's death certificate.

Subsection (3)(L) carefully defines how an ODDA prescription may be obtained. A doctor may dispense directly. Very few doctors, however, are state certified to dispense prescriptions. A different way of saying it is that few doctors want to include a dispensary (with the need to learn and keep track of changes in regulations, the record-keeping requirements, the need for secure premises, additional liabilities, and so on) in their practice, so few seek state certification. For most people, therefore, a pharmacist's services will be necessary. The amendment prohibits a patient from presenting a prescription to a pharmacist himself or herself. Instead, with the patient's consent the prescribing physician must present the prescription in person or by mail. The filled prescription may then be dispensed either to the patient, the prescribing physician, or the patient's agent. Additionally, pharmacists must be informed that they are being asked to dispense an ODDA prescription.

CLARIFYING THE CIVIL LAW CONSEQUENCES OF THE ODDA

Section 5a enables any governmental entity that might incur costs resulting from a person using the act, in a public place, to have a claim against the estate to recover costs and reasonable attorney fees.

Affording Doctors a Secure Legal Position

Section 6 suggests the attending physician recommend rather than merely ask the patient to notify the next of kin of his or her request for medication pursuant to the act.

The purpose and intent of Section 8 is to clarify residency requirements for purposes of the act. The bill uses the *indicia* approach rather than the "domicile" approach. "Domicile" is a legal term that is subject to litigation and is not workable in a clinical medical setting. The intent is to say that any of a number of *indicia* of residency will suffice to demonstrate residency. Examples may include registration to vote in Oregon, evidence that a person leases or owns property in Oregon, filing of an Oregon tax return in the most recent year, or any other evidence.

Quality Control of ODDA Practice

Section 9 modifies the reporting requirements. The OHD shall require any health care provider upon dispensing medication pursuant to the act to file a copy of the dispensing record with the division.

The Sanctioning Power

Section 10, containing language on conscientious objection, or "opt-outs," is the most complex part of the bill. Providence Health System and the Oregon Health Care Association, representing long-term care facilities, thought that the current law was ambiguous concerning the ability of a health care facility to sanction an employee or independent contractor who violated policies prohibiting participation in the ODDA. This was despite the fact that the attorney general issued an opinion that the current immunities clause is fully comprehensive and applies to all health care providers and facilities.

Through negotiation involving the interested parties, this section of the bill clarifies the ability of a "sanctioning" provider, like a hospital, to sanction other medical providers in a variety of circumstances and within appropriate limits.

To clarify the intent, here are a few examples:

1. An independent contracting physician, leasing space in an office building owned by Providence Health System, could potentially be subject to loss of lease if participating in the act is prohibited by the lease, but could not be subject to the loss of medical staff privileges.
2. Similarly, an independent contracting physician could be subject to termination of contract or other specified nonmonetary remedies for participating in the act while acting within the course and scope of his or her capacity under a contract that prohibits participation.
3. In the case of a long-term care facility, where physicians don't have staff privileges, the sanction is more prospective. The facility may prohibit a provider from participating in the act on its premises if it has notified the provider of its policy prohibiting participation in the act. The bill specifically provides, however, that nothing in this sanctioning language prevents such physicians from providing other services to terminally ill patients that do not constitute death with dignity services.

This section also clarifies that sanctions cannot be imposed when a provider participates in the act while acting outside the course and scope of the provider's capacity as an employee or independent contractor. Subsection (5)(b)(C)(ii) ensures that patients have the right to contract with an attending physician and consulting physician to act outside the course and scope of the provider's capacity as an employee or independent contractor. Subsection (5)(d) clarifies sanctioning providers' notification requirements, and in (B) defines what "participation" in the act means and doesn't mean for purposes of imposing sanctions.

Finally, to underscore the improvements that have been made in end-of-life care, Subsection (7) clarifies that nothing in the act is to be construed to allow a lower standard of care for patients. This directly parallels language in the Oregon Medical Practices Act.

One concern that some working group members had with implementation was that the state had sought access to complete patient records from which to abstract the information needed to meet the OHD's reporting and surveillance requirements. Again, the issue of confidentiality was paramount to the OMA, to ODDA proponents, and to other health care lobbyists. They convinced the state to make a clear distinction between which forms physicians were required to submit and which were strictly voluntary.

While the House Speaker wanted a more stringent residency requirement (at least six months in Oregon), legislative counsel analyzed the issue and concluded that a more stringent requirement would violate U.S. Supreme Court decisions regarding the fundamental right to travel. On this basis, the speaker was convinced to drop her proposed amendment and allow the bill to be passed (Shetterly 1999). The speaker was convinced that any proposals to amend the law that would lead to a veto by Governor Kitzhaber would leave the status quo intact, a situation significantly less desirable than any outcome under the proposed legislation, which was aimed at establishing a sober range of policy implications that could be expected to come about from the processes of implementing the law (Bryant 1999).

REFORMER LOBBYISTS

The Oregon Right to Die lobbyist was a Republican who had good rapport with members of the Republican-controlled legislature, a good reputation, and many years' experience lobbying for health care interests, including a long tenure with an Oregon health system (Statsman 2000; Telfer 2000). One of his first efforts was to produce what he called a "litmus test." The official title was "Oregon Right to Die's Guiding Principles for End-of-Life Care." The guiding principles were distributed to all Oregon legislators. The guidelines were possible because of the governor's position that he would veto any law attempting to overturn or block implementation of the law, which voters had passed and later confirmed by a great margin.

Essentially, the bill worked through the legislative process. This included choosing not to adopt amendments that would have released data gathered by the OHD for academic research regarding the effectiveness of the monitoring protocols. A consensus was reached among most parties that such expansion of access to the state's data—collected for the purpose of complying with the reporting and surveillance requirements of the ODDA—simply had no merit in light of the countervailing interests in the confidentiality of patients, their families and physicians and pharmacists. The weight of the countervailing interests was established by the OMA and Oregon Right to Die's ardent defense of confidentiality, Providence's disavowal of any effort to overturn or block the law, and the strong probability of a governor's veto. Collective agreement to omit the consortium's amendments strengthened the key parties' individual commitments and tightened the circle around the work group's unyielding resolution to improve the law.

This made it possible to work through the more politically sensitive issues presented by the pharmacists' association, whose "corporate opt-out" would have limited patient access. It also made it possible to address the house speaker's concern about residency requirements.

Oregon Right to Die was most concerned with the possibility that the opt-out provisions could be interpreted to encompass any Catholic interest, which could have had the effect of blocking patient access to the law. Any broad exercise of group consciousness that could too easily lead to literal efforts to block patient access (here the anti-abortion movement is an obvious parallel) was precisely what Oregon voters rejected in 1994 and defied in 1997.

In the end, the key stakeholders from several branches of Oregon's health communities and government apparatus worked together with great resolve and cooperation to fashion a bill that reflected the voice of the electorate from 1997 and took a pragmatic approach to advancing the implementation of the ODDA. As we have described, it was not a simple matter, nor a preordained matter. The key actions of several legislators and representatives of key interests coalesced to bring S.B. 491 to a successful conclusion. If the Measure 16 contest and the Measure 51 repeal had suggested that key Oregonians would reach an impasse on the ODDA, the 1999 Oregon legislature dispatched that notion effectively.

CONGRESSIONAL LEGISLATION TO BLOCK THE ODDA: HYDE/NICKLES II, 1999

With the failure of the Hyde/Nickles I bills in 1998, opponents of the ODDA went back to the drawing table and tried to determine what they needed to craft a bill that could pass in the United States Congress. The opposition of the AMA to the 1998 bill had been a crucial obstacle to the passage and those trying to block the Oregon law through federal preemption turned to modifying their bill.

To Richard Doerflinger, sssociate director for policy development at the Secretariat for Pro-Life Activities of the National Conference of Catholic Bishops, "Last year's bill gave priority to stating a new policy against assisted suicide, then explained that this policy does not forbid the legitimate use of controlled substances to control pain. In H.R. 2260 the emphasis is reversed" (Doerflinger 1999).

Crucial changes were needed to get the AMA on board. In a letter to Representative Hyde, AMA Executive Vice President Ratcliffe Anderson, Jr., stated what shape that took:

> The AMA, as you know, is squarely opposed to physician-assisted suicide and believes it is antithetical to the role of physician as healer. In crafting an appropriate legislative response, physicians have been deeply concerned that legislation must recognize that aggressive treatment of pain carries with it the potential for increased risk of death, the so-called "double effect."
>
> Thus, we are very pleased to note that the bill would recognize the "double effect" as a potential consequence of the legitimate and necessary prescribing of controlled substances for pain management, and explicitly include this as a "safe harbor" provision for physicians in the Controlled Substances Act. This is a vital element in creating a legal environment in which physicians may administer appropriate pain care for patients without the threat of criminal investigation and prosecution for fully legitimate medical decisions, and we appreciate its inclusion. (Anderson 1999)

Pleased with the reversal in priorities, and with a $5 million palliative care allotment in the new bill, the AMA and NHO reversed their opposition. The 1999 act sought to expressly legalize routine practices at the legal fringes of end-of-life care. To the AMA, that was the major advantage of the 1999 act. It was what the AMA bargained for, and it was why the AMA helped pass the 1999 act, as far as it has progressed.

According to United States Conference of Catholic Bishops official Richard Doerflinger, a key architect of the Hyde/Nickles repeal efforts, the 1999 Pain Relief Promotion Act addressed these concerns of critics in several ways (Doerflinger 1999):

1. A new explicit statement ... in H.R. 2260 ... that a state, by enacting a law permitting assisted suicide, does not succeed in changing the separate federal standard that already applies to all other states—in other

words, a law like Oregon's has no "force and effect" in determining whether a practitioner has violated separate federal standards for protecting patients' health and safety.

2. It contains a forthright and explicit declaration on the legitimacy of using controlled substances to control pain, then adds that this and other policy statements in the relevant section of the CSA do not authorize the use of controlled substances for assisted suicide.
3. H.R. 2260 contains a new mandate that the DEA's continuing education programs for federal, state and local law enforcement personnel include education in how their enforcement procedures can better accommodate the legitimate medical use of controlled substances for pain relief.

Doerflinger concludes: "[The bill] underscores the federal policy that pain control is an important and legitimate purpose for the use of federally regulated drugs—a policy that has never before been so explicitly stated in federal statutes." Moreover, he argues:

> The Pain Relief Promotion Act is carefully tailored to clarify federal law on assisted suicide only to the minimum degree needed to correct the Attorney General's ruling, so that the federal government will no longer actively *facilitate* assisted suicide in any state that has legalized the practice. It does not give new enforcement authority to the DEA, and does not change the law at all in the vast majority of states—*except* to give new emphasis to the legitimate use of federally regulated drugs to control pain.

While some of the initial opponents of Hyde/Nickles I changed sides with the redrafting contained in Hyde/Nickles II, others did not. For example, the American Pain Foundation noted its objections:

> In our initial review of H.R. 2260 we have heard widely different legal interpretations of the bill and confusion about how it will be interpreted, how it will be implemented, whether or not it will increase DEA's regulatory authority or actions in states that do not have laws permitting physician-assisted suicide, whether it will result in new DEA regulations, whether it will shift any of DEA's attention away from its proper role of regulating diversion into the improper role of overseeing and investigating patient care and medical practice, how charging the DEA with determining a physician's or pharmacist's "intent" in using opioids will affect their care of patients, what role federal, state and local law enforcement officials would now play in medical oversight, how the bill will impact access to opioids for chronic pain patients who are not in end-of-life sit-

> uations, and many other serious questions concerning how the bill will affect the practice of pain and symptom management and end-of-life care.
>
> In addition, the bill is wholly inadequate in its provisions for promoting pain relief. Its new initiatives are very limited, and the provisions focus on a narrow subgroup of persons who suffer from unrelieved pain while ignoring the much larger group of patients whose pain is often undertreated or mistreated, the 50 million Americans with chronic pain. As we see it at this point, if the goal is to effectively improve pain management, this bill as drafted won't do it. If the goal is to prevent physician-assisted suicide, this bill won't do it. If the goal is a uniform approach to using opioids in all 50 states, this bill won't do it. (American Pain Foundation 1999)

Ann Jackson, executive director of the OHA, was critical of the unforeseen consequences of Hyde/Nickles II:

> A goal of the Pain Relief Promotion Act is to make a clear distinction between an appropriate use of controlled substances to manage pain, even if death is hastened inadvertently, and an inappropriate use of controlled substances to assist in a suicide. It attempts to make black and white a very grey area, creating a tightrope, when a balance beam or even a bench would be both more acceptable and defensible. The use of controlled substances is always subject to question, when our society has invested so much time to curb their abuse. Questions will be raised by pharmacists, nurses, health aides, or family members, any of whom may be alarmed by what they perceive to be unusually large doses of narcotics or other drugs—or a death following soon on the heels of a prescription. These questions will precipitate an investigation. These investigations will significantly undermine physicians' prescribing practices. (Jackson 1999)

David Orentlicher, a legal and medical expert, sounded a similar warning:

> The Act will compromise the quality of palliative care in this country. Physicians are very sensitive to the possibility of criminal prosecution, and this Act's emphasis on enforcement actions by federal, state and local law enforcement personnel will discourage the aggressive and appropriate treatment of pain at the end of life.
>
> As several major studies indicate, the reality is that legal concerns already make physicians overly cautious about prescribing the medications necessary to relieve the pain of their patients. Given the seriously disruptive and traumatic nature of criminal prosecutions, this Act will make

> physicians err even more on the side of caution. Often extra caution is good, but in this case it means that tens of thousands of patients will continue to die without adequate treatment of their pain. No matter how many words you attempt to write into this Act to define and encourage good pain management and palliative care, the reality of the practice of medicine all over the country is that doctors would rather avoid risk, interrogation and investigation at all costs. (Orentlicher 1999)

Even as it endorsed Hyde/Nickles II, the AMA itself was a site of contestation over endorsement. At the AMA 1999 meeting in San Diego, testimony was presented by delegates from several state delegations and by organizations such as Physicians for Compassionate Care, Academy of Family Physicians, American Society of Clinical Oncology, American Academy of Pain Medication, AMA Board of Trustees, AMA Council on Legislation, American Pain Foundation, and the American Psychiatric Association. At issue was what some perceived as the precipitous action by the AMA in supporting the Pain Relief Promotion Act. While opponents of the action argued strenuously against what they claimed was inappropriate use of AMA authority—some supporters even conceded that the AMA had somewhat circumvented the association's normal procedures for full hearing on the topic—in the end the opposition fell short, and the AMA support for Hyde/Nickles II stood.

Even with the 106th Congress ending soon after the November 2000 election, the full Senate had not moved on Hyde/Nickles II by June 2000 for several reasons. Oregon Senator Ron Wyden had worked tirelessly in lobbying against the bill and had threatened a filibuster, even as observers were unsure if he had the forty votes to prevent cloture or whether President Clinton—who had signed the Assisted Suicide Funding Restriction Act in 1997—would sign the bill. Indeed, Vice President Gore, the Democratic nominee for president, had been able to effectively evade taking a public stand on the bill while campaigning in Oregon in 2000, as he sensed Republicans lying in wait to make assisted suicide a campaign issue and hurt Gore's chances in more conservative states. As it was, Gore narrowly carried Oregon in his close loss to George W. Bush.

Wyden, a Democrat, hoped to be joined in opposition to Hyde/Nickles II, and in the threat to Oregon's autonomy, by his colleague, Oregon Republican Senator Gordon Smith, but Smith eventually sided with the Republican leadership, explaining his position as a moral, not political, calculation (Hosaka 2000). Meanwhile, Wyden was faced with the prospect of federal funding for Oregon projects being pulled because of his opposition (Barnett and Hogan 2000).

Wyden made a parliamentary move that further complicated matters. He reintroduced Hyde/Nickles II verbatim as S.B. 2607.IS– the bill he was lobbying against—in efforts to have the bill directed to the Health, Education, Labor and Pensions Committee, chaired by Vermont moderate Republican James Jeffords (Barnett 2000). Wyden's move was aimed at undoing the original decision to send the completed House version of the bill to the Senate Judiciary Committee, where the chair, Senator Orrin Hatch, was known to be supportive of it.

When Hyde/Nickles II hadn't been passed by the Senate by the end of the 106th Congress, it faced an uncertain fate in the 107th Congress. While a president had been elected who would be more certain than either Clinton or Gore to sign the bill, the loss of four Senate seats made the Republicans less potent in fending off effective blocking of proposed legislation, such as Sen. Wyden's moves ("Legislation Approved Before Adjourn" 2000).

OREGON HEALTH DIVISION SECOND-YEAR REPORT, 2000

In an almost anti-climactic way, the second-year ODDA report of the OHD was issued in February 2000 (Sullivan et al. 2000).

The Associated Press reported: "Seventeen of the 27 who took lethal drugs last year were cancer patients. The others had chronic lung disease, AIDS or Lou Gehrig's disease. The median age of the those who took their lives was 71; all patients had health insurance and 21 were in hospice care before death" (Associated Press 2000).

According to the OHD (Hedberg 2000), the flurry of interest that followed the 1998 report hasn't followed the 1999 report. *The Oregonian* was appropriately quite interested, but few reporters called. There was greater international than national interest, and even that was generally over in a week.

The lead sentence in a story by the *Washington Post* was typical of the restrained response given to the year two report, in comparison to its predecessor: "There is no evidence that the poor, uneducated, mentally ill or socially isolated are disproportionately seeking—or getting—lethal prescriptions of drugs under the country's only legal program for physician-assisted suicide" (Brown 2000).

CONCLUSION

To look back from June 2000, several factors loom large in the implementation of the ODDA. Maybe with a governor other than Kitzhaber, the reformers wouldn't have succeeded in Oregon. Perhaps, without Measure 51, they would have been playing a weaker hand, based on the 51–49 vote in 1994. But the downside for opponents was that Measure 51 overwhelmingly displayed Oregonian's support for the reform and the desire to let it go forward (Duncan 1998). With that as prelude, implementation actions after November 1997 followed up on activities undertaken from November 1994 onward. Through it all, key Oregonians moved forward to close a circle of pragmatic implementation. The reformers kept their strategy, their team, and their message together as the process moved forward.

While congressional action in Washington threatened to thwart the ODDA, key stakeholders in Oregon had moved forward to activate the implementation of the assisted suicide reform. Senator Neil Bryant indicated in an interview that he had voted in opposition to the ODDA in both 1994 and 1997 (Bryant 1999). Yet he flatly opposed the request to gut the ODDA. Key players in the ODDA implementation process had predicted this, as the will of the voters was institutionalized. There is simply no doubt that the different cultural views that predominated during the fight to pass the ODDA, and perhaps even facilitated it, have been superseded by a concerted effort to make the law work better. Oregon voters have clearly spoken, and physicians are legally helping people die in Oregon. For these reasons primarily, all groups except the Catholic Church—even eventually ORL and Not Yet Dead—endorsed the collective wish list that was S.B. 491, and the ODDA moved forward.

The Supreme Court's decision not to grant certiorari in *Lee v. Oregon* in 1997 and the first ODDA death in March 1998 created a variety of new actions, spurring assisted suicide opponents to use whatever means remained, such as the Congress, to block the ODDA. At the same time, with *Quill* and *Glucksberg* also decided, states that had been waiting for these decisions were now motivated to use the initiative or legislative process to try to emulate Oregon's success.

In Chapter 7, we examine the two initiative attempts that followed, as well as some legislative bills, and also place the American experience against the efforts in other countries, some of which, like the Netherlands, have a much longer experience with end-of-life reform.

7

Death with Dignity in Other States and Other Countries

This bill is about compassion, but more than that, it is about choice. This is about how people spend the last days of their lives.

—California Assembly member Dion Aroner,
as her death with dignity bill passed the California Assembly
Judiciary Committee ("Assisted Suicide Bill Moves Ahead" 1999)

Nowhere else in the world are these questions being discussed so openly, so systematically, so calmly and thoughtfully, and with such a lack of ideological rigidity as in the Netherlands.

—Dutch sociolegal scholar John Griffiths (Griffiths 1995:378)

Oregon was not the first state to vote on a ballot measure to legalize physician-assisted suicide. Nor would it be the last by the end of the century. While Oregon's success emboldened reformers in other states, the usual route to possible legalization was legislative. Between 1994 and 2000, at least fourteen American states entertained the possible legalization of physician-assisted suicide, some more seriously than others, and some on multiple occasions.

Only one state voted on an initiative on assisted suicide, when Michigan turned down the reform by a 2–1 vote in 1998. As the year 2000 unfolded, however, Maine presented itself as the next state with a chance to replicate the Oregon reform.

OTHER AMERICAN STATES' INITIATIVE EFFORTS

Michigan

Michigan has the unique history of being the locale for most of Dr. Jack Kevorkian's at least 130 assisted suicides (Murphy and Swickard 1999). In 1997, a group called Merian's Friends, named in memory of an Ann Arbor woman with Lou Gehrig's disease whom Jack Kevorkian had helped to die in 1993, gathered enough signatures to place a measure to legalize physician-assisted suicide on the 1998 ballot.

If Oregon represented the triumph of informed discussion of medical choices and ethics, and post-1997 reflected a consensus toward implementing the ODDA, Michigan had been described as a "sideshow of dying and politics" (Zalman et al. 1997). Michigan's profile never lent itself to being high on the list of states targeted for changes in the assisted suicide law. Its cultural politics are more conservative than those of Washington, California, and Oregon. Its large Catholic population, 23 percent according to one source, had made it one of the exemplars of the "Reagan Democrat" focus of the Republican party in the 1980s, when that party appealed to blue-collar voters who were more socially conservative than the Democratic party. While a bellwether state in national politics in part because of the social conservatism of some its blue-collar Catholic (and Protestant) voters, it had elected Governor John Engler twice in the 1990s.

When Michigan finally had an assisted-suicide decriminalization measure on the ballot in 1998, the strong presence of the Catholic Church and Catholic voters was instrumental in the initiative's defeat. Thirty groups, including the Medical Society, the Catholic Church of Michigan, and Right to Life of Michigan, combined in the Citizens for Compassionate Care. Together, they raised and spent over $5 million in defeating Proposal B, which went down in a more than 2–1 defeat in November 1998 (Cain and Kiska 1998). The *Detroit Free Press* and other media editorialized against Proposal B.

Polls had shown Proposal B to be ahead in August, before the media campaigns for both sides began. This was not unlike Washington and California, where similar measures had also lost after early support, as described in Chapter 2. The common thought in politics is that such early polls don't reflect the commitment of time, groups and politicians, and money in the heat of the final weeks. In Michigan, this was certainly true. While Citizens for Compassionate Care raised their $5 million, the proponent group spent most of what it raised on qualifying for the ballot and could allocate only $75,000 for television ads in the final months. It was unable to challenge the criticisms of its opponents, in what one reporter referred to as a "virtually uncontested television campaign against Proposal B" (Murphy 1998).

Maine

When some observers of American assisted suicide reform considered where the next battleground states would be for the decriminalization of assisted suicide, Vermont sprung to mind. Vermont is a state with a small and independent population, a history of progressive politics in its largest city, a destination for "back to the earth" activists in the 1970s, and the election of a socialist (now independent) congressman in the 1990s. It also passed a gay rights landmark bill with its "civil union" legislation in 2000 (Goldberg 2000). It also does not possess a large Catholic population, a feature that had characterized the previous initiative states.

While Vermont did not become an important battleground, neighboring states' decriminalization bills were introduced in the early 1990s in New Hampshire and Maine. While none passed, Maine set out in 1999 to be the next state to follow in the steps of Oregon in decriminalizing physician-assisted suicide.

Maine had been a leading state in other innovative measures, such as being the first state to pass comprehensive campaign finance reform with full funding. One-third of the 115 state legislative candidates are running without using their own funds or those of outside funders (Cooper 2000). Two senators in Congress are moderate Republicans, and there is an independent governor. Its repeal of a statewide gay rights bill made it a hard state to easily categorize as a progressive state.

In November 1999, the Maine secretary of state approved Question 1 for the November 2000 ballot. The reformers, Mainers for Death With Dignity, submitted 48,566 valid voters signatures to send the issue before the legislature, and then to voters when the legislature didn't approve the measure.

The secretary of state's ballot language for Question 1 read as follows:

> This initiated bill creates the Maine Death With Dignity Act. It allows a mentally competent adult who is suffering from a terminal illness to request and obtain medication from a physician to end that patient's own life in a humane and dignified manner, with safeguards to ensure that the patient's request is voluntary and based on an informed decision.

The ballot measure itself read: "Should a terminally ill adult who is of sound mind be allowed to ask for and receive a doctor's help to die?" ("Assisted Suicide Top Questions" 2000) According to a news report:

> Advocates say their proposal only allows medication to hasten death to be self-administered. Only terminally ill patients with less than six months to live would be covered, and a second doctor's opinion would be required. The proposal also prohibits mercy killing and requires that the patient be informed of feasible alternatives such as hospice care and pain management, advocates say. It includes two waiting periods—15 days and 48 hours—before death-inducing medication can be administered. (Associated Press 1999)

According to the Mainers for Death With Dignity, their initiative:

- Allows a patient to request from his or her physician medication that would hasten death. The medication must be self-administered by the patient.
- Applies only to competent, terminally ill adults with less than six months to live, as verified by two physicians.
- Mandates a second medical opinion by a doctor with expertise in the patient's disease regarding the diagnosis and prognosis of the terminal illness.
- Requires consultation with a palliative care specialist to ensure that the patient is aware of and receiving the best possible pain relief.
- Requires consultation with a professional licensed counselor to validate that the patient is in possession of independent and competent judgment and to discuss the decision to hasten death.
- Provides sanction-free nonparticipation for any health care providers or pharmacists who have a conscientious objection to participation.
- Prohibits mercy killing and active euthanasia and does not allow for lethal injection.
- Requires that the patient be fully informed of feasible alternatives, including hospice care, comfort care, and pain control.
- Promotes full involvement of the family.
- Requires two personally communicated requests and one written request.
- Requires two waiting periods, one of fifteen days and the second of forty-eight hours. (Mainers for Death With Dignity 2000)

This in fact coincides with the model law set out by the Hemlock Society (Hemlock Society 2000) and with the typology of state laws we have already examined.

Earlier, the Maine legislature had been unwilling to support decriminalization legislation ("Maine House Rejects Assisted Suicide" 1998). In 1998, the House voted down the bill, 99–42, after the Judiciary Committee had recommended against it by a 12–1 vote. Representative Joseph Brooks reminded his colleagues of a January poll by Strategic Marketing Services that said 71 percent of Mainers supported doctor-assisted suicide. Maine lawmakers had considered doctor-assisted suicide three times before, most recently in 1995, when the Senate defeated an amended bill 24–10 and the House voted 105–35 against it. At that time, The Portland Roman Catholic Diocese, the Maine Hospice Council, and the Maine Medical Association (MMA) opposed the legislation.

Testimony was held before the Maine Senate on February 16, 2000. At that time, Gordon H. Smith, the executive vice president of the MMA, testified that the legislative act to enact the Maine Death With Dignity Act was a "radical proposal, fraught with legal difficulties" and that "Maine should not be the 2d state to enact it" (Smith 2000). Smith articulated two reasons for the MMA's opposition, which resonated with the opposition of many before him: the negative effect upon the role of physicians and the fear of the slippery slope. He cited the common concern about the Dutch experience that Hendin and others have raised, that of nonvoluntary euthanasia. Finally, he pointed to the increased training in palliative care among Maine physicians as a sign that the concerns of patients in pain were being addressed and that cultural changes were taking place in the medical profession there.

A hospice nurse who testified against the reform argued, like other hospice providers had before her in other settings, that "we should not try to control and choose the time of our death." Rather, she added, hospice experience indicates the opposite—that "the final days of life are a precious gift that they would not want to miss" (Demosthenes 2000).

The Maine Osteopathic Association argued that the availability of assisted suicide would crowd out alternatives such as hospice and that adoption of assisted suicide as a reform could impede progress on palliative care (Miller 2000). In addition, representatives of the American Cancer Society, the Maine Consortium for Palliative Care and Hospice, and the Disability Rights Center testified or sent testimony on a number of overlapping bases of opposition. Like others, Maine's Chief Health Officer objected to the reform because of slippery slope objections and because the reform did not "address the need for improved palliative care for terminally ill people" (Mills 2000). The Christian Civic League weighed in with its opposition, with special mention that "passage of this legislation might make Maine a state in which our elderly may feel an obligation to die" (Heath 2000). To the representative of the Catholic Church, "the legalization of Physician Assisted Suicide corrupts all of health care" (Mutty 2000).

One proponent of legal reform used Oregon data to argue against the palliative care specialists, showing the rise in hospice use and the rise in morphine use after the passage of Measure 16. She expressed hope that "these two movements for better end-of-life care can work together" (Melanson 2000). State Representative Joseph Brooks, who has been a major legislative sponsor of assisted suicide reform legislation, urged his colleagues to let the bill pass to the initiative stage, in honor of the many persons who had signed the petitions and the majority of Maine residents who had responded positively to polls regarding assisted suicide reform. One physician described the bill as written by "caring cautious people" (Weiss 2000). The Maine Civil Liberties Union (MCLU) spoke in favor of the liberty elements of the reform, raising the issue of "back-alley" euthanasia, in a clear parallel to the liberalization of abortion debates (Sutton 2000).

Not all representatives of Christian churches were in opposition—a representative of the Bagaduce Interfaith Peace and Justice Committee testified of his personal family experiences and of support he had found in audiences he had spoken to. His group had assisted in gathering signatures for a ballot measure for the assisted suicide reform (Lippke 2000). A Presbyterian minister appealed to support for autonomy and to "give our doctors the authority to deal caringly, professionally, and medically with all the options that are available to the terminally ill" (Bonthius 2000).

Two testifiers were central to that day's discussion. Darlene Grover, a critical care nurse who has assumed a significant role in the reform campaign, testified of her own father's ordeal—a common theme in the framing of the need for compassion by movement activists. She finished: "In my nursing career, I've seen so many people die with no control over what happens to them . . . only focused on their fears and suffering. . . . This bill will allow the terminally ill the choice over this most private of decisions to spend their energies on *living* and not just dying" (Grover 2000). Finally, a medical ethicist argued that the law needed to change before medicine would change, rather than the opposite: "Without this option, many patients will not get the pain relief and palliative care that would make unnecessary their request for assisted dying" (Gelwick 2000).

In May 2000, a new group opposing physician-assisted suicide announced its formation. The director of The Maine Citizens Against the Dangers of Physician-Assisted Suicide (hereafter, Citizens Against) announced that his group hoped to raise $1.3 million to get its message out. He stated the message as: "It's a very, very innocent question, but the law itself . . . is dangerous, fatally flawed, has various loopholes that could turn out to be disastrous to Maine people who have illness."

Mainers for Death With Dignity stated that they expected to be outspent by 4 to 1 or so, given the experience of reformers in other states. Our Oregon data and the Michigan experience indicate that this was risky indeed. In the end, the reformers raised more funds than the opponents (Maine Secretary of State, 2001b).

The coalition included the MMA, the Maine Hospice Council, the Organization of Maine Nursing Executives, and the disability group Alpha One (Moore 2000a). By comparison, in Oregon, the Oregon Medical Association was neutral in 1994, as described in Chapter 3, and the Oregon Hospice Association eventually embraced the legal reform, as described in Chapter 6.

A colleague who was the director of the Maine Hospice Council promoted the alternative of better palliative care, arguing that death with dignity should mean "promoting hospice care, palliative care and effective pain management" instead of suicide (Weinstein 2000).

Citizens Against tried early in the campaign to introduce and combine two issues that opponents of most legal reforms hope can stick to their opponents:

1. The reformers represent "special interests." In Citizens Against's language, the proponents of the referendum represent "the Hemlock Society and other well-funded special interest groups." (Weinstein 2000)
2. The reformers come from out of state and have just landed in Maine as their best chance to succeed. Thus, Citizens Against attempted to portray the reformers as "...targeting Maine as the next battleground in their national campaign to promote physician-assisted suicide and euthanasia." (Weinstein 2000)

Using common political and sports strategies, a representative of the opponents cast her group at the "underdogs" in the ballot contest ("Assisted Suicide Top Question" 2000). The director of Mainers for Death With Dignity challenged the Citizens Against statement as a "scare tactic."

An editorial in the *Journal Tribune* urged that voters take the first claim with a grain of salt.

> The act was not, as opponents imply, brought to the state fully formed by national advocates with a larger agenda. It began with the efforts of Darlene Grover, a critical care nurse . . . who made a deathbed promise to her father that she would fight for the right of other terminally ill patients to escape the pain he suffered at the end of his battle with colon cancer. ("An Emotional Debate" 2000)

While not supporting the November measure, the *Journal Tribune* editorial argued that the law was carefully crafted and would, like Oregon's, be used by a small number of people. The newspaper urged careful consideration of the measure, in an atmosphere in which: " . . . the act will be portrayed as a first step down a slippery slope toward extermination of people with disabilities and as a measure to allow doctors to show compassion toward people in the final stages of suffering" ("An Emotional Debate" 2000).

Much as Dutch case were used—and often misrepresented—in Oregon campaigns, supposed negative information from Oregon's experience was used by reform opponents in Maine (Bradbury 2000). Oregon reformers claimed that the ad referred to dubious information on the use of the ODDA.

Maine opponents had taken their information from an opinion-editorial in *The Oregonian* by associated editor David Reinhard, whose opposition to the ODDA was described in Chapter 4 (Moore 2000b).

Maine television stations allowed that ad to air. However, another opponent ad, claiming potential HMO decisions under the proposed law, was pulled from television stations ("Suicide Opponents Regroup After Ad Loss" 2000).

In the end, the Maine effort resembled the Washington and California defeats. After leading in the polls significantly, support for the measure began to fade after ads claiming lack of safeguards and negative experience began to air widely (Young 2000). Maine voters rejected Measure 1 by a 51–49 margin on November 7. At the same time, voters surprised some analysts by rejecting another measure that would have prohibited discrimination based on sexual orientation. In keeping with our analysis of close reformer victory in Oregon, and close losses in Washington and California, Maine may not have been as conducive as backers hoped. Whether proponents could have operated a more successful campaign will be a topic which reformers in other states return to the future.

STATE LEGISLATIVE EFFORTS FOR REFORM

After Oregon's success with Measure 16 in 1994, legislators in at least fourteen American states introduced similar legislation in their respective state legislatures. California, Colorado, Hawaii, Maine, New Hampshire, Washington, Illinois, Iowa, Florida, Louisiana, New York, Arizona, Michigan, and Rhode Island entertained bills.

In general, the bills followed the Oregon model, with common features on qualifications, witnesses, alternatives and revocation, psychiatric examinations, time periods, immunities and liabilities, residency requirements, and the role of surrogates. In this way, they also shared elements with the model law on the Hemlock Society's web site (Hemlock Society 2000).

California

In California, bills had been introduced in prior legislatures, such as in the 1995 legislature by assembly members Kerry Mazzoni and Diane Martinez, but they were not heard by any committee (California Legislature 1999).

In 1999, however, assembly member Dion Aroner introduced A.B. 1592. Like many reformers, Aroner had faced an experience with a loved one's end of life that was "not a happy one" (Gladstone 1999). Aroner emphasized that her bill would enable mentally competent adults who were terminally ill to self-administer a fatal dose of drugs and characterized the bill as "full of safeguards," an issue of contestation for previous reform campaigns. Aroner emphasized that she is strongly opposed to suicide, but that A.B. 1592 was narrowly tailored to allow physician-assisted suicide only for terminally ill, competent patients. She expressed her belief that doctors should not be criminally sanctioned for permitting a compassionate act, and that patients should not be treated differently than those who can refuse or withdraw treatment:

> Our systems of health care have produced a modern dilemma: Under current California law, terminally ill patients who want to die may request that the medical system not treat them further but may not request medication to hasten their death. . . . [This] bill simply provides compassionate medical assistance by a willing physician to dying patients who choose a humane and dignified death. (California Legislature 1999:9)

Aroner sought to clarify how outlaw physicians like Jack Kevorkian would fall outside the design of her bill and be sanctioned as he was in his last Michigan court case, in which he was sentenced to a prison sentence of ten to twenty-five years. Like the Oregon reformers, she was careful to make Kevorkian an example of what her law would not permit.

Her bill came at a time when a Field Poll showed widespread support in California for right-to-die proposals, with over 70 percent of respondents supporting the concept of allowing terminally ill patients to request and receive life-ending medications ("Assisted-Sucide Bill" 1999). A question asked by the Field Poll, which showed similar results, was whether respondents would want their own doctor to be able to provide suicide assistance if they faced imminent death. An assembly staffer commented that only fresh air and water bills were tracking as high in poll support (Hemann 2000). Despite that, death with dignity bills have not advanced far in any state legislature, and they are untested and viewed as risky, even by reliably liberal civil rights members on other issues (Stefanics 1995).

A.B. 1592 brought swift opposition from the California Medical Association (CMA), which testified against the Aroner bill, charging that physician-assisted suicide, "however well-intentioned," diminishes the right of every dying person to "pass their last days in the most comfort and dignity possible." The CMA president noted that his organization had joined with the California Hospice Association to sponsor legislation that would have mandated health plans to offer hospice care to enrollees as well as a bill that would have increased access to end-of-life care (CMA 1999). The CMA also spoke to the educational programs on pain management they were sponsoring for health professionals.

A Los Angeles oncologist, a member of the CMA's Council on Ethical

Affairs, added: "Doctors must not give up on terminally ill patients. Instead, they must make sure that dying patients' depression is treated and that their pain is fully managed" (CMA 1999). The oncologist, Dr. Rex Greene, characterized the bill as "a way of opening the door for expanding this for people who aren't terminal, who aren't adults, who aren't competent mentally" (Gladstone 1999:A13).

Aroner's bill passed the Assembly Judiciary and passed the Appropriations Committee, but was pulled before it could come to the Assembly floor for lack of votes, despite the support of the then assembly speaker. The bill died as an inactive bill in the 2000 session.

STATE LEGISLATIVE EFFORTS AGAINST REFORM

While Dr. Jack Kevorkian gained recognition in the 1990s for his string of over one hundred assisted suicides and Washington, California, and Oregon voted on decriminalizing physician-assisted suicide, several states were acting in the opposite direction. Since the end of 1994, new statutes against assisted suicide have been enacted in Louisiana (1995); Rhode Island and Iowa (1996); Virginia, Michigan, and South Carolina (1998); and Maryland (1999). In 1998, three states (Kansas, Oklahoma, and South Dakota) added to their existing criminal prohibitions by providing civil penalties as well. The new Michigan law did not include an explicit disclaimer on the legitimacy of pain control, but such legislation was later enacted separately. Kevorkian's flagrant but effective misuse of the principle of double effect in his trials made Michigan legislators hesitant to include such language in their ban.

Other states prohibit assisted suicide by statute (Missouri, New Hampshire, Tennessee) or by common law or interpretation of the state homicide law (Vermont, West Virginia).

OTHER COUNTRIES

The Netherlands

As the country with the longest experience with decriminalization of euthanasia, the Netherlands has drawn worldwide attention, praise, scrutiny, opprobrium, and interest. Of the nearly 35,000 requests made each year, physicians assist in about 9700 patient deaths, usually with a lethal injection, according to a 1995 study of euthanasia in the Netherlands published in the *New England Journal of Medicine* (van der Maas et al. 1996). In 2000, the Dutch have movded beyond their model of 25 years, and have formal legalization of euthanasia ("Dutch Take Step" 2000).

In 1984, the Executive Board of the Royal Dutch Medical Society (KNMG) announced guidelines that formalized emerging court decisions on euthanasia that had begun in the Netherlands in 1973.

In their guidelines, the KNMG established that five criteria must be met for a physician to have observed the "requirements of careful practice," and therefore not be subjected to criminal prosecution:

1. The request for euthanasia must be voluntary.
2. The request must be well-considered.
3. The patient's desire to die must be a lasting one.
4. The patient must experience his suffering as unacceptable for him.
5. The doctor concerned must consult a colleague. (Griffiths et al. 1998:66)

In 1992, a fully documented written record was added as a requirement. Dillman indicates that the fundamentals of the KNMG approach to assisted suicide and euthanasia is found in three concepts: "respect for human dignity, accountability and scrupulousness" (Dillman 1996:100).

Dutch experts have testified before various bodies in other countries that have looked at liberalization of euthanasia laws. In all of these venues, Dutch legal and medical experts have warned of the nonimportability of the Dutch models to other countries with different medical delivery systems and philosophy (Battin 1994; Griffiths et al. 1998:304–305).

The Dutch example has been attacked in various writings in English in medical and other journals, in other articles, in briefs filed in the American test cases *Quill* and *Compassion*, and throughout the debate carried on in the ethics literature.

Critics such as American psychiatrist Herbert Hendin, a vocal critic of Dutch euthanasia policies in *Seduced by Death* (Hendin 1997), make a number of charges that attempt to undermine the idea of Dutch discussion and consensus on this issue, among them: "Despite Dutch acceptance of euthanasia, hard facts about it have not been easy to come by" (Hendin 1997a:49). He asserts that Dutch medical and legal critics of the government policy on euthanasia are made into pariahs in their professions, thus making the Dutch debate a hollow or invisible one. He considers the physicians to be well-intentioned in the Netherlands (Hendin 1997a:11); he knows there is public support for this, but aims his critique at practice—there are not sufficient safeguards. "Virtually every guideline established by the Dutch to regulate euthanasia has been modified or violated with impunity" (Hendin 1997a:23).

Griffiths et al. reject the criticisms of Hendin and British scholar John Keown as being anecdotal and wrong in their emphasis on the expansion of nonvoluntary euthanasia in the Dutch case. In their view, Keown, Hendin, and Carlos Gomez have fixated on the Dutch experience without sufficient reference to the legal experience in their own countries of medical decisions at the end of life. With axes to grind, in Griffiths et al.'s view, they have used anecdotes and insufficient data to make their claims. Keown in particular is critical of the effectiveness of Dutch regulation, especially given reporting levels, a statement Griffiths et al. show some support for (and which the emerging legalization regime should change).

> Keown is so anxious to prove his point that he seems to lose sight of the implications of what he is saying. He has not uncovered evidence of a slope in the Dutch data, let alone of a slippery one. What he really calls attention to is quite a different problem, namely that both in the Netherlands and elsewhere the widespread use of abstinence and administration of pain relief to shorten life calls for much more adequate regulation than it currently receives. (Griffiths et al. 1998:28)

Griffiths et al. show how the Dutch euthanasia cases—2.4 percent of the total Dutch deaths in 1995, according to the work of Paul van der Maas and colleagues—pales in comparison to the other nearly 40 percent of Dutch deaths attributable to either pain relief (18.5 percent) or abstinence (20 percent). In this way, they assert, critics who ignore their own countries' experience with double effect and terminal sedation overemphasize the Dutch experience with euthanasia out of context (van der Maas et al. 1996).

The Dutch are often described as pragmatic in their legal rule-making, and are known for their approach to drug control and prostitution, which emphasizes tolerance and decriminalization (Downes 1988). Leuw and Marshall have characterized the Dutch drug policy as "pragmatic" and "non-moralistic," concepts that stand in opposition to other countries' prohibitionist approaches (Leuw and Marshall 1994: vii). The emphasis in drug policy—as well as euthanasia—has been on the maintenance of the criminal sanction, with the use of guidelines, regulation, and toleration to allow for controlled operation.

To counter criticism of their neighboring countries over their drug policies, the Dutch have lately drawn a bright line between "hard drugs" and "soft drugs," and their increased punitiveness in certain spheres has announced to some the diminution of the "progressive paradigm" (Punch 1996).

The work of the Dutch medical profession, through the KNMG, has been central to the reform of the criminal law regarding euthanasia. The Dutch have embraced physician administration of drugs by injection as their preferred method, and, while assisted suicide is a method that may ensure greater autonomy to many, it is a smaller category there. As Battin points out, the Dutch are far different from the American experience, not only in their provision of health care for all citizens, but in the delivery of health services and the close and long-standing relationship between Dutch physicians and their patients (Battin 1995).

The Dutch have been singular in their approach to euthanasia worldwide, since 1973, when a court in Leeuwarden absolved a physician of criminal responsibility for putting a patient to death. Over the subsequent twenty-seven years, Dutch law has gone through a more common law evolution, as the legislative path to legal change has been blunted by the presence, until 1994, of the Christian Democrats as the major party in the ruling coalition.

Professor Johan Legemaate has described Dutch euthansia developments as having four periods. In the first, a legal opening was created between 1973 and 1984. A debate following the Leeuwarden decision prompted other similar cases and led to the 1984 *Schoonheim* decision by the Dutch Supreme Court, which declared that while the Penal Code defines euthanasia as a crime, doctors may invoke the defense of necessity when they are confronted with a conflict of duties. "A conflict of duties arises when the doctor's professional ethical obligations to honor a patient's request to die with dignity force the physician to act inconsistently with the formal provisions of the Penal Code."

Several experts argue that the secularization and "depillarization" of Dutch society, processes that characterized social changes in the 1960s forward, and the gradual diminution of the importance of organized religion, coincided with these legal changes (Ester et al. 1993). De Moor observes that the combination of individualization and secularization in the Dutch case accounts for rising public support of euthanasia (de Moor 1996).

The Leeuwarden court in 1973 had formulated criteria for the claim of such a defense, and the KNMA clarified the criteria in 1984 with the following requirements: (1) there is voluntary, competent, and durable request on the part of the patient; (2) the request is based on full information; (3) the patient is in a situation of intolerable and hopeless suffering (either physical or mental); (4) there are no acceptable alternatives to euthanasia; and (5) the physician has consulted another physician before performing euthanasia. By 1995, the KNMG would add the need for a written report to its criteria. These criteria have guided Dutch legal and medical practice and policy in this area.

Legemaate allows that the debate over whether to reform the Dutch situation by legislation started in the mid-1980s, but had not resulted in significant legislative reform (the 1994 changes to the Burial Act were largely procedural which changed in 2000).

In our 1996 interviews with Dutch legal and medical experts, the theme emerged of the political impracticality of forging legalization legislation during the many years when the Christian Democratic party was the lead party in the Dutch government. This took place simultaneously with a Ministry of Justice policy that took the court rulings, incorporated the medical association's leadership (for which it has been vilified in some cases in the Netherlands, as well as in medical gatherings abroad [van Leeuwen 1996]), and advanced a policy of nonprosecution.

A series of state commissions and study efforts, including a 1985 state commission and the 1991 Remmelink Commission, have weighed in on the utility of various policy options. The latter was more in the form of an empirical study of doctors' attitudes and reporting, conducted by Paul van der Maas and his colleagues, and has resulted in a firestorm of controversy, mostly abroad, over the issue of nonvoluntary euthanasia. Within the Dutch medical profession and legal circles, the van der Maas data have focused discussion on the level of reporting rates by medical professionals.

How Nonprosecution by Policy Works

Several Dutch legal experts emphasize that their model has evolved because of legislative blocking, rather than through design, and that there have been some recent calls for the movement to legalization of a decriminalized regulatory model.

Dutch prosecutors can choose not to prosecute in the public interest, as opposed to other systems, where the prosecutor is supposed to go forward if there will be a conviction. Euthanasia prosecution is often an example of conflict—between local and national prosecution decision makers. The national prosecutorial body does review decisions by the local prosecutors, given that the Dutch have a national system of prosecution. In some cases, even as the Dutch model was evolving toward nonprosecution in most cases of euthanasia, the decision not to prosecute by local prosecutors was on occasion overridden.

In this atmosphere, the decisions by physicians to report the cases of euthanasia in which they were involved—which, after all, is a central feature of all the proposed forms of regulation—were inevitably affected by prosecutorial power. Some local prosecutors took a more pragmatic approach and adopted an infrastructure and advertised to physicians that if they reported more frankly, the prosecutor would be more cautious of recommending cases for prosecution.

The political party and personal or political leanings of the justice minister can influence prosecution policy in this area significantly. While the Ministry of Justice initially explicitly excluded from prosecution physicians who had followed the criteria, changes in the Ministry could and did lead to other policy decisions in time. The Minister of Justice during the 1990–1994 period (Ernest Hirsch Ballin) indeed stepped up the prosecution of such cases, impressing upon some the need for legislative change to prevent the shifting of policy as a result of cabinet membership and government change.

Often Catholic prosecutors, mostly in the southern part of the country, decided to prosecute. Without case law, they were finding all sorts of cases to prosecute—they said they would only prosecute in cases where there was a new issue, and there were truthfully new issues in many cases.

Indeed, the few prosecutions—with approximately 1500 cases reported a year only five were prosecuted in 1995—that have taken place in the current government have mostly been aimed at rule development. For example, the 1995 prosecution of Doctors Kadike and Prins were for cases involving newborn babies, which the courts upheld as justifiable, since the babies were already on resuscitation (Sutorius 1996). The argument has been made by legal experts that such "test case prosecution" is an unwise use of prosecutorial power, and some judges are beginning to resist this approach.

The national committee procurie general, which includes the head of every court of appeals district, serves as a national decision-making body for prosecution decisions. Since the early 1990s, there was a centralization of decision making. Hirsch Ballin cut a deal with KNMG: If physicians would report and meet guidelines, they would not be prosecuted. This prosecutorial decision was the precursor of the largely administrative legislation of 1994 that ratified these changes through the Burial Law.

The size and power of Dutch opponents to the evolving euthanasia policy have dwindled, again giving support to the observers' assessment of societal consensus. One interview subject considers it "hard to find respectable opponents" and that those who challenge do so with quotes from the Bible or the Pope. Even in the United States, religious groups have often couched their opposition on other issues on which there is secular concern, like safeguards in the case of the 1992 California assisted suicide initiative. Other interview subjects concede that there are some groups that are small but thoughtful opponents.

In the Australian Northern Territories' effort at legal reform on euthanasia, elements closely paralleled the Dutch model, and also resembled the defeated 1991 and 1992 state initiatives in Washington and California, respectively. When the state of Oregon passed its 1994 initiative and upheld it in a 1997 repeal vote, the role of the physician as provider of an injection was removed to make the initiative more palatable to a larger number of voters. One result is that the American model is developing with assisted suicide as the central core of its delivery system. While there is concern from various quarters—Derek Humphry of the Euthanasia Research and Guidance Organization (ERGO) and the proponents of the failed 1997 Oregon repeal law, for example—that some percentage of assisted suicides fail and could benefit from a physician's perspective, assisted suicide—with the physician in the background—has become the American politically preferred model.

By comparison, in the Netherlands, assisted suicide has been less prominent, and the role of the physician, who can and does administer injections, is more prominent.

In this way, the Dutch model has been a medicalized model, not unlike the American abortion law in several states during the liberalization that preceded *Roe v. Wade* (1973). The KNMG is an important party to the negotiations and discussions in a way that the American Medical Association may turn out not to be, given its strenuous opposition to these laws (Dillman 1996; Spreeuwenberg 1996).

By 1999, legislation was once again introduced into the Dutch parliament to fully legalize euthanasia. With some 90 percent of the Dutch citizenry backing the twenty-five-year Dutch experience with euthanasia under guidelines and with the guidance of the medical profession, the bill, sponsored by a progressive party, encountered less opposition than the idea had in the past. At the same time, the Dutch have embraced formal legalization of prostitution after many years of a similar regime with statutory prohibition and official tolerance (Daley 2000; Deutsch 1999; "Dutch Take Step 2000).

Switzerland

The Swiss approach to euthanasia has been on a much smaller scale and is at odds with the Dutch model. It is not based on the physician, instead endorsing assisted suicide without physicians. The Swiss, who have also been more pragmatic and progressive in their drug policy (MacCoun and Reuter 1998), have followed a course of allowing nonphysicians to assist in suicide in certain prescribed cases over a sixty-year period, according to the president of EXIT, the Swiss Society for Humane Dying (Schaer 1999).

In Switzerland, by comparison to the Netherlands, the Swiss medical organization does not support the practice of doctors helping patients die. According to the EXIT president, "Swiss laws stipulate that persons who assist a suicide do so for humane reasons with no chance of personal gain. EXIT requires that the applicant be at least 18 years old, a Swiss resident, mentally competent and suffering from intolerable health problems" (Schaer 1999).

EXIT offered such assistance to a total of 119 persons in 1996 (Schaer 1999). According to a 1999 news report:

> Exit operates in a legal grey area. Under strictly defined circumstances, its "companions in death" are able to procure a fatal drug overdose from sympathetic doctors for a member who has been diagnosed as terminally ill and has repeatedly asked to die.
>
> But the companions are permitted only to hand the lethal cocktail to the person seeking to die. They may not put the drug to the person's lips, administer an injection or turn on an intravenous drip.
>
> After each death, Exit volunteers notify police and provide a detailed written account with dates, times and witnesses. No Exit member has ever been prosecuted [according to the EXIT official]. (Nullis 1999)

In 1999, a group of physician specialists proposed that Switzerland should legalize euthanasia under certain conditions. The group, Help In Dying, argued for a Dutch-type model, with direct active euthanasia remaining illegal, and authorities not prosecuting doctors involved.

According to a news report, the specialists were advising the Swiss Minister of Justice and Police in response to a parliamentary bill. Currently, Article 114 of the Swiss penal code provides for the sentencing of anyone assisting in suicide to imprisonment (Agence France-Presse 1999).

Colombia

In 1997, Colombia's highest court legalized euthanasia for terminally ill people who clearly have given their consent (Sequera 1997). According to one report, "the court decided that a person acting under strict guidelines cannot be held criminally responsible for taking another's life ... [but] ... judges would have to come up with the guidelines and consider on a case-by-case basis whether a person is terminally ill" (Sequera 1997).

Australia

After the Oregon success in 1994, Australia seemed poised to become the second country to legalize physician-assisted suicide in one of its states. In 1995, the legislature in the sparsely populated Northern Territory voted to allow physician-assisted suicide in their territory (Magnusson 1996). The territory—twice the size of Texas with a population of about 170,000 (Ryan 1996:326)—passed a law with features similar to Oregon's and those in the Netherlands. The patient needed to be eighteen years of age, of sound mind, suffering from a terminal illness, and experiencing severe pain or suffering (Ryan 1996:326). After consultation with a second physician with psychiatric credentials, who confirmed the diagnosis and prognosis, and letting a waiting period transpire, the physician could assist in euthanasia, including: "prescribing or preparing a lethal substance, providing such a substance for self-administration, and administering the substance directly to the patient" (Ryan 1996:327).

Magnusson has written a thorough and learned examination of the factors leading to the Northern Territory's passage of an assisted suicide reform law (Magnusson 1996). In his view, the passage of the law was due to a combination of influences. The Rights of the Terminally Ill Act resulted from a bill introduced by the former chief minister, Marshall Perron. Debate over the issue had occurred elsewhere in Australia during the prior decade, when physicians in Melbourne had admitted their participation in euthanasia and called for introduction in the parliament of legislation drafted by the Voluntary Euthanasia Society of Victoria (Magnusson 1996:3). As in the United States, he points out, a combination of factors related to personal autonomy, compassion, the possible declining influence of organized religion, and growing technology as central to modern medicine helped shape the debate (Magnusson 1996:6). In addition, legal and moral issues dealing with the withdrawal of treatment had prepared the way for the discussion of active euthanasia. As he writes:

> The Australian legislation thus includes a variety of mechanisms (advance directives, including "living wills" and proxy decision-making under a court appointed guardian, or pursuant to one during medical power of attorney), which enables patients to exercise—to varying degrees—a right of bodily self-determination encompassing a right to hasten death by refusing life-preserving medical treatment. (Magnusson 1996:20)

The Northern Territory's reform generated a reaction in the Australian parliament; parliament members felt that they could overturn territories' laws. This is exactly what happened in 1997. The territory's controversial Rights of the Terminally Ill Act was overturned by the federal parliament that year, when Victorian Liberal Minister of Parliament Kevin Andrews's private member's bill was passed. Prime Minister John Howard supported the Andrews Bill. The Catholic Church, among others, threw its support into government efforts to rescind the law ("The Catholic Church" 1999).

One report of the 1997 defeat explains: "The pro-euthanasia forces, just a few disorganized and poorly funded voluntary euthanasia groups with a handful of political supporters, had been comprehensively outmanoeuvred" (Brough 1997). It was a success for the fundamentalist Christian faction of the Australian legislature. Although described as a conscience vote, it was the urging of the prime minister that had the effect of influencing votes on a party basis. Moreover, as Brough notes, "Territory rights disappeared as an issue as the anti-euthanasia juggernaut of the Catholic Church, Right to Life and the Anglican Church rolled into Canberra."

With public support for law reform remaining high in Australia generally, a Kevorkian-type physician-challenger emerged in Dr. Phillip Nitschke, who had been active in the Northern Territory, where he had helped four people kill themselves when the law was in effect. After the parliamentary overturn, Nitschke began to operate "death centers" in Brisbane, Sydney, and Melbourne, challenging the authorities there. Nitschke told a reporter, "We have got some decent legal advice, and I'm interested in pushing the limits." Characterized by the media as Australia's "Dr. Death," he also mounted an unsuccessful challenge to Andrews in parliamentary elections. Victoria's Medical Practitioners Board fielded a complaint about Nitschke, which alleged that he encouraged patients to obtain drugs illegally for the purpose of suicide in media reports promoting the Melbourne clinic (Hannan and Naidoo 1999).

In 2000, Nitschke found support in Tasmania for clinics he would operate there. The clinics, educational forums according to an Australian news report, do not "advise, counsel or assist" a patient to die. However, Dr. Nitschke said he could tell a patient if a certain course of action would result in a quick death or if they risked "liver failure and intensive care" (Haley 2000).

Nitschke's clinics coincided with strong support found in Tasmanian polls for both the clinics and assisted suicide generally. According to Haley, "An exclusive Mercury newspaper poll found 64.8 percent approve of euthanasia advisory clinics being held in Tasmania.... While the poll result does not necessarily indicate direct support for euthanasia, it does suggest a gap exists between public attitudes on the issue and the position being taken by health and government officials" (Haley 1999). A 1997 *Mercury* poll found that 54.3 percent of Tasmanians surveyed supported legalizing voluntary euthanasia.

A 1996 poll in the Northern Territory found that 48 percent of Northern Territory doctors supported physician-assisted suicide for terminally ill patients who requested it, and 73 percent of the community supported euthanasia (Alcom 1999).

Meanwhile in Western Australia, Democrat Norm Kelly introduced a Voluntary Euthanasia Bill in the state parliament in May 2000, for the third time. The bill allows a dying patient who is mentally sound to request a doctor's assistance to hasten death. One doctor who supported the bill, speaking as a colleague was facing criminal prosecution for similar acts, stated, "I believe that community attitudes are changing and that the majority of people would be in favour of this sort of legislation" (Ashworth 2000).

The report explains,

> The bill would legalise euthanasia for adults with an incurable illness causing them unbearable and constant suffering and who are of sound mind and have clearly asked to die.
>
> Euthanasia would also be legalised for anyone in a coma with no prospect of recovering consciousness and who had requested, before two witnesses, to have their life ended in such circumstances within the previous five years. (Reuters News 1999)

Belgium

Those working in the euthanasia law and medicine area (van Leeuwen 1996) in the Netherlands had long found themselves at odds with their Belgian neighbors to the south. On a host of social issues, the largely Catholic Belgium society has been at odds with Dutch attitudes and reduced use of the criminal law in areas such as drugs, abortion, prostitution, and euthanasia.

However, by 2000, even the Belgian government was moving closer to the Dutch on the issue of euthanasia. According to a 1999 Reuters report, the ruling coalition of French and Flemish Socialists was considering liberalization.

Liberals and Greens have moved fast to legalize euthanasia since coming to power in mid-1999. Previously, the Christian Democrats, who had been the major partner in forty years of government, had suppressed attempts to decriminalize euthanasia, as the Dutch parallel political party had slowed its use. According to the report, euthanasia is widely practiced in Belgian hospitals, but doctors can be prosecuted under the current penal code.

According to Schotsmans (1996), the Flemish Welfare Committee in 1993 and the Green Party in 1994 started, in different ways, to open the debate on "the right to die with dignity," with the Greens linking it closely to self-determination. To do this, the reformers have had to overcome the Code of the Order of Physicians, Article 95, stating, "Deliberately causing the death of a patient for whatever reason is a criminal act," which is "in no way justified by having been explicitly requested by the patient."

Belgian Doctor Y. Kenis (Kenis 1996) had argued for the legalization of euthanasia in a minority position before the National Colloquium on Bioethics (1985–1987), and told a 1994 European Conference that his 1984 physician survey had found a significant proportion of doctors engaged in euthanasia and supportive of changes in the law.

England

British legal and medicical experts began holding serious debates on the practices surrounding end-of-life care in the 1990s. A lengthy House of Lords debate by the Select Committee on Medical Ethics reported that British law should not change in this area.

The British were tracing some of the 1970s American reforms in the removal of artificial nutrition and other machines. According to a British Broadcasting Corporation (BBC) report, the High Court ruling in 1994 in the case of Tony Bland, who was in a persistent vegetative state, stated that artificial feeding was a medical treatment and could be withdrawn. Bland had been injured in a soccer tragedy that left ninety-five dead. His condition made him the British equivalent of Karen Ann Quinlan.

The Select Committee on Medical Ethics, in their 1994 report, came down strongly opposed voluntary euthanasia. While they cited their sympathy with the stories of individual witnesses, they came down on the side of the British jurist Devlin, who had argued against Mill, Hart, and others regarding the liberalization of victimless crimes laws. To the committee, "dying is not only a personal or individual affair. The death of a person affects the lives of others.... [T]he issue of euthanasia is one in which the interest of the individual cannot be separated from the interest of society as a whole" (Select Committee on Medical Ethics 1994:48).

At the same time, the committee thought double effect was fine. They concluded: "[W]e are satisfied that the professional judgment of the health-care team can be exercised to enable increasing doses of medication ... to be given in order to provide relief, even if this shortens life" (Select Committee on Medical Ethics 1994:48).

Currently, the British Medical Association has guidelines that give doctors the go-ahead to withdraw artificial feeding and hydration from severely incapacitated patients (British Broadcasting Company [hereafter BBC] 1999). Meanwhile, a physicians group calling itself First Do No Harm is trying to counter what they believe is "pro-euthanasia propaganda" as the British Medical Association conducts research to "gauge the public's attitude towards the issue and others connected with euthanasia" (Doctors Campaign against Euthanasia" 1998). At the same time, a bill that would have outlawed the withdrawal of treatment, food, or drink that might lead to death, a bill inspired in part by the Bland case, died in Parliament (BBC 2000). While the public health minister noted that such was the law in Britain currently, and thus the law was unnecessary, the British Medical Association and other health organizations predicted prosecutions of physicians and mobilized against the "draconian" aspects of the bill.

Canada

Like other Commonwealth countries, Canada has seen a great deal of discussion and legal action around the topic of euthanasia and assisted suicide.

In 1993, the Supreme Court of Canada came close to establishing a *Quill*-like ruling in the case of Sue Rodriguez, a severely disabled woman who sought the right to be killed, arguing that her disability prevented her from options that the nondisabled had. According to a Canadian legislator:

> The most famous one is probably the story of Sue Rodriguez, a woman with amyotrophic lateral sclerosis who, under the Canadian Charter of Rights and Freedoms, challenged the ban on assisted suicide in the Criminal Code.
>
> In December 1992, the Supreme Court of British-Columbia turned down her request, stating that section 241 of the Criminal Code did not go against the charter. On March 8, 1993, the Court of Appeal of the same province rejected the appeal by Ms. Rodriguez. Lastly, on September 30, 1993, the Supreme Court of Canada put an end to her crusade, with a close five to four decision that did not quash the debate, far from it. (Picard 1998)

That same year, the Canadian Medical Association completed a series of reports that examined end-of-life issues from the physician's perspective. Following those two leads, the Senate of Canada began a lengthy examination of the topics of assisted suicide and euthanasia in 1994. In hearing from dozens of witnesses of various viewpoints and examining the Dutch experience in depth, the Senate made a serious and thorough inquiry.

In 1995, the Senate completed its report. Because of several factors, including possible risks associated with legalization, a majority of the Special Senate Committee supported no substantial changes in the Canadian laws regarding assisted suicide and euthanasia. There were minority positions on both items.

Witnesses such as Marilynne Seguin of Dying With Dignity saw the suffering of Sue Rodriguez and others as a call to reform of the law: "That is the whole issue—the freedom for that person to choose and to define what is tolerable and not tolerable for them." (Seguin 1995).

The committee did recommend lesser sentences to take into account the elements of compassion and mercy, while at the same time upholding the existing criminal code criminalizing voluntary euthanasia, nonvoluntary euthanasia, and assisted suicide (Special Senate Committee 1995:88).

In 2000, the Canadian high court was considering the appeal of Robert Latimer in a celebrated case engendering high emotion among the farmer's supporters and the disability community over Latimer's necessity defense of himself for the killing of his severely handicapped ten-year-old daughter in 1993.

In February 2000, the Subcommittee to Update "Of Life and Death" of the Standing Senate Committee on Social Affairs, Science and Technology began holding hearings to examine the developments since the tabling in June 1995 of the final report of the Special Senate Committee on Euthanasia and Assisted Suicide. However, the current consideration, in the words of the Senate Chair, "is not reopening the debate on assisted suicide and euthanasia" (Carstairs 2000).

Even in an area in which the 1995 report had been in agreement, there was dismay that issues such as palliative care had not been adequately addressed in the medical culture and the state funding mechanisms. As LaPointe stated, "Despite all we know about the growing need for end-of-life care and the explosion of clinical knowledge in the field, only a minority of medical, nursing, social work, psychology and other health care programs offer palliative care training" (LaPointe 2000).

CONCLUSION

In countries around the world, varied in their developed legal and religious traditions, challenges have been made to the existing law governing end-of-life decisions. Even as several countries hardened their laws toward physician-aided death, reforms were discussed in many countries.

For example, a South African commission has issued a report in which the legalization of euthanasia is considered as a policy option (South African Law Commission 1999). The report noted that "the South African Law Commission has proposed allowing doctors to switch off life support machines, withhold food and water and even administer lethal injections under certain circumstances." The health minister added, "Morally speaking, therefore, it would seem to me that each individual adult citizen in South Africa has to answer the question about the moral defensibility for herself or himself according to the dictates of his or her conscience" (Lovell 1999).

The Israeli Knesset has been directed by the Supreme Court there to determine the conditions under which a person may choose withdrawal of feeding tubes and other end-of-life decisions (Izenberg 1999).

In France, the French penal code distinguishes between "active" euthanasia and "passive" euthanasia. Active euthanasia is regarded as murder, while passive euthanasia is considered an offense against a French law that makes it a crime not to help a person in danger. Nonetheless, a 1998 study reported that almost half the deaths recorded as taking place in intensive care units in France resulted from a decision to stop treatment and could be classed as acts of "passive" euthanasia (Agence France-Presse 1998). In addition, a committee recommended that euthanasia be considered in certain cases (Daley 2000).

In Brazil (Associated Press 1999a), a congressional commission recently recommended liberalization of Brazil's abortion law and reducing punishment for assisted suicides of the terminally ill, from twenty years in prison to five years.

In Russia, approximately 40 percent of respondents to a 2000 poll favored euthanasia as a justified intervention (Tass 2000).

In China, a lawmaker who was a deputy to China's top legislature suggested in 1998 that China should enact a law on euthanasia. The lawmaker, an honorary president of Beijing Children's Hospital, suggested that the aging of China's population encouraged consideration of such practices. "Euthanasia can only be applied to patients suffering from incurable diseases under the precondition that it is the patients' own wishes and has the consent of their family members," the lawmaker said (Xinhua English Newswire 1998).

In Hong Kong (Chan 1999), a survey found physician support for turning off life support systems at a patient's request. The survey found general acceptance of withdrawal of treatment among doctors and the public, but less support for Dutch-type regulations. In Hong Kong, turning off life support machines or prescribing life-ending drugs is considered murder.

The debate in New Zealand over euthanasia law reform took shape at roughly the same time as the debate was enlarging in Australia and other Commonwealth counties. The chairman of the New Zealand Medical Association commented that doctors had no problem with "double-effect" death; it was not seen as euthanasia as the intention was to control pain.

In all these countries, the sea change that Griffiths depicts is taking place (Griffiths et al. 1998), some in smaller ways than others, some at greater speeds than others. The wave of legal reform that took place from the 1960s forward in the area of abortion in Western industrialized societies parallels the current combination of compassion and autonomy as values leading to legal reform. Within the unique cultural and religious traditions of these countries, and against a backdrop of governing parties and coalition politics that either thwart or prod such reforms, activists have mobilized reformers, identified and reached out to stakeholders, and tried to capitalize on growing popular sentiment for greater individual control over the events at the end of life. In the concluding chapter, we will again examine how these themes and forces came together in the successful Oregon legalization effort, and what the lessons of its path indicate for other jurisdictions.

8

The Good Death

CHANGING MORAL BOUNDARIES

> Two-thirds of all deaths in the U.S. each day involve the doctor in participation, at least indirectly.
>
> —Dr. Timothy Quill (Quill 1996:208)

> What I do has nothing to do with the right to die. I don't want the right to die—we'll all die anyway. What I am talking about is the right not to suffer. That's an important distinction, which would be a common and accepted practice in a rational society.
>
> —Dr. Jack Kevorkian (Lessenberry 1996)

> This is not suicide in the normal use of that word. Suicide is usually a secretive, violent act by a despondent person. It cuts short a life and leaves a family traumatized. This is very different.... It is hastening death for someone who is already dying. And it is not secretive or traumatic. They are at home. The family is brought together. They say their final good-byes. And then they simply fall asleep.
>
> —Compassion in Dying's Reverend Ralph Mero (Savage 1996)

INTRODUCTION

In this book, we have presented a sociohistorical description of the death with dignity movement. Three functions are served by the various analytical perspectives taken in this book. First, in a limited sense, *Dying Right* tells the stories of intense political struggles at the ballot box and in the courts. The centerpiece of our analysis is the state of Oregon and its watershed passage of the Oregon Death With Dignity Act (ODDA) in 1994. Oregon is the only state in America where death with dignity (physician-assisted suicide) has been legalized. But Oregon does not stand alone in death with dignity reform efforts. Reformers in Washington and California attempted ballot initiatives several years before. And during the time when implementation of the ODDA was blocked by court challenges and a repeal effort within the state of Oregon, two federal court challenges moved their way to the U.S. Supreme Court. Each of these political actions is described in great detail in this book.

Second, in a broader analytical sense we derive empirical explanations for why further death and dying reform is happening. As the Dutch legal scholar John Griffiths has stated, current events in the right-to-die arena are indicative of a growing sea change worldwide in the relationships between patients, doctors, and the state (Griffiths et al. 1998).

In this broader analysis of the death with dignity movement, we also explain why it is occurring here in the United States. Since 1976, drawing the line between killing and letting die has been a matter of major policy innovation in the United States (Glick 1992). A list of the once-fundamental distinctions that have been erased include withholding versus withdrawing treatment, the rights of competent patients versus incompetent patients, the rights of terminal patients versus nonterminal patients, and the distinction between extraordinary treatments (e.g., artificial respiration) and ordinary treatments (e.g., artificial food and water). The legal mechanisms that have accomplished these changes include living wills, powers of attorney, substituted judgment, and rules of evidence. Between 1977 and 1996, moreover, public support for the following statement—"a person has the right to end his or her life if this person has an incurable disease"—increased steadily from 38 percent to 61 percent (CNN/USA Today Gallup Poll 1996; Glick 1992). And in a poll conducted at the request of California legislators considering a change in California's assisted suicide law in 1999, pollsters found that voter interest in death with dignity was second only to interest in clean air and water (Hemann 2000).

The long history of right-to-die reform enshrined the values of autonomy and choice in medical decision making, especially at the end of life. Popular beliefs about medicine and personal freedom, plus the maturing history of laws and clinical practices permitting control of the time, place, and manner of death, provided reformers with a proven political framework. Also in this broader analytical sense, we have examined why the death with dignity movement is happening through direct legislation and litigation. In this sense, *Dying Right* provides a detailed empirical account of how proposed changes in criminal law and medical practice are actually contested. Our analysis of how legal reformers succeeded in Oregon centers on how reformers framed what might be considered a radical notion—physician-assisted suicide—in the context of personal freedom. From the data that we have collected since 1990—at the front lines and from behind the scenes—we examined how the need for change was conceptualized, argued for, and communicated to a public that has been somewhat interested in but also quite wary of some of the implications of legalizing physician-assisted suicide.

Broadly speaking, therefore, we have described this reform using the dynamics of law and social change. Beginning with an empirical look at changes in the nature of dying, we explored the right-to-die movement in terms of changing relationships between doctors, patients, and the state. Autonomy and compassion were shown to be the two major themes that have been championed by reform proponents. On the other side of the debate, arguments that physician-assisted suicide is tantamount to killing patients, that legal change will result in the wrong persons using the law for the wrong reasons, or that the economically marginalized will be pressured to die against their will were closely considered. Other opposition arguments were also contemplated, including fears of a slippery slope to more active or involuntary forms of euthanasia, the potential for an erosion of trust and good care in the patient-physician relationship, and the ramifications of physician-assisted suicide on the reputation of the medical profession generally. Our detailed description of the strategies of death with dignity reformers and opponents, and their use of the citizens' initiative and litigation, provided an exhaustive case study of direct democracy.

A final function of the book is to analyze the more nuanced ways in which the death with dignity movement is impacting law and society. Of primary interest is the growing recognition, at least among clinicians, that human intervention in the timing and manner of death is already as invasive as, and as risky as, assisted suicide. Some people close to the debate argue that de jure decriminalization of assisted suicide is preferable to de facto decriminalization because only in the former case are regulation and oversight truly possible. In this way, assisted suicide criminal law reform reflects the earlier debates over the proper use of the criminal law in the regulation of gambling, drugs, prostitution and abortion. Of related interest are the semantic arguments that in some measure have led to redefining suicide. Here our analysis draws several parallels with the abortion movement and a variety of other activities under the control of the criminal law—some of which have undergone significant change in recent decades. In addition to the fact that abortion and physician-assisted suicide reform efforts each affect laws and policies that regulate death, they also have in common a divisive cultural struggle in which the changing conceptualization of a medical practice has accompanied a shift in public opinion and legal reform.

COMPETITION OVER RELATIVE MORAL STANDING

In this book we have illustrated how legal activities in the movement to sanction hastened death have involved competition over relative moral standing. We have described the relation between the organized death with dignity movement, attitudes toward hastened death, and conflicts between divergent subcultures in American society. In this final chapter, our task is to incorporate these themes into our examination of the legal activity that affected the shift of those who would hasten death from one social category to another. Our observational focus follows a line of study in which legal activities to produce or block moral reform are analyzed as one way through which "a cultural group acts to preserve, defend, or enhance the dominance and prestige of its own style of living within the total society" (Gusfield 1963:3). Both sides in the death with dignity debate have used legal activities to seek moral dominance. In legal activities for and against the death with dignity movement, "autonomy," "compassion," "protecting the vulnerable," and "the sanctity of human life" have all been terms by which people have expressed approval or disapproval of cultures by reference to the moral positions they accord hastened death. Legal activities on both sides have sought to deviantize competing moral positions. In this sense, this chapter concludes, while demands for hastened death cut across various social categories, legal activities concerning hastened death have been one way Americans have defined their own cultural commitments.

It is worth elaborating on the last paragraph for the purpose of laying out the framework for this chapter. First, following Gusfield's (1972) study of the temperance movement and Duster's (1970) study of American drug legislation, this is a study of moral reform as a political and social issue. In other words, it is within an analytical context of concern with noneconomic issues that we have studied the death with dignity movement. We see the death with dignity movement as a reflection of clashes and conflicts between rival social systems, cultures, and status groups.

In this context, we focus on the historical processes by which moral claims are made and negotiated, a scholarly approach that Jenness (1993) has characterized as one of the dominant sociological frameworks of the last few decades. From the constructionist approach to social problems, the "objective" conditions that underlie social problems are less significant than the processes by which human actors collectively define and interpret social conditions. In the pages that follow, we recapitulate the "natural history" (Spector and Kitsuse 1977) of the death with dignity movement. That history includes efforts to overcome the cultural perception of those whose physical anguish supersedes their will to live as sick, inept, or despondent. It also includes efforts to remove the stigma from physicians who help patients expedite death, so that they would be viewed not as killers, but as "midwives throughout the dying process," as one prominent physician activist has called himself. The central theme in this discussion is the claim that "specific individuals and groups must promote or resist particular ways of conceptualizing deviance and policies toward it. Hence the inevitable links between deviance, political action, and social change" (Schur 1980:23).

Schur (1980) explains that deviance struggles involve competition over relative moral standing. The early history of the right to die is an example of politicization of deviance, a term Schur applied to collective attempts to resist or reduce being labeled as deviant. Other historical examples of the politicization of deviance include the questionable application of the amorphous "psychopath" diagnosis to a range of sexual offenses (Sutherland 1950), the deletion of homosexuality from the American Psychiatric Association's published list of sexual disorders (Dombrink 1988), the movement by prostitutes to take ownership of the problem of prostitution away from experts (Jenness 1993), and efforts to decriminalize marijuana use (DiChiara and Galliher 1994), among others.

A major focal point for such studies of collective definition has to do with the processes through which, and conditions under which, particular deviance categories develop and change. Schur (1980) identified continuing struggles over competing social definitions in terms of power. Says Schur:

> At all levels, deviance situations reflect some people's response to other people's behavior as being troublesome, offensive, problematic, or unsettling—as being, in one way or another, personally or socially threatening. . . . The perceived threat may be direct or indirect, patently economic or largely symbolic, and grounded in rational assessment, irrational response, or mistake. What is most important . . . is the perception itself. (Schur 1980:229)

In the following pages, we emulate Schur's assertion that "deviance is always a social construction, brought about through a characteristic process of social definition and reaction" (Schur 1980:18). The sociologist's endeavor in explaining the collective definition of a social problem, and the commencement of a political movement, is to determine who feels threatened and whose interests are at stake (Schur 1980). We apply these propositions to the conditions under which the death with dignity movement commenced in America.

EARLY HISTORY

In general, physicians have not been trained to treat patients and families facing death. Moreover, for both psychological and cultural reasons, they typically shunned the actual experience of death when it happened to their own patients. Under these conditions, physicians labored under their own inadequacies whenever patients and families sought advice. These inadequacies were both personal and structural. The concept of planning for and perhaps even hastening death had no place in the discourse and practices of institutionalized end-of-life care. In reality, however, the prevailing discourse and practices caused greater problems for those who encounter death in their medical practices.

Telling and interpreting personal histories and interpretations given to these histories became ways of construing meaning to events and situations that would later become the basis of discourse on legal change. For example, Dr. Peter Goodwin, a chief petitioner of the ODDA, told how his own life was profoundly affected the first time a patient asked him for assistance with dying. "It felt as if my blood froze," he said. "I realized that with all my technical knowledge about diagnosing and treating, I knew nothing about helping people die. And there was nowhere to turn—not to my colleagues, my association, the literature. There was literally no guidance anywhere" (Goodwin 1996). So Dr. Goodwin joined the Hemlock Society and served as a board director, just waiting for an opportunity for legal reform to come along, an opportunity like the ODDA.

The harmful burdens of heroic medicine became anecdotal inside and outside hospitals and nursing homes. People were angry at their own doctors and the medical profession generally for being so patronizing as to decide how their lives would be lived. Largely because of such tragedies, and reinforced by sympathetic media coverage of them, patients and their families began demanding more control over treatment decision making, especially at the threshold of death. But doctors like Timothy Quill in New York and Peter Goodwin in Oregon said they could not practice end-of-life medicine any better without professional and legal acquiescence in helping patients to exercise choice before death is imminent. For example, a doctor speaking on behalf of the Hemlock Society stated, "It's a very very fine line between increasing a dose knowing we are shortening the dying process, on the one hand, and on the other saying, 'Okay, today is the day—this is certainly enough medication that we will certainly end the patient's suffering on this particular day.' " Some physicians expressed reluctance to help patients to die for fear of being drawn in: "It's difficult to act in the present legal climate" (Goodwin 1996). Some crossed the line. Operating in fear, they linked up with leaders in the legal profession, and this professional alliance advocated reform of assisted suicide law.

For physicians who felt that the present legal climate "put the monkey around their necks" (Goodwin 1996), a decision by the people at large to change the law seemed both desirable and worth pursuing.

As dying patients and their families have entered the professional aided-dying discourse, they have brought their own experiences and insights to bear on political analysis. They have sought to transform the cultural image of suicide as a violent, lonely, despairing act that leaves survivors confused and guilty for not having seen it coming to a compassionate act of self-deliverance that honors choice and relieves suffering. According to these reformers, the fear of death in Western, Judeo-Christian culture, and the resulting laws for dealing with a person who no longer wishes to live, compound the disasters of heroic medicine. Viewed in this light, they say, any facial ban against assisted suicide prevents dying people from deciding the circumstances of their own death, denigrates their moral judgment, and limits their freedom. Most importantly, choice in dying is more than an individual need, private crisis, or hospital staff problem: It is a collective need because each of us will experience our own and maybe another's death some time or another.

Patients and professionals looked at physician-aided dying from different standpoints, but patients, as sufferers and political actors, moved physicians to a more radical political position. Dying patients and/or their families insisted that the medical profession listen. Many in the medical profession heard the general message as well as individual patients' demands. Now, however, communication and negotiation occurred in public forums between institutions, organizations, and professional movements rather than in the seclusion of hospitals and courtrooms. What had been the private problem of death had become political, and what had been the subject of personal discussions had turned into a public debate.

We aver from these data that changes in the doctor-patient relationship have been, and are being, stirred by wider social movements to protect consumers' rights and patients' rights. The paternalism of the old ethics has been largely abandoned along with the power shift that has occurred as informed consent and similar ethical principles have transformed common social practices (Darvall 1993; Jonsen 1990; Griffiths et al. 1998). One dramatic empirical example is the abandonment of the belief among doctors that patients do not really want to know what is wrong with them or that they cannot possibly understand. In 1961, JAMA published a study of physicians' practices in telling or not telling patients about a diagnosis of cancer. The results were that cancer patients were rarely told of their diagnoses or prognoses. But less than twenty years later, an AMA report stated that diagnoses and prognoses are the least amount of information most patients are given (Council on Scientific Affairs 1996).

As Porter describes in *The Greatest Benefit to Mankind: A Medical History of Humanity*, "new tensions and uncertainties in the patient-doctor relationship are in many ways a response to the modern medicalization of life" (1997:690). In recent decades, many protests have arisen against the medical system and the medical establishment. Porter calls attention to:

> the widening provision of medical explanations, opinions, services and interventions; the infiltration of medicine into many spheres of life, from normal pregnancy and childbirth to alcohol and drugs related behavior, in line with a philosophy that assumes the more medicine the better.... Today's complex and confused attitudes towards medicine are the cumulative responses to a century of the growth of the therapeutic state and the medicalized society. (Porter 1998: 690–691)

As Griffiths explains, physicians' practices are coming under greater legal control in all sorts of countries, and the legal position of patients is growing stronger. This general domestication of medicine is the major sea change that is taking place, and particular legal battles are but local manifestations (Griffiths et al. 1998).

As these changes have taken place, dying has increasingly moved from the private sphere into the center of public debates (Callahan 1987, 1990, 1992, 1993; Englehardt 1989; Glick 1992; Jonsen 1990; Meisel 1992; Vaux 1992). To Porter, "What has occurred is not a conspiracy by medical elites to push professional dominance into domains traditionally outside medicine's province, but rather the destabilization of the boundaries of lay and professional competence" (Porter 1997:702).

Because the line between letting die and inducing death is very unclear, and because the legal and professional ramifications of falling on the wrong side of the line are potentially devastating, many physicians will not do what they would do if it were legal, and whatever does occur occurs secretly. In Washington, an op-ed piece in the *Seattle Times* in 1991 by Nicolas Canaday noted: "Some doctors help patients when asked, others won't. Rather than depend on how lucky we are in a choice of physicians, we want our decision in such an important matter to be authorized by law" (Canaday 1991).

An analysis of the evolution of problem identification demonstrates that, much like the decriminalization of abortion, assisted suicide law is changing because a grassroots movement of patients, family, and physicians made people aware that accepted medical practices such as orders not to resuscitate, removing breathing and feeding apparatuses, and sedating the imminently dying are all strong indicators that choice in dying occurs already.

THE CENTRALITY AND MARGINALITY OF EARLY MOVEMENT LEADERS

Another example of competition over relative moral standing is the potential undermining of reform by more radical public figures associated with the movement. At the time of this writing, Derek Humphry, the so-called father of the death with dignity movement in America, has been in the news again. Humphry's controversial book, *Final Exit*, has been reproduced on video, and several cable stations across the nation have opted to air it, even in the face of strong opposition from not only the right-to-life camp, but also death with dignity supporters. As base as Humphry's book seems to some—it details the amounts of prescription medications needed to overdose as well as promotes the added measure of a tying a plastic bag around one's head as a way of making sure that death results if not by drugs alone, then by the combination of drugs and suffocation—it has not only been a best-seller in the United States, but has also been published in seven languages.

Yet as we discussed in Chapter 3, reformer leaders in Oregon have persisted in distancing themselves from Humphry. In 1994, while Oregon voters were debating the provisions of the ODDA, distancing Humphry was a precarious move. The reformers needed Humphry's widespread base of political supporters, especially the financial contributions that he could muster from them. Humphry, on the other hand, wanted progress in the movement he had started, and the movement in Oregon placed him back in the public eye. Oregon Right to Die and its affiliated organizations could not afford to suffer a backlash from Humphry and Hemlock Society members, since neither group could benefit from the appearance of major factions within the death with dignity movement. Therefore, leaders of the Oregon campaign carefully orchestrated a fine strategy of simultaneously courting Humphry, yet keeping him out of their strategy sessions and, more importantly, the public eye.

We interviewed Humphry in 1996, at a point when reformers in Oregon were painstakingly trying to defeat the injunction issued by a federal judge. Even then Humphry persisted in his view that the ODDA would be a first step in legalizing the use of lethal injections by physicians who were willing to step into the controversial, and perhaps career-ending, practice of hastening death. Humphry's characterization of the ODDA clearly controverted the stated goals of the reform leadership. Somehow, however, they managed to keep Humphry's vision of the ODDA out of public debate. Using the colloquialism "half a loaf is better than none at all," Humphry, we can only guess, moved aside in hopes that this strategy was the best way to further the social movement he had started. If the ODDA paved the way for lethal injections,

Humphry would win the debate between himself and reform leaders in Oregon. If it didn't, so be it—legalizing lethal doses of prescription medications would advance his social cause.

Now we turn to the problem of—in the eyes of Oregon reform leaders—Jack Kevorkian. When death was raised as an issue of discussion in America in the 1990s, it wasn't the genteel approach of a surgeon general, a PBS discussion led by Bill Moyers, or an earnest religious debate that piqued public interest. Instead, it was the continuing saga of Dr. Jack Kevorkian—his patients and the legal controversies that followed him.

In advocating his vision of freedom from suffering, Kevorkian made a point of stepping on toes—often with a bizarre relish and fascination with things related to dying. Whether it was proposing to allow prisoners on death row to donate their organs (Kevorkian 1991), displaying his macabre artwork on the television program *60 Minutes*, or appearing in a Michigan courtroom in a powdered wig and judicial gown, Kevorkian cut a unique swath through American culture in the 1990s.

It is remarkable that Kevorkian became such a cultural icon in such a relatively short period. He has been the butt of many political cartoons and late-night talk-show monologues. References to him have been made during congressional hearings. Even cyber language reveals the popularity of Jack Kevorkian: To "kevork" has become synonymous with killing something (Kakutani 2000). He appeared on a *Time* magazine cover—yet so did John Gotti (Gibbs 1993). He also appeared at a *Time* party celebrating cover story subjects and the end of the century, and Kevorkian's table-hopping with the likes of more traditional cultural icons and political movers and shakers seemed against the image of him as Dr. Death.

What is less remarkable about Kevorkian is that he exemplified a consistent pattern in the decriminalization of contested moral activities. Mangione and Fowler (1979), for example, have shown that gambling laws were ripe for change, and legalization became imminent when juries typically wouldn't convict illegal gamblers, judges wouldn't pronounce prison sentences for the few who were convicted, and prosecutors and the police took notice.

Kevorkian challenged the law by claiming that end-of-life practices are simply not a matter for lawmakers and judges. Popular appeal covered him as long as it was understood that he went no further than giving people the means to bring about their own deaths. That was more than courts and legislators would allow, and as long as juries remained willing to acquit Kevorkian, even when he acted beyond what legal institutions would permit, his seditiousness and odd charm appealed to the public and put him at the forefront of the movement generally. But unlike Humphry, Kevorkian had no organized following, meaning no votes and no money, so he was never a player who had to be placated. Mainstream movement leaders who worked to change the law—not defy it—persisted in distancing themselves from Kevorkian, and that didn't hurt them in the court of public opinion. Conversely, they benefited from the popular appeal Kevorkian engendered for the twin themes of compassion and legal autonomy. Still, like Humphry, Kevorkian was at once a spur for the death with dignity movement and a lightning rod for criticisms of its potential excesses. In other ways, however, Kevorkian played a functional role for reformers who came after him, reformers like Timothy Quill who by refraining from Kevorkian-like zeal could lay claim to cultural centrism.

This discussion has illustrated how death with dignity proponents have worked to align their goals with the values of voters, from the perspectives of people who have suffered through the prolonged death of loved ones, those who are suffering prolonged deaths, physicians who treat and counsel patients and their families, and political activists who want the laws changed. The following section details how social reformers in Oregon captured these sentiments to advance their cause.

MOVEMENT ACTIVISTS, PUBLIC ATTITUDES, AND SOCIETAL CONFLICTS

A major activity of the death with dignity movement has been to gain legitimacy for its claims by linking them with broadly accepted cultural values and beliefs. This linkage is a process known as "frame alignment" (Snow and Benford 1988; Snow, Rochford, Worden, and Benford 1986). Snow and Benford explain:

> We use the verb framing to conceptualize this signifying work precisely because that is one of the things social movements do. They frame, or assign meaning to and interpret, relevant events and conditions in ways that are intended to mobilize potential adherents and constituents, to garner bystander support and to demobilize antagonists. In an earlier paper, we argued that the mobilization and activation of participants are contingent upon "the linkage of individual and [social movement organization] interpretive orientation, such that some set of individual interests, values, and beliefs and organization activities, goals and ideology are congruent and complementary" (Snow et al. 1986:464). We referred to this linkage as "frame alignment." (Snow and Benford 1988:198)

The phrase "frame alignment processes" refers to the linkages between individual and movement interpretive orientations. "So conceptualized, it follows that frame alignment is a necessary condition for movement participation, whatever its nature or intensity" (Snow et al. 1986).

To begin the processes of frame alignment, the movement hired professionals to (1) collect data from focus groups and (2) collect opinion data from the Oregon electorate. In the focus groups, people were asked to read the ballot question and then were asked if they would vote for or against the law. A moderator facilitated open discussion to determine the bases for the respondents' opinions. Then the moderator presented the opponents' arguments and asked whether the participants' opinions had changed and why. The moderator also tested reactions to a variety of slogans for the purpose of determining which slogans would win over public acceptance of death with dignity. Reactions to a variety of television advertisements were also assessed. The procedures permitted the detection of subtle differences in participants' reactions to particular phrasings and images. These data were summarized in a report to movement activists, and generalizations were drawn about the levels of support for the movement's preferred frames.

Proponents also used baseline poll data to identify the characteristics and demographics of voters who identify with choice and autonomy. Then, throughout the course of the campaign, tracking polls were used to detect voter response to advertisements. Reactions to their own ads and to opponents' ads were closely monitored. Even shoppers in malls were randomly selected to test the campaign's messages. Television and newspaper interviews were arranged whenever the data indicated a new need for frame reinforcement or realignment. The gap in support for proponents and opponents was very closely watched, and so was the sway of undecided voters. These tactics, which are commonplace in candidate campaigns, are far more sophisticated than the tactics typically employed by leaders of ballot measure campaigns (Jenness 1999).

Yet Tarrow notes that not all framing is controlled by movement activists; rather, they compete with the media for attempts to shape messages. He also argues that movement activists are careful to define the "us" and "them" in a movement, and to define their enemies "by real or imagined attributes and evils" (Tarrow 1998:22).

Moreover, frame alignment processes differ with the constraints inherent in different reform strategies. As earlier chapters have shown, proponents and opponents of assisted suicide reform resorted to different discourses and tactics depending on whether they were in court or running a ballot initiative campaign. However, despite these differences, sociologist Valerie Jenness makes it clear that "frame alignment processes nonetheless remain critical to the successful negotiation of the larger sociopolitical environment that crusaders of any type must participate in and ultimately be responsive to" (Jenness 1993).

Proponents of expanding the right to die continuously and firmly situated the death with dignity movement within larger publicly legitimated issues and community values. As we have striven to demonstrate throughout this book, the death with dignity movement has symbolically and literally linked the right to seek a physician's active, intentional assistance in causing death to principles and beliefs emanating from the right to die movement, the movement to decriminalize the harm caused by criminalization of activities that are happening anyway (e.g., drugs, abortion), the larger efforts in this nation and others to bolster the position of patients against the harms of medicalized life, and the widespread public support—sometimes more than 70 percent—among Americans who voice approval for physician aid in hastening death. These issues and their attendant discourse constitute not only the political backdrop for the death with dignity movement but also a rhetorical and cultural resource for it.

Reformers framed their appeals for change along four distinct yet complementary lines: (1) compassion for suffering patients; (2) patient autonomy; (3) recognition that underground practices of assisted suicide exist already, and (4) the benefits of bringing underground practices into the open. In these ways, they articulated recurrent themes from reform movements to decriminalize other activities such as abortion, gambling, and drugs.

The perception that modern medicine does little to reduce suffering has been a major impetus for the right to die movement. Philosopher Margaret Pabst Battin identifies mercy, or compassion, as a fundamental moral principle on which the case for euthanasia rests:

> The principle of mercy asserts that where possible, one ought to relieve the pain or suffering of another person, when it does not contravene that person's wishes, where one can do so without undue costs to oneself, where one will not violate other moral obligations, where the pain or suffering itself is not necessary for the sufferer's attainment of some overriding good, and where the pain or suffering can be relieved without precluding the sufferer's attainment of some overriding good. (Battin 1994:101)

Similarly, in 1958 Glanville Williams, a British scholar of jurisprudence, argued for legal reform of euthanasia laws as a way of preventing cruelty to patients and relatives: "Those who plead for the legalization of euthanasia think that it is cruel to allow a human being to linger for months in the last stage of aging, weakness and decay, and to refuse him his demand for merciful release" (Williams 1969:134). A quarter-century later, Williams's urgings have been echoed by physicians like Timothy Quill and other American physicians who have led the movement for assisted suicide reform. In 1993,

Quill wrote, "A patient's request for assisted death often seemed simultaneously legitimate, heartbreaking, and terrifying to the caregivers. Watching patients beg for assistance that did not come seemed cruel, adding a final humiliation to a process that was already grueling and undermining" (Quill 1993:130–131).

Nonphysician reformers similarly argue that patients with terminal illnesses are primarily asking for refuge from suffering, which they characterize as unwanted, horrible, and essentially unproductive. For example, compassion for suffering was articulated in campaign ads during all three of the state ballot initiative campaigns detailed in Chapters 2 to 4 and in the legal arguments presented in two federal court challenges that were eventually rejected by the U.S. Supreme Court (Chapter 5).

A second primary rhetorical and cultural resource that has been offered in support of reform is patient autonomy. Battin identifies the principle of patient autonomy as a rationale for euthanasia: "[O]ne ought to respect a competent person's choices, where one can do so without undue costs to oneself, where doing so will not violate other moral obligations, and where these choices do not threaten harm to other persons or parties" (Battin 1994:107).

In 1994, federal District Court Judge Barbara Rothstein rooted part of her opinion favoring the reformers in this manner:

> The liberty interest protected by the Fourteenth Amendment is the freedom to make choices according to one's individual conscience about those matters which are essential to personal autonomy and basic human dignity. There is no more profoundly personal decision, nor one which is closer to the heart of personal liberty, than the choice which a terminally ill person makes to end his or her suffering and hasten an inevitable death. (Compassion I 1994, at 16)

Although Judge Rothstein's ruling was eventually rejected by the U.S. Supreme Court, it became a powerful rhetorical resource for framing issues in the campaign urging Oregon voters to pass Measure 16—the ODDA. For example, a television ad broadcast during the campaign stated:

> This is my body. I don't need you, I don't need government, I don't need any church playing politics with my choices, with my life. If I'm terminally ill, I'll decide how and when and in what way I will end my life. Measure 16 has all the safeguards you and I need. And it ends government and religious interference in a part of our lives that is strictly personal. Vote yes on Measure 16. ("Faces" 1994)

Ads like this illustrate the ways in which Oregon reformers used attempts to change the law as a way to define their own moral positions regarding hastened death. In this way, their efforts to deviantize competing moral positions contradicted the usual sentiment that a wish to die is always a sign of mental weakness. Instead of the image of a jilted lover or a financially ruined businessman who just wants to end it all, the images offered in the campaigns—and in prior legal reform efforts—personified the tragedy of a physically miserable existence made worse by the excesses and paternalism of modern medicine. Although moral opposition to hastening death made sense to many people, the passage of the ODDA suggests that many felt even stronger that they would not want to be forced by law to suffer until the bitter end. Why, then, did similar campaigns in Washington and California fail? What did Oregon reformers do differently to get their law passed?

MOVEMENT MOBILIZATION

By 1994, thanks in part to the continued interest in Jack Kevorkian, people's understanding of the issues surrounding death and dying went beyond the scope of public knowledge during the earlier campaigns in Washington and California. Three things happened in Oregon: (1) Communities around the state were joined via satellite for a public debate on the merits of physician-assisted suicide, (2) a small group of prominent citizens (including the parents of Janet Adkins) started an organization called Oregon Death With Dignity, and (3) a campaign to get the issue of physician-assisted suicide on the Oregon ballot was mobilized. Barbara Coombs Lee and Peter Goodwin, two of the chief petitioners of the ODDA, each had excellent community and professional standing with many years of experience and service in health care. Together with a third petitioner—Al Sinnard, whose wife had died a lonely death—they sought to build a coalition of people with professional and community integrity and reputations. Their goal was to secure voter confidence that the coalition truly aimed to achieve what is best for patients, and physicians, in terms of what could actually be accomplished by changing the law.

POLITICAL STRATEGIES

The discursive themes proceeding from the rights movements of the 1960s and 1970s have formed the sociopolitical terrain that has inspired and fueled the contemporary death with dignity movement, while the conservative politics of the 1980s has presented obstacles for the movement. At present, pro-life groups are increasingly including euthanasia in their anti-abortion campaign. The death with dignity movement, however, has succeeded in tapping into the discourse from rights movements and their attendant arenas of debate to frame its grievances, press its claims, and seek support for the movement. It is this discourse that has been the backdrop of, and resources for, the death with dignity movement's moral contestation of assisted suicide laws.

The small coalition of professionals started with two goals. First, they wanted to obtain the voters' confidence that the coalition truly aimed to achieve what is best for patients and physicians. Second, they wanted to be realistic about what could actually be accomplished by changing the law. This framework led to two vital strategies: proposing a prescribing bill only (omitting injections) and conceptualizing the law as a safe harbor for Oregonians and by Oregonians.

Reformers have stressed the point that they started without a law in mind, believing instead that they should first learn what degrees of death with dignity people actually wanted. To gain that knowledge, leaders of the newly formed organization Oregon Right to Die held a forum for physicians, nurses, hospice workers, and pharmacists, as well as terminal patients and their families and people who had watched loved ones suffer protracted deaths or botched suicides. The goal was to get a bare-bones view of the problems surrounding the care of the dying and to develop possible options that could realistically work.

Consensus is reported to have been achieved without regard to the foreseeable counterattacks by the opposition. For example, Dr. Goodwin stresses that while omitting injections from the consensus and subsequent legislation had a very favorable political impact, that is not why they were omitted. "They were omitted because doctors overwhelmingly felt like they could not and would not provide them, and patients expressed very little interest in having them available" (Goodwin 1996). Chapter 3 of this book described the unofficial survey of physicians around the Portland area. It indicated that a majority of doctors would like their patients to have the option of taking a prescribed lethality, but none were interested in injecting their patients. Patients in the coalition also said that they did not like the idea of injections, but they would like the option of swallowing a lethal dose of medicine. From this process of determining what could work for both patients and doctors, the coalition decided it was realistic to seek assisted suicide, but not injections.

Another crucial strategy was to strive to distinguish death with dignity from suicide. This was not just a repetition of the claim that there is a moral distinction between a fifty-four-year-old blasting his head off after being fired (suicide) and a thirty-four-year-old in the final ravages of AIDS feeding himself a deadly amount of prescription medicine mixed in chocolate pudding and dying restfully, accompanied by friends and family, in the comfort of his own bedroom (death with dignity). Assisting someone in the first scenario is still illegal in Oregon, said Coombs Lee. Instead, the ODDA created a "safe harbor," which means that there is now a set of statutory guidelines that allow physicians and loved ones to aid or abet the inevitable, imminent death of a suffering person, as in the second case just described, without fear of coming into the reaches of the assisted suicide law.

The point is that in Oregon the death with dignity movement proceeded to a second stage, which moderated between the interests of patients and the interests of physicians and sought only what people really wanted. The coalition came up with new ideas for strategies, and its leaders had better know-how about deploying resources. Much like movement organizers in McCann's scholarship on pay equity (1994) and Silverstein's (1996) on animal rights, reformers in Oregon deployed legal resources within the context of a broad-based movement campaign and with an eye toward tactical coordination. They were hardly naive or narrow about the law's promises for advancing the cause of death with dignity. Most significantly, they characterized their efforts in terms of likely outcomes and decisions for dying patients and the doctors who care for them.

REFORM STRATEGIES

The bulk of scholarship examining the relationship between law and the politics of social reform advocacy in the United States has been "highly circumspect" regarding the progressive potential of legal tactics and legal activists in struggles for social change (McCann and Silverstein 1998). Yet in the view of reformers who succeeded in passing and implementing the ODDA, they did not win a concession from defenders of the status quo—by contrast, they literally took their victory (Stutsman 2000). Variables attributed to this success include a demographically homogenous voter population, a geographically small campaign area, an affordable media market, strength in the polls, and the political ability to control wayward activists in the right-to-die movement. More importantly, the reform leaders planned and implemented reform strategies that are typically more familiar to candidate campaigners than to ballot measure campaigners.

Oregon organizers realized that successful reform requires more than formally enacting a law (Duncan 1996). To build political credibility they were careful to propose only what people would actually feel comfortable doing. That was one lesson from the failure of the initiatives in Washington and California, both of which included lethal injections even though few doctors care to provide them. Oregon reform seekers enhanced their credibility by organizing a broad coalition of people whose professional and personal lives would be directly affected by changing the law. They developed a political platform and moral rationale for allowing physicians to prescribe lethalities, but not to inject patients or otherwise intentionally end their lives. By frankly looking ahead at what physicians and other health care providers, patients, and potential patients can live and die with, Oregon reformers have distinguished themselves from reformers in Washington and California, who apparently made a crucial political mistake when they put formal law before social experience.

Another strategy used by reform leaders was the framing of reform goals in a way that would win over the many professionals in health care who would actually be faced with implementing the ODDA—those who actually have a stake in the law. The importance of stakeholders can be summarized this way. First, it's one thing to get popular will and grassroots support; second, it's quite another to present the movement goals and proposed law in a way that stakeholders can go along with. Third, the movement must be able to organize and execute information gathering and media buys so well that they can overcome the money and institutions that defend the status quo by getting half-plus-one of the voters to vote for their proposal. By their own admission, the reform leadership did not fully realize the key importance of stakeholders at the time the ODDA was passed. Ironically, however, the legal challenges that lasted four years and included two votes bought time for rules and protocols to be developed, not to mention the formation of the prestigious Task Force to Improve the Care of Terminally-Ill Oregonians—producers of the ninety-one-page *Guidebook for Health Care Providers* concerning the ODDA. The activities of opposition forces also gave reformers time to increase their understanding of stakeholder participation by the time they cleared the way for implementing the ODDA.

The fact that the movement leaders in Oregon didn't fully realize the key importance of stakeholders at the time the ODDA was passed apparently didn't hurt them because the opponents were even less politically savvy. One of the observations of the reformers in Oregon is that they were blessed with the political miscalculations by their opponents on several occasions. To them, the strategy mistakes of the opponents started in 1993. At that time, the opponents severely underestimated what was new about Measure 16. For one, the people behind the law weren't the same old Hemlock Society people, and the law wasn't the same old broad euthanasia proposal. Instead of burying their disdain and evaluating the proposed law on its own merits, the reformers felt that their opponents resorted to legalistic tactics that in hindsight truly helped the death with dignity movement reformers.

Litigation over the title of the ballot measure is the second example of this mistaken strategy. Opponents did it to keep the signature gatherers off the streets. When at first they lost this battle, they challenged the decision, delaying the process until the end of April 1994, giving them just a few months to fight the initiative once their effort to keep it off the ballot was soundly defeated.

The third perceived mistake was seeking an injunction on grounds that were ultimately unsupportable. While the litigants' strategy did succeed with injunctions from Judge Hogan in *Lee v. Oregon*, they were ultimately overturned by the Ninth Circuit and were not granted review by the Supreme Court.

The 1997 repeal campaign (Measure 51) was the death with dignity opponents' fourth and greatest mistake. They suffered serious repercussions from their legalistic tactics. While the opponents might have accepted the "draconian" compromises the Oregon reformers were willing to accept in order to avoid a second ballot measure campaign, they pressed ahead with a repeal. Their tactics backfired with the citizens of Oregon in November 1997, when the reformers received a 60–40 windfall, plus the support of a governor's veto against future efforts to defeat, block, or negatively amend Measure 16. In 1997, the opponents might have commanded major concessions. A year later—and mostly because of their own tactics—they were left only with dealing with the reformers on the reformers' chosen terms.

This outcome comports with Bowler and Donovan's conclusion that offering a counterinitiative to increase confusion and deplete the rival campaign's resources may be unsuccessful when policy consequences are localized. "[V]oters make decisions on the basis of how initiatives might affect them, and their local community's interests" (Bowler and Donovan 1998:107).

LAW AND POLITICS

Three interrelated political schemas have accounted for the movement's successes in Oregon. From the start, Oregon leaders of the right-to-die movement recognized the superiority of using the ballot initiative over legislative and judicial efforts. The legislatures and courts were the forums of choice in the 1970s and 1980s when right-to-die efforts involved treatment withholding and withdrawal, advance directives, and standards for permitting substituted judgment—all rights derived from the laws and ethical principles of informed consent. But legislators and judges never had the political backing to recognize a right of a patient to request and receive a physician's explicit assistance in hastening death.

Yet lawmaking by initiative offered movement leaders a second political schema—the base political utility of frequent random voter surveys and focus group data to wage a media campaign wherein erosion of support could be tolerated as long as supporters systematically maintained 50 percent approval plus a single vote. Media buys represented a key battle. In Oregon, a lower-cost, sophisticated, empirically driven media strategy was more salient than the relative amounts of money spent by the opposing campaigns. This was a huge difference from California three years before the Measure 16 vote and Michigan three years later. Two years before Oregon's Measure 16, Washington proponents maintained a hybrid strategy between soft-spoken educational media messages and messages tested for their political impact; however, leaders there didn't execute a good media buy in the last week of the campaign—a period when these methods must be adroitly adapted to last-minute voter changes.

A third political schema (detailed earlier) that wasn't fully appreciated by Oregon leaders in 1994—but that they fully exploited in 1997—involved the role of stakeholders. Stakeholders were initially brought into the campaign and given a true role in forming and fighting for—or at least remaining neutral toward—the proposed law. As one reformer noted regarding the Oregon Medical Association, "Physician neutrality was key because it removed a well-organized, well funded power group from the fight" (Duncan 1996). This initial investment was truly real enough to cause those who would have to implement the ODDA at the clinical level naturally to take ownership of the law and its implementation once the voters had spoken. According to the reformers' legal counsel and chief political strategist, California and Michigan completely failed to realize this (Stutsman 2000). Washington reformers in 1991 and Oregon reformers in 1994 were more savvy about this aspect of political maneuvering, and in 1997 ODDA proponents seem to have attended to this task nearly perfectly.

To this point we have been describing the relation between the organized death with dignity movement, public attitudes toward hastened death, and conflicts between divergent subcultures in American society. Our goal has been to examine social reform activities—both for and against physician-assisted suicide—which changed the status quo in Oregon. We have further illustrated ways in which legal activities are one way Americans have defined their own cultural commitments to moral positions they accord hastened death. We now aim to extend this analysis to the ebbs and flows of the criminal law in competition over relative moral standing.

REDUCING THE USE OF THE CRIMINAL LAW

The expansion of law into end-of-life medicine runs headlong into another dimension of social life: the criminal sanction in law and morality. Other studies of law and morality illustrate a high degree of individual and social ambivalence about the proper balance between choice and harm in many illegal activities (Skolnick 1988). Like laws and mores about drugs, prostitution, pornography, homosexuality, gambling, and abortion, laws and mores about death and dying have fluctuated over time. Typically, these activities are said to be victimless, meaning that those who commit them harm themselves, not others. But other arguments point out, for example, that one who gambles away a paycheck, or who dies from a drug overdose, or who commits suicide harms his family and his community if his dependents must go on the public dole.

During the past forty years, Western industrialized societies have rethought the problem of the use of criminal law in areas of personal morality. From the time of the Wolfenden report in Great Britain Committee on Homosexual Offences and Prostitution (1957) through the Model Penal Code in the United States and the work of legal scholars such as Edwin Schur, Herbert Packer, Gilbert Geis, Jerome Skolnick, Sanford Kadish, Francis Allen, Norval Morris, and others, legal reform both for the sake of philosophical reasons (harm, civil liberties, and privacy) and practical reasons (cost of law enforcement, opportunities for corruption) has been suggested in many areas of criminal law.

In some cases, such as gambling, the reasons for the legal reform efforts have been the attractiveness of legal commercial alternatives. In the case of legal gambling, the revenue-raising attraction of gambling harkens back to colonial days, when the legal lottery was used as a revenue-raising mechanism for public works and institutions of higher learning, such as Harvard. In the case of illegal gambling, studies of American attitudes toward crime have indicated that gambling is viewed as far less serious than most other crimes, and this attitude has been confirmed by the reluctance of juries to convict persons accused of illegal gambling, and even eventually by the reluctance of prosecutors to prosecute such crimes. During the 1970s, similar evaluations of the seriousness of harms associated with illicit drugs resulted in the reduction of penalties for possession of small amounts of marijuana in eleven American states, yet the decriminalization movement was unsuccessful in reducing penalties for the use of other illicit drugs.

In other cases, such as abortion, legal reform passed through a relatively lengthy period of liberalization, during which state legislatures acted to permit physicians more latitude in allowing women to terminate a pregnancy under a model of enforcement that viewed abortion as more of a medical problem than a criminal one. While the women's movement activated a large constituency that promoted the shift from viewing abortion as a medical "problem" to a woman's right to choose, it was through the Supreme Court's ruling in *Roe v. Wade* in 1973 that abortion was legalized.

Given the mixed nature of public opinion and private behavior surrounding so-called victimless crimes, one theme running through modern studies of crime has focused on the benefits of removing criminal sanctions against such activities on the basis that the criminal law is overextended, and, as a result, many people have lost respect for the law. Still other studies have followed the sentiments of John Stuart Mill in asserting principled opposition to laws that impinge upon personal liberty.

It was in this tradition of appeal to Millian principles and the proper use of the criminal law in sanctioning morality that British jurisprudential scholar Glanville Williams wrote in 1958, when he engaged in a spirited debate with American legal scholar Yale Kamisar over the wisdom of decriminalizing euthanasia. Unknowingly, Williams anticipated the arguments by physicians such as Timothy Quill and others who have lead physicians in the modern movement to reform assisted suicide laws in the United States when he wrote: "If the doctor honestly and sincerely believes that the best service he can perform for his suffering patient is to accede to his request for euthanasia, it is a grave thing that the law should forbid him to do" (Williams 1958).

But at the time when Williams was writing—forty-three years ago—the nature of dying was far different from the conditions now experienced since the modern "medicalization of death" (Illich 1994), and the impetus for a social reform movement grounded in public consciousness around the issues Williams identified had not yet arisen. More importantly, at that time the experience of Nazi Germany's experiments with euthanasia—*Lebensunwertes Leden*, "life unworthy of life"—and the experience of the Holocaust, were not far in the past, and fears of history repeating itself dominated any discussion of possible decriminalization of euthanasia laws. The groups that sought legal reform were small and easily marginalized, and, except in a few instances, their efforts at legislative reform garnered very little support. The discursive themes proceeding from the rights movements of the 1960s and 1970s were not yet fully developed, and the example of abortion law reform that took place throughout the 1960s—relying as it did upon changing social mores about sexual relations, women's roles, the appropriate responsibilities of physicians, and the influence of religious organizations—was not yet available. Indeed in all spheres of life, the nature of rights-claiming was less developed, and as a result, the earliest attempts at decriminalization of euthanasia and assisted suicide did not go far.

By 1976, however, collective efforts to challenge laws and traditional medical practices concerning treatment withdrawal renewed the arguments about redrawing the line between killing and letting die and transformed them into a matter of major policy innovation (Glick 1992) and an area of continued cultural controversy. Twenty-five years later, attempts to keep a bright line between withdrawal of treatment and assisted suicide are still being hotly contested, and competition over relative moral, legal, and political standing remains problematic, as we have demonstrated. The distinction between killing and letting die appears to be fluid, as it has been repeatedly reconstructed by human actors in the course of collective action, definitional processes, interpretive procedures, and claims-making activities.

Given this history, we can compare the argument by proponents of euthanasia reform to some of the arguments of people who successfully mobilized changes in abortion, gambling, and marijuana laws. The argument is, "It happens anyway." Under the ethical principle of "double effect," which *Quill* appears to have enshrined in American law, doctors have escaped both professional sanction and criminal prosecution when they have simply averred that the potentially lethal quantities of drugs they have prescribed or administered to dying patients were intended to ease pain and suffering, not cause death. Add to this the regularity of physicians' orders to withhold or withdraw treatment, plus orders not to resuscitate, and some proponents for reforming laws that prohibit physicians from intentionally hastening death argue that such medical practices are a form of de facto decriminalization of assisted suicide. Thus, to physician activists such as Timothy Quill, the efforts of people who want to relax proscriptions against assisting in hastened death—like those who have contested criminal laws against abortion, gambling, and marijuana use—are aimed at bringing into the open what occurs now in secret—what occurs now, according to the *New York Times*, with "a wink and a nod" ("Assisted Suicide and the Law" 1997).

THE NEW GOOD DEATH

While the reasons and strategies offered by Quill and others for changing the law have varied, there is near unanimity among their conceptions about what is wrong with the current state of dying in America. The title of Bill Moyers's September 2000 PBS series—"On Our Own Terms"—captures the sentiment of those arguing for greater choice and self-determination in the American way of dying.

The reformers have crafted a strategy and message reflecting public fear of what we call the "bad death." In this current way of dying, a patient may die in a hospital, in intractable pain, hooked up to tubes, surrounded by strangers, and at the mercy of events beyond his or her control. Death was in the often-cruel hands of fate, and it was controlled by often indifferent doctors. Patients' rights were not foremost in the doctor-patient relationship, and death without horrible suffering was certainly not perceived as a right. *New England Journal of Medicine* editor Marcia Angell, whose own aged father committed suicide while suffering from a terminal disease, wrote editorials in support of assisted suicide reform. Judge Reinhardt made reference to this when he ruled in *Compassion III*: "A competent, terminally ill adult, having lived nearly the full measure of his life, has a strong liberty interest in choosing a dignified and humane death rather than being reduced at the end of his existence to a childlike state of helplessness—diapered, sedated, and incompetent" (*Compassion III* 1996, at 3161–3162).

In its place, reformers have suggested a patient-controlled alternative, which emphasizes choice, freedom from pain, a greater role for the patient, and acknowledgment that the current legal and medical practice allows for such deliverance, under the concept of "double effect." We call this construct "the reformers' good death."

Opponents of assisted suicide reform, however, have not accepted these conceptions and arguments. There is some argument in places like the Supreme Court brief of the National Hospice Organization that the appellate courts had failed to consider the "opportunities to find value during the last stage of life" (National Hospice Organization 1996:6). Others speak to the importance of the last days of life, even in pain and in hospitals, as a time when closure can be made, conflicts resolved, families brought together, and lasting sentiments restated.

In general, however, opponents of assisted suicide reform have been careful not to romanticize the attributes of death. They have not led their arguments with the idea that the current "bad death" of the reformers is indeed a "good death," a chance for growth, and the way things should be. They have been savvy enough to discern from the Gallup polls over the years the growing sentiment of Americans for greater control over their end-of-life experiences. Rather than trumpeting the positive values of pain, those who oppose assisted suicide reform have their own conception of a good death, which we shall call "the opponents' good death." Now, many of those who are lumped together in the "opponent" side would bristle at their approach to end-of-life care being so classified in this crude way, without much nuance. They might also object to their views and practices, many long-developed through years of efforts in palliative care medicine, as being constructed only in opposition to the arguments of the assisted suicide reformers.

Nonetheless, there are elements of "the opponents' good death" that are consistent, especially the reliance upon proper palliative care. Many in the medical profession have tried to change the direction of the assisted suicide reform, without denigrating its leaders and supporters. Many have in essence said, thanks for raising the issue, but we can now resolve it within the power of the medical profession—through better training, more attention to palliative care, and better communication.

A recent Milbank Memorial Fund report (Foubister 2000) summarized the principles of a collaboration of several major medical associations in establishing core principles for end-of-life care, such as providing access to palliative care and hospice care, while respecting the dignity of patients and caregivers (Cassel and Foley 2000).

Thomas Reardon, a Portland physician who was President of the American Medical Association, said: "It was a wake-up call to everyone that we needed to do a better job." Sherwin Nuland, a surgeon whose book *How We Die* was a national bestseller, is representative when he writes: "If it has accomplished nothing else, the debates over assisted suicide, euthanasia and advanced directives have forced clinical scientists into a heightened awareness of what can be done to relieve suffering. Doctors are improving palliative care and their own behavior. Patients are becoming more aware of the options before them as they live out their days" (Nuland 1997:A15).

In the amicus briefs before the various courts, and in initiative arguments, as noted above, the report of the New York Task Force on Life and the Law was often cited, especially in its conclusion that more attention be paid to training in and provision of palliative care.

The Robert Wood Johnson Foundation recently awarded $12 million to Last Acts, an national coalition of more than 120 organizations committed to common goals and areas of concern related to death and dying issues. The coalition includes the American Cancer Society, American Nurses Association, Choice in Dying, hospice organizations, and Catholic lay organizations. The mission of the campaign is to engage both health professionals and the public in efforts to improve care at the end of life, including:

- Improving communication between dying people and their loved ones and between dying people, families, and health professionals.
- Reshaping the medical care environment to better support high-quality end-of-life care.
- Changing American culture so that people can more comfortably face death and the issues raised by care of the terminally ill.
- Recognizing that dying is more than a medical event; it has emotional and spiritual components as well.
- Realizing that improvement is needed in all the care settings where people die, including the home, hospitals, and long-term care facilities.
- Acknowledging that pain and symptom control should be high priorities and could be improved starting today.
- Asserting that caregiving by family members and friends is an invaluable gift not sufficiently recognized by society.

The opponents also warn that the "reformers' good death" may instead lead to another reality, something we'll call the "reformers' risky death." It can be found in the specter of managed care displayed in The International Anti-Euthanasia Task Force's Supreme Court brief in *Quill* and *Glucksberg*, in Hebert Hendin's charges that the Dutch experience portends a slippery slope of nonvoluntary euthanasia and expansion of an initial limited right to assisted suicide among terminally ill competent adults, and in Not Dead Yet's claim that the disabled, the poor, and other marginalized groups will be the focus of even involuntary euthanasia.

Quill et al. argue in a 1998 article (1998:1) that consensus might be built among those with divergent views in this area. Still, to many reformers the "opponents' good death" is an optimistic spin on a cynical return to the doctor-controlled construct of the "double effect" dose of painkillers, Preston's morphine drip, as the current practice of assisted suicide (Preston 1994). It certainly rankles many reformers that the 1999 Hyde/Nickles II bills explicitly embraced the double effect, with the blessing of the United States Conference of Catholic Bishops and the American Medical Association. It is a repackaging of what Dworkin contends is a two-tiered system that provides "a chosen death and an end of pain outside the law for those with connections and stony refusals for most other people" (Dworkin 1997:41).

These competing visions of the "good death" and the "bad death" continue as the frameworks of the contesting movements and activists. Events in the coming decade will determine whether the death with dignity movement can successfully translate this sentiment—and public fear of a protracted death hooked up to machines—into a successful movement for assisted suicide reform in more places than Oregon. Conversely, events will affect whether the "third way" of increased attention to good palliative care or the "middle ground" of a continued availability of double-effect painkiller use—the "terminal sedation" that some Supreme Court justices embraced in *Quill* and *Glucksberg*—becomes the accepted policy option. The paradox is that, to many, this would just be sweeping under the societal rug the practice that has helped give rise to reformers' calls for greater uniformity and transparency in end-of-life care. What's clear to date, however, is that the Oregon reformers have been able to successfully frame the twin themes of compassion and autonomy and to carefully chart a path to their desired "safe harbor."

References

INTERVIEWS

Bonanno, Mark (1999). Attorney, Cooney and Crew law firm, Portland, representing Oregon Medical Association, June 15.

Bonanno, Mark (2000). Attorney, formerly of Cooney and Crew law firm, Portland, representing Oregon Medical Association, February 28.

Bostick, Warren, M.D. (1994). University of California Irvine professor emeritus, former president of the California Medical Association and Proposition 161 supporter, January 18.

Bryant, Senator Neil (1999). Chair of the Oregon State Senate Judiciary Committee, Salem, June 14.

Budetti, John L. (1998). Legislative director for Powers, Pyles, Sutter & Verville, PC, firm representing the National Pain Care Coalition. Washington, DC, November 16.

Coombs Lee, Barbara, R.N. (1997a) Legal reform activist, executive director, Compassion in Dying, Seattle, May 21.

Coombs Lee, Barbara, R.N. (1997b) Legal reform activist, executive director, Compassion in Dying, Portland, November 4.

Coombs Lee, Barbara, R.N. (1998). Legal reform activist, executive director, Compassion in Dying, Portland, July 20.

Cooper, Karen (1998). Campaign director of Washingtion initiative and campaign consultant in California and Oregon initiatives, June 12–13.

Davidson, Hannah (1997a). Assistant director of Oregon Death With Dignity Legal Defense and Education Center, Portland, November 4.

Davidson, Hannah (1997b). Assistant director of Oregon Death With Dignity Legal Defense and Education Center, Portland, July 20.

Davidson, Hannah (1997c). Assistant director of Oregon Death With Dignity Legal Defense and Education Center, November 9 (telephone).

Davidson, Hannah (2000). Executive director of Oregon Death With Dignity Legal Defense and Education Center, Portland, February 29.

de Wachter, Maurice A. M. (1996). Ethicist, Brussels, Belgium, September 10.

Dillman, R. J. M., M.D. (1996). Official of the Dutch Royal Medical Society, Utrecht, the Netherlands, September 4.

Dolin, Leigh, M.D. (1996). Physician and president of Oregon Medical Association, during Measure 16 campaign, July 11.

Duncan, John (1996). Executive director of Oregon Death With Dignity Legal Defense and Education Center, Portland, July 10.

Duncan, John (1997a). Executive director of Oregon Death With Dignity Legal Defense and Education Center, January 16 (telephone).

Duncan, John (1997b). Executive director of Oregon Death With Dignity Legal Defense and Education Center, Portland, November 4.

Duncan, John (1997c). Executive director of Oregon Death With Dignity Legal Defense and Education Center, November 9 (telephone).

Duncan, John (1998). Executive director of Oregon Death With Dignity Legal Defense and Education Center, Portland, July 20.

Dupuis, Heleen (1996). Ethicist and university professor, University of Leiden, the Netherlands, September 5.

Field, Daniel (2000). Vice president and general counsel, Oregon Association of Hospitals and Health Care Systems, Portland, February 29.

Fiskum, David (2000). Partner, Conkling, Fiskum & McCormick, Inc., lobbyist for Sisters of Providence Health Care Systems, Portland, March 1.

Gallant, Scott (1999). Director of Government Affairs, Oregon Medical Association, Salem, June 14.

Gallant, Scott (2000). Director of Government Affairs, Oregon Medical Association, Portland, February 28.

Geiger, Lisa M. (1998). Associate director, Legislation and Political Action, American Pharmaceutical Association, Washington, DC, November 16.

Gevers, Joseph (1996). Professor, University of Amsterdam, the Netherlands, September 18.

Gibson, Mark (1998). Health advisor and spokesperson for Governor John Kitzhaber, Salem, July 21.

Gibson, Mark (1999). Health advisor and spokesperson for Governor John Kitzhaber, Salem, June 14.

Giglio, John (1998b). Director, National Hospice Organization, Alexandria, Virginia, November 17.

Goodwin, Peter (1996). Physician and cosponsor of Measure 16, Portland, July 10.

Griffiths, John (1996). Dutch sociolegal scholar, Utrecht and Groningen, the Netherlands September 2, September 10.

Gunning, Karl (1996). Physician and anti-euthanasia activist, Rotterdam, the Netherlands, August 30.

Hagan, Kelly (1998). Attorney, Cooney and Crew law firm, Portland, and member, Task Force to Improve the Care of Terminally-Ill Oregonians, June (telephone).

Haley, Kathleen, J.D. (1998). Executive director, Oregon Board of Medical Examiners, Portland, July 20.

Haney, Cynthia, J.D. (1998). Washington counsel, Division of Legislative Counsel, American Medical Association, November 16.

Hedberg, Katrina, M.D., M.P.H. (1998). Epidemiologist, Oregon Health Division, Portland, July 20.

Hedberg, Katrina, M.D., M.P.H. (1999). Epidemiologist, Oregon Health Division, Portland, June 15.

Hedberg, Katrina, M.D., M.P.H. (2000). Epidemiologist, Oregon Health Division, Portland, February 29.

Hemann, Hans (2000). Staff member of Assembly member Dion Aroner's office, June 21 (telephone).

Holt, Thomas (2000). Executive director, Oregon State Pharmacists Association, and member, Oregon Society of Health Systems Pharmacists, Salem, March 1.

Humphry, Derek (1996). Founder of the Hemlock Society, director of Euthanasia Research and Guidance Organization (ERGO), author of the best-selling book *Final Exit*, and so-called father of the right-to-die movement, July 9.

Jackson, Ann (2000). Executive director and chief executive officer of the Oregon Hospice Association, and member, Task Force to Improve the Care of Terminally-Ill Oregonians, February 28.

Jonsen, Albert R. (1993). Professor and chair of medical history and ethics, University of Washington, November 12 (telephone).

Jonsen, Albert R. (1997). Professor and chair of medical history and ethics, University of Washington, May 20.

Kits Nieuwekamp, Johanna. (1996). Health policy expert, Health Council of the Netherlands, The Hague, the Netherlands, August 27.

Kleemans, Kees (1996). Official, National Hospital Association, Utrecht, the Netherlands, September 17.

Lee, John (1997). Compassion in Dying board member, Seattle, May 21.

Legemaate, Johann (1996). Professor, Erasmus University, Rotterdam, the Netherlands, September 10.

McCormick, Thomas (1997). Professor of medical ethics, University of Washington, May 20.

McDevon, Michael (1997). Terminally ill man walking anti-Measure 51 picket, Portland, November 4.

McGough, Peter, M.D. (1997). Health-care medical director and key physician spokesperson against Washington initiative, Seattle, May 20.

Park, Sister Sharon (1997). Lobbyist and chief spokesperson for the Washington Catholic Conference, Seattle, May 22.

Price, Deborah A. (1998). Legislative aide, Senator Don Nickles's office, Washington, DC, November 16.

Reagan, Bonnie, M.D. (1998). Physician and member, Task Force to Improve the Care of Terminally-Ill Oregonians, Portland, July 20.

Risley, Robert, J.D. (1994). Attorney and Proposition 161 cosponsor, Los Angeles, March 18.

Robleski, Sister Eileen (1998). Official, Providence Health System, Portland, July (telephone).

Roell, Jean (1996). Representative, Dutch Voluntary Euthanasia Association (NVVE), September 17 (telephone).

Schnabel, Gary, R.N. (1998). Official, Oregon Board of Pharmacy and member, Task Force to Improve the Care of Terminally-Ill Oregonians, Portland, July 20.

Schroten, Egbert (1996). Ethicist, Utrecht University, the Netherlands, September 3.

Shetterly, Representative Lane (1999). Chair, Oregon House Judiciary Committee; cochair, joint interim judiciary committee, Salem, June 14.

Spreeuwenberg, Cor (1996). Official of the Royal Dutch Medical Society, Utrecht, the Netherlands, September.

Stefanics, Elizabeth (1995). New Mexico state senator, Santa Fe, July.

Stutsman, Eli, J.D. (1996). Legal counsel for Oregon Death With Dignity Legal Defense and Education Center, Portland, July 11.

Stutsman, Eli, J.D. (1997). Legal counsel for Oregon Death With Dignity Legal Defense and Education Center, Portland, November 18.

Stutsman, Eli, J.D. (1998). Legal counsel for Oregon Death With Dignity Legal Defense and Education Center, Portland, July 21.

Stutsman, Eli, J.D. (2000). Legal counsel for Oregon Death With Dignity Legal Defense and Education Center, Portland, March 1.

Sugerman, Geoff (1997). Campaign director and consultant for Washington and Oregon ballot initiatives, Portland, November 4, 5.

Sutorius, Eugene, J.D. (1996). Leading attorney in euthanasia cases, Bosniak and Winters Advocaten, Arnhem, the Netherlands, September 16.

Taylor, William (1999). Legal counsel, Senate Judiciary Committee, state of Oregon. Salem, June 14.

Telfer, Steve (2000). Official, The Telfer Company; lobbyist for Oregon Right to Die, Portland, February 28.

Tucker, Kathryn, J.D. (1997). Attorney for Compassion in Dying, Seattle, May 21.

van der Maas, Paul (1996). Professor, Erasmus University, Rotterdam, the Netherlands, August 26.

van Leeuwen, Menno (1996). Official, Gezondsheidraad, Health Council of the Netherlands, The Hague, the Netherlands, August 27.

Williams, William, J.D. (1997). Chief counsel for the state of Washington, Olympia, May 23.

Winchler, Susan C. (1998). Pharmacist; director of Policy and Legislation, American Pharmaceutical Association, November 17.

Yanow, Morton (1997). Washington attorney and ACLU consultant, Seattle, May 19.

BOOKS AND JOURNAL ARTICLES

Allen, Francis (1964). *The Borderland of Criminal Justice: Essays in Law and Criminology.* Chicago: University of Chicago Press.

Anspach, Renee R. (1993). *Deciding Who Lives: Fateful Choices in the Intensive-Care Nursery.* Berkeley: University of California Press.

Bachman, J. G., K. H. Alcser, D. J. Doukas, R. L. Lichtenstein, A. D. Corning, and H. Brody (1996). "Attitudes of Michigan Physicians and the Public Toward Legalizing Physician-Assisted Suicide and Voluntary Euthanasia." *New England Journal of Medicine* 334, no. 5, February 1, pp. 303–309.

Baron, C. H., C. Bergstresser, D. W. Brock, G. F. Cole, N. S. Dorfman, J. A. Johnson, L. E. Schnipper, J. Vorenberg and S. H. Wanzer (1996). "A Model State Act to Authorize and Regulate Physician-Assisted Suicide," *Harvard Journal of Legislation* 33, no. 1, pp. 1–34.

Battin, Margaret Pabst (1995). *The Least Worst Death: Essays in Bioethics on the End of Life.* New York: Oxford University Press.

Battin, Margaret, Pabst et al., eds. (1998). *Physician Assisted Suicide: Expanding the Debate.* New York: Routledge.

Biggar, Joanna (1995). "Compassion in Dying's Suicide Policy Walking Legal Tightrope." *Las Vegas Review-Journal,* March 12, pp. 75–85.

Boehm, Frank H., M.D. (1996). "Physician-Assisted Suicide Is a Very Bad Idea." *The Tennessean,* October 1, p. 11A.

Boston Women's Health Book Collective (1971). *Our Bodies, Our Selves.* Boston: Boston Women's Health Book Collective and New England Free Press.

Bowler, Shaun, and Todd Donovan (1998). *Demanding Choices: Opinion, Voting, and Direct Democracy.* Ann Arbor: The University of Michigan Press.

Byock, Ira (1997). *Dying Well: The Prospect for Growth at the End of Life.* New York: Riverhead Books.

Callahan, Daniel (1987). *Setting Limits: Medical Goals in an Aging Society.* New York: Touchstone/Simon and Schuster.

Callahan, Daniel (1990). *What Kind of Life? The Limits of Medical Progress.* New York: Simon and Schuster.

Callahan, Daniel (1992). "'Aid-In-Dying': The Social Dimensions." *Commonweal,* Special Supplement, September, pp. 12–16.

Callahan, Daniel (1993). *The Troubled Dream of Life: Living with Mortality.* New York: Simon and Schuster.

Cantor, Norman L. (1993). *Advance Directives and the Pursuit of Death with Dignity.* Bloomington: Indiana University Press.

Capron, Alexander Morgan, and Vicki Michel (1992). "Be Sure to Read the Fine Print: Will California Legalize Euthanasia?" *Commonweal,* Special Report. "Euthanasia: California Proposition 161." September 25, pp. 16–20.

Cassell, Christine K., M.D., and Kathleen M. Foley, M.D. (1999). *Principles for Care of Patients at the End of Life: An Emerging Consensus among the Specialities of Medicine.* New York: Milbank Memorial Fund.

Chin, Arthur E., Katrina Hedberg, Grant K. Higginson, and David W. Fleming (1999a). "Legalized Physician-Assisted Suicide in Oregon—The First Year's Experience." *New England Journal of Medicine* 340, no. 7, February 18, pp. 577–583.

Chin, Arthur E., Katrina Hedberg, Grant K. Higginson, and David W. Fleming

(1999b). "Legalized Physician-Assisted Suicide in Oregon—Reply." *New England Journal of Medicine* 341, no. 3, July 15, pp. 212–213.

Cohen, Jonathan S., et al. (1994). "Attitudes toward Assisted Suicide and Euthanasia among Physicians in Washington State." *New England Journal of Medicine* 331, no. 2, July 14, pp. 89–94.

Committee on Homosexual Offences and Prostitution (1957). *Report.* London: Her Majesty's Stationery Office.

Condit, Celeste Michelle (1990). *Decoding Abortion Rhetoric: Communicating Social Change.* Champaign: University of Illinois Press.

Council on Scientific Affairs, American Medical Association (1996). "Council Report." *JAMA*, vol. 275, no. 6, pp. 474–478.

Cooper, Mark (2000). "Clean Money in Maine." *The Nation* 270, no. 21, May 29, pp. 22–24.

Cox, Donald W. (1993). *Hemlock's Cup: The Struggle for Death with Dignity.* Buffalo, N.Y.: Prometheus Press.

Craig, Barbara Hinkson, and David M. O'Brien (1993). *Abortion and American Politics.* Chatham, NJ: Chatham House.

Darvall, Leanna (1993). *Medicine, Law and Social Change: The Impact of Bioethics, Feminism and Rights Movements on Medical Decision-Making.* Aldershot, England: Dartmouth.

de Hennezel, Marie (1997). *Intimate Death: How the Dying Teach Us How to Live.* New York: Alfred A. Knopf.

de Moor, R. (1996). "Euthanasia and Moral Permissiveness," pp. 87–101 in *Euthanasia and Assisted Suicide in the Netherlands and in Europe: Methodology of the Ethical Debate.* Proceedings of a European Conference, June 10 and 11, 1994. Luxembourg: European Commission, Directorate—General Science, Research and Development.

de Wachter, Maurice A. M. (1992). "Euthanasia in the Netherlands." *Hastings Center Report*, March–April, pp. 23–30.

DiChiara, Albert, and John F. Galliher (1994). "Dissonance and Contradictions in the Origins of Marijuana Decriminalization." *Law & Society Review* 28, pp. 41–47.

Dillman, R. J. M. (1996). "Euthanasia in the Netherlands: The Role of the Dutch Medical Profession." *Cambridge Quarterly of Healthcare Ethics* 5, pp. 100–106.

Dombrink, John, and Daniel Hillyard (1998). "Manifestations of Agency in the 1994 Reform of Oregon's Assisted Suicide Law." *Sociology of Crime, Law and Deviance* 1, pp. 127–154.

Dombrink, John, and William N. Thompson (1990). *The Last Resort: Success and Failure in Campaigns for Casinos.* Reno: University of Nevada Press.

Downes, David M. (1988). *Contrasts in Tolerance: Post-War Penal Policy in the Netherlands and England and Wales.* New York: Oxford University Press.

Duster, Troy (1970). *The Legislation of Morality: Law, Drugs, and Moral Judgment.* New York: The Free Press.

Dworkin, Ronald M. (1993). *Life's Dominion.* New York: Alfred A. Knopf.

Dworkin, Ronald (1996). "Sex, Death and the Court." *New York Review of Books*, August 8, pp. 44–50.

Dworkin, Ronald (1997). "Assisted Suicide: The Philosophers' Brief." *New York Review of Books*, March 27, p. 41–47.

Edwards, Miles J., M.D. and William E. Connor, M.D. (1999). Letter to the Editor, "Legalized Physician-Assisted Suicide in Oregon." *New England Journal of Medicine* 341, no. 3, July 15, pp. 212.

Elster, P., L. Halman, and R. de Moor (1993). *The Individualizing Society: Value Change in Europe and North America*. Tilburg, the Netherlands: Tilburg University Press.

Emanuel, Linda L., ed. (1998). *Regulating How We Die: The Ethical, Medical, and Legal Issues Surrounding Physician-Assisted Suicide*. Cambridge: Harvard University Press.

Englehardt, H. Tristam, Jr. (1989). "Death by Free Choice: Modern Variations on an Antique Theme," pp. 251–280 in Baruch A. Brody, ed., *Suicide and Euthanasia: Historical and Contemporary Themes*. Dordrecht, the Netherlands: Kluwer Academic Publishers.

Fins, Joseph J., M.D., and Elizabeth A. Bancroft, M.D. (1999). Letter to the Editor, "Legalized Physician-Assisted Suicide in Oregon." *New England Journal of Medicine* 341, no. 3, July 15, p. 212.

Fletcher, Joseph F. (1954). *Morals and Medicine: The Moral Problems of the Patient's Right to Know the Truth: Contraception, Artificial Insemination, Sterilization, Euthanasia*. Princeton, NJ: Princeton University Press.

Gallagher, Hugh Gregory (1990). *By Trust Betrayed: Patients, Physicians and the License to Kill in the Third Reich*. New York: Henry Holt.

Garrett, Valery (1999). "The Last Civil Right? Euthanasia Policy and Politics in the United States, 1938–1991." Unpublished doctoral dissertation, Department of History, University of California, Santa Barbara.

Garrow, David J. (1994). *Liberty and Sexuality: The Right to Privacy and the Making of Roe v. Wade*. New York: Macmillan.

Garrow, David J. (1997). "The Oregon Trail," *New York Times*, November 6, p. A27.

Geis, Gilbert (1972). *Not the Law's Business?* Washington, DC: U.S. Government Printing Office.

Gevers, J. K. M. (1992). "Legislation on Euthanasia: Recent Developments in the Netherlands." *Journal of Medical Ethics* 18, pp. 138–141.

Gibbs, Nancy (1993). "Rx for Death." *Time* 141, no. 22, May 31, pp. 34–40.

Glick, Henry R. (1992). *The Right to Die: Policy Innovation and Its Consequences*. New York: Columbia University Press.

Gomez, Carlos F. (1991). *Regulating Death: Euthanasia and the Case of the Netherlands*. New York: Free Press.

Gomez, Carlos F. (1992). "Consider the Dutch." *Commonweal*, Special Supplement, September, pp. 5–8.

Griffiths, John (1994a). "The Regulation of Euthanasia and Related Medical Procedures That Shorten Life in the Netherlands." *Medical Law International* 1, pp. 137–158.

Griffiths, John (1994b). "Recent Developments in the Netherlands Concerning Euthanasia and Other Medical Behavior That Shortens Life." *Medical Law International* 1, pp. 347–386.

Griffiths, John (1995). "Assisted Suicide in the Netherlands: The Chabot Case." *The Modern Law Review* 58, no. 2, March, pp. 232–248.

Griffiths, John, Heleen Weyers, and Alex Bood (1998). *Euthanasia and Law in the Netherlands.* Amsterdam and Ann Arbor: Amsterdam University Press and University of Michigan Press.

Gusfield, Joseph R. (1972). *Symbolic Crusade: Status Politics and the American Temperance Movement.* Chicago: University of Illinois Press (paperback edition).

Hagan, Kelly (1998). "Liability and Negligence," pp. 46–55 in The Task Force to Improve the Care of Terminally-Ill Oregonians. *The Oregon Death With Dignity Act: A Guidebook for Health Care Providers.* Portland: The Center for Ethics in Health Care, Oregon Health Sciences University.

Heilig, Steve, Robert Brody, Fred S. Marcus, Lonny Shavelson, and Patricia Carson Sussman (1997). "Physician-Hastened Death: Advisory Guidelines for the San Francisco Bay Area from the Bay Area Network of Ethics Committees." *Western Journal of Medicine* 166, no. 6, pp. 370–378.

Hendin, Herbert, M.D. (1997a). *Seduced by Death: Doctors, Patients, and the Dutch Cure.* New York: W. W. Norton.

Hendin, Herbert, M.D., Chris Rutenfrans, M.D., and Zbigniew Zylicz, M.D. (1997). "Physician-Assisted Suicide and Euthanasia in the Netherlands: Lessons from the Dutch." *Journal of the American Medical Association* 277, no. 21, pp. 1720–1722.

Hentoff, Nat (1988). "The 'Small Beginnings' of Death." *The Human Life Review* 114, Spring, pp. 53–58.

Hessing, Dick J., John R. Blad, and Roel Pieterman (1996). "Practical Reasons and Reasonable Practice: The Case of Euthanasia in the Netherlands." *Journal of Social Issues* 52, no. 2, Summer, pp. 149–168.

Himmelstein, Jerome L. (1983). *The Strange Career of Marihuana.* Westport, CT: Greenwood Press.

Hoefler, James M., with Brian Kamoie (1994). *Deathright: Culture, Medicine, Politics and the Right to Die.* Boulder, CO: Westview Press.

Illich, Ivan (1976). *Medical Nemesis: The Expropriation of Health.* New York: Pantheon Books.

Jenness, Valerie (1993). *Making It Work: The Prostitute's Rights Movement in Perspective.* New York: Aldine de Gruyter.

Joffe, Carole E. (1995). *Doctors of Conscience: The Struggle to Provide Abortion before and after Roe v. Wade.* Boston: Beacon Press.

Jonsen, Albert R. (1990). *The New Medicine and the Old Ethics.* Cambridge, MA: Harvard University Press.

Jonsen, Albert R. (1991). "Initiative 119: What's at Stake?" *Commonweal,* vol. 118, Supplement, August, pp. 466–468.

Kadish, Sanford (1967). "The Crisis of Overcriminalization." *Annals* 374, pp. 157–170.

Kamisar, Yale (1996). "Why So Many People Support Physician-Assisted Suicide: And Why These Reasons Are Not Convincing." *Law Quadrangle Notes*, Fall/Winter, pp. 83–88.

Kaplan, John (1970). *Marijuana—The New Prohibition.* New York: World Publishing.

Kass, Leon H. (1991). "Why Doctors Must Not Kill." *Commonweal*, v. 118, Supplement, August, pp. 473–474.

Kenis, Y. (1996). " First European Roundtable: Questions from Abroad and Practices across Europe: Belgium," pp. 23–24 in *Euthanasia and Assisted Suicide in the Netherlands and in Europe: Methodology of the Ethical Debate.* Proceedings of a European Conference, June 10 and 11, 1994. Luxembourg: European Commission, Directorate—General Science, Research and Development.

Kevorkian, Jack (1991). *Prescription—Medicide: The Goodness of Planned Death.* Buffalo, NY: Prometheus.

Kubler-Ross, Elisabeth (1969). *On Death and Dying.* New York: Collier Books.

Kubler-Ross, Elisabeth (1978). *To Live Until We Say Goodbye.* Englewood Cliffs, NJ: Prentice Hall.

Lee, M. A., H. D. Nelson, V. P. Tilden, L. Ganzini, T. A. Schmidt, and S. W. Tolle (1996). "Legalizing Assisted Suicide—Views of Physicians in Oregon." *New England Journal of Medicine* 334, no. 5, pp. 310–315.

Lee, Melinda (1997). "The Oregon Death With Dignity Act: Implementation Issues. " *Western Journal of Medicine* 166, no. 6, June, pp. 398–401.

Legemaate, Johan (1995). "Legal Aspects of Euthanasia and Assisted Suicide in the Netherlands, 1973–1994." *Cambridge Quarterly of Healthcare Ethics*, vol. 4, pp. 111–121.

Lessenberry, Jack (1996). "Kevorkian Unplugged." *George* 1, no. 6, August, pp. 52–54

Leuw, Ed., and I. Haen Marshall (1994). *Between Prohibition and Legalization: The Dutch Experiment in Drug Policy.* Amsterdam: Kugler Publications.

Logue, Barbara J. (1993). *Last Rights: Death Control and the Elderly in America.* New York: Lexington Books.

Lowenstein, Daniel H. (1982). "Campaign Spending and Ballot Propositions: Recent Experience, Public Choice Theory and the First Amendment." *UCLA Law Review* 29, pp. 505–641.

Luker, Kristin (1984). *Abortion and the Politics of Motherhood.* Berkeley: University of California Press.

Lupia, Arthur (1992). "Busy Voters, Agenda Control and the Power of Information." *American Political Science Review*, vol. 86, pp. 390–403.

Macklin, Ruth (1993). *Enemies of Patients.* New York: Oxford University Press.

MacCoun, Robert, and Peter Reuter (1998). "Drug Control," pp. 207–238 in Michael Tonry, ed., *The Handbook of Crime and Punishment.* New York: Oxford University Press.

Magelby, David B. (1984). *Direct Legislation: Voting on Ballot Propositions in the United States.* Baltimore: Johns Hopkins University Press.

Magelby, David B. (1986). "Legislatures and the Initiative: The Politics of Direct Democracy." *State Government* 59, p. 32.

Magelby, David B. (1994). "Direct Legislation in the American States," pp. 218–257 in David Butler and Austin Ranney, eds., *Referendums around the World.* Washington, DC: The AEI Press.

Magnusson, Roger, J.D. (1996). "The Sanctity of Life and the Right to Die: Social and Jurisprudential Aspects of the Euthanasia Debate in Australia and the United States." Unpublished paper, Faculty of Law, University of Melbourne, Australia.

Magnusson, Roger, J.D., and Peter H. Ballis (2000). *Angels of Death: Exploring the Euthanasia Underground.*

Maguire, Daniel C. (1984). *Death by Choice.* Garden City, NY: Image Books/Doubleday.

Mangione, Thomas W., and Floyd J. Fowler, Jr. (1979). "Enforcing the Gambling Laws." *Journal of Social Issues* 35, no. 3, pp. 115–128.

McCann, Michael W. (1994). *Rights at Work: Pay Equity Reform and the Politics of Legal Mobilization.* Chicago: University of Chicago Press.

McCann, Michael, and Helena Silverstein (1998). "Rethinking Law's 'Allurements': A Relational Analysis of Social Movement Lawyers in the United States," pp. 261–292. In Austin Sarat and Stuart Scheingold, eds., *Cause Lawyering: Political Commitments and Professional Responsibilities.* New York: Oxford University Press.

McInerney, F. (2000). "'Requested Death': A New Social Movement." *Social Science & Medicine* 50, no. 1, pp. 137–154.

Meisel, Alan (1989). *The Right to Die.* New York: Wiley Law Publications.

Meisel, Alan (1992). "The Legal Consensus about Forgoing Life-Sustaining Treatment: Its Status and Its Prospects." *Kennedy Institute of Ethics Journal* 2, no. 4, pp. 309–345.

Mill, John Stuart (1859, 1956). *On Liberty.* Indianapolis: The Bobbs-Merrill Company.

Musto, David (1999). *The American Disease: Origins of Narcotic Control.* New York: Oxford University Press.

Neff, David (1991). "The Wrong Way to Go (Washington State's Initiative 119." *Christianity Today* 35, no. 12, October 28, p. 15.

New York State Task Force on Life and the Law (1994). *When Death Is Sought: Assisted Suicide and Euthanasia in the Medical Context.* New York: The New York State Task Force on Life and the Law.

Nuland, Sherwin (1994). *How We Die: Reflections on Life's Final Chapter.* New York: Alfred A. Knopf.

Nuland, Sherwin B. (1997). "How We Die Is Our Business." *New York Times,* January 13, p. A15, col. 2.

Oken, Donald, M.D. (1961). "What to Tell Cancer Patients: A Study of Medical Attitudes." *Journal of the American Medical Association* 175, no. 13, pp. 86–94.

Oregon Health Division (1997). "Physician-Assisted Suicide." *CD Summary, Centers for Disease Prevention and Epidemiology* 46, no. 23, November 11.

Orentlicher, David (1996). "The Legalization of Physician-Assisted Suicide." *New England Journal of Medicine* 335, no. 9, August 29, pp. 663–667.

Otlowski, Margaret (1997). *Voluntary Euthanasia and the Common Law.* Oxford: Clarendon Press.

Packer, Herbert (1968). *The Limits of the Criminal Sanction.* Stanford, CA: Stanford University Press.

Porter, Roy (1998). *The Greatest Benefit to Mankind: A Medical History of Humanity.* New York: W. W. Norton.

Preston, Thomas A. (1994). "Killing Pain, Ending Life: Morphine Drip Euthanasia." *New York Times*, November 1, p. A15.

Punch, Maurice (1996). "The Dutch Criminal Justice System: A Crisis of Identity." Paper Presented at the International Perspectives on Crime, Justice and Public Order Conference, Dublin.

Quill, Timothy E., M.D. (1991). "Death and Dignity: A Case of Individualized Decision Making," *New England Journal of Medicine* 324, no. 10, March 7, p. 693.

Quill, Timothy E., M.D. (1993). *Death and Dignity: Making Choices and Taking Charge.* New York: W. W. Norton.

Quill, Timothy E., M.D. (1996). *A Midwife through the Dying Process.* Baltimore: The Johns Hopkins University Press.

Quill, Timothy E., M.D., Diane E. Meier, M.D., Susan D. Block, M.D., and J. Andrew Billings, M.D. (1998). "The Debate over Physician-Assisted Suicide: Empirical Data and Convergent View." *Annals of Internal Medicine* 128, April, pp. 552–558.

Reagan, Leslie J. (1997). *When Abortion Was a Crime: Women, Medicine, and Law in the United States, 1867–1973.* Berkeley: University of California Press.

Reinarman, Craig, and Harry G. Levine (1997). *Crack in America: Demon Drugs and Social Justice.* Berkeley: University of California Press.

Rothman, David (1991). *Strangers at the Bedside: A History of How Law and Bioethics Transformed Medical Decision Making.* New York: Basic Books.

Schneiderman, Lawrence J., and Nancy S. Jecker (1995). *Wrong Medicine: Doctors, Patients, and Futile Treatment.* Baltimore: The Johns Hopkins University Press.

Schotsmans, P. (1996). "Second European Roundtable: Toward a European Consensus? Belgium," pp. 153–156 in *Euthanasia and Assisted Suicide in the Netherlands and in Europe: Methodology of the Ethical Debate.* Proceedings of a European Conference, June 10 and 11, 1994. Luxembourg: European Commission, Directorate—General Science, Research and Development.

Schur, Edwin H. (1965). *Crimes without Victims.* Englewood Cliffs, NJ: Prentice-Hall.

Schur, Edwin H. (1980). *The Politics of Deviance: Stigma Contests and the Uses of Power.* Englewood Cliffs, NJ: Prentice-Hall.

Shavelson, Lonny (1995). *A Chosen Death: The Dying Confront Assisted Suicide.* New York: Simon & Schuster.

Silverstein, Helena (1996). *Unleashing Rights: Law, Meaning and the Animal Rights Movement.* Ann Arbor: University of Michigan Press.

Singer, Peter (1995). *Rethinking Life & Death: The Collapse of Our Traditional Ethics.* New York: St. Martin's Press.

Skolnick, Jerome H. (1968). "Coercion to Virtue: The Enforcement of Morals." *Southern California Law Review* 41, pp. 588–641.

Skolnick, Jerome H. (1988). "The Social Transformation of Vice." *Law and Contemporary Problems* 51, pp. 9–29.

Skelton, George. (1994). "Sending a Message with Initiative (California Ballot Propositions)." *Los Angeles Times,* September 29, p. A3 at col. 1.

Smith, Wesley J. (1997). *Forced Exit: The Slippery Slope from Assisted Suicide to Legalized Murder.* New York: Times Books.

Smith, Wesley J. (1999). "Dependency or Death? Oregonians Make a Chilling Choice." *Wall Street Journal,* February 25, p. A18.

Snow, David A., and Robert D. Benford (1988). "Ideology, Frame Resonance, and Participant Mobilization." *International Social Movements Research* 1, pp. 197–217.

Snow, David, E. Burke Rochford, Steven K. Worden, and Robert D. Benford (1986). "Frame Alignment Processes, Micromobilization, and Movement Participation." *American Sociological Review* 51, August, pp. 464–481.

Spector, Malcom, and John I. Kitsuse (1977). *Constructing Social Problems.* Menlo Park, CA: Cummings.

Spindelman, Marc (1999). "Flaws Mar Oregon Report on Dying Law." *Detroit News,* March 7.

Sprung, Charles L. (1990). "Changing Attitudes and Practices in Forgoing Life-Sustaining Treatments. " *Journal of the American Medical Association* 263, no. 16, pp. 2211–2215.

Staggenborg, Suzanne (1991). *The Pro-Choice Movement: Organization and Activism in the Abortion Conflict.* New York: Oxford University Press.

Starr, Paul (1982). *The Social Transformation of American Medicine.* New York: Basic Books.

Steinhoff, Patricia G., and Milton Diamond (1977). *Abortion Politics: The Hawaii Experience.* Honolulu: University of Hawaii Press.

Sullivan, Amy D., Katrina Hedberg, and David W. Fleming (2000). "Legalized Physician-Assisted Suicide in Oregon—The Second Year." *New England Journal of Medicine* 342, no. 8, February 24, pp. 598–604.

Sutherland, Edwin H. (1950). "The Diffusion of Sexual Psychopath Laws." *American Journal of Sociology* 56, September, pp. 142–148.

Tarrow, Sidney (1998). *Power in Movement: Social Movements and Contentious Politics.* Cambridge, England: Cambridge University Press.

Traynor, Michael P., and Stanton A. Glantz (1996). "California's Tobacco Tax Initiative: The Development and Passage of Proposition 99." *Journal of Health Politics, Policy and Law* 21, no. 3, Fall, pp. 543–585.

Tribe, Laurence (1992). *Abortion: The Clash of Absolutes.* New York: W. W. Norton.

van der Maas, Paul, and Linda L. Emanuel (1998). "Factual Findings," pp. 151–174 in Linda L. Emanuel, ed., *Regulating How We Die: The Ethical, Medical, and Legal Issues Surrounding Physician-Assisted Suicide.* Cambridge, MA: Harvard University Press.

van der Maas, Paul J., Johannes J. M. van Delden, and Loes Pijnenborg (1992). *Euthanasia and Other Medical Decisions Concerning the End of Life.* Health Policy Monographs 22/1+2, 1992, Special Issue. Amsterdam: Elsevier.

van der Maas, Paul J., G. Vanderwal, et al. (1996). "Euthanasia, Physician-Assisted Suicide and Other Medical Practices Involving the End of Life in the Netherlands, 1990–95." *New England Journal of Medicine* 335, no. 22, November 28, pp. 1699–1705.

Vaux, Kenneth L. (1992). *Death Ethics: Religious and Cultural Values in Prolonging and Ending Life.* Philadelphia: Trinity Press International.

Weiner, Joshua M. (1992). "Oregon's Plan for Health Care Rationing." *The Brookings Review,* Winter, pp. 26–31.

Wennberg, Robert N. (1989). *Terminal Choices: Euthanasia, Suicide and the Right to Die.* Grand Rapids, MI: W.B. Erdmans.

Wilkes, Paul (1997). "Dying Well Is the Best Revenge." *New York Times Magazine,* July 6, pp. 32–38.

Williams, Glanville (1957). *The Sanctity of Life and the Criminal Law.* New York: Alfred A. Knopf.

Williams, Glanville (1958). "Euthanasia Legislation: A Rejoinder to the Non-Religious Objections." *Minnesota Law Review* 43, no. 1, pp. 134–147.

Williams, Glanville (1969). "Euthanasia Legislation: A Rejoinder to the Non-Religious Objections," in A. B. Downing, ed., *Euthanasia and the Right to Death: The Case for Voluntary Euthanasia.* London: Peter Owen.

Zalman, Marvin, J. Strate, D. Hunter, and J. Sellars (1997). "Michigan's Assisted Suicide Three Ring Circus—An Intersection of Law and Politics." *Ohio Northern University Law Review* 23, no. 3, pp. 863–968.

Zussman, Robert (1992). *Intensive Care: Medical Ethics and the Medical Profession.* Chicago: The University of Chicago Press.

CAMPAIGN RECORDS

Washington (1991)

Cooper, Karen (1991a). Handwritten notes on memorandum from Ralph Mero (1991a).

Cooper, Karen (1991b). Handwritten notes on memorandum from Marvin Evans (1991).

Cooper, Karen (1991c). "The Campaign Message—Defining the Campaign." Undated memorandum to Initiative 119 Leadership.

Cooper, Karen (1991d). "1991 Campaign Plan for Citizens' Initiative for 'Yes' on 119."

Cooper, Karen (1991e). "Strategic Considerations." Undated memorandum to Initiative 119 Leadership.

Evans, Marvin (1991). "Framing the Message." Memorandum to Washington Citizens for Death With Dignity, February 26.

Mero, Ralph (1991a) "Framing the Message." Memorandum to Washington Citizens for Death With Dignity, February 18.

Mero, Ralph (1991b). Untitled memorandum to Initiative 119 Campaign Leadership, April 24.

Robinson, Kirk (1991). "An Urgent Message from Initiaitve 119 Washington Campaign for Death With Dignity. " Undated video message.

State of Washington Secretary of State (1991). "Voters Pamphlet."

California (1992)

State of California Secretary of State (1992). "Voter's Pamphlet."

Oregon (1994)

Cooper, Karen (1994). *1994 Campaign Plan for Oregon Right to Die.*

Fairbanks, Bregman, and Maulin (1994b). Untitled memorandum dated October 5.

Stutsman, Eli, J.D. (1994a). "Letter to Peter Norton." Regarding the Oregon Death With Dignity Act, June 2.

Stutsman, Eli, J.D. (1994b). "Letter to Stephen D. Brummer, M.D." Regarding the Oregon Death With Dignity Act, June 10.

Sugerman, Geoff (1994). "Oregon Right to Die Earned Media Plan."

Oregon (1997)

Admiraal, Pieter (1997). "A letter to Mr. Duncan," July 25.

Coombs Lee, Barbara (1997). Personal correspondence.

Kimsma, Gerrit K. (1997). "To the People of Oregon," July 3.

TELEVISION ADS

Washington (1991)

"An Urgent Message from Initiative 119 Washington's Campaign for Death with Dignity," Kirk Robinson, President of Washington Citizens for Death with Dignity (1991). 1) Proponent ad.

"Susan Baron." (199. 1) Proponent ad.

"Rose Crumb." (199. 1) Opposition ad.

"Dr. C. Everett Koop." (199. 1) Opposition ad.

"William A. Mahoney." (199. 1) Opposition ad.

"Pat Nugent." (199. 1) Proponent ad.

"Parent of a Young Son." (199. 1) Opposition ad.

"Sarah Jane Rudiger." (199. 1) Opposition ad.

"This Isn't What Dad Wanted—These Machines." (199. 1) Proponent ad.

California (1992)

"Conrad Bain." Proponent ad.
"Jim Curly." Opposition ad.
"Kelly Markham." Opposition ad.
"Secret Suicide." Opposition ad.
"Steel Syringe." Opposition ad.

Oregon (1994)

"Billy." Opposition ad.
"Difficult Diagnoses." Opposition ad.
"Doctors Make Mistakes." Opposition ad.
"Faces." Proponent ad.
"Patty Rosen." Proponent ad.
"Skull and Crossbones." Opposition ad.

Oregon (1997)

"Don't Let 'Em Shove Their Religion Down Your Throat." Proponent ad.
"Dr. Glen Gordon." Proponent ad.
"Dorothy Hoogstraat." Proponent ad.
"Show Me the Study." Proponent ad.
"Al Sinnard." Proponent ad.

NEWSPAPER AND RADIO SOURCES

About Washington (1991 Initiative)

Balzar, John (1991). "Washington Voters Weigh Right to Die." *Los Angeles Times* (October 6). A1.

Brown, Charles E. (1991). "Initiatives 119, 120 Denounced in Mass by Archbishop Murphy." *Seattle Times* E1.

Canaday, Nicholas (1991). "Why We Back an Initiative That Provides Legal Aid in Dying." *Seattle Times* (July 3). A7.

Cantwell, Brian J. (1991). "Suicide Handbook a Fast Seller Locally." *The Columbian* (August 14). A1.

Dority, Barbara (1992). "Civil Rights Watch: Report from Washington State." *The Humanist* (January/February) 37–38.

Gilmore, Susan (1991a). "Church Joins the Campaign—Initiatives Push Catholic Leaders into Voter Drive." *Seattle Times* (September 21). A1.

Gilmore, Susan (1991). "Death Initiative Splits Clergy." *Seattle Times* (April 20). A16.

Gilmore, Susan, and Jim Simon (1991). "Death, Abortion, and Catholics—Church's Political Thrust Debated." *Seattle Times* (November 10). B1.

"Initiative Campaign Contributors." (1991). *Seattle Times* (November 3). B7.

King, Warren (1991a). "Doctors Group Declares War on 'Death with Dignity' Initiative," *Seattle Times* (October 24). B6.

King, Warren (1991b). "Both Sides Claim Victory in 119 Vote." *Seattle Times*, (November 7). A3.

Knox, Richard A. (1991). "64 Percent Back Aid in Dying, Poll Finds—In National Survey, Majority Wants Option." *Seattle Times* (November 4). C1.

Krauthammer, Charles (1991). "'Aid in Dying' Means 'Put to Death.'" *Seattle Times* (October 28). A11.

Leo, John (1991). "Cozy Little Homicides," *U.S. News & World Report* (November 11). 28.

McGough, Peter, and Hugh Straley (1991). "The Dangerous Possibilities of 'Physician Aid in Dying.'" *Seattle Times* (June 25). A7.

Neff, David (1991). "The Wrong Way to Go." *Christianity Today* (October 28). 15.

"Northwest Bishops Denounce Euthanasia" (1991). *Seattle Times* (October 11). C1.

Ostrom, Carol M. (1993). "Helping Other People Die." *Seattle Times* (May 20). B2.

Ostrom, Carol M. (1991). "Small Donations Push Death-With-Dignity Initiative Near Record." *Seattle Times* (July 18). A1.

Paulson, Tom (1993). "Helping Those Who Ask to Die." *Seattle Post-Intelligencer* (May 20). A1.

Pinette, John (1990). "Death and Dying in Washington State." *America* (October 20). 267–268.

Robinson, Anthony B. (1991). "Death with Dignity in Washington State." *The Christian Century* (October 30). 988–989.

Robinson, Herb (1991). "Strong Support for 'Dignity in Death'" (Editorial). *Seattle Times* (July 15). B1.

Shukovsky, Paul (1994). "Assisted Suicide Upheld." *Seattle-Post Intelligencer* (May 4). A1.

Simon, Jim (1991a). "Initiatives Hit the Big Time—National Groups, Huge Budgets Invade Former Turf of the Little Guy." *Seattle Times* (October 4). A1.

Simon, Jim (1991b). "Church to Spend $280,000 More to Fight Death, Abortion Initiatives." *Seattle Times* (October 15). A1.

Simon, Jim (1991c). "Out-of-State Cash Is Rolling in to Beat Initiatives Deadline—Term Limits, Abortion, 'Death with Dignity' Bills on U.S. Stage." *Seattle Times* (October 16). A1.

Snow, Katrin (1991). "AIDS Survivors Reflect on Euthanasia Option." *National Catholic Reporter* (November 8). 3–4.

Spencer, Hal (1991). "'Living Will' Revision Derailed—Amendments Held Back by Initiative 119's Defeat." *Seattle Times* (November 9). A10.

About California (1992 Initiative)

Associated Press (1987). "CMA Resists Any Laws Making Doctors Aid Patients in Suicide." *Orange County Register* (March 12). A3.

Associated Press (1990). "Poll Finds Most Back Right to Die." *Sacramento Bee* (June 13). A10.

Associated Press (1994). "Measure on Suicide Fought by Churches." *Los Angeles Times* (November 5). B12.

Associated Press (1996). "Catholic Bishop Threatens to Expel Abortion, Right-to-Die Supporters." *Los Angeles Times* (March 24). A44.

Colbert, Treacy (1992). "Prop. 161: A 'Rationing' of Individual Health Care." *Los Angeles Times* (October 22). B12.

Ellingwood, Ken, and J. R. Moehringer (1995). "Son Won't Face Charge of Aiding Suicide Attempt." *Los Angeles Times* (June 9). B1.

Harrison, Eric (1991). "Jury Told Abetted-Suicide Case May Establish Rights." *Los Angeles Times* (May 10). A26.

Harrison, Eric (1991). "Man Acquitted of Abetting Ill Wife's Suicide." *Los Angeles Times* (May 11). A1.

Humphry, Derek (1987). "Catholics and Doctors' Groups Oppose Change." *Hemlock Quarterly* 29 (October) 1.

Humphry, Derek (1988). "1988: Hemlock's Most Important Year." *Hemlock Quarterly* 30 (January) 1.

Humphry, Derek (1992a). "Why Were They Beaten in Washington?" *Hemlock Quarterly* 86 (January) 4.

Humphry, Derek (1992b). "Death with Dignity Effort May Be Tried Here Again." *San Francisco Chronicle* (November 13). A25.

"The Indignity of Prop. 161" [Editorial] (1992) *Orange County Register* (October 30). B8.

Jacobs, Paul (1992a). "Quietly, Doctors Already Help Terminal Patients Die." *Los Angeles Times* (September 29). A1.

Jacobs, Paul (1992b). " Prop. 161—A Matter of Life or Death at the Polling Place." *Los Angeles Times* (October 10). A24.

Jacobs, Paul (1992c). "Proposition 161: Suicide Measure Losing Cash Battle." *Los Angeles Times* (October 18). A3.

Jacobs, Paul (1992d). "Emotions Run High over Doctor-Aided Death Issue." *Los Angeles Times* (October 22). A1.

Jacobs, Paul (1992e). "Proposition 161: Initiative Fuels Debate over Morality of Euthanasia." *Los Angeles Times* (October 31). A28.

Journal of Human Dignity (1987). "AAHS Moves Forward on Right-to-Die Legislation in California" vol. 1, no. 1, July, p. 3.

Kershner, Vlae (1992). "State Poll Finds Voter Support for Congressional Term Limits." *San Francisco Chronicle* (September 23). A4.

"Kevorkian's Proposition" [Editorial] (1992). *Orange County Register* (October 26). B8.

Llewellyn Jr., David L. (1992). "Is Proposition 161 a License to Kill?" *Orange County Lawyer* (November) 20–27.

Lostin, Don (1992). "Bishops Fight Right-to-Die Initiative." *San Francisco Chronicle* (October 1). A1.

Maharaj, Davan (1993). "Most Would Let Terminally Ill Die." *Los Angeles Times* (March 9). A10.

Monmaney, Terence (1996a). "Doctors Divided over End of Ban on Aided Suicide." *Los Angeles Times* (March 8). A1.

Monmaney, Terence (1996b). "Doctors in Surveys Back Aided Suicides." *Los Angeles Times* (February 1). A3.

Monmaney, Terence (1997). "More Doctors Found Willing to Assist Suicide." *Los Angeles Times* (February 6). A3.

Nauss, Donald W., and Judy Pasternak (1996). "Kevorkian Freed in Assisted-Suicide Case." *Los Angeles Times* (May 15). A3.

Olsyewski, Lori (1992a). "Right-to-Die Advocate in S. F." *San Francisco Chronicle* (August 28). A25.

Olsyewski, Lori (1992b). "State's Controversial Choice." *San Francisco Chronicle* (October 20). A1.

Olsyewski, Lori (1992c). "Tight Race Likely on Prop. 161." *San Francisco Chronicle* (October 29). A9.

Olsyewski, Lori (1992d). "Right-to-Die Law Apparently a Loser." *San Francisco Chronicle* (November 4). A12.

Parachini, Allan (1987). "Bringing Euthanasia to the Ballot Box: Group Sponsors State Initiative to Legalize 'Physician-Assisted Suicide,'" *Los Angeles Times* (April 10). Part V, 1.

"Petition Failure Is Spur to 1990" (1988). *Hemlock Quarterly* 32 (July) 1.

Religion News Service (1992). "Matters of Life and Death Are Also Questions of Ethics and Morals." *Los Angeles Times* (April 4). B8.

Religion News Service (1995). "Document Forbids Assisted Suicide." *Los Angeles Times* (April 1). B12.

Robinson-Haynes, Ellen (1988). "Should Doctors Kill Terminally Ill Who Ask to Die?" *Sacramento Bee* (April 6). A1.

Seiler, John (1992). "Proposition 161: In 1920, Germany Was Introduced to 'Death With Dignity.'" *Orange County Register* (November 1). K3.

"Signatures Sought For Initiative" (1988). *Hemlock Quarterly*. 30 (January) 1.

Stammer, Larry B. (1996). "Bishops Vow to Fight Assisted Suicide as Much as Abortion." *Los Angeles Times* (March 1996). B6.

Steinfels, Peter (1992). "Beliefs: California Considers a Bold Course on Euthanasia but Leaves Some Paths Unexplored." *New York Times* (October 10). L7.

Stolberg, Sheryl (1996). "Kept Alive, But to Live What Kind of Life?." *Los Angeles Times* (October 22). A1.

"Supporters to Get Signatures for Euthanasia Poll" (1987). *Hemlock Quarterly* 28 (July) 1.

Warrick, Pamela (1991). "Cruzan Case: Flash Point for Opposing Beliefs." *Los Angeles Times* (January 10). E1.

Williams, Mike (1990). "Morality Debate: Is Death on Demand a Right of Humans?" *Orange County Register* (November 11). N1.

About Oregon (1994 Initiative)

Appleby, Timothy (1994). "Suicide Law Falls Short, Activist Says." *The Globe and Mail* (November 21). A10.

Associated Press (1994). "Foe Decries Initiative for Assisted Suicide." *The Register-Guard* (May 9). 1A.

Bates, Tom, and Mark O'Keefe (1994). "On Suicide Measure, Oregon Is a Maverick Again." *The Oregonian* (November 13). A1.

Cain, Brad (1994). "Sponsors File 17 Initiatives for November Ballot." *The Register Guard* (July 9). 6B.

Carney, Bob (1994). "Issue That Refuses to Die." *Spectrum/Portland* (March) 2.

Castagna, Robert (1994). "Assisted-Suicide Initiative Opens Door to Killing the Powerless." *The Oregonian* (September 19). B5.

Fredrickson, Keith (1994b). "Torn Mother: I Helped Her Pass On." *The Bulletin, Bend Oregon* (May 16). A2.

"How Many Voted for Measure 16" (1994). *The Oregonian* (November 11). A16.

Leary, Lynda (1994a). "Oregon Group Files for Vote on Assisted Death." *Spectrum/Portland* (February) 3.

Leary, Lynda (1994b). "Wife's Pain Drives Leader of Right-to-Die Ballot Issue." *Spectrum/Portland* (March) 4.

Mapes, Jeff (1994). "Doctor-Aided Suicide Measure Shows Support." *The Oregonian* (September 8). C10.

McLaughlin, K. (1994). "History Points to Failure for Illegal Immigrant Initiative." *The Oregonian* (September 18). A19.

McQuire, Terry (1994). "Assisted Suicide Proposal Gets Another Test in Oregon." *The Catholic Northwest Progress* (September 29). 3.

"No License to Kill" [Editorial] (1994). *The Oregonian* (October 20). D6.

"Offer Dignity without Death" [Editorial] (1994). *The Oregonian* (November 2). C6.

O'Keefe, Mark (1994a). "Catholic Church Plans to Fight Suicide Measure." *The Oregonian* (September 9). A1.

O'Keefe, Mark (1994b). "Catholic Leaders to Use Pulpit to Fight Initiative." *The Oregonian* (September 10). A1.

O'Keefe, Mark (1994c). "AMA's National Board Opposes Measure 16." *The Oregonian* (October 23). A1.

O'Keefe, Mark (1994d). "Founding Father: Derek Humphry Began the Assisted-Suicide Movement, but His Views May Be Too Extreme for Measure 16 Strategists." *The Oregonian* (November 2). C1.

O'Keefe, Mark (1994e). "TV Ad on Assisted Suicide Leaves Out Part of Story." *The Oregonian* (November 5). C1.

O'Keefe, Mark (1994 f). "Churches Urge Voter Turnout: Their Way." *The Oregonian* (November 8). A1.

O'Keefe, Mark (1994g). "Assisted-Suicide Measure Survives." *The Oregonian* (November 10). A1.

O'Keefe, Mark (1994h). "Opponents of Measure 16 Concede Defeat." *The Oregonian* (November 11). A1.

O'Keefe, Mark (1994i). "Suicide: The World Focuses on Oregon." *The Oregonian* (November 1). A1.

O'Keefe, Mark (1995). "Catholics Keep Lonely Vigil on Suicide." *The Oregonian* (September 25). A1.

O'Keefe, Mark, and Tom Bates (1994). "Oregon Morality, Issues Divided." *The Oregonian* (November 10). A1.

O'Neill, Patrick (1994). "Initiative Supporters, Candidates Make Final Push as Election Nears." *The Oregonian* (November 7). B7.

O'Neill, Patrick, and Foster Church (1994). "Physician-Assisted Suicide Stirs Up Emotional Maelstrom." *The Oregonian* (May 5). A1.

"Oregon Democrats Support Rights of Terminally Ill" (1984). *Port Orford News* (March 30). 3.

"*The Oregonian's* Recommendations" [Editorial] (1994). *The Oregonian* (November 2). B10.

Pfohman, Robert (1994). "Oregonians to Face Suicide Initiative." *Catholic Sentinel* (July 15). 1.

Putnam, Judy (1994). "Kevorkian Case Goes to State's High Court." *The Oregonian* (October 2). A17.

Reinhard, David (1994). "Measure 16: The Vote of Your Life." *The Oregonian* (October 27). D8.

Religion News Service (1997). "Catholic Church Alters Tactics on Suicide Law." *Los Angeles Times* (November 1). B8.

Rojas-Burke, Joe (1994a). "Time to Die: Who Makes the Choice?." *Eugene Register Guide* (May 2). 1A.

Rojas-Burke, Joe (1994b). "Meetings to Discuss Doctor-Assisted Suicide." *Eugene Register Guide* (August 11). 1A.

Rubenstein, Sura (1994). "Voters Split over Initiative." *The Oregonian* (November 7). A1.

Rubenstein, Sura, and Mark O'Keefe (1994). "Poll Shows Early Support for Doctor-Assisted Suicide." *The Oregonian* (October 10). A1.

"Securing the Right to Die" (1994). *The News-Review* (March 28). 3.

"State Demos Urge Party to Support 3 Initiatives" (1994). *The Oregonian* (August 30). B6.

About Oregon (1997 Initiative)

Benson, Arden R. (1997). "Series of Editorials on Suicide Law Overdone," Reader Response. *The Oregonian* (October 26). E5.

Dietz, Diana (1997). Comments of reporter for the *Register-Guard* (Eugene) on "Seven Days," Oregon Public Broadcasting, October 17.

"Editorial" (1997). *The Oregonian* (October 9). D6.

Fogarty, Colin (1997). Comments of radio reporter for Oregon Public Broadcasting on "Seven Days." Oregon Public Broadcasting, October 17.

Hill, Gail Kinsey (1997b). "More Stations Reject Measure 51 Ad. *The Oregonian* (October 9). 6.

Hill, Gail Kinsey (1997c). "Repeal Opponents Swipe Proponents' Slogan for Ads." *The Oregonian.* (October 15). A14–A15.

Humphry, Derek, William K. Kaula, and Geoffrey N. Fieger (1994). "To the Editor." *New York Times* (December 3) 14.

Lunch, Bill (1997). Comments of political science professor and political analyst on "Seven Days," Oregon Public Broadcasting, November 7.

McAtee, Shendy (1997). "Assisted Suicide Better than Violent Alternative." Reader Response, *The Oregonian.* (October 29). B15.

O'Keefe, Mark (1997). "The Pursuit of Liberty and Death." *The Oregonian* (October 19). A1, A20.

Reinhard, David (1997a). Comments of associate editor of *The Oregonian* "Seven Days." Oregon Public Broadcasting (October 17).

Reinhard, David (1997b). "Liar, Liar." *The Oregonian* (October 19). E4.

Religion News Service (1997). "Catholic Church Alters Tactics on Suicide Law." *Los Angeles Times* (November 1). B8.

Rohas-Burke, Joe (1997). "Suicide Bill to Go Back to Voters." *Eugene Register Guard* (June 10) 22–24, 26, 28–32.

Shurman, Jerry (1997). "Illogic of Editorials a Disservice to Oregon," Reader Response. *The Oregonian* (October 29). B15.

Smigelski, David (1997). "To Lie For." *Willamette Week* (September 17) 1.

OTHER NEWSPAPER ARTICLES ABOUT ASSISTED SUICIDE

"A Better Death in Oregon" [Editorial] (1998). *New York Times* (March 28).

Agence France-Press (1998). "Euthanasia Debate Reopens in France." July 25.

Agence France-Presse (1999). "Experts Want Switzerland as First Nation with Legal Euthanasia." April 29.

Alcom, Gay (1999). "Euthanasia Poll Shows Divided Attitudes in NT." *The Age* (Melbourne) (February 26).

"Appeal to High Court Certain, Lawyers and Doctors Say" (1996). *Los Angeles Times* (March 8) A34, at col. 1.

Ashworth, Keryn (2000). "New Push for Death Choice." *West Australian* (May 22).

"Assisted Suicide and the Law" [Editorial] (1997). *New York Times* (January 6) A12, at col. 1.

"Assisted-Suicide Bill Moves Ahead: Assembly Panel Supports Plan" (1990). *Sacramento Bee* (April 21).

"Assisted Suicide, in Practice" Editorial (1999). *New York Times* (February 27) A14.

"Assisted Suicide Lesson Learned in Oregon" (1999). *American Medical News* (March 22/29).

"Assisted Suicide Top Question on State's Ballot" (2000). *Portland Press Herald* (May 26) 2b.

Associated Press (1998a). "Group Unveils Guidebook on Physician-Assisted Suicide." March 3.

Associated Press (1998b). "Oregon Medical Professionals Wrap up Netherlands Tour." April 3.

Associated Press (1999a). "Latin American Briefs." January 30.

Associated Press (1999b). "Experts Want Switzerland as First Nation With Legal Euthanasia." April 29.

Associated Press (2000). "Assisted Suicides Increase in Oregon." February 24.

Associated Press (2000.) "Legislation Approved Before Adjourn" December 15.

Barnett, Erin Hoover, and Lisa Grace Lednicer (1999). "Bill Would Tighten Assisted Suicide Restriction." *The Oregonian* (January 22) 3.

Barnett, Jim (2000). "Wyden Uses Pain Relief Bill as Stall." *The Oregonian* (May 24).

Barnett, Jim, and Dave Hogan (2000). "Suicide Bill Feud Grows Intense." *The Oregonian* (May 7).

Belkin, Lisa. (1993b). "There No Simple Suicide." *New York Times Magazine*, November 14, pp. 487.

Biskupic, Joan (1997). "Justices Skeptical of Assisted Suicide." *Washington Post* (January 9) A1, at col. 4.

Blumenfeld, Laura (1997). "At Dawn, Activists Greet Matters of Death in Shades of Gray." *Washington Post* (January 9) A1, at col. 3.

Bradbury, Dieter (2000). "Ad Angers Backers of Assisted Suicide." *Portland Press Herald* (October 25) 2B.

British Broadcasting Company (1999). "British Medical Association Stands by End-of-Life Guidance." July 8.

British Broadcasting Company (2000). "Euthanasia Bill Blocked." April 14.

Brough, Jodie (1997). "The Last Rights." *The Sydney Morning Herald* (March 29) New review section, 22.

Brown, David (2000). "A Picture of Assisted Suicide." *Washington Post* (February 24) A03.

Cain, Brad (1999). "Oregon MDs Wary of Suicide Law." Associated Press, March 5, p. 1.

Cain, Charlie, and Tim Kiska (1998). "Voters Overwhelmingly Reject Assisted Suicide." *Detroit News* (November 4).

Castaneda, Carol J. (1996). "Appeals Court Backs Right to Assisted Suicide." *USA Today* (March 7) 1A, at col. 2.

"The Catholic Church: Mandate of Heaven" (1999). *Sydney Morning Herald* (July 31).

Chan, Quinton (1999). "Doctors Give Support to Euthanasia." *South China Morning Post* (December 30) 1.

Daley, Suzanne (2000). "The Dutch Seek to Legalize Long-Tolerated Euthanasia." *New York Times* (June 20) A1, at col. 1.

Deutsch, Anthony (1999). "Dutch Debate Legalized Euthanasia." Associated Press, September 24.

"Doctors Campaign against Euthanasia" (1998). *Daily Telegraph* (October 15).

"Dutch Take Step to Make Assisted Suicide Legal" (2000). *Los Angeles Times* (November 29) A4.

"An Emotional Debate Leaves Room for Rational Argument" [Editorial] (2000). *Journal Tribune* (May 20–21).

Foubister, Vida (2000). "Medical Experts Agree on Guide for End-of-Life Care." *American Medical News* (February 7).

Gladstone, Mark (1999). "Assisted-Suicide Debate Shifts to State." *Los Angeles Times* (April 20) A3, at col. 2.

Goldberg, Carey (2000). "Vermont's House Backs Wide Rights for Gay Couples." *New York Times* (March 17) A1.

Goldstein, Amy (1998). "No Drug Law Penalty for Assisted Suicide." *Washington Post* (June 6).

Greenhouse, Linda (1997). "High Court Hears 2 Cases Involving Assisted Suicide." *New York Times* (January 9) A1, at col. 5.

Haley, Martine (2000). "Euthanasia Clinics Win Public Support." *The Mercury* (January 24).

Hannan, Ewin, and Manika Naidoo (1999). "Kennett Caution on Death Clinic." *The Age* (April 16).

Hill, Gail Kinsey (1997a). "Kitzhaber Supports Assisted Suicide," *The Oregonian* (August 3) A1, A20.

Hoover, Erin (1998). "Assisted-Suicide Guide Expands Ethics Debate." *The Oregonian* (March 6).

Hosaka, Tomoko (2000). "Smith Defends His Vote Against Suicide Law." *The Oregonian* (April 29).

Humphry, Derek (1996). "Perspectives on Assisted Suicide: Self-Determination Is Affirmed." *Los Angeles Times* (March 8) B11, at col. 3.

Izenberg, Dan (1999). "Court Calls for Knesset to Spell Out Euthanasia Laws." *Jerusalem Post* (June 3) 4.

"Justices' Ruling Won't End the Assisted-Suicide Issue" (1997). *Los Angeles Times* (June 27) B8, at col. 1.

Kakutani, Michiko (2000). "Critic's Notebook: When the Geeks Get Snide; Computer Slang Scoffs at Wetware (the Humans)." *New York Times* (June 27) B1.

Kmiec, Douglas W. (1996). "Perspectives on Assisted Suicide: There Is No Right to Kill." *Los Angeles Times* (March 8) B11, at col. 3

Kolata, Gina (1997). "Passive Euthanasia in Hospitals Is the Norm, Doctors Say." *New York Times* (June 28) 1.

Lewin, Tamar (1996). "Ruling Sharpens Debate on 'Right to Die.'" *New York Times* (March 8) A8, at col. 1.

Lovell, Jeremy (1999). "South Africa Opens National Debate on Euthanasia." Reuters, September 8.

"Maine House Rejects Assisted Suicide." *Patriot Ledger* (1998). (Quincy, MA) (February 12), 11.

"Mercy in Oregon." (1999). *Times Union* (February 22).

Monmaney, Terence (1996). "Doctors Divided over End of Ban on Aided Suicide." *Los Angeles Times* (March 8) A1 at col. 5.

Moore, Michael O'D (2000). "Maine Group Fights Death Assistance." *Bangor Daily News* (May 18).

Moore, Michael O'D (2000b). "Anti-Assisted Suicide Ad Factually Shaky." *Bangor Daily News* (October 26).

Murphy, Brian (1998). "Suicide Law Trounced." *Detroit Free Press* (November 4).

Murphy, Brian, and Joe Swickard (1999). "Convicted of Murder." *Detroit Free Press* (March 27).

National Public Radio. (1998a). "Morning Edition." March 4.

National Public Radio. (1998b). "Morning Edition." August 31.

Nullis, Clare (1999). "Debating Dignified Death." *The London Free Press* (Canada) (September 23) C8.

Oregon Public Broadcasting (1998b). "Pharmacists vs. Doctors." April 8.

Price, Richard, and Tony Mauro (1997). "Advocates Promise to Press the Fight." *USA Today* (June 27) 4A, at col. 1.

Reuters News (1999). "Euthanasia Bill Highlights Belgian Political Split." December 23.

Savage, David G. (1996a). "Northwest Effort on Right to Die Faces High Court." *Los Angeles Times* (September 30) A1.

Savage, David G. (1996b). "Administration Asks Court to Reject Assisted Suicide." *Los Angeles Times* (November 13) A3 at col. 1.

Savage, David G. (1997). "Justices Signal Rejection of Right to Die." *Los Angeles Times* (January 9), A1, at col. 4.

Savage, David G., and Henry Weinstein (1996). "Court Strikes Down N.Y. Ban on Assisted Suicide." *Los Angeles Times* (April 3) A19, at col. 1.

"Suicide Opponents Regroup After Ad Loss." *Bangor Daily News* (November 3).

Sequera, Vivian (1997). "Colombia's High Court Legalizes Euthanasia." Associated Press, May 21.

Tass (2000). "Russians Differ on Euthanasia—Poll." April 29.

United Press International (1999). "Few Use Oregon's Assisted Suicide Law" (February 17).

Vitez, Michael (1999). "Oregon Assisted-Suicide Law Little Used But Well Regarded." *Philadelphia Inquirer* (January 19).

Weinstein, Henry and Larry B. Stammer (1996). "Court's Ruling on Physician-Assisted Suicide Ignites Strong Emotions." *Los Angeles Times* (March 7) A16, at col. 1

Weinstein, Joshua (2000). "Sides Square Off on Assisted Suicide." *Portland Press Herald* (May 18) 1B.

Xinhua English Newswire (1998). "Lawmaker Calls for Experiment on Euthanasia." March 10.

Young, Susan (2000). "Poll Shows Support Slipping for Two Citizen Initiatives." *Bangor Daily News* (October 18).

COURT CASES

Barber v Superior Court, 147 Cal. App. 3d 1066 (1983).

Bartling v Superior Court, 163 Cal. App. 3d 186 (1984).

Bouvia v Superior Court, 179 Cal. App. 3d 1127 (1986).

Bowers v Hardwick, 478 U.S. 186 (1986).

Brophy v New England Sinai Hospital, Inc., 398 Mass. 417, 497 N.E. 2d 626 (1986).

Compassion I: Compassion in Dying v Washington, 850 F. Supp. 1454 W. D. Wash. (1994).

Compassion II: Compassion in Dying v Washington, 49 F. 3d 586, 9th Cir. (1995).

Compassion III: Compassion in Dying v Washington, 79 F. 3d 790, 9th Cir. (1996).

Compassion IV: Washington v Glucksberg, 521 U.S. 702. (1997).

Conservatorship of Drabic, 245 Cal. Rptr. at 840: 855 (1988).

Cruzan v Director, Missouri Dept. of Health, 497 U.S. 261 (1990.

Dandridge v Williams, 397 U.S. 471 (1969).

Griswold et al. v Connecticut, 381 U.S. 479 (1965).

In re Eichner, decided with *In re Storer.*

In re Jobes, 108 N.J. 394, 529 A. 2d 434 (1987).

In re Quinlan, 355 A. 2d 647 (1976).

In re Storer, 52 N.Y. 2d 363, 420 N.E. 2d64, cert denied 454 U.S. 858 (1981).

Lee v State of Oregon, 107 F. 3d 1382, 9th Circuit (1997 [overturning of injunction]).

Lee v State of Oregon, 869 F. Supp 1491, D. Or. (1994 [preliminary injunction]).

Lee v State of Oregon, 891 F. Supp. 1429, D. Or. (1995 [permanent injunction]).

New State Ice Co. v Liebmann, 285 U.S. 262 (1932).

Planned Parenthood v Casey, 112 S. Ct. 2791 (1992).

Poe v Ullmann, 367 U.S. 497 (1961).

Quill I: Quill v Koppell, 870 F. Supp. 78 (S. D. N. Y. 1994).

Quill II: Quill v Vacco, 80 F. 3d 716 2nd Cir. (1996).

Quill III: Vacco v Quill, 521 U.S. 793 (1997).

Roe v Wade, 410 U.S. 113 (1973).

Superintendent of Belchertown State School v Saikewicz, 373 Mass 728, 370 N.E. 2d 417 (1977).

COURT BRIEFS

36 Religious Organizations (1996). Brief of 36 Religious Organizations, Leaders and Scholars as Amici Curiae in Support of Respondents, *Vacco v Quill* and *Washington v Glucksberg*, In the Supreme Court of the United States, December 10.

American Civil Liberties Union et al. (1996). Brief Amici Curiae Supporting

Respondents of the American Civil Liberties Union, American Civil Liberties Union of Washington, National Gray Panthers Project Fund, Gray Panthers of Washington, Gray Panthers of New York, Japanese American Citizens League, Pacific Northwest District of the Japanese American Citizens League, Humanists of Washington, Hemlock Society USA, Hemlock Society of New York State, Hemlock Society of Washington State, Euthanasia Research Guidance Organization, AIDS Action Council, Northwest AIDS Foundation; Seattle AIDS Support Group, Local 6 of Service Employees International Union, Temple de Hirsch Sinai Social Action Committee, Seattle/King County Chapter of the Older Women's League, December 10.

American Civil Liberties Union of Washington et al. (1994). Brief of Amicus Curiae (American Civil Liberties Union of Washington; Northwest AIDS Foundation; Seattle AIDS Support Group; Older Women's League; Gray Panthers of Seattle; Hemlock Society of Washington State; National Organization for Women, Seattle Chapter; Humanists of Washington; National Lawyers Guild, Seattle Chapter; Local 6 of Service Employees International Union; Temple de Hirsch Sinai) in support of plaintiffs, *Compassion in Dying v Washington*, United States District Court for the Western District of Washington at Seattle, February 24.

American Hospital Association (1996). Brief Amicus Curiae of the American Hospital Association in Support of Petitioners. *Vacco v Quill* and *Washington v Glucksberg*, in the Supreme Court of the United States, November 12.

American Suicide Foundation (1996). Brief of the American Suicide Foundation, *Amicus Curiae*, Supporting Reversal, *Vacco v Quill* and *Washington v Glucksberg*, in the Supreme Court of the United States, November 12.

Bioethicists (1996). Brief of Amicus Curiae Bioethicists Supporting Respondents, *Vacco v Quill* and *Washington v Glucksberg*, in the Supreme Court of the United States, December 9.

Bioethics Professors (1996). Brief for Bioethics Professors Amicus Curiae Supporting Petitioners, *Vacco v Quill* and *Washington v Glucksberg*, in the Supreme Court of the United States, November 12.

Choice in Dying, Inc. (1996). Brief of Amicus Curiae Choice in Dying, Inc., *Vacco v Quill* and *Washington v Glucksberg*, in the Supreme Court of the United States.

Coalition of Hospice Professionals (1996). Brief of the Coalition of Hospice Professionals as Amicus Curiae for Affirmance of the Judgments Below, *Vacco v Quill* and *Washington v Glucksberg*, in the Supreme Court of the United States.

Dworkin, Ronald, et al. (1996). Brief for Ronald Dworkin, Thomas Nagel, Robert Nozick, John Rawls, Thomas Scanlon, and Judith Jarvis Thomson as Amici Curiae in Support of Respondents. *Vacco v Quill* and *Washington v Glucksberg*, in the Supreme Court of the United States, December.

Gay Men's Health Crisis et al. (1996). Brief of the Amici Curiae: Gay Men's Health Crisis and Lambda Legal Defense and Education Fund: On Behalf of Their Members with Terminal Illnesses; and Five Prominent Americans with Disabilities: Evan Davis, Hugh Gregory, Gallagher Swarz, Michael Stein, and

Susan Webb, in Support of Respondents, *Vacco v Quill* and *Washington v Glucksberg*, in the Supreme Court of the United States.

Glucksberg, Harold, M.D. (1994). "Declaration of Harold Glucksberg, M.D." *Compassion in Dying v Washington*, United States District Court, Western District of Washington at Seattle, February 3.

Hatch, Senator Orrin (1996). Brief of Senator Orrin Hatch, Chairman of the Senate Judiciary Committee; Representative Henry Hyde, Chairman of the House Judiciary Committee; and Representative Charles Canady, Chairman of the Subcommittee on the Constitution of the House Judiciary Committee, as Amicus Curiae in Support of the Petitioners, *Vacco v Quill* and *Washington v Glucksberg*, in the Supreme Court of the United States, November 12.

International Anti-Euthanasia Task Force (1994). Brief of the International Anti-Euthanasia Task Force as Amicus Curiae in Support of Defendants/Appellants' Brief, *Compassion in Dying v Washington*, United States Court of Appeals for the Ninth Circuit, July 3.

International Anti-Euthanasia Task Force (1997). "Caring, Not Killing, Wins." Press release, June 27, www.iaetf.org.

Lambda Legal Defense and Education Fund et al. (1995). Brief of Amici Curiae in Support of Reversal, Lambda Legal Defense and Education Fund, Inc., National Association of People with AIDS, the Unitarian Universalist Association, Americans for Death With Dignity, Death With Dignity Education Center, the Gray Panthers Project Fund, the Hemlock Society, and Minna Barrett, *Quill v Vacco*, in The United States Court of Appeals for the Second Circuit, March 3.

Law Professors (1996). Brief Amicus Curiae of Law Professors in Support of Respondents, *Vacco v Quill* and *Washington v Glucksberg*, in the Supreme Court of the United States, December 10.

Legal Center (1996). Brief Amici Curiae of the Legal Center for Defense of Life, Inc. and the Pro-Life Defense Fund in Support of Petitioners, *Vacco v Quill* and *Washington v Glucksberg*, in the Supreme Court of the United States, November 12.

Members of the New York State Legislature (1995). Brief Amicus Curiae of Members of the New York State Legislature in Support of Defendants-Appellees, *Quill v Vacco*, in The United States Court of Appeals for the Second Circuit, April 3.

Members of the New York and Washington State Legislatures (1996). Brief Amicus Curiae on Behalf of Members of the New York and Washington State Legislatures in Support of Petitioners, *Vacco v Quill* and *Washington v Glucksberg*, in the Supreme Court of the United States, November 7.

National Center for the Medically Dependent & Disabled, Inc. (1996). Brief Amici Curiae of the National Center for the Medically Dependent & Disabled, Inc., et al., *Vacco v Quill* and *Washington v Glucksberg*, in the Supreme Court of the United States, November 12.

National Hospice Organization (1996). Brief *Amicus Curiae* for the National Hospice Organization in Support of Petitioners, *Vacco v Quill* and *Washington v Glucksberg*, In the Supreme Court of the United States.

National Right to Life Committee (1996). Brief Amicus Curiae of the National Right to Life Committee, Inc., in Support of Petitioners, *Vacco v Quill* and *Washington v Glucksberg*, in the Supreme Court of the United States, November.

Project on Death in America (1996). Brief of the Project on Death in America. Open Society Institute, as Amicus Curiae, for Reversal of the Judgments Below, *Vacco v Quill* and *Washington v Glucksberg*, in the Supreme Court of the United States, November 12.

Public Disclosure Commission (1991). State of Washington. Summary, Full Report Recipts and Expenditures on I–119 for: Citizens for Patient Self-Determination; Washington Physicians Against 119; Washington State Catholic Conference/I–119 No !; Washington Hemlock PAC; 119 Vote No; People Against Legalized Murder; Concerned Women for America of Washington; Yakima County Pro-Life Action League; Physicians for Initiative 119; Interfaith Clergy for "Yes" On Initiative 119; Unitarian Univeralists for Death with Dignity, Olympia.

Quill III and *Compassion IV* (1997a). Transcripts. United States Supreme Court Official Transcript. West Publishing Company. WL13671. Database: SCT.ORALARG, January 8.

Quill III and *Compassion IV* (1997b). Transcripts. United States Supreme Court Official Transcript. West Publishing Company. WL13672. Database: SCT.ORALARG, January 8.

State Legislators (1996). Brief Amicus Curiae of State Legislators in Support of Respondents, *Vacco v Quill* and *Washington v Glucksberg*, in the Supreme Court of the United States, November 12.

States of California et al. (1996). Brief of Amicus Curiae States of California, Alabama, Colorado, Florida, Georgia, Illinois, Iowa, Louisiana, Maryland, Michigan, Mississippi, Montana, Nebraska, New Hampshire, New York, South Carolina, South Dakota, Tennessee, and Virginia and the Commonwealth of Puerto Rico in Support of Petitioners, State of Washington, et al., *Vacco v Quill* and *Washington v Glucksberg*, in the Supreme Court of the United States.

Surviving Family Members (1996). Brief Amicus Curiae of Surviving Family Members in Support of Physician-Assisted Dying, in Support of Respondents *Vacco v Quill* and *Washington v Glucksberg*, in the Supreme Court of the United States.

United States Catholic Conference (1994). Brief of the United States Catholic Conference; Washington State Catholic Conference; Oregon Catholic Conference; California Catholic Conference; Roger Cardinal Mahony; Archbishops William Levada, Thomas Murphy, and John Quinn; as Amici Curiae in Support of Appellants State of Washington et al., *Compassion in Dying v Washington*, in the United States Court of Appeals for the Ninth Circuit, July 11.

United States Catholic Conference (1995). Brief of United States Catholic Conference and New York State Catholic Conference as Amici Curiae in Support of Appellees Dennis C. Vacco et al., *Quill v Vacco*, in the United States Court of Appeals for the Second Circuit.

Washington State Hospital Association (1994). Brief of Amici Curiae Washington State Hospital Association and Catholic Health Association of the United States *Compassion in Dying v Washington*, in the United States Court of Appeals for the Ninth Circuit, July 11.

Washington State Psychological Association et al. (1996). Brief of the Washington State Psychological Association, the American Counseling Association; the Association for Gay, Lesbian and Bisexual Issues in Counseling, and a Coalition of Mental Health Professionals as Amici Curiae in Support of Respondent, *Vacco v Quill* and *Washington v Glucksberg*, in the Supreme Court of the United States, December 10.

TESTIMONY AND ORAL PRESENTATIONS

American Pain Foundation (1999). Letter from American Pain Foundation to House Judiciary Committee Chairman Hyde, June 24.

Anderson, E. Ratcliffe, Jr., M.D. (1999). Letter to Judiciary Committee Chairman Rep. Henry Hyde re: Support for HR 2260, the "Pain Relief Promotion Act of 1999" from AMA Executive Vice President, June 28.

Bonthius, Robert K., Ph.D. (2000). Testimony of Presbyterian minister before the Joint Standing Committee on the Judiciary, Maine legislature, February 16.

Carstairs, Sharon (2000). Statement of Senator before the Subcommittee to Update "Of Life and Death" of the Standing Senate Committee on Social Affairs, Science and Technology Evidence, Senate of Canada, Ottawa, Tuesday, February 15 (from transcript).

Castagna, Robert J. (1998). Written testimony of the General Counsel and Executive Director, Oregon Catholic Conference to the Hearing of the Oregon Health Division on the Death With Dignity Act, March 20.

Coombs Lee, Barbara (1998). Written testimony of the Executive Director of the Compassion in Dying Federation to the Hearing of the Oregon Health Division on the Death With Dignity Act, March 20.

Demosthenes, Debbie (2000). Testimony of hospice nurse before the Joint Standing Committee on the Judiciary, Maine legislature, February 16.

Doerflinger, Richard M. (1999). Testimony of the Associate Director for Policy Development at the Secretariat for Pro-Life Activities, National Conference of Catholic Bishops at the Hearing on H. R. 2260, the "Pain Relief Promotion Act of 1999," Subcommittee on the Constitution, Committee on the Judiciary, U.S. House of Representatives, June 24.

Foley, Kathleen, M.D. (1996). Testimony before the United States House of Representatives Committee on the Judiciary Subcommittee on the Constitution, April 29.

Gelwick, Rev. Richard (2000). Testimony of medical ethicist before the Joint Standing Committee on the Judiciary, Maine legislature, February 16.

Grover, Darlene (2000). Testimony of nurse before the Joint Standing Committee on the Judiciary, Maine legislature, February 16.

Hagan, Kelly (1997). "The Feasibility of Appropriate Regulations." Presentation at University of Southern California, Pacific Center for Health Policy and Ethics

Conference, Physician Assistance in Bringing About Death: Can Regulation Work?" November 18.

Hamilton, N. Gregory, M.D. (1998a). Written testimony of the President, Physicians for Compassionate Care to the Hearing of the Oregon Health Division on the Death With Dignity Act, March 15.

Hamilton, N. Gregory, M.D. (1998b). Testimony of the President, Physicians for Compassionate Care, U.S. House of Representatives, Committee on the Judiciary, Subcommittee on the Constitution, Hearing on H.R. 4006 (Lethal Drug Abuse Prevention Act of 1998). Washington, DC, July 14.

Heath, Michael S. (2000). Testimony of Executive Director of the Christian Civic League of Maine before the Joint Standing Committee on the Judiciary, Maine legislature, February 16.

Hendin, Herbert M.D. (1997b). Presentation at University of Southern California, Pacific Center for Health Policy and Ethics Conference, "Physician Assistance in Bringing about Death: Can Regulation Work?" November 18.

Hendin, Herbert, M.D. (1998). Testimony, U.S. House of Representatives, Committee on the Judiciary, Subcommittee on the Constitution, Hearing on H.R. 4006 (Lethal Drug Abuse Prevention Act of 1998). Washington, DC, July 14.

Higginson, Grant, M.D., M.P.H. (1998). Written testimony of the Deputy Administrator, State Health Officer, State of Oregon, to the Hearing of the Oregon Health Division on the Death With Dignity Act, March 20.

Hofmann, Chuck E., M.D. (1998). Written testimony of the President, Oregon Medical Association, to the Hearing of the Oregon Health Division on the Death With Dignity Act, March 20.

Hyde, Henry (1998). Statement of House of Representatives Judiciary Committee Chair to the Subcommittee on the Constitution, Committee on the Judiciary, U.S. House of Representatives H.R. 4006, the "Lethal Drug Abuse Prevention Act of 1998." July 14.

Jackson, Ann M. (1999). Testimony of the Executive Director and Chief Executive Officer of the Oregon Hospice Association at the Hearing on H.R. 2260, the "Pain Relief Promotion Act of 1999," Subcommittee on the Constitution, Committee on the Judiciary, U.S. House of Representatives, June 24.

Jenkins, Alitha (1999). Testimony before Senate Judiciary Committee from Providence Health Systems, March 17.

Kitzhaber, John A., M.D. (1998). Testimony of Oregon Governor, U.S. House of Representatives, Committee on the Judiciary, Subcommittee on the Constitution, Hearing on H.R. 4006 (Lethal Drug Abuse Prevention Act of 1998). Washington, DC, July 14.

Knowlton, Calvin H., R.Ph., M.Div., Ph.D. (1998). Testimony of the American Pharmaceutical Association to the Subcommittee on the Constitution, Committee on the Judiciary, U.S. House of Representatives H.R. 4006, the "Lethal Drug Abuse Prevention Act of 1998." July 14.

Lapointe, Bernard (2000). Statement of the President of the Canadian Palliative Care Association, before the Subcommittee to Update "Of Life and Death" of the Standing Senate Committee on Social Affairs, Science and Technology Evidence, Senate of Canada, Ottawa, Tuesday, February 15, 2000 (from transcript).

Lippke, James (2000). Testimony of Chair of the Bagaduce Interfaith Peace and Justice Committee before the Joint Standing Committee on the Judiciary, Maine legislature, February 16.

Lynn, Joanne, M.D. (1998). Testimony of the President of Americans for Better Care of the Dying before the United States Senate Judiciary Committee, Washington DC, July 31.

Marzen, Thomas J. (1998). Testimony, General Counsel, National Legal Center for the Medically Dependent and Disabled, U.S. House of Representatives, Committee on the Judiciary, Subcommittee on the Constitution, Hearing on H.R. 4006 (Lethal Drug Abuse Prevention Act of 1998), Washington, DC, July 14.

Melanson, Dorothy, R.N. (2000). Testimony of registered nurse before the Joint Standing Committee on the Judiciary, Maine legislature, February 16.

Miller, Kellie P. (2000). Letter of the Executive Director of the Maine Osteopathic Association to the Joint Standing Committee on the Judiciary, Maine legislature, February 15.

Mills, Dora Anne (2000). Testimony of Chief Health Officer of Maine before the Joint Standing Committee on the Judiciary, Maine legislature, February 16.

Mutty, Marc R. (2000). Testimony of representative of Roman Catholic Diocese before the Joint Standing Committee on the Judiciary, Maine legislature, February 16.

Onek, Joseph (1998). Testimony of the Principal Deputy Associate Attorney General, United States Department of Justice, before the United States Senate Judiciary Committee, Washington DC, July 31.

Orentlicher, David, M.D., J.D. (1999). Testimony of Professor of Law and Codirector, Center for Law and Health, Indiana University School of Law–Indianapolis, Hearing on H.R. 2260, the "Pain Relief Promotion Act of 1999" Subcommittee on the Constitution," Committee on the Judiciary, U.S. House of Representatives, June 24.

Picard, Pauline (1998). Floor statement of Canadian representative, Hansard transcript, February 2.

Reardon, Thomas R., M.D. (1998). Testimony of the President of the American Medical Association before the Subcommittee on the Constitution, United States House of Representatives Committee on the Judiciary, Washington, DC, July 14.

Seguin, Marilynne (1994). Statement of Dying With Dignity Executive Director before the Senate of Canada, May 25. Reported in Special Senate Committee 1995 "Of Life and Death" Report of the Special Senate Committee on Euthanasia and Assisted Suicide, Senate of Canada, Ottawa.

Smith, Gordon H. (2000). Testimony of the Executive Vice President of the Maine Medical Association before the Joint Standing Committee on the Judiciary, Maine legislature, February 16.

Sox, Harold C. Jr., M.D. (1998). Testimony of the President of the American College of Physicians—American Society of Internal Medicine, before the United States Senate Judiciary Committee, Washington, DC, July 31.

Stevens, Kenneth R., Jr., M.D. (1998). Written testimony of a board member of Physicians for Compassionate Care to the Hearing of the Oregon Health Division on the Death With Dignity Act, March 20.

Stutsman, Eli, J.D. (1997). "Permissible Regulation: The Oregon Death With Dignity Act. " Presentation at University of Southern California, Pacific Center for Health Policy and Ethics Conference, "Physician Assistance in Bringing About Death: Can Regulation Work?" November 18.

Sutton, Sally (2000). Testimony of the Executive Director of the Maine Civil Liberties Union before the Joint Standing Committee on the Judiciary, Maine legislature, February 16.

Weiss, Elizabeth, M.D. (2000). Testimony of physician before the Joint Standing Committee on the Judiciary, Maine legislature, February 16.

NEWSLETTERS

Compassion in Dying Federation of America (1998). "Compassion of Oregon Gets Going," Vol. 6, no. 1.

The Oregon Report on the Right to Die (1998a). "The Death With Dignity Act Finally Reaches Implementation," Vol. IV, no. 1, Winter/Spring, pp. 1–2.

The Oregon Report on the Right to Die (1998b). "Congress Steps In As Justice Rules in Favor of Oregon & Death With Dignity." Vol. IV, no. 2, Spring/Summer, pp. 1–2.

REPORTS

California Legislature (1999). Assembly Committee on the Judiciary, Analysis of AB 1592.

Oregon Health Division (1997). "Physician-Assisted Suicide." *CD Summary*, Centers for Disease Prevention and Epidemiology Vol. 46, no. 23, November 11.

Oregon Health Division (1998). Hearings Officer Report—Oregon Death With Dignity Act for Hearing of March 20. Portland, April 3.

Select Committee on Medical Ethics (1994). Report of the Select Committee on Medical Ethics, House of Lords, Session 93–94. London: HMSO.

South African Law Commission (1999). "Investigation into Euthanasia and the Artificial Preservation of Life."

The Task Force to Improve the Care of Terminally-Ill Oregonians (1998). *The Oregon Death With Dignity Act: A Guidebook for Health Care Providers.* Portland: The Center for Ethics in Health Care, Oregon Health Sciences University.

WEB SITES

Hemlock Society (2000). www.hemlock.org.

Hughes, John (1997). "Court Ruling Won't Change Kevorkian." http://www.washingtonpost.com, June 27.

Mainers for Death With Dignity (2000). " What the Maine Death with Dignity Act Is All About," www. mdwd.org.

Schaer, Meinrad (1999). "The Practice of Assisted Suicide in Switzerland," www.opn.org:8080/finalexit/swiss.html.

Taylor, Stuart (1997). "High Court Analysis." Online Backgrounders, www.pbs.org.

OTHER

CNN/USA Today Gallup Poll (1996). "Should a Doctor Aid Suicide?"

California Medical Association (1999). "California Medical Association Opposes Physician-Assisted Suicide: Legalization Will Abuse Dying Patients' Rights and Dignity." Press release, April 21.

Constantine, Thomas A. 1997. Letter from DEA Administrator Thomas A. Constantine to Representative Henry Hyde, November 5.

Dolstra, Diana M. (1998). "New Administrative Rules." *BME Report.* Spring/Summer, p. 3.

Giglio, John (1998b). Comments made at a press conference in Washington concerning the Lethal Drug Abuse Prevention Act. Washington Transcript Service, August 20.

International Anti-Euthanasia Task Force (1997). "Caring, Not Killing, Wins." Press release, June 27, www. iaetf. org.

Maine Secretary of State (2001a). Elections division. Telephone conversation, January 5.

Maine Secretary of State (2001b). Ethics division. Telephone conversation, January 5.

Sutin, L. Anthony (1998). Letter to Oregon Senator Ron Wyden from Acting Assistant Attorney General L. Anthony Sutin.

Index